Palgrave Macmillan Studies in Banking and Financial Institutions

Series Editor
Philip Molyneux, Bangor University, Bangor, UK

The Palgrave Macmillan Studies in Banking and Financial Institutions series is international in orientation and includes studies of banking systems in particular countries or regions as well as contemporary themes such as Islamic Banking, Financial Exclusion, Mergers and Acquisitions, Risk Management, and IT in Banking. The books focus on research and practice and include up to date and innovative studies that cover issues which impact banking systems globally.

Marco Bodellini · Gabriella Gimigliano ·
Dalvinder Singh
Editors

Commercial Banking in Transition

A Cross-Country Analysis

palgrave
macmillan

Editors
Marco Bodellini
University of Luxembourg
Luxembourg, Luxembourg

Dalvinder Singh
School of Law
University of Warwick
Coventry, UK

Gabriella Gimigliano
Dipartimento di Studi Aziendali e Giuridici
University of Siena
Siena, Italy

ISSN 2523-336X ISSN 2523-3378 (electronic)
Palgrave Macmillan Studies in Banking and Financial Institutions
ISBN 978-3-031-45288-8 ISBN 978-3-031-45289-5 (eBook)
https://doi.org/10.1007/978-3-031-45289-5

Cover illustration: Alexander Spatari/getty images

This Palgrave Macmillan imprint is published by the registered company Springer Nature Switzerland AG
The registered company address is: Gewerbestrasse 11, 6330 Cham, Switzerland

Paper in this product is recyclable.

Foreword

The editors of the volume on *Commercial Banking in Transition: a Cross-Country Analysis* asked me for a brief presentation, and I agreed as I hold all of them in high regard thanks to my reading of their writings as well as my personal acquaintance with some of them.

I was rewarded with the opportunity to read a preview of the numerous writings collected in the volume, all of good, and in some cases excellent quality. I can thus wholeheartedly recommend the book to readers for thorough reading.

If I had to sum up in a few words the book's subject as well as what will be of the greatest interest to the reader, I would say that the authors all converge around analysing finance law that makes use of advanced technology. In short, the focus is on new developments and the greatest challenges that commercial banking transactions present to scholars.

Actually, if we look at the history of business law, there is nothing revolutionary in this: commercial law has always dealt with the most innovative practices, including technology.

If I were to then add what I consider the volume's main merit, I would say it is the fact of having brought together around this theme scholars of varied backgrounds and geographical provenance. The authors have found common ground for useful discussion and, often, convergence of ideas. This is particularly important at a moment in history like our current one in which, outside of scientific activities, polarizing positions tend to be trumpeted. This leads me to conclude on a note of cautious optimism for the future of humanity.

Vittorio Santoro
Full Professor of Business
and Company Law, Law School
University of Siena
Siena, Italy

Contents

Notes on Contributors

Folashade Adeyemo is a Lecturer in law at the University of Reading, where she teaches both Company Law and Banking Law at the Undergraduate level. She is also the Co-Director of Admissions and Recruitment for the School of Law. Her recently published monograph is titled *Banking Regulation in Africa: The Case of Nigeria and Other Emerging Economies* (Routledge, 2021). The book's core jurisdictional focus is Nigeria; however, it also provides a holistic overview of the South African and Kenyan banking regulatory environments. She has published in the field of banking and financial regulation and has a specific interest in financial and economic crime, bank insolvency, company law and whistleblower protection.

Patrick Barban is Professor of Law at the Law Faculty of CY Cergy Paris Université in France and a member of LEJEP ("Laboratoire d'études juridiques et politiques"). His research is mainly on securities and banking law, especially on market infrastructures and on the European financial regulation system. He is also leading several research projects on blockchain technology in a consortium including economists and computer scientists.

Marco Bodellini is a Senior Research Scientist in Sustainable Finance at the ADA chair in financial law and inclusive finance—University of Luxembourg—House for Sustainable Governance and Markets and a Lecturer in Banking and Financial Law—University of Bergamo. His main areas of research include bank crisis and resolution, corporate governance of financial institutions, systemic risk and financial stability, shadow banking and investment funds, fintech and sustainable finance. He is a member of the expert group advising the European Parliament on bank crisis management matters, a member of the Advisory Panel of the International Association of Deposit Insurers (IADI) and a Special Advisor to the Unidroit Secretariat on bank insolvency.

Antonella Brozzetti is Full Professor of Economics Law at the Business and Law Department of the University of Siena where she teaches Italian and European Union banking law to bachelor's and master's degree students. Her main area of research covers banking conglomerates, prudential supervision, green transition and sustainable development of the financial system. She is a member of the board of directors of the Bank of Italy located in Florence.

Ding Chen is currently a Senior Lecturer at the School of Law, University of Sheffield, and a Research Associate at the Centre for Business Research, Cambridge University. She has undertaken extensive research on law and finance, with a particular interest on rule of law, political economy, corporate finance, corporate governance and digital economy.

Xuejun Cheng, Assistant Professor, Law School of Tongji University (TJU), Doctor of Law of Shanghai Jiao Tong University (SJTU) and Doctor of Economics of Chinese Academy of Social Sciences (CASS). His research interests include economic law, financial law, data law, etc. He has written *Digital Consumer Finance, Internet Consumer Finance: Technology, Finance and Regulation, On Legal Regulation of Internet Consumer Finance*, and published more than 30 papers in CSSCI journals including *Law Science, China Economic Transition,* etc.

Iris H. Y. Chiu is Professor of Corporate Law and Financial Regulation at the Faculty of Laws, University College London. She joined the Faculty in 2009. She is also Director of the UCL Centre of Ethics and Law. She has interests in financial regulation and governance, law and technology, corporate law and governance and the law and policy for business and finance generally. She is a Research Fellow of the European Corporate Governance Institute, and most recently, a Senior Scholar at the European Central Bank's Legal Research Programme.

Anne Corrigan is a Deputy Head of Legal at the Bank of England with a particular responsibility for climate matters across the Legal Directorate. Anne trained as a lawyer in the Government Legal Services. In her early career, she conducted charity litigation and advised the Department for Culture Media and Sport and the Advisory Committee on the Export Control of Works of Art. Anne then moved to the Treasury and has since followed a career in financial services spanning the Treasury, the Department for Work and Pensions, the Financial Services Authority prior to legal cutover and now the Bank of England.

Shalina Daved is a Senior Legal Counsel and Manager in the Bank's Financial Stability Division, where she advises the Bank in its capacities as the UK's resolution authority, payment systems and other financial market infrastructure supervisor and the Financial Policy Committee. Shalina joined the Bank from Allen & Overy's financial services regulatory team. Prior to her time in private practice, Shalina worked in the European Parliament in Brussels assisting an MEP with her legislative work in the Civil Liberties, Justice and Home Affairs (LIBE) Committee. Shalina studied Law at the University of Nottingham and has a Master of Law from the University of Cambridge.

Nikita Divissenko is Assistant Professor at the International and European Law (IER) Department of the Utrecht School of Law, Utrecht University (The Netherlands). He holds a Ph.D. in law (2022) from the European University Institute, Florence (Italy).

Gabriella Gimigliano is Lecturer in Law at the Business and Law Department of the University of Siena. She holds a Ph.D. in banking law and the law of financial markets and has been working as a research fellow in business and economics law; she held a Jean Monnet Chair in EU Money Law from 2018 to 2022 and before she was already been awarded with a Jean Monnet Module (2013–16) on the Europeanisation of the payment systems.

Weronika Herbet-Homenda is a Ph.D. candidate in the Department of Commercial Law at the Faculty of Law and Administration at the University of Warsaw. Graduate of postgraduate studies in competition law at the Institute of Legal Studies of the Polish Academy of Sciences. Specializes in Polish and EU competition and consumer protection law and company law.

Pablo Iglesias-Rodríguez is Senior Lecturer in International Finance Law at the Sussex Law School, where he convenes the LL.M. in International Financial Law. He is a member of the Consultative Working Group of the CCP Policy Committee of the European Securities and Markets Authority (ESMA). He graduated from the University of Vigo (*Licenciatura en Derecho* and M.Phil. in Applied Finance and Environmental Resources) and the EUI (M.Res. and Ph.D. in Law). His main areas of professional experience, research, publications and teaching are financial law and corporate law.

Johannes Langthaler is a Senior Group Regulatory Transformation Manager at Raiffeisen Bank International AG with a focus on Basel-Regulations, Bank Resolution and ESG/Sustainable Finance. Before he worked at the European Central Bank, the European Commission, the Austrian Financial Market Authority and the Austrian Central Bank. He is Lecturer at the Applied University BFI Vienna, a regular speaker at conferences and training and regularly publishes in national and international journals.

Zhirou Li is a Ph.D. student at the Centre for Commercial Law Studies, Queen Mary University of London. She earned her Bachelor of Economics (Actuarial Science and Risk Management) degree from the University of International Business and Economics in China and her M.A. (Regulation and Compliance) and LL.M. (Law and Economics) from Queen Mary University of London. Zhirou is a co-chair of the Centre for Commercial Law Studies China Chapter; this committee is responsible for organizing academic, professional and social events for alumni of Queen Mary University of London.

Joy Malala is an Assistant Professor at the University of Warwick who has a special interest in researching financial regulation and supervision, the legal accountability of regulators, corporate governance, as well as the regulation of financial innovation and technology. She particularly researched the legal and regulation of mobile payment systems which she examines in her book, *Law and Regulation of Mobile Payment Systems: Issues Arising 'post' Financial Inclusion in Kenya*. She moreover researches financial sector reform through the consideration of the role of Central banks, and systemically important financial institutions and their impact on developing economies.

Lela Mélon is the 2021 MDPI Emerging Sustainability Leader winner, a former Marie Curie Research Fellow, coming from a legal and economic background. She is currently the director of the postgraduate programme on Sustainability Transition at ESCI-UPF as well as assistant director of the Masters of Science in Sustainability Management at ESCI-UPF and UPF-BSM. She specializes in EU law, with a focus on corporate conduct and sustainability and is currently researching policy coherence for sustainability at the EU level, with particular interest in corporate law policies as well as its expression in terms of sustainable tourism through the Greentour project.

Alenka Recelj Mercina M.Sc., is Sustainable Development Lead at NLB d.d., Ljubljana, Slovenia. Competencies related primarily to strategy and business development, environmental sustainability and social responsibility, with the ability to recognize and implement innovations in banking, with extensive experience in project management and with a master's degree focused on finance from Bayes Business School, London. She is currently also a Sustainable Finance Group Lead at Slovenian Banking Association, a member of Sustainable Finance Expert Group at European Banking Federation (EBF) and Slovenian representative in the EBF's Chief Sustainability Officers' Roundtable.

Clare Merrifield is a Senior Legal Counsel and Manager in the Bank of England's Financial Stability Division. She advises the Bank in its capacity as the UK's resolution authority. Clare has a background in insolvency law. She joined the Bank from Linklaters, where her experience included advising the administrators of Lehman Brothers International Europe, in particular on the return of trust assets to the bank's clients. While at Linklaters, Clare completed a secondment to the policy unit of The Insolvency Service, an executive agency of the Department for Business, Energy and Industrial Strategy. Clare has a degree in Modern & Medieval Languages (Russian and French) from the University of Cambridge and completed her postgraduate conversion to law at BPP Law School.

Anne-Christin Mittwoch holds the chair of Private Law, European and International Business Law and is the Executive Director of the Institute of Economic Law at the faculty of Law, Economics and Business at Martin Luther University Halle-Wittenberg. She recently authored the monograph "Nachhaltigkeit und Unternehmensrecht" ("Sustainability and Company Law"), which was awarded the scientific award of the Esche

Schümann Commichau Foundation in 2022 and funded by the DFG (Deutsche Forschungsgemeinschaft). Prof. Dr. Anne-Christin Mittwoch teaches company law, capital market law, European private law, private international law and comparative law.

Jack Parker is a Legal Counsel in the Legal Directorate of the Bank of England. He was previously a lawyer at international law firm Clifford Chance where he practised in London, the Middle East and continental Europe and has worked within the Compliance function of Goldman Sachs in London. He read Law at the London School of Economics and Political Science, University of London, where he graduated with first-class honours. He also holds a Bachelor of Civil Law from Brasenose College, University of Oxford.

Lucia Quaglia (D.Phil. Sussex, M.A. Sussex) is Professor of Political Science at the University of Bologna. She has published 9 books, 7 of which with Oxford University Press. Her most recent books are *The Perils of Internal Regime Complexity in Shadow Banking*, Oxford University Press (2022); *The Politics of Regime Complexity in International Derivatives Regulation*, Oxford University Press (2020); *The UK and Multi-Level Financial Regulation: From Post-Crisis to Brexit*, Oxford University Press (with S. James) (2020).

Bruno Meyerhof Salama is a Lecturer at UC Berkeley Law School and a partner at Salama Silva Filho Advogados in São Paulo. He is licensed to practice law in New York and in Brazil and holds a J.S.D. from UC Berkeley Law School. He has 20 years of experience with banking and monetary law in government, academia and private practice.

Michael Salib is the Deputy Secretary at the Bank of England. He was formerly Deputy Head of Legal in the Financial Stability Division, where he advised the Bank in its capacity as the UK's resolution authority. Prior to this, he worked in the Bank's EU Withdrawal Unit and as the Private Secretary to the General Counsel. He joined the Bank from the law firm Freshfields Bruckhaus Deringer, where he trained and qualified as a lawyer in the firm's litigation department. Michael studied Law at the University of Oxford and holds a Master's in Banking and Financial Regulation from the London School of Economics. He has published a number of articles in relation to legal issues affecting the Bank, including its statutory immunity from damages and HM Treasury's powers of direction over the Bank.

Dalvinder Singh is a Professor of Law at the University of Warwick, School of Law. He is an author and editor of several monographs and a number of research papers on banking supervision, resolution and crisis management. Most notably, *European Cross Border Banking and Banking Supervision*, Oxford University Press, 2020. He is a contributing author to *Debt Restructuring*, Oxford University Press, (2022). He has been Editor of the *Journal of Banking Regulation*, since 2003 and Financial Regulation International, since 2006; He is also a member of the Advisory Panel of the International Association of Deposit Insurers (IADI) Basel, Switzerland.

Weronika Stefaniuk is a Ph.D. candidate in the Department of Commercial Law at the Faculty of Law and Administration at the University of Warsaw. Trainee Advocate at the District Bar Association in Warsaw. She specializes in commercial law, capital markets, corporate disputes and unfair competition.

Feimin Wang Professor, School of Humanities and Law, North China University of Technology (NCUT); and Director, Fintech and Information Security Law Research Institute in NCUT. Feimin Wang is a member of anti-money laundering committee in National Internet Finance Association of China (NIFA). His research interests mainly focus on Data Law, Financial Law and Bankruptcy Law. Many of his works have been published in CSSCI journals including *Political Science and Law*, *Studies in Law and Business*, etc. He now serves as Deputy Director of the Beijing Bankruptcy Law Society and Deputy Director of the Beijing Cyber Law Society.

Anne-Marie Weber holds the position of Assistant Professor at the Chair of Commercial Law of the University of Warsaw, where she has defended her doctoral thesis, which was then awarded by the Chairman of the Polish Financial Supervision Authority in the competition for the best doctoral thesis in the field of financial market regulation and published as a monograph entitled "Wpływ instytucji prawnych rynku kapitałowego na efektywność spółek Skarbu Państwa" ("The influence of capital market institutions on state-controlled companies" efficiency'). Dr. Anne-Marie Weber teaches company law and financial market law.

Duoqi Xu Professor, Fudan University Law School; and Director, Center for Law and Digital Economy, Fudan University. Duoqi Xu is an affiliated professor at Shanghai Advanced Institute of Finance (SAIF). Her research mainly focuses on Data Law, Financial and Tax Law. Many of her works have been published in SSCI and CSSCI journals including *Computer Law & Security Review*, *Social Sciences in China*, etc. She has visited and taught at Harvard University, New York University and other academic institutions around the world. She now serves as Member of Shanghai Government Legislative Expert Pool and Deputy Director of Shanghai Fiscal and Tax Law Society.

Yangguang Xu graduated from the School of Law of Renmin University of China with a Ph.D. in law. He worked as a postdoctoral researcher at the School of Law of Peking University and as a visiting scholar at the University of Cambridge. He is a professor and Ph.D. supervisor at the School of Law of Renmin University of China. He is also the Deputy Director and Secretary-General of the Bankruptcy Law Research Center of Renmin University of China, President of the Beijing Bankruptcy Law Society and a member of the working group for the revision of "Enterprise Bankruptcy Law" of the Financial and Economic Committee of the China National People's Congress.

GiJin Yang is a Law Professor at Jeonbuk National University, Jeonju, Korea; Director of the Korea Financial Law Association; Director of the Korea Business Law Association; Director of the Korea Commercial Law Association; Director of International Academy of Financial Consumers; member at the Korean FSS Financial Supervisory Advisory Committee; ex-member at the FSS Disciplinary Decision Committee. She has Ph.D. in Law (Seoul National University 2007); M.P.M. (KDI School of Public Policy and Management 2013); LL.M. (Seoul National University 1997) and LL.B. (Seoul National University 1995).

Sung-Seung Yun is a Law Professor at Ajou University, Suwon, Korea. Former President of the Korea Financial Law Association; Vice President of the Korea Commercial Cases Association; President of the Korean Association of Police & Law; Director of the Korea Business Law Association; Director of the Korea Commercial Law Association. He is a U.S. attorney at law, admitted both in California and New York; Ph.D. in Law (Seoul National University 2021); M.B.A. (University of Washington 1999), LL.M. (Golden Gate University 2002 and Seoul National University 1989); LL.B. (Seoul National University 1989).

Leonidas Zelmanovitz earned a law degree from the Federal University in Porto Alegre, Brazil, and a master's and a doctorate in economics from the King Juan Carlos University in Madrid. He is a Senior Fellow with Liberty Fund, in Indianapolis, USA. Before that, he was a businessman in Brazil.

List of Figures

List of Tables

CHAPTER 1

Introduction

Marco Bodellini, Gabriella Gimigliano, and Dalvinder Singh

1 Aims and Pillars of the Book

Over the last few years, commercial banks, and more in general the commercial banking business model, have been impacted by three main different forces, namely: the advent of fintech-related innovations (such as artificial intelligence, cryptocurrencies, blockchain, algorithmic trading, machine learning and electronic payments, to name a few), the Covid-19 pandemic and the government measures adopted to tackle it and the sustainable development goals-related initiatives undertaken at both international and domestic levels. Such forces have changed the way commercial banks are organized and operate, and they are expected to

M. Bodellini (✉)
University of Luxembourg, Esch-sur-Alzette, Luxembourg

G. Gimigliano
University of Siena, Siena, Italy
e-mail: gabriella.gimigliano@unisi.it

D. Singh
School of Law, Warwick University, Coventry, England
e-mail: dalvinder.singh@warwick.ac.uk

M. Bodellini et al. (eds.), *Commercial Banking in Transition*, Palgrave Macmillan Studies in Banking and Financial Institutions,
https://doi.org/10.1007/978-3-031-45289-5_1

keep on affecting such institutions as well as the banking system as a whole.

On these grounds, *Commercial Banking in Transition* investigates how the impact of such driving forces has unfolded in recent times and to what extent they will keep on impacting commercial banks. The analysis is conducted taking a comparative approach, whereby three main geographies are explored, namely: the European Union, United States and United Kingdom (the Anglo-Saxon systems) and some prominent Asian jurisdictions (China and South Korea).

Leveraging on lessons learnt from the recent past, this co-edited book aims at discussing how commercial banking will look like in the forthcoming future, what commercial banks are expected to be and to do in the new economic and social reality, and how banking supervision and market competition will develop as a result of these structural changes.

Referring to the impact of those three driving forces, this work explores three intertwined dimensions of commercial banking, which broadly relate to the core business model of commercial banks, their prudential supervision and competition issues.

The advent of financial technologies (Fintech) may reduce commercial banks' operating costs thereby increasing their profits, but—it goes without saying—this is also triggering a disintermediation process both on the asset and liability sides, which lowers the market entry barriers to newcomers. This is seen as beneficial since banks have been pressured to become more efficient, but it has also affected their income base. On these grounds, it is crucial to investigate if there is still (and there will be in the future) a market space for the traditional commercial banking business model (namely: taking reimbursable deposits from the public and extending loans) and to which extent fintech-based payment service providers interfere with the traditional monetary function performed by commercial banks.

On the other hand, the Covid-19 pandemic has spurred States to intervene much more vigorously in the economy than it used to be in the past. If this is only a transitory situation or if a new role for the State in the economy has become necessary is still to be seen. It seems that expansionary fiscal policies and public intervention (also in the banking sector) are here to remain at least until the post-Covid 19 economic downturn and the impact of the war in Ukraine on the economy will be fully overcome. Against this background, it is worth reflecting upon the role of commercial banks as the *longa manus* of governments and the impact of the new State interventionism on the corporate governance of commercial banks. The Covid-19 pandemic has been faced through the use of a huge amount of public money. When such relief measures will be lifted, even commercial banks might be hit, mostly through a relevant increase in their stock of non-performing assets. In this respect, supervisors have temporarily relaxed some rules concerning capital requirements and the accounting treatment of assets, whereas central banks have provided a huge amount of liquidity to market players. Still, banks will likely need to recapitalize when losses will be recorded but recapitalizations may be challenging should private investors be unwilling and/or unable to buy banks' capital instruments. As a result, effective bank crisis management regimes will be instrumental in keeping financial stability.

Sustainable development has become a key priority which is now placed at the very top of the policy makers' agenda. The UN Sustainable Development Goals (SDGs) are spurring on the development of new economics theories—like *doughnut economics*—which try to tackle social and financial inequality by critically revising the 'capitalistic' approach. Against this background, sustainable finance has gained momentum on the assumption that a massive amount of resources are needed to reach the UN SDGs. Such enormous resources can be successfully mobilized only with a key role being played by the financial system. In other words, as public money in and of itself will not be sufficient to finance the transition to sustainability, financial institutions, including commercial banks, are now requested to play a role in facilitating the flow of financial resources to sustainable-related business initiatives.

2 Structure of the Book

The comparative approach featuring this study is reflected in the structure of the book which is divided into three parts, whereby Part 1 is dedicated to the EU legal regime, Part 2 deals with the Anglo-Saxon systems (i.e. US and UK) and Part 3 focuses on the Chinese and Korean frameworks. Fintech-related issues are in the view of the contributors the main driver of change impacting commercial banking.

Part I of the book, on the EU legal framework, is made up of 9 chapters.

From Chapter 2 to Chapter 5, the book considers how fintech is changing the banking business organization, value chain and market structure. In Chapter 2, Patrick Barban investigates how fintech-led developments are challenging the role of banks as the traditional middlemen in financial intermediation. He moves from the analysis of the universal banking model, applied in the EU banking harmonization process, to argue then that fintech innovations are deeply challenging credit institutions as one-stop-shop business organizations in that such innovations may *de facto* remove market entry barriers. And this holds true despite the EU policy choice of requesting an *ad-hoc* authorization to engage in activities entailing the collection of deposits or other reimbursable funds from the public and the extension of credit (core banking business), the provision of payment services as well as other financial and investment services. In Chapter 3, Gabriella Gimigliano explores more in-depth on how fintech deals with competition concerns in the banking sector. This chapter focuses on two of the main policy priorities addressed in the 2007 Competition Report, namely, the price and non-price agreements applied in the payment systems, and the interoperability between credit data platforms: the aim is to ascertain how command and control strategy as well as antitrust enforcement dealt with them and whether fintech may give proper answers to the pending issues. In Chapter 4, Iris H.Y. Chiu looks at how cryptofinance may create new market opportunities for traditional banks while challenging the prudential regulatory policies, where the three areas of business expansion envisaged are "crypto-based secured lending", provision of "custodial and payment services intermediation for crypto-finance" and dealing services in crypto-currencies.

In Chapter 5, Anne-Christine Mittwoch, Anne-Marie Weber, Weronika Herbert-Homenda and Weronika Stefaniuk analyse digitalization from the standpoint of the risk of financial exclusion. This is a relevant issue, particularly for elderly people; discussing the case for legislative action, the Authors consider "the growing tendency to view access to the financial market (the right to financial inclusion) as a human right", on "the assumption that financial institutions carry a particular social responsibility, (…). As a consequence, a limitation of commercial banks' freedom in shaping their business models would be justified". This raises questions on the legal nature of commercial banks and what "social responsibility" means for them.

Chapters 6, 7 and 8, by Lucia Quaglia, Marco Bodellini and Johannes Langthaler, focus on how the commercial banking business model has changed as a result of the Covid-19 pandemic and Covid-19-related regulatory actions. Their studies emphasize how the economic and financial crisis—triggered by the Covid-19 health emergency—made it necessary for European policymakers to further integrate the banking system; on these grounds in Chapter 6, Lucia Quaglia points that "we need European solutions for European problems". Yet, while in the context of the policy measures taken during the 2008 international financial crisis, aimed at stabilizing the euro-area, banks were perceived as part of the problem, in the Covid-19-related regulatory measures banks performed a critical role in lending money to firms and households. However, establishing an effective legal framework for ailing banks was (and still is) one of the key regulatory challenges; the lack of such harmonized framework has caused divergent approaches to be taken among member states as to the allocation of costs and risks and has shown asymmetries across the different levels of EU governance arrangements covering powers, responsibility, accountability and competences in bank crisis management.

These issues are discussed also in Chapters 7 and 8 where Marco Bodellini and Johannes Langthaler both focus on the bank crisis management framework considering, from different perspectives, banks' access to external financial resources.

Particularly, Marco Bodellini deals with "problem banks"—i.e. banks facing a crisis—and looks at how they can raise finance. On these grounds, he analyses the European legal framework on Emergency Liquidity Assistance (ELA) and Deposit Guarantee Schemes (DGSs). Despite the importance of both of them, the chapter argues that there is no one-size-fits-all financing tool and "a sensible legal framework is one that provides the authorities with a large toolkit, allowing them to pick the most effective instrument after a case-by-case assessment. To do so, authorities need to be given some discretion in their choices. Yet such discretion needs in turn to be counterbalanced with proportional accountability". Focusing on some critical shortcomings currently affecting the EU legal framework he advances policy considerations that could lead to law reforms.

As a complementary piece of the puzzle, Johannes Langthaler investigates the EU rules requiring credit institutions to improve their resolvability by issuing and maintaining a sufficient level of loss-absorbing capacity. He focuses mainly on the Minimum Requirement of Eligible Liabilities and Own Funds (MREL), introduced at the EU level consistently with the international FSB Standards on Total Loss Absorbing Capacity (TLAC). Keeping the eyes on the building of MREL capacity, he discusses the potentially fruitful synergies between the EU crisis management framework and the Capital Markets Union (CMU), as the CMU rules and regulations might "encourage and facilitate MREL exposures of long-term institutional investors".

Part I ends with a discussion on the "sustainability" driver. In Chapter 9, Pablo Iglesias-Rodriguez analyses the EU policies, legal reforms and actions aiming to improve commercial banks' sustainability by pursuing a three-tier objective. He wonders whether such policies and reforms will be effective to mitigate agency problems between commercial banks and those stakeholders affected by or having an interest in sustainability and redefine the corporate objective of commercial banks and the role of directors. Chapter 10 by Lela Mélon and Alenka Recelj Mercina analyses an interesting case of sustainability transition: namely NLB Group, which is a leading commercial bank operating in the Balkan area, that aligned its business model to the United Nation Sustainable Development Goals. Conducting a critical assessment of the quality of the EU legal framework, while Pablo Iglesias-Rodriguez stresses the need to strike a balance between the fulfilment of sustainability goals and "guaranteeing critical societal objectives", Lela Mélon and Alenka Recelj Mercina argue, inter alia, that "all in all, the EU activity in the field of narrowing down the meaning of what 'sustainable' activity is (…) is welcome, but it needs to be reconciled with the need for clarity and simplicity in order to be adequately supporting and incentivizing the sustainable corporate transition in general as well as sustainable transition of commercial banking in particular".

Part II is dedicated to the Anglo-Saxon systems and is made up of five chapters. Chapters 11–13 investigate the fintech-led developments and how they influence the regulatory approach not only in terms of trade-offs between private and public and/or market and State-led intervention but also in terms of new forms of regulation tailored to the decentralized structure of finance.

In Chapter 11, Leonidas Zelmanovitz and Bruno Meyerhof Salama critically explore the creation of a CBDC having regard to the US legal regime, advancing considerations which can apply even elsewhere. The starting point of their analysis is that "retail CBDCs represent yet another step towards the devolution of monetary powers from commercial banks to the state" thereby revising the trade-off achieved between private and sovereign money and the establishment of the fractional reserve system. In other words, the launch of a retail CBDC might be a policy choice to tip the regulatory balance towards sovereign money: according to the Authors, most CBDC proponents "dispute the ability of the banking system to efficiently allocate capital, whether due to the shortsightedness or inability to factor broader societal goals into their decisions to price or extend credit". The "financial repression" might be one of the expected results together with the growth of new forms of shadow banking; therefore, they suggest moving from a retail CBDC to a wholesale CBDC working as money base "to settle payments between stablecoins".

The issue of the regulatory trade-off between market-led and State-based actions is investigated also in Chapter 12, by Nikita Divissenko, moving from the UK strategy to fintech-led developments. The starting point is the report on the state of the banking market in the United Kingdom, which shows a high level of concentration on the demand-side and the supply-side and a very low level of customer mobility; the scarce customer engagement is assumed to slow down innovation and competition. The solution was found in the Open Banking strategy, established by the Open Banking Implementation Body, whereby the largest banks were mandated to cooperate with each other. However, a few years later, no remarkable change has been reached in the level of customer mobility, despite the significant increase in the number of competitors. The reason for that might be—according to the Author—that the open banking strategy is based on a co-opetition approach and this makes it advisable to change the way to assess the competitiveness of the banking market: "(...) it is the infrastructure created by the Open Banking framework that allows millions of users to benefit from new products and services. This narrative (...) places the size of the ecosystem and the availability of new payment or account aggregation options based on API-fuelled data sharing framework alongside the growing number of users at the centre of the impact assessment of the frameworks on customer engagement". On the other hand, Joy Malala and Folashade Adeyemo in Chapter 13 question "whether regulatory tools in relation to systemic stability in conventional finance (...) are applicable in crypto finance", since crypto-finance is based on decentralized participation; they argue that there is no one-size-fits-all solution to protect retail investors. Indeed, in their view "given the very structure and evolving nature of cryptocurrencies and crypto-assets, it seems impossible to simply transpose existing legislation to regulate this".

The last two chapters of Part II concern respectively the UK legal framework for bank resolution and the response of the Bank of England to climate change. Chapter 14, by Shalina Daved, Clare Merrifield, and Michael Salib, analyses the UK framework on the recognition of foreign resolution procedures focusing particularly on the importance of reaching a "cooperative solution with foreign resolution authorities" despite—as the Financial Stability Board noted in its Principles for Cross-border Effectiveness of the Resolution Actions—any contractual recognition clauses suffer from some limitations. In Chapter 15, Jack Parker and Anne Corrigan analyse how the legal framework on climate-related financial risks and the central banking policy have developed. On these grounds, they look at "how the work of the Bank of England fits into the overall effort, including ensuring the financial system is resilient to climate change-related financial risks".

Part III, from Chapter 16 to Chapter 19, on commercial banking in China and South Korea gives priority to the fintech driver, while Chapter 19 covers also the regulatory challenges and changes triggered by Covid-19 and sustainability.

On these grounds, Chapter 16 by Ding Chen takes a snapshot of the structure of the Chinese banking market: in the relationship between fintech companies and commercial banks, it seems that the former boomed also because they were able to fill into two market gaps, namely: (1) the provision of transaction account services through mobile payments and the offering of "money market funds" and, (2) lending to small borrowers taking advantage of big data, real-time and behavioural data, rather than financial information, to assess credit score. However, as the Author argues "(…) banks are not as conservative as they are often thought to be" and this explains why the reaction from the incumbents was not long in coming. In Chapter 17, Feimin Wang, Duoqi Xu and Xuenjun Cheng investigate the digitalization of the private and public banking sector in China; they explore the regulatory development of the banking business from off-line to on-line provision of lending and trade finance services taking advantage of the platforms of third-party payment institutions and blockchain infrastructures. They also consider a Chinese CBDC that may prevent financial disintermediation of commercial banks, helping them reduce operating costs and improve the level of financial risk prevention. The leading role performed by the public sector in the fintech-led innovation process, already discussed in Chapter 16, is emphasized by arguing that "The public sector, as a party in trade finance, is primarily engaged in providing public services and maintaining trade order. Therefore, the trade finance blockchain platform led by the public sector is distinctive for its social public utilities". However, in the Chinese banking experience, fintech is not only a driver of competition between newcomers and incumbents but it also encourages cooperative agreements between them. This aspect is analysed in Chapter 18 by Yangguang Xu and Zhirou Li; they emphasize how fintech applications allow commercial banks to lower their operational costs, increase efficiency and improve risk control. On the other hand, banks are at risk of "catfish effect" because fintech firms provide several banking-like services without being regulated by a proper legal regime, as to some extent Patrick Barban stresses in Chapter 5 with regard to the EU framework. Cooperation is then seen as a way of managing the catfish risk but this may create different risks, therefore it is argued that "activity-based regulation should be viewed as a complement to entity-based regulation rather than an alternative. (…) Hence the need for a more holistic approach to regulation that simultaneously focuses on entities, activities and the wider ecosystem".

In the end, Sung-Seung Yun and GiJin Yang in Chapter 19 provide an overview of ongoing banking business model changes in South Korea; commercial banks turn out to be under severe financial, market and reputational stress. Indeed, due to fintech growth and open banking, commercial banks are challenged by big techs "seeking growth as comprehensive financial platforms through SNS services, and/or simple payment/remittance service". Sung-Seung Yun and GiJin Yang raise an interesting point relating to the "normative wall" between finance and industry. Indeed, "although BigTechs are now gradually penetrating the financial industry, typical financial companies like banks are unable to engage in non-financial businesses due to long lasting Korean policies of banking and commerce separation. Therefore, the argument that the business environment of BigTechs is relatively advantageous in terms of regulation, the so-called 'unlevel playing field' between financial companies and BigTechs recently gained strength in Korea". The authors also point out that the government Covid-19 emergency measures, that provided, inter alia, extremely low interest rates for loans to small businesses, reduction of the debt burden for vulnerable people, as well as a State-grant (so-called Disaster Emergency Payment), considerably affected commercial banks. With regard to sustainability-related issues, it is stressed that the largest financial institutions and commercial banks are now used to prepare ESG reports which are made available on their websites. This is often done in order to benefit from comparative reputation advantages and "avoid any indirect sanction from the government and from the public".

In Chapter 20 Antonella Brozzetti draws conclusions on the regulatory challenges that lie ahead.

3 Looking Ahead

The "transition" offers a period to reflect on the opportunities and threats that lie in this period of considerable change from financial innovation and the need for sustainable finance. The threats and opportunities that have arisen from endogenous and exogenous shocks have not been entirely understood. But these shocks have pushed the move towards financial technology and regulatory technology to improve existing products and processes.

The opportunity during the transition gives us time to design new regulatory systems for these innovations to co-exist with conventional forms of finance, to ensure appropriate measures are in place to protect consumers and financial stability. The lessons we can learn do not exist in one jurisdiction or a single discipline hence the opportunity to learn from experiences across the world to advance best practices. The systemic importance of these new market innovations is not so clear yet. However, as we open the regulatory space to these new instruments and innovations, new threats will enter the formal regulatory financial markets. It is evident from history that regulation and supervision do not completely bridge the asymmetry of information gaps between different stakeholders in financial markets. Those threats need to be understood in the transition period to design new tool kits and modify old tools to ensure they are fit for purpose. Certainly, a risk-based approach is necessary, and experience would suggest sound judgement is needed now more than ever going forward to ensure we minimize those informational problems in new and traditional financial markets. The judiciary will play an important role as disputes arise and conventional commercial law evolves to capture new risks.

The current legislative reforms initiated recently are simply the starting points for regulating and supervising these innovations rather than the endpoint. It will be important over time to fill the space created by those legislative frameworks as we better understand the risks. There is equally a need for a level playing field across jurisdictions to minimize the opportunities for fraudulent and criminal activities which are so prevalent at the moment. Whether a discretion or rules-based approach is not so important, but both will need to capture functional and institutional aspects—conduct of business and prudential safety and soundness. Each financial regulator, bank and non-bank, will need to understand how new product innovations can be managed alongside conventional financial products in their specialism. Equally, it is important to start thinking of these innovations from a macroprudential and microprudential perspective to ensure financial integrity and stability. Currently, it is arguable that the former is more of a concern than the latter. Since the current lack of coherent oversight of the crypto asset and crypto firm market has partially curtailed its growth and so does not pose risks to financial stability. However, once these products come within the formal regulatory space, a significant degree of regulatory legitimacy will fuel these markets, so making the risks to financial stability material overtime. The co-existence and cross fertilization of conventional and non-conventional risks can create unintended consequences which will need understanding and capturing. This requires, as a starting point, a focus on a special resolution regime for such firms and markets to minimize disruption and protect different stakeholder interests.

PART I

The European Union

CHAPTER 2

Intermediaries' Model in Banking and Finance and the Treatment of Fintech in the European Union: A Critical Approach

Patrick Barban

1 Introduction

Intermediation as a major economic phenomenon. Intermediation has become one of the models of the modern economy. Using a smartphone, one can ask for an Uber vehicle to drive us from point A to point B while later asking for food delivery through, using the same Uber app or one from other competitors on the food delivery market. The "Middleman"[1] helps to conclude contracts on many daily life transactions but also for

[1] The word is used in the work of K. Judge, Direct, The rise of the Middleman economy and the power of going to the source, Harper Business, 2021, spec. preface X: "*Middlemen are the connectors. They help people and companies overcome the informational, logistical, and other hurdles that stand in the way of an exchange that would otherwise make them both better off*".

P. Barban (✉)
CY Cergy Paris University, Cergy, France
e-mail: patrick.barban@cyu.fr

M. Bodellini et al. (eds.), *Commercial Banking in Transition*, Palgrave Macmillan Studies in Banking and Financial Institutions,
https://doi.org/10.1007/978-3-031-45289-5_2

asset and wealth management operations. Realtors help real-estate sellers and buyers to make a deal and banks manage payment accounts, loans and mortgages while also facilitating initial public offerings. People helping a client to get access to a service, a good or a contractor go by many names: agents, intermediaries... The activity of a middleman can be defined by two elements: (1) the middleman is not the beneficiary of the contract, good or service sought; (2) the middleman manages a supply chain that is often characterized by its length, to help his client reach the desired goal. There is no need to focus on a particular contract to define the intermediary as long as he is a professional connecting two parts of the market through a supply chain. Even if diversity is key to understanding the activity—ultimately Amazon, Walmart, Über, Blackrock or JP Morgan are all middlemen—they operate using the same pattern.

The fact that a large part of the economy requires today to go through Middlemen is not surprising. Middlemen are essential for the economy as they offer expertise and rapidity to meet their clients' needs. They have used their time to build their network and do not suffer from informational asymmetry as is the case for non-professionals in a market.

Critics of the middlemen economy. However, the middlemen's economy has also been criticized as major middlemen have gained a large market influence—such as Amazon which is part of the GAFAM—and because of the effect they can have on the market and the wellness of their clients. In her book, K. Judge analyzes the advantages and disadvantages of what she calls the middlemen economy.[2] In brief, a number of issues have been detected such as the market power of middlemen (especially in the real estate market) and the risk attached to long supply chains that appear to be fragile in times of uncertainties.[3] K. Judge also shows how a more direct approach is possible and highlights the benefits in terms of cost and wellness before addressing some principles toward consumers and public actors to promote it.

The idea behind the book of K. Judge is to blame the abuse which results from a very powerful position as a middleman and to offer remedies. This will not be the objective of this chapter. The idea is rather to analyze intermediation in the banking and finance industries, mainly

[2] See K. Judge, Direct, *op. cit.*

[3] The attack of Russia against Ukraine highlighted the importance of the cereal market from Ukraine and strengthened the instability of the market, brought inflation and also raised major concerns as a high risk of starvation for some countries.

in the European Union as the European system makes the intermediary mandatory. Such monopoly led to a large number of attempts to bypass the professional monopoly with a clear and express desire to abolish intermediaries or reduce the supply chain. Financial innovations such as crowdfunding or blockchains and other distributed ledger technologies come to mind. Confrontation between the old and established system and the new actors translates into a reaction from the public authorities, especially through new regulation at the highest level. The goal of the chapter is to analyze this confrontation and its consequences.

Professional monopoly in Europe and the intermediation principle.[4] In the European Union, the intermediary is not only suitable: he is mandatory. Historically, the creation of a professional monopoly in France followed the major financial crisis known as the Law's system crisis, when the open trading venue of rue Quincampoix led to a Ponzi Scheme, bankrupting many investors.[5] In reaction, the King's Council took a bill in 1724 imposing that all financial transactions had to be concluded through an intermediary (a registered change agent). Sanction was the voidance of the contract. Today, this monopoly is central to all European regulation.

The pattern between banking, finance and, on a smaller scale, insurance is the same as in the EU. Whenever the EU decides to harmonize the rules governing a given market, a directive or a regulation,[6] it will define the activities that are placed under a professional monopoly. A professional monopoly can be defined as a legal monopoly on certain services. Under such a monopoly, the law prohibits any individual or entity that has not been licensed by a public authority to provide such services. A license is granted based on experience, honorability and prudential rules.

By adopting this type of legislation, the European system has in fact consolidated an old model where each individual or entity had for their banking or financial operation only one intermediary. Latterly, consumers or professionals had only one bank for their banking operations (deposits

[4] The scope of the study will be European Laws studied through French doctrine, as they are the main field of studies of the author.

[5] See R. Bigo, Les bases historiques de la finance moderne, Armand Colin, Paris, 1922, 29; A. Colling, *La prodigieuse histoire de la bourse*, S.E.F., Paris, 1949, 59.

[6] A directive is an act that is not directly enforceable but the member states will have to integrate the act in their law system. A regulation is, on the opposite, directly enforceable.

and loans), one investment firm for everything related to market transactions, such as brokers, and one payment system often provided by their bank. This is particularly true in France where the model of a universal bank has been widely defended.[7] But the universal model can create the illusion where only one person is acting as intermediary. In reality, there is always a specific supply chain. For instance, in the financial market, a lot of credit institutions request several investment firms to fulfill the order of a client.

That complex and intricate web of intermediaries can have direct consequences and bear a systemic risk mitigated, when possible, by a netting system.[8] In the banking system, the industry came close to collapsing during the subprime crisis. The ties between the real-estate market and banking—through mortgage loans—were the main cause of the economic crisis in 2008: massive securitization of such mortgages occurred, with a view to offer better services for investors. Also, intermediation can be very costly in certain transactions such as initial public offerings ("IPO").[9]

Newcomers and technological innovation in bank and finance. Therefore, the public called for a more direct relation rather than being connected to an intermediary. Technical innovations helped. Firstly, the Internet allowed partners to interconnect directly without the help of a third party. If new Middlemen appeared rapidly (as Uber or AirBnb for the two most known), the Internet helped nonetheless to create a more direct connection. Crowdfunding is one example and has been rendered possible as a result of web 2.0. It helped actors in need of investment to directly submit their projects to individuals willing to invest their savings. Studies have shown that the cost is lower and once the economic benefits have been taken, there can be a feeling of fulfillment that a more

[7] See J.-B. Bellon, G. Pauget, Union bancaire et évolution du modèle des banques universelles, Revue d'économie financière, 2015/2 (n° 118), 79–91. https://doi.org/10.3917/ecofi.118.0079. URL: https://www.cairn.info/revue-d-economie-financiere-2015-2-page-79.htm.

[8] Governed by the Regulation (EU) N°648/2012 of the European Parliament and of the Council of 4 July 2012 on OTC derivatives, central counterparties, Official Journal of European Union, L 201, 27.7.2012, a netting system is a system where an entity mitigate the counterpart risk and can offer its own capital as guaranty if deemed necessary.

[9] *Infra*, n° 14.

traditional approach does not provide.[10] A more diverse approach will translate in two different ways. First, clients will not transit through only one agent. They will ask for direct access to any node in the supply chain. Not only such change can occur without legal evolution, but it might also not even need one. For the latter, the payment services industry is an example as new services have been created alongside an opening of the access to payment accounts which was exclusively reserved for credit institutions[11]. Second, the elimination of all agents in order to create a direct link between an individual/entity and the good, service or contractor they seek. At one time, this direct approach has been made possible through crowdfunding and explains the rise of blockchain technology. Called sometimes Web 3.0, this technology has been deployed with a public goal of creating a trustless system, without intermediaries, such as central or commercial banks.[12]

Toward a change of paradigm in European rules? This chapter analyses the deep technological impact that occurred in the last decades in the banking and finance industry. The focus will be held primarily on the finance and banking industries, for two reasons: firstly, these markets have been deeply altered by the Internet and, more recently, by the distributed ledger technology; secondly, these markets are highly regulated with binding and developed rules emanating from the EU legislator and applied by the supervisory authorities in each Member-State. Those rules are based on a principle of intermediation and a legal monopoly, which reduces the potential of new actors to directly compete with the bigger and more settled actors of such markets. The rise of new technologies and markets could also lead to a change of paradigm by the EU. Therefore, the reaction of the European legislator has to be analyzed.

To assess the impact of new technologies on the more traditional banking and financial system, it is first necessary to study the fundamentals of the European system, based on a professional monopoly and on mandatory intermediation (**2**). Only then can a review of the changes that occurred in the industry through new practices or infrastructures be analyzed (**3**). Lastly, and before concluding (5), the reaction of the

[10] See K. Judge, *op. cit.*, 199.

[11] *Infra*, n° 23.

[12] See S. Nakamoto: https://bitcoin.org/bitcoin.pdf [as of 29 September 2022].

authorities toward such new markets will be studied to identify the evolution, if any, of the rules and determine whether the old model will be maintained or if the EU will change its approach (**4**).

2 The European Model of Intermediation in Bank and Finance Markets

The Intermediation Principle and Professional Monopolies. The intermediation principle has been built in Europe by always using the same mechanisms. Based on the idea that some services can only be rendered by experienced and honorable professionals, the system is built around an activity broken down into several services. Any professional wishing to provide such services on a regular basis has to be licensed by an Authority (either European or national). A license provides a way to supervise the professionals. The system often offers for the main services provided a "European passport" in order to open the whole European Union market (The Single Market) to said professional. That construction renders the need for an agent for such operations mandatory and has been duplicated in the banking, finance and insurance fields. We have to study each step to fully understand how solid and inevitable the system appears.

Defining a Market. The first step for the Authorities is to consider that a market is of major importance for the Single Market and requires harmonization of national laws or protection against systemic risk. Defining a brand of activities central to this market is the first step. For instance, the Investment services Directive,[13] first directive to regulate the financial market, has defined a number of services around Financial Instruments ("ISD"). Section B of the annex of the directive targeted the main tools that were widely used at that time by the market: transferrable securities, monetary instruments, derivatives... Defining such tools was necessary to define the services professionals could offer on these instruments (section A). The professional rendering such service was named by that directive an "investment firm" (ISD, art. 1). Some ancillary services were also mentioned but of second importance. The core of the system revolved around investment services that could only be offered by licensed (and registered) professionals. Investment firms were (and

[13] Council Directive 93/22/EEC of 10 May 1993 on investment services in the securities field, Official Journal of the European Union, L 141, 11/06/1993 (no longer in force).

still are) defined by their activities (to provide an intermediation service related to financial instruments) and by their status comprising a set of duties and rights.

Supervising the Agents. The definition of the market has regulatory consequences. The purpose is to subject the professional to scrutiny and duties. They are generally divided threefold. Firstly, some governance requirements are prescribed and the firms must have honorable and experimented management and a process to avoid conflicts of interest. Secondly, a set of prudential duties is required—especially for credit institutions. Lastly, the relation with clients revolves around strong rules such as council obligations. When providing an investment service, the professional must act honestly, fairly and professionally in accordance with the best interests of its clients.

Access to the Single Market. The heavy duties come also with a powerful market power as the investment firm benefits from a professional monopoly. It comes with a set of rights in order to ensure a Capital Market Union inside the Single Market. The monopoly is based on the principle of the sole license. It means that an investment firm has to obtain a license granted for each service provided by its national authority, i.e., the authority competent for the place it has its registered office or its central administration. Once the license is granted, the investment firm can provide its services inside the member state but also in any other member state without the need to obtain for each one a new license.[14] As a result, investment firms benefit from the freedom to provide investment services and activities[15] which is based on both freedom to provide services and freedom of establishment, two major freedoms provided for in European Union Treaties.[16]

Extension of Financial and Banking Monopolies. As the services targeted in ISD were few, ever since the trend has been to add new

[14] Even if the firm must notify its national authority and also the authority of the state where the service is offered. The goal of such notification is to coordinate the supervision of the firm but only the initial authority is competent to sanction the firm in case of a breach of regulation.

[15] Directive 2014/65/EU of the European Parliament and of the Council of 15 May 2014 on markets in financial instruments ("MiFID 2"), Official Journal of European Union, L 173, 12.6.2014 (in force), art. 34.

[16] Treaty on the Functioning of the European Union (TFEU), Articles 26 (internal market), 49–55 (establishment) and 56–62 (services).

services with the purpose of filling any regulatory gap that could remain. One radiant example is the treatment of crossing networks. To understand what a crossing network is, a detour through trading venues must be made. Trading venues or trading facilities are financial markets: platforms where the financial instruments of public companies are listed and offered to investors. The function of a trading venue is to allocate in the central ledger orders on financial instruments and match them to form selling contracts on such instruments. The old Market in Financial Instruments Directive of 2004 (MiFID 1)[17] only recognized two trading venues: Regulated markets and multilateral trading facilities ("MTF"). Such actors had to be registered and were monitored and submitted to transparency. But certain actors started on their own account to trade clients' orders in their internal systems. Such behavior was not restricted but, soon enough, a large part of transactions was held on such systems and therefore not subject to transparency. That is why in 2014 the new MiFID 2 created a new kind of trading venue and characterized as an investment service subject to licensing: Organized trading facilities. Such a phenomenon can also be seen in other fields such as payment services.[18]

The Power of Intermediation. European regulation created a middlemen economy for the banking and financial markets. Investment firms, credit institutions and payment institutions are major actors in the markets. Any client wishing to pay for a good, collect salary on an account, get a loan or invest on the market will have to request a licensed firm to provide such services. If we take a look at a service as simple as buying a stock on the financial market, several services are offered in a long supply chain. The non-professional buyer will generally ask directly his bank to carry out the operation. As the access to the central order ledger of a financial market is limited, quite often that bank will not have direct access thereto: only market members are entitled to do so once they have obtained a license for the following services: "Execution of orders on behalf of clients" or "Dealing on own account". The client's bank will not have such kind of activity most of the time and will instead be agreed to "Reception and transmission of orders in relation to one or more financial instruments" ("RTO"). He will then ask his own services

[17] Directive 2004/39/EC of the European Parliament and of the Council of 21 April 2004 on markets in financial instruments, Official Journal of European Union, L 145, 30.4.2004 (no longer in force).

[18] *Infra*, n° 16 and 23.

provider (maybe another RTO service provider or directly an executor of orders on behalf of a client to place the order on the market).

Any company competing without having followed the licensing process will be prosecuted.[19] Only a set of exemptions exist but they address situations where a state company or authority provides such service, for facilitating money transfer inside groups of companies and also for the small operations called "de minimis". There was virtually no way to circumvent the monopoly outside these exemptions. So, we can see that both criteria defined by K. Judge can be found in the banking and financial industry (powerful market power and long supply chain) and that the intermediary is mandatory. But the changes in technology, especially linked to innovation processes around the Internet, have brought a lot of tension around these monopolies.

3 Fintech and Circumvention of the Intermediaries' Model

The development of the Internet (web 1.0) made information more accessible but it is with the establishment of web 2.0 that new fintech services were able to start before the distributed ledger technology known as blockchain (Web 3.0) could offer the possibility of trustless systems that do not require intermediaries.

Internet and the Availability of Information

Availability of Information on the Internet. The Internet has become a major information system in our modern economy and simplifies access to information. As one of the advantages presented by agents and other intermediaries is to provide their clients a true and fair information—as the intermediary is a professional player in his market—it is quite normal that some clients try to lower the cost of their operation by seeking themselves the needed information. Before the internet era, such information was often only available inside a closed network of professionals who knew

[19] In France, such breach of law will not void the contract (French Cassation Court, Com. 15 juin 2022, n° 20–22.160) but will be prosecuted under criminal law (French Monetary and Financial Code, art. L. 511–5 and L. 571–3 and can lead to an imprisonment of 3 years and 375 000 € for a physical person and 1 875 000 € for a moral person).

how to find and exploit it. Now, it is accessible to anyone but finding it is time-consuming and often requires some experience. That is also why the shift from inaccessible information to accessible information was not the end of the intermediary system: getting access to information is not the same as analyzing it, understanding it, classifying it and being able to exploit it. Agents still render a convenient and useful service for people who have neither the time nor the willingness to do so. A simple look at Tour operators shows how people can now manage their own holidays without these actors. Two examples will be further studied to show the consequences that the Internet has on the system.

The Internet and the Consequences on Real-Estate Sector. The first one is the real-estate sector. Studies have shown that the information about the selling of houses in the U.S. is not easily accessible. As often is the case in the U.S., the rules that govern the market were created by the professionals themselves decades or even centuries ago. Today, in the U.S., the seller will bear the cost of intermediation (roughly 6% of the estate selling price). The payment will be made to his agent who will equally share with the agent of the buyer. The principal tool for the agents is what is called a "Multiple-listing service", or "MLS".[20] These systems work as local exchanges. Even if these local exchanges could easily become transparent to sellers and buyers, allowing for a more direct approach, studies have shown that these essential facilities give the realtor a great market power, often to the detriment of the owners of real estate. The latest studies and the activities of certain start-ups show that clients wish for a change of market.[21]

The Internet and the Consequences on Financial Sector. The same applies to the financial sector. A quick look at the market of Initial Public Offerings shows the same pattern: a mandatory market organized by agents with heavy costs for the issuer. When a company decides to go public, it will have to first offer shares to a large public of investors on a trading venue. To do so, the company will request a consortium of

[20] The centrality of real estate agents in the buying and selling of homes in the United States goes back to the 1800s. At that time, local real estate agents would gather together to exchange information about their listings. These "exchanges" served the interests of both buyer and seller clients by making it more likely that each would find the right match. Over time, these exchanges became formalized through a multiple-listing service, or MLS", K. Judge, *op. cit.*, 69.

[21] See K. Judge, *op. cit.*, 121 on the company "Trelora" and critical infrastructures like MLS.

banks to manage the operation. As the operation is related to transferable securities, it is characterized in Europe as an investment service. The Banks will provide several services and rely on their network of clients to help the IPO to succeed. They act both as investors (they buy some of the securities through underwriting services) and intermediaries (they find subscribers among their clients through placement services)[22] and often will pool together in case the IPO is a major one. During such a process, the banks will usually keep a part of the securities for themselves in order to trade them, following the first listing. They have therefore an incentive to value high-potential securities at a lower price, in order to get the capital gain perceived as a bonus after market correction. A study covering more than 650 IPOs between 2015 and 2021 shows that the median company going public incurred costs that totaled 21.9% of the funds raised (both by direct costs paid as fees to the intermediaries but also by cost of underpricing).[23] Although more direct approaches are possible as, for instance, direct listing,[24] the risk attached thereto remains high. The company can feel more comfortable with an agent that is contractually obliged to bear a part of the risk attached to the operation.[25] The high cost of intermediation can also be of prejudice for small and medium businesses who wish to rely on the market.[26]

Binding Two Parts of the Market Through a Sole Intermediary

Crowdfunding. The development of web 2.0 has permitted exchanges between users, thus making direct contacts much easier. Crowdfunding is an example of such innovation through which companies were able to

[22] See the list of services in MiFID 1, Annex 1, section A.

[23] See M. Gahng, J. R. Ritter, D. Zhang, "SPACs": https://ssrn.com/abstract=3775847 (revised in July 2022).

[24] In a direct listing, the issuer will not go through a process of finding securities holders: it will directly put a part of the securities on the market for seeling. See T. Bonneau, P. Pailler, A.-C. Rouaud, e.a., *Droit financier*, 3e éd., n° 1104.

[25] Such as the placing of financial instruments on a firm commitment basis, where the bank must acquire for themselves all the securities that were not subscribed by their clients.

[26] OICV-IOSCO published a report in 2015 about listing of SME: https://www.iosco.org/news/pdf/IOSCONEWS348.pdf; on that report: P. Barban, "Rapport OICV de juillet 2015 sur le financement des PME au travers des marchés de capitaux: état des lieux des meilleures pratiques de régulation", RISF 2015/4, 49–53.

raise capital money or take out loans. Crowdfunding is defined as "*an open call to the public to raise funds for a specific project. Crowdfunding platforms are websites that enable interaction between fundraisers and the crowd. Financial pledges can be made and collected through the platform*".[27] Several types of platforms exist and can be classified as follows: Investment based crowdfunding (issuance of equity or debt instruments), Lending-based crowdfunding (for a direct loan related to a project), invoice trading crowdfunding (selling of unpaid invoices or receivables), reward-based crowdfunding (donation to a project in exchange of a non-financial reward, such as goods or services), donation-based crowdfunding (for a direct donation for a charitable project with no financial or material return) and even hybrid platforms mixing these categories.[28]

Crowdfunding, as it will be described below,[29] has been harmonized within the EU in 2020,[30] but it originated long before and dates back to the year 2000. As public listing is primarily meant to allow a company to get financing through its general activity, crowdfunding is more project-related.[31] But even if there is a change of scope, the way to carry out crowdfunding was the same: a sole intermediary created an Internet platform to allow companies and investors to meet. The operator of the platform offered services such as reception and transmission of orders, placement of securities or facilitation of obtaining loans. All these services are now comprised of the monopolies mentioned above. To allow such activity on its territory, France relied on the exemptions offered in the regulation and enacted them in 2014 the crowdfunding Order.[32] If once again the system requires an agent and regulates it, there is a drastic diminution in the number of intermediaries. As the crowdfunding agent

[27] See European Union, "Crowdfunding in the EU Capital Markets Union", SWD (2016) 154 final, 3d of May 2016, 8.

[28] Ibid.

[29] *Infra*, n° 29.

[30] Regulation 2020/1503 of 7 October 2020 on European crowdfunding service providers for business, Official Journal of the European Union, 20.10.2020, L 317/1.

[31] The Crowdfunding regulation does not mention "issuers" or "companies" but a "project owner", making the project central in the comprehension of what crowdfunding is. See previous regulation, art. 2.

[32] Order n° 2014–559 of 30th may 2014 regarding crowdfunding, French Republic Official Journal, 31th may 2014, text n° 14.

is able to solely offer all services required and facilitates contact between the two parts of the market, it has become more direct. The French legislation also created specific instruments called "Minibons" that replicated the common bonds to lighten the burden of such issuance[33] and to avoid the banking monopoly regime on credit operations. Such instruments vanished after transposition of the regulation.[34]

The development of crowdfunding and its regulation both show the need for a more direct approach.[35] As only one crowdfunding service provider is needed to connect the company and the investors, the long and costly chain of intermediation is set aside. It helps to have a more direct approach where the project is directly assessed by the investors and not placed through an agent who can also be the buyer of the shares. Moreover, direct communications are allowed between the project holder and the investors. But the internet has not only helped that more direct approach. It has also led to a multiplication of providers who are not linked in a vertical chain but can offer direct services.

Expanding the Services—the Example of the Payment Regulation. Another clue that a more direct approach is researched can be noticed in the efforts to set aside the monopoly on essential facilities. Essential facilities are systems that are mandatory for certain activities. For instance, in the banking industry, payments revolve around a bank account and, for a long time, the account manager bank had few competitors in some services. With regard to payment services, the economy has been built in Europe—especially in France—around the idea to have a unique Bank providing an array of services. The bank account serves both as a deposit account, a credit account and a payment account, and all these services are often provided by a sole intermediary. The bank in charge of all these services has a powerful market power as the clients often have only one account, meaning that changing from one account to another

[33] See R. Vabres, "Bons de caisse, minibons, blockchain... résurrection ou révolution?", *Droit des sociétés* 2016, n° 7, 1.

[34] See M. Julienne, Le droit européen du financement participatif; Note sous Règlement (UE) 2020/1503 du Parlement européen et du Conseil du 7 octobre 2020 (...), RDBF 2021, n° 2, 26; J.-M. Moulin, Le cadre juridique français du financement participatif s'adapte après l'adoption du règlement européen relatif aux prestataires de services de financement participatif, RDBF 2021, n° 2, 61; P. Barban, Le nouveau cadre français du financement participatif, Banque & Droit 2022, n° 201, 52.

[35] See K. Judge, *op. cit.*, 199.

can be complicated. Further, allowing access to the account for third-party services could be difficult. In addition to digital innovations, a new payment services market has been instituted by the EU[36] to achieve greater mobility of bank accounts.[37] Opening access to infrastructures as sensible as bank accounts helps to diversify the services and the providers based on that account. The account ceases to be an anchor, restraining the options of the client, and becomes a tool providing them more choice and freedom and allowing them to have several direct intermediaries from which they can choose and change more freely. The trend is therefore to reduce the supply chain and get for each service one intermediary. But innovation also helps to define systems that do not require at all intermediaries.

The End of Mandatory Intermediaries in the Blockchain System

Blockchain and the Trustless System. Blockchain technology is a mix of computer technics such as databases, cryptography, peer-to-peer systems and consensus mechanisms often revolving around a Merkle Tree. Blockchains were born when Satoshi Nakamoto published a manifesto to create the Bitcoin protocol in 2008.[38] Satoshi Nakamoto directly linked the apparition of the bitcoin to the subprime crisis that was devastating the global economy at that time. The technology was created to eliminate middlemen, such as central and commercial banks, from the economy. As a preliminary to his demonstration, Satoshi Nakamoto stated the disadvantage of a third-party relying economy for electronic business and electronic payment:

> *Commerce on the Internet has come to rely almost exclusively on financial institutions serving as trusted third parties to process electronic payments. While the system works well enough for most transactions, it still suffers from the inherent weaknesses of the trust based model. Completely non-reversible transactions are not really possible, since financial institutions cannot avoid mediating disputes. The cost of mediation increases transaction costs, limiting the minimum practical transaction size and cutting off the possibility for*

[36] *Infra*, n° 23.

[37] See J.-M. Jude, La mobilité bancaire, Les enjeux de la mobilité interne et internationale, IFJD, 2021, 231.

[38] See S. Nakamoto: https://bitcoin.org/bitcoin.pdf [as of 29 September 2022].

> *small casual transactions, and there is a broader cost in the loss of ability to make non-reversible payments for non-reversible services. With the possibility of reversal, the need for trust spreads. Merchants must be wary of their customers, hassling them for more information than they would otherwise need. A certain percentage of fraud is accepted as unavoidable. These costs and payment uncertainties can be avoided in person by using physical currency, but no mechanism exists to make payments over a communications channel without a trusted party.*[39]

The goal of a blockchain protocol—in its public form[40]—is to avoid the power of a small group of third parties. It is not a surprise that the first use of a blockchain was for virtual money. Indeed, bitcoin can be exchanged through the blockchain without the need for a payment service provider. It relies on validators running nodes of the system. To understand such an evolution, it is necessary to describe the manner in which payment services function and are regulated.

Payment Process. When a payment occurs, the payer is a person who holds a payment account and allows a payment order from that payment account (although sometimes there is no payment account but the payment can be made directly to the payee). The payee is the beneficiary of the payment. For most of the transactions, an intermediary is mandatory. In the European Union, the market of payment services is regulated through the Payment Services Directive that harmonized the member states' legislations.[41] The payee will give an order to the payment service provider, who will initiate the transfer of funds, usually by using the funds from an account. If the payer and payee do not have the same intermediary, then a relationship is necessary where the payer agent will transfer the order to the payee agent. The role of the intermediaries is essentially to verify the possibility of the payment and the existence of the

[39] Ibid.

[40] A protocol can be defined as public or private depending on the possibility for anyone to intervene on the chain as a node. On public blockchain, the distributed ledger is public and anyone can use the infrastructure (through a user profile) and be a node running the consensus. On a private or consortium chain, access to the blockchain, either for using it or becoming a node, is restrained: see P. De Filippi, A. Wright, *Blockchain and the law, the rule of code*, Harvard University Press, 2018, 31.

[41] Directive (EU) 2015/2366 of the European Parliament and of the Council of 25 November 2015 on payment services in the internal market, Official Journal of the European Union, L 337/35, 23.12.2015.

funds, as well as avoid duplicate payments, which can occur with very rapid payment systems.[42] Therefore, such intermediaries need to asses prior to the payment that the funds exist but must also cancel a payment if an error occurred. Given the regulated nature of their activity, they have legal duties such as "Know your Customer" and will request a considerable amount of information related to clients. Building a trust relationship brings along mediation costs, losses due to fraud and will also make it necessary to multiply verifications such as double verification systems in online payments (where the payers receives a text message containing a code to link the order to their phone and help to verify their identity).

Functionning of a Blockchain System: Validation Nodes. Bitcoin in conjunction with public blockchain protocols relies on a trustless system which can be defined as a payment infrastructure permitting the issuance of bitcoins or monetary tokens (also named virtual money or cryptocurrency). Such an infrastructure needs therefore to build another kind of trust which is intricately connected to the protocol and the operating nodes. A blockchain is a distributed ledger made of several blocks relied on in a chronological order from one to another. Each block contains data.[43] In the case of bitcoin, the data makes it possible to identify each bitcoin and link it to the user profile of the owner of that bitcoin. When a payer wants to initiate a payment in bitcoin, they will request a transaction. Such transaction is carried out through the nodes which will first assess the right to initiate a payment by analyzing if the payer has enough bitcoins for the operation and then queue it for integration in a validated block.

Functioning of a Blockchain System: Validation of Transaction. The validation of the block of transactions is based on a consensus method, which helps to build a truthless system and avoid intermediaries. Regarding the bitcoin protocol, for instance, the nodes will compete to be the first to find the exit hash of the block. Indeed, a block of transactions is protected against hacking by encrypting two hashes. The first one, which is similar to the prior block on the chain, has a time and date stamping function. The second one, which closes the block, depends on the precise data

[42] SWIFT for instance is a secured messenger service used by credit institutions for payment services: see S.V. Scott, M. Zachariadis, Origins and development of SWIFT, 1973–2009. Business History, 54 (3), 462–482. ISSN 0007-6791, https://doi.org/10.1080/00076791.2011.638502 [as of 29 September 2022].

[43] See P. De Filippi, A. Wright, *op. cit.*, 20.

contained in the block. It is unique and any alteration of the block will show that it has been compromised. As the block is linked in an interconnected chain of blocks using that hash system (a Merkle tree), all the following corrupted blocks will be dismissed. Writing that hash needs a "proof-of-work" which is the CPU effort to find the good hash and reward it with generated bitcoins. Any change in the validated block will lead to incompatibility between the content of the block and the exit hash and invalidate the block: the system will end the chain on a node and replicate a sane block on the same node.

Technology Improvement: Smart Contracts and Third-Parties' Applications. The use of blockchain goes beyond a cashless system. Ethereum has widened the possibilities by facilitating third-party application to use the protocol and by allowing these apps to rely on Smart contracts. They are basically programs that will operate if certain prerequisites are fulfilled. For instance, the delivery of data will automatically prompt a payment by the smart contract. If we put aside law and regulations restrictions, it is now virtually possible to create financial instruments on blockchain and a variety of services working through a distributed ledger system. In France, for instance, a recent law has allowed non-public companies to register their securities on a distributed ledger rather than on a financial instrument account,[44] as it was the case since the dematerialization of securities in France 40 years ago.[45] The change is not only formal as companies are now able to simulate a stock market for their shares, even if the system stays quite rudimentary.[46] The perspectives opened by the distributed ledger technology are important, even if the European Union, after years of studies, is currently working on a regulation of the market based on establishing a monopoly for licensed service providers.[47]

Potentially, the use of DLT could also change substantially the supply chain of services in financial markets. DLT markets are one of several possible innovations: they can offer a more direct approach and also build

[44] Order n° 2017–1674 of 8 décembre 2017 related to the use of a distributed ledger for representation and transmission of financial securities. About that law, see P. Barban, V. Magnier (dir.), Blockchain and Company Law, Dalloz, 2019.

[45] French law related to Public Finance, n° 81–1160, of 30 December 1981.

[46] For a study on the impact of such system on the selling of shares of non-public companies, see: P. Barban (coord.), "Le recours à la technologie Blockchain en droit des sociétés", *Actes pratiques et ingénierie financière*, 2021, n° 178, Dossier, 3–50.

[47] *Infra*, n° 28.

synergies among infrastructures. For a more direct approach, the use of blockchain could allow users to access directly the market as participants, without the need for an agent. Activities built around multiple market infrastructures, such as a trading venue and then a securities settlement system, can now be undertaken on the same system using blockchain.[48] Such technological possibilities have been taken into account by the EU legislator as it will be explained below.[49]

4 Approaches of European Authorities

Innovation improves the way services are provided in the banking and finance industry. However, it is also a breach of a monopoly defined by the European authorities allowing for better consumer and investor protection. The EU can react in different ways. First, it can help achieve a more open market by diminishing the scope of the monopoly regime as it has been the case for payment services. It can also go further and help to suppress certain intermediaries. But most of the time, the EU will create new monopolies and align them with the standard that has become the financial monopoly.

Opening New Services and Diminishing the Scope of the Monopoly

Fintech as an Innovation on Process. Fintech is born from the new opportunities created by technology improvement, especially the evolution of the Internet, artificial intelligence and distributed ledger technologies. Therefore, the new actors born from the rise of fintech are not offering new services: they are offering other means to provide the same service. A loan granted through a credit institution or a crowdfunding platform is still a loan. Its nature does not change, only the means to obtain it.

In the European system, in particular, in the banking, financial and insurance system, such innovation can be blocked by the existing monopolies, where a loan provider must most of the time request a credit institution or investment firm license. Although a lot of exemptions exist, they are often based on either the public nature of the actor (which is

[48] See The financial markets and blockchain: outline of a blockchain infrastructure. Blockchain et droit des sociétés, dir. P. Barban, V. Magnier, Dalloz, 2019, 295.

[49] *Infra*, n° 28.

not the case of the fintech model) or the *de minimis* characteristic of the operation.[50] As only small operations can be offered freely, the new actors cannot compete equally with already settled actors.

Increasing the Number of Services and Opening Access to Accounts in the Payment Industry. In order to offer better services to clients of credit institutions in the Single Market, the EU has however modified its Payment services directive to add new actors whose services are based on accounts held by other companies. PSD2[51] distinguishes two types of payment institutions. The account servicing payment service provider is a payment institution that holds an account on behalf of its client and provides related payment services. Such providers are the historical payment providers. Two new services have been created: payment initiation services and account information services. The first service is meant to initiate a payment order at the request of the payment service user with respect to a payment account held with another payment service provider. The second one is an online service to provide consolidated information on one or more payment accounts held by the payment service user with either another payment service provider or with more than one payment service provider.[52] There are specific services where the provider has access with consent from the client to their account data. The company offering such services is often smaller than a credit institution and, therefore—and as it does not hold funds from the public—they are subject to less prudential regulation, which opens access to the market and helps break some market barriers. As described above,[53] access to the account which represents an essential facility is required to provide such services. The directive specifies the rights of the new providers to access the data despite criticism by professionals arguing that this generates a potential systemic risk.[54] By creating these two new services, the European authorities decided that a payment account must not reinforce the

[50] For example in the Financial sector: MiFID 2, art. 2.

[51] Directive (EU) 2015/2366 of 25 November 2015 on payment services in the internal market, Official Journal of European Union, 23.12.2015, L337/35 ("PSD").

[52] See PSD, art. (4, 15, and 16).

[53] *Supra*, n° 18.

[54] See T. Bonneau, X. Verbiest, Fintech et droit, RB éditions, 2017, 69.

monopoly and that by recognizing the new actors, this may emulate the market and lower the costs for clients.[55]

Offering a More Direct Approach Through Exemptions

Single Distributed Ledger Technology Market Infrastructure. Rather than increasing the number of providers in order to get a better access to services, EU regulation has recently opted for a new method. Regarding Blockchain and distributed ledger technology, automatization and transparency allow for an amelioration of the existing market infrastructure, if we set aside the scaling issue alongside the slowness of DLT transactions. Studies have forecast the possibility for DLT infrastructure to combine in a sole infrastructure the functions of all the infrastructures of the title chain (trading, netting, settlement).[56] The pilot regime for market infrastructures based on DLT[57] allows for operators to request for an exemption from the constraining rules of the Market in the Financial Instruments directive such as (1) restriction of access to specified members or (2) necessity for a license for a settlement system. It would be possible for investors to directly access the trading venue. Moreover, the trading venue will be able to associate direct settlement whereas, in a traditional market, the settlement system is operated by another company than the market operator. Costs could be consecutively reduced.

Choice for an Experimental Regulation. The Financial markets in Europe are under strict regulation. The current regulation has taken into account the subprime crisis and addressed the issue of the systemic risk. The operators wishing to operate a DLT infrastructure will have to request specific exemptions from their local supervisory authority and must in this regard demonstrate the risk mitigation that has been taken. The license is only granted to registered multilateral trading facilities. But to allow DLT infrastructure in such a model is to allow exemptions that bear some risk for the whole single market. The choice has been made to create an experimental regulation called "pilot regime". To maintain

[55] PSD, recitals 27 and 28.

[56] See P. Barban, ibid.

[57] Regulation (EU) 2022/858 of 30 May 2022 on a pilot regime for market infrastructures based on distributed ledger technology, Official Journal of European Union, 2.06.22, L 151/1.

systemic risks at a reasonable level, some limitations are fixed.[58] The experiment will last for six years, following which a decision will be made: take another six years experimentation time, abandon the experiment or integrate the experiment into the general regulation.

Such an experiment, given the adequate guarantees, will help to test new technologies on a wide scale and might improve the intermediary system by reducing the number of middlemen and the supply chain. This method is very promising but the results will only be known approximately in 2030 once the experiment time has elapsed. Such an approach allows us to assess on the ground how the new system works. Nonetheless, it is a new approach for the EU and, more frequently, European regulations rely too much on a hard monopoly with heavy prerequisites, as highlighted by both the current discussions around a proposal to regulate crypto assets and the recent crowdfunding regulation[59]

Extending Monopolies to New Market and Technics

Cryptoassets Regulation. Cryptoassets are defined by the European Bank Authority as: "*a type of private financial asset that depend primarily on cryptography and distributed ledger technology as part of their perceived or inherent value. A wide range of crypto-assets exist, including payment/ exchange tokens (for example, so-called virtual currencies (VCs)), investment tokens and tokens to access a good or service (so-called "utility" tokens)*".[60] There is not only one type of cryptoassets. Under those terms, a vast variety of tokens exist, allowing their bearers to get a variety of rights. Cryptoassets are in fact merely vehicles of rights.[61] Therefore, to determine the nature of a given cryptoasset, it is necessary to define the rights attached to it. This raises questions as complex as the monetary nature of Bitcoin and other virtual moneys and as delicate as the qualification as a financial instrument or utility token.[62]

[58] Aforementioned Regulation, art. 3.

[59] *Infra*, n° 26.

[60] See EBA, Report with advice for European Commission on cryptoassets, 9 January 2019, 4.

[61] See H. de Vauplane, From paper securities to digital securities, Blockchain et droit des sociétés, dir. P. Barban, V. Magnier, Dalloz, 2019, 239.

[62] *Supra*, n° 21.

Such a qualification of securities tokens has raised numerous questions around the globe. In the U.S., the Howey Test was deemed necessary to characterize such tokens as securities and firmly regulate them. The test relies on the three characteristics of an investment contract. The instrument is qualified as an investment contract under the Securities Act when it is "*a contract, transaction or scheme whereby a person invests his money in a common enterprise and is led to expect profits solely from the efforts of the promoter or a third party*".[63] Under that test, the S.E.C. qualified several tokens as investment contracts and submitted them to a thorough and harsh regulation.[64]

Qualification of the Cryptoasset. In Europe, the qualification of such tokens is required to determine whether or not the financial directives should apply. The Prospectus (the documentation asked for any public offer of securities) and the MiFID 2 regulations both limit the liberty of the issuers of a token in case of IPOs and the service providers on tokens, would they offer a token qualifiable as a financial instrument. In such a case, transactions and services provided on such a token will fall under the strict scrutiny, regulation and sanctions of the MiFID 2 and Prospectus regulation. If the token does not qualify as a financial instrument, then the market is still open but it can prove dangerous for investors.[65]

Extention of Monopoly to Cryptoassets That Do Not Qualify as Securities. This freedom is about to end as the European Union has recently adopted a regulation for a Market in Cryptoasset known as "MICA".[66] The purpose of the regulation is to regulate all the EU transactions and services regarding all tokens that do not fall under the scope of MiFID 2. The regulation is closely linked to MiFID 2 in two ways: firstly, it works on the basis of a monopoly where only agreed professionals can provide services on cryptoassets; secondly, the regulation offers investment firms an advantage as they can more easily provide such services compared to newcomers.

The European approach has been criticized by the actors of the cryptomarket for two reasons: One reason is that they impose a strong

[63] S.E.C. v. W. J. Howey co., 328 U.S. 293 (1946).

[64] See B. François, Initial Coin Offering. (ICOs) in French Law and comparative law, Blockchain et droit des sociétés, dir. P. Barban, V. Magnier, Dalloz, 2019, 273.

[65] See P. de Filippi, A. Wright, *op. cit.*, 140–141.

[66] Regulation (EU) 2023/1114 of 31 May 2023 on markets in crypto-assets., Official Journal of EuropeanUnion, 9.06.23, L. 150/40 (MICA).

intermediary system to invest in cryptoassets with high prudential regulations and sanctions' risk.[67] The second is that by putting a quite low threshold for the *de minimis* exemption[68] and by allowing already settled investment firms to provide services on cryptoasset,[69] the regulation appears to be in favor of the already settled investment firms. Though, "mifidization"[70] seems to be a new paradigm as all kinds of markets tied to invest slowly falls under the system clearly inspired by aforementioned directive.

Creation of a European Crowdfunding Monopoly. Crowdfunding has been regulated by member states for some time. It is only recently that the European Authorities focused on crowdfunding for investments and loans. The European regulation has a very wide scope. In fact, it is an implementation of the methods used in the directive and regulations related to the general financial markets, credit institutions and insurance. In the regulation, the activity is defined either as the facilitation of granting loans or the placement, reception and transmission of transferable securities on a crowdfunding platform, *i.e.*, a website where the project is explained and the public can decide to participate in the project.

There again there is a "mifidization" of crowdfunding: a new monopoly is created with mandatory intermediaries. Needless to say, it comes with the same constraints with very high standards. Concerns have been expressed about those standards as the *de minimis* exemption is quite low and the whole system appears quite distant from the roots of crowdfunding. Initially, crowdfunding was a new type of service allowing for a more direct approach between issuers and shareholders. More concerning, however, the major actors already regulated through MiFID 2 will be exempted from many constraints, as they are already monitored under such regulation. As for MICA, it offers a market advantage to the already settled actors of the finance and banking industry and may create a barrier for newcomers in this field.

[67] See H. de Vauplane, RTDF 2020/3, 74.

[68] MICA, art. 4.

[69] MICA, art. 59.

[70] The term refers to a model (the MiFID directive) expanded toward other fields of regulation: see Th. Bonneau, La directive "crédit hypothécaire", sa genèse, ses objectifs, son périmètre, RDBF 2015, study 21; M. Rousille, "Mifidisation" des règles de commercialisation des produits bancaires: l'ACPR relaye les orientations de l'ABE, *Banque & Droit* 2017, n° 175, 41.

5 Conclusions

Maintaining a professional monopoly is not an easy task and needs a lot of adjustment. However, the way European rules are built does not incline to flexible regulations. Services are strictly defined in order to avoid any gap. However, rapid innovation leads to a more rapid obsolescence. To avoid that, the EU reacts either by strengthening the monopoly or by weakening it, depending on economic politics. Most of the time, the monopoly will be strengthened but the EU can also act to experiment with exemptions and weaken barriers to enter the market. Nonetheless, most of the time, it appears that the legislation will maintain a strict approach and define precisely monopolies, thus strengthening already settled actors.

CHAPTER 3

FinTech and Competition Regulatory Concerns in the EU Banking Business Framework

Gabriella Gimigliano

1 Introduction

FinTech—described as 'technology-enabled innovation in financial services, regardless of the nature or size of the provider of the services'—covers the automation process for activities like the provision of payment services, the lending business, advising and consulting, etc.,[1] by means of blockchain and decentralized ledger technology (DLT), Artificial Intelligence (AI), the Internet of Things (IoT), as well as big data, machine

[1] Expert Group on Regulatory Obstacles to Financial Innovation (ROFIEG), 30 Recommendations on regulation, innovation and finance, December 2019; COM (2020) 591 final. Here, the single forms of FinTech innovation are broadly explained and analyzed from a regulatory standpoint.

G. Gimigliano (✉)
University of Siena, Siena, Italy
e-mail: gabriella.gimigliano@unisi.it

M. Bodellini et al. (eds.), *Commercial Banking in Transition*, Palgrave Macmillan Studies in Banking and Financial Institutions,
https://doi.org/10.1007/978-3-031-45289-5_3

learning and so on.[2] In this chapter, the key question is: can FinTech-based applications improve banking competition in the internal market? To what extent could FinTech help European policymakers deal with competition law concerns in the retail banking business?[3]

Before beginning this legal analysis, it is important to reiterate the complex dialectical relationship between competition and regulation in the market sector concerned. It has been emphasized that 'The complex nature of the industry not only creates threats to stability in periods of crisis but also makes the application of a standard model of competition, which emphasizes cost minimization and allocative efficiency, difficult. In particular, according to OECD and Carletti and Vives, certain idiosyncratic features existing in the financial sector, such as asymmetric information in corporate relationships, switching costs and networks in retail banking, have as a consequence that competition cannot always promote efficiency there'.[4] Therefore, liberalization[5] processes were regularly followed by re-regulation. This, as Rosa Maria Lastra argued, should not be viewed as a paradox. On the contrary, the two-tier regulatory strategy may be explained in terms of the need to address 'the externalities of private risk-taking behavior creating a systemic crisis'.[6]

[2] Commission, Consultation Document on "Fintech: a more competitive and innovative European financial sector," 15 June 2017; its follow-up: COM (2018) 109 final.

[3] The concept of the retail banking business comprises banking services provided to consumers and small and medium enterprises (COM (2007) 33 final). It is worth noting that, since the beginning, there has been no distinction in the European legal framework between retail and wholesale, investment and commercial banks.

[4] See Ilias Kapsis, Competition law and policy for the EU banking sector in a period of increased economic uncertainty, in International Journal of Law and Management, 2012, vol. 54 (4), 284–301.

[5] We should keep in mind the conceptual difference between liberalization and privatization. The liberalization process concerns any regulatory actions aiming to remove any regulatory burdens to the market entry. See: Reiner schmidt, La liberalizzazione dei servizi di interesse economico generale, in Riv. trim. dir. pubbl., 2003 (3), 687. Therefore, in the EU the idea of liberalization is closely connected with the construction of the internal market defined, according to Art 26 (2) of the Treaty on the Functioning of the European Union (TFEU), as "an area without internal frontiers in which the free movement of goods, persons, services and capital is ensured in accordance with the provisions of the Treaties."

[6] See R. M. Lastra, Multilevel governance in banking regulation, in M. P. Chiti & V. Santoro (eds), The Palgrave handbook of European Banking Union Law, Palgrave-Macmillan, 2019, 3–17.

The recent global financial crises are increasingly eroding space for competition especially concerning the regulatory approach to state aid.[7] However, this topic falls beyond the scope of this legal analysis, which will focus on antitrust enforcement according to Articles 101 and 102 TFEU. While the former provision concerns the prohibition of 'agreements between undertakings, decisions of associations of undertakings and concerted practices that may affect the trade between the Member States and which have as their object or effect the prevention, restriction or distortion of competition within the internal market', the latter covers unilateral conduct that may affect trade between Member States by means of abuse of dominant position. Both of them are applied by the Antitrust Network Authorities on the basis of the Council regulation enacted ex Article 103 TFEU. In 2003, Council Regulation n. 1 enabled the Commission—as *primus inter pares* in the national antitrust authorities network—to perform sector inquiries into a particular sector or a particular type of agreement whenever the 'rigidity of prices or other circumstances suggest that competition may be restricted or distorted within the common market'. Indeed, the Commission may require the enterprises or associations of enterprises concerned to communicate all agreements, decisions and concerted practices.[8]

As for the banking sector, the last sector inquiry dates back to January 2007. According to the final report, there were three main areas of concern regarding competition. Firstly, inter- and intra-system competition for payment card services raised issues in terms of price and non-price standards: reference was made especially to the level and structure of the multilateral interchange fee (or MIF)[9] as well as to membership fees

[7] Namely, Article 107 TFEU.

[8] Article 17, Council Regulation (EC) No 1/2003, of 16 December 2002 [2003] L1/1 (consolidated version).

[9] When the Commission settled the 2001 Visa decision on MIF it provided that 'the Visa multilateral interchange fee is a fee per payment transaction that has to be paid according to the Visa rules between the two banks involved in a Visa card payment. Currently, it is paid by the merchant's bank to the cardholder's bank' (Commission decision of 9 August 2001 published in OJEC L293/2001). There is internal consistency between the 2001 MIF definition and the definition of interchange fee established in the 2015 MIF Regulation meaning 'a fee paid for each transaction directly or indirectly (i.e. through a third party) between the issuer and the acquirer involved in a card-based payment transaction. The net compensation or other agreed remuneration is considered to be part of the interchange fee' (European Parliament and Council, Regulation [EU]

and requirements. Secondly, customer mobility is impaired by information asymmetries and high switching costs. In the end, lack of open and affordable access to good quality credit data may make consumer loans and credit cards more expensive. The following legal analysis will skip the second point because there is no antitrust case on this point while, at the same time, the 2014 PAD Directive strongly encouraged customer mobility by compelling Member States to make comparison websites available for free and empowering consumers with the right to switch, on a cross-border basis, all or part of the incoming credit transfers, standing orders for credit transfers or direct debit mandates, with no further cost.[10]

In the following sections, this paper aims to prove that in the years following the 2007 Competition Report, many further steps were made toward a level playing field for banks thanks to synergies between antitrust enforcement and command and control strategy but there are several grey areas to deal with. Therefore, using the 2007 Sector Inquiry Report as the starting point of this legal analysis, this chapter aims to investigate the following research questions with regard to the EU-based regulatory framework: (i) whether the social role of commercial banks might have impaired the applicability of competition law and, in this context, what role the digital euro might play; (ii) whether FinTech may improve the European regulators' ability to deal with the cost and the drawbacks of two-sided payment platforms; (iii) in the end, whether FinTech could improve the interoperability of national credit registers. While sections II–IV cover the above-mentioned research questions, section V draws conclusions arguing that FinTech may not be a panacea for banking competition.

No 751/2015 on interchange fees for card-based payment transactions, in OJ [2015] L123/1).

[10] European Parliament and the Council, Directive (EU) No 92/2014, of 23 July 2014 on the comparability of fees related to payment accounts, payment account switching and access to payment accounts with basic features, in OJEU [2014] L257/214.

2 From the Liberalization Process for Commercial Banks to the project of a Digital Euro

The social function of commercial banks has traditionally raised doubts about the construction of the banking business or the identification of some banking activities as services of general economic interest (SGEI), questioning the full applicability of competition law. This first part of Section II leads us to the role of credit institutions in the provision of payment account services. In this context, it seems easier to understand the role of the digital euro.

The starting point of this legal analysis is the definition of credit institutions: these are defined by what they do, regardless of the business model or the legal form they take. In fact, the EU legal framework refers to banks as credit institutions, and this concept comprises any 'undertaking the business of which is to take deposits or other repayable funds from the public and to grant credits for its own account'[11] The banking business is a regulated activity, therefore any business entities wishing to enter the bank market must obtain a banking authorization issued by the competent Home State supervisory authority. The banking authorization covers the operation of the credit intermediation function but it may also cover the provision of one or more passported activities.[12] Furthermore, in compliance with the universal banking model, credit institutions may also operate investment services as long as they obtain an ad-hoc authorization, and they may distribute insurance products,[13]

It goes without saying that among the various business activities mentioned above, only credit intermediation is really deemed a social function,[14] thus raising the question of whether this is enough to consider

[11] European Parliament and the Council, Regulation (EU) no 575/2013 of 26 June 2013 on prudential requirements for credit institutions and investment firms and amending Regulation (EU) No 648/2012, in OJ [2013] L176/1 (Art 4, let. a).

[12] Annex I, European Parliament and the Council, Directive (EU) no 36/2013 of 26 June 2013 on access to the activity of credit institutions and the prudential supervision of credit institutions and investment firms, amending Directive 2002/87/EC and repealing Directives 2006/48/EC and 2006/49/EC, in OJ [2013] L176/238.

[13] See J. H. Dahuisen, Financial liberalisation and re-regulation, in European Business Law Review, 2000, 373–380.

[14] R. M. Lastra, Multilevel governance in banking regulation, 4.

the banking business a service of general economic interest (SGEI) and, if so, whether competition law is still applicable. As for the first issue, we should keep in mind what SGEIs are: as the 2000 Commission Communication stated, they are 'different from ordinary services in that public authorities consider that they need to be provided even where the market may not have sufficient incentives to do so' to promote the social and territorial cohesion and overall competitiveness of European industry.[15] Therefore, SGEIs demonstrate the existence of a market failure: States entrust some undertakings to operate SGEIs as they are 'services that all citizens should have access to at an affordable price because they are indispensable for their welfare'.[16] However, it is worth mentioning that being treated as an SGEI does not automatically exempt an enterprise from competition law and, moreover, any compensation provided by State, regional, or local authorities may fall within the scope of state aid law unless exempted according to Articles 93, 106(2) and 107(3) TFEU.[17] So, the key question concerns the nature of the European regulatory approach to the banking business.

As for the negative harmonization process, the European Court of Justice (ECJ) has not excluded that some banks' businesses may be deemed SGEIs, but the operation of banking business in terms of credit intermediation function is not per se a service of general interest of an economic nature for its social importance. In fact, in the Züchner case,[18]

[15] COM (2000) 580 final. It is up to the Member States to establish whether an economic activity is to be considered as a service of general interest, how it should operate and, in the case, it is such a service, whether compensation may be provided, while the Union through the Commission is in charge of performing a check for manifest error. More recently: COM (2011) 900 final.

[16] See A. M. Collins & M. Martínez Navarro, Economic activity, market failure and services of general economic interest: it takes two to tango, in Journal of European Competition Law & Practice, 2021, vol. 12 (5), 380–386; L. Gyselen, Services of general economic interest and competition under European law—a delicate balance, in Journal of European Competition Law & Practice, 2010, vol. 1 (6), 491–499.

[17] COM (2000) 580 final, 14 f.

[18] EU Court of Justice, Gerhard Züchner *v.* Bayerische Vereinsbank AG, 14 July 1981, C-172/80. The defendant maintained that 'by reason of the special nature of the services provided by such undertakings and the vital role which they play in transfers of capital they must be considered as undertakings (...) entrusted with the operation of services of general economic interest within the meaning of Article 90 (2) and thus are not subject, pursuant to that provision, to the rules on competition in Articles 85 and 86 of the Treaty'.

the ECJ held that 'Although the transfer of customers' funds from one Member State to another normally performed by banks is an operation that falls within the special task of banks, particularly in connection with international movements of capital, that is not sufficient to make them undertakings within the meaning of Article 90 (2) of the Treaty unless it can be established that in performing such transfers the banks are operating a service of general economic interest with which they have been entrusted by a measure adopted by the public authorities'.[19] This legal conclusion was to some extent confirmed in the 1998 Commission Report to the Council of Ministers about the banking sector, planning more in-depth investigations. There it was established that the Member States tend to consider one banking activity or another as an SGEI: some of them opt for the promotion of small and medium enterprises, others for the provision of social loans or municipal financing and still others for the granting of guarantees of export credits.[20]

By contrast, in the positive harmonization process, there is no mention of banking activities as SGEIs. The entire harmonization process has always been aimed at removing internal frontiers and carrying on a liberalization process. Indeed, the First Banking Directive,[21] in the second half of the Seventies, laid down the definition of credit institution and dealt with the banking business as a regulated activity.[22] Moreover, in an effort to keep under control any national attempt to protect national champions, this Directive established that the 'economic needs of the market' may no longer work as a condition of authorization, with the

[19] Gerhard Züchner *v.* Bayerische Vercinsbank AG, § 7–8.

[20] See Report of European Commision to the Council of Ministers: services of general economic interests in the banking sector, adopted on 17 June 1998. These results were also mentioned in the COM (2000) 580 final, 15.

[21] First Council directive of 12 December 1977 on the coordination of laws, regulations and administrative provisions relating to the taking up and pursuit of the business of credit institutions, OJ [1977] L322/30.

[22] Indeed, any business entity having its legal seat and central administration in a Member State may enter the internal market as a credit institution as long as it has obtained the proper authorization. More details in: J Dalhuisen, *Home and Host Country regulatory control of trans-border banking services in the EU* 20 (Guido Alpa & Francesco Capriglione eds, Utet 2002); C. Rossini, Cross-border banking in the EC: host country under the Second Banking Directive, in European Review of Private Law 1995, vol. 4, 571–590.

consequence that the national competent authorities were no longer entitled to issue or refuse banking authorization on the grounds of 'economic needs of the market'. However, whenever technical and structural difficulties in a national banking system kept Member States from abandoning this criterion, the State concerned was allowed to continue applying it for a period of seven years after the directive implementation. Where this temporary exception was employed, the First Banking Directive provided that the 'economic needs' criterion should be applied on the basis of general predetermined standards aiming to promote '(i) security of savings, (ii) higher productivity in the banking system; (iii) greater uniformity of competition between the various the banking networks; (iv) a broader range of banking services in relation to population and economic activity'.[23]

Despite further steps taken, the fragmentation along the national lines survived in the form of business commencement authorizations for branches whose head office was located in another Member State. This regulatory mechanism was overcome thanks to the Second Banking Directive[24] which inverted the balance between the home and the host Member State. Indeed, any credit institution having its legal seat and central administration in a Member State may operate banking business and any other business activities covered by the authorization issued (known as passported activities) on the basis of the home State regulation and under the supervision of the home state authority, extending to banks the conclusion reached in the 1979 Cassis de Dijon case.[25]

Coming to recent years, the regulatory effort to liberalize the banking market was slowed down, but not stopped, by the last financial crises.[26] Indeed, the EU State Aid law and, consistently, the Bank Recovery

[23] Article 3, lett. (d), First Banking Directive.

[24] Second Council directive of 15 December 1989 on the coordination of laws, regulations and administrative provisions relating to the taking up and pursuit of the business of credit institutions and amending Directive 77/780/EEC, in OJ [1989] L386/1.

[25] See M. Björkland, The scope of the general good notion in the Second EC Banking directive according to recent case law, in European Business Law Review, 1998, 227–243.

[26] See M. Passalacqua, Profili giuridici del governo del rischio, in A. Brozzetti (ed), L'ordinamento bancario europeo alla ricerca di un assetto stabile, Bologna: Il Mulino 2022, 39–67.

and Resolution Regulatory Package,[27] have established that all economic operators, not only legal entities but also capital providers, should be accountable for their choices and actions[28]; this means in other words that '(...) public resources can be used only as a last resort and subject to strict requirements' and only when the application of insolvency proceedings and the liquidation procedure are likely to impair the bank's critical functions[29] or may have significant adverse effects on financial stability.[30]

In the end, both negative and positive harmonization try to foster the liberalization process in times of growth and in times of distress. But neither the banking business nor any other banking activities (passported activities) were deemed at the Union level as services of general economic interest in themselves. Similarly, banking activities listed as critical activities by the European Supervisory Risk Board were in no way considered as services of general economic interest despite—as already mentioned above—the fact that deposit-taking and lending activities, payment, clearing, settlement, cash and custody services, capital markets and wholesale funding are considered as businesses and operations 'the discontinunance of which is likely in one or more Member States, to lead to the disruption of services that are essential to the real economy or to disrupt financial stability due to the size, market share, external and internal interconnectedness, complexity or cross-border activities of an

[27] This regulatory package is made up of European Parliament and the Council, Directive (EU) No 59/2014 of 15 May 2014 establishing a framework for the recovery and resolution of credit institutions and investment firms and amending Council Directive 82/891/EEC, and Directives 2001/24/EC, 2002/47/EC, 2004/25/EC, 2005/56/EC, 2007/36/EC, 2011/35/EU, 2012/30/EU and 2013/36/EU, and Regulations (EU) No 1093/2010 and (EU) No 648/2012, of the European Parliament and of the Council, in OJ [2014] L173/190 (hereafter, BRRD); European Parliament and the Council, Regulation (EU) No 804/2014, of 15 July 2014 establishing uniform rules and a uniform procedure for the resolution of credit institutions and certain investment firms in the framework of a Single Resolution Mechanism and a Single Resolution Fund and amending Regulation (EU) No 1093/2010, in OJ [2014] L225/1 (hereafter, SRMR).

[28] See M. Maggiolino, EU State aid law in the banking sector: the story of a revelatory change, in Law and Economics Yearly Review, 2019, 64–124.

[29] With regard to the "critical functions," see: Single Resolution Board (SRB), Public interest assessment: SRB approach, available at: http://srb.europa.eu.

[30] Olina Capolino, The Single Resolution Mechanism: authorities and proceedings, in Mario P. Chiti & V. Santoro (eds), The Palgrave handbook of European Banking Union Law, Palgrave-Macmillan, 2019, 247–269.

institution or group, with particular regard to the substitutability of those activities, services or operations'.[31]

However, the PAD directive and the earlier 2011 Commission Communication on access to a basic payment account seem to take a different direction in order to pursue a financial inclusion objective: the right to a payment account is conferred on any consumer who is legally resident in the Union, and this right may be exercised in any Member State. In fact, the payment account with basic features is fully comparable to the regular payment account. Indeed, account holders are entitled to make and receive payment transactions by means of credit transfers, direct debits or debit cards, for free or at a 'e payment fee'.[32] It is consistently stated that 'consumers (...) who do not hold a payment account in that Member State should be in a position to open and use a basic payment account in that Member State. In order to ensure the widest possible access to basic payment accounts, Member States should ensure that consumers have access to such an account in spite of their financial circumstances, such as unemployment or personal bankruptcy'.[33]

The PAD directive set the category of potential beneficiaries and the needs to be fulfilled, picked out a category of payment service providers (namely, credit institutions) and imposed on them a duty of service defining the contents of the mission, while it left to Member States the task of establishing how many banks are entrusted with this task in such a way as to cover all the territory concerned, at affordable rates and with similar conditions. Therefore, the provision of payment accounts with basic features looks like an EU-based SGEI pursuing financial inclusion.[34] Behind all of this, there is the awareness that the electrification process of retail payment services inverted the ratio between public (banknotes and coins) and private (scriptural) money in the internal market, giving priority to the latter over the former, and this means that one must necessarily hold a payment account to access the payment system.

However, holding a payment account is not enough to fully participate in the payment system: it does not work like a light switch. Consumers,

[31] Supra nt. 28.

[32] Article 17 PAD.

[33] COM (2011) 4977 final (preamble 7).

[34] The same conclusions were raised by: José luis Gómez-Barroso & Raquel Marbán-Flores, Basic financial services: a new service of general economic interest?, in Journal of European Social Policy 2013, vol. 23 (3), 332–339.

especially vulnerable consumers should—but it is likely they will not—be able to deal with digital threats hiding behind the everyday use of payment accounts as well as with (strong) authentication mechanisms set up for protection from digital threats on an ongoing basis. Both of these may impair the effective fulfillment of the financial inclusion objective because vulnerable consumers may not live up to the EU policymaker's expectations. Neither do credit institutions have enough business incentives to deliver proper or better payment account services and customer-based ancillary services, especially because they are not compensated at all for the payment account service provided. This may trigger a race-to-the bottom mechanism.[35]

In this context, the launch of a digital euro may seem like an extremely interesting project in the pursuit of financial inclusion, but this achievement depends on the basic elements of its business model and the main requirements of the legal framework. It should be noted that, in the third report on the digital euro,[36] the European Central Bank and euro area national central banks clarified that the digital euro (i) works through an app provided by the Eurosystem as the basic alternative to the PSP's existing banking or payment apps, (ii) does not depend on mobile device manufactures, because anyone must be able to have access regardless of the type of device; (iii) may be used in online and offline payment transactions and, in the latter, through QR codes. But, at the same time, this Report imposes on payment service providers, as laid down in the 2015 Payment Service Directive, the provision of onboarding services, in terms of identification and authorization steps required to open a digital euro account for end users, both consumers and merchants. So, the question is whether this may raise the same type of financial exclusion concerns that are still on the table.

[35] See J. Hoffmann, Implementation of the Payment Accounts Directive, 20 *ERA Forum*, 2019, 241.

[36] This document is available at: https://www.ecb.europa.eu/paym/digital_euro/investigation/governance/shared/files/ecb.degov220929.en.pdf?c7289d0032238188c71a4803112ea552.

3 Price and Non-Price Competition Among Card-Based Payment Systems

Price and non-price competition concerns focus on the role of match-maker: the regulatory challenge at the EU level is to figure out whether and to what extent decentralized ledger technology (DLT) may provide for a feasible alternative form of coordination.

The starting point is to understand what competition concerns were about. The 2007 sector inquiry into card-based payment systems underscored that Member States took different approaches to the price levels and structures of inter-bank, card-holder and merchant fees which, according to the Commission, was a clear sign of market fragmentation. Moreover, the Report emphasized that membership conditions and governance arrangements in several Member States (Belgium, Denmark, Finland, Hungary, Ireland, Italy and so on) reserved the right to issue and acquire solely for credit and/or financial institutions and their subsidiaries, while others, such as France and Spain, compelled associate members to report business-sensitive information to the principal members without reciprocal data sharing.[37]

As for price competition concerns, the main point was the multilateral interchange fee (or MIF), set by the governing body of VISA and applied by default whenever there was no bilateral agreement between the financial intermediaries of the cardholder and of the merchant concerned. In fact, MIF is a fee paid by acquirers to issuers for services provided by the latter to merchants without a direct contract relationship.

According to VISA rules, MIF was nothing more than a 'transfer between undertakings that are cooperating in order to provide a joint service in a network characterized by externalities and joint demand'. VISA thus concluded that MIF should fall beyond the scope of competition concerns. However, the European Commission did not agree with the VISA approach in full: while the MIF agreement may not be considered a restriction (of competition) by object because it improved inter-system competition (between four-party and three-party platforms) and increased the stability and efficiency of operation card payment markets, it may be deemed a restriction of competition by effects following the

[37] COM (2007) 33 final, 4 ff.

2002 decision.[38] More specifically, the Commission stated that for the provision of card payment services, it was necessary to set 'a remuneration paid between banks who must deal with each other for the settlement of a card payment transaction and thus have no choice of partner. The absence of some sort of default rule on the terms of settlement could lead to abuse by the issuing bank, which is in a position of monopsony as regards the acquiring bank for the settlement of an individual payment transaction. Thus, some kind of default arrangement is necessary, but the question of whether it qualifies for exemption or not will depend on the details of the arrangement'.[39] Therefore, the Commission temporarily authorized the new MIF scheme ex Article 101(3) TFEU (old 81(3) Treaty of the European Community) and no longer critically contended the MIF structure, endorsing the interactions required by two- or multi-sided platforms. By contrast, in 2015 European lawmakers decided to regulate the MIF level: while after the 2002 VISA decision, the level of MIF had been set according to an objectively cost-based approach, regulation n. 751 of 2015 imposed a maximum interchange fee rate for debit and credit card payments in business-to-consumer payment transactions.[40]

Turning to non-price competition restrictions, the most interesting case is the antitrust proceeding on Groupment Cartes Bancaires, but, well before its settlement, Article 28 of the 2007 Payment Services Directive (PSD1) stated that 'rules on access of authorized or registered payment service providers that are legal persons to payment systems shall be objective, non-discriminatory and proportionate and that those rules do not inhibit access more than is necessary to safeguard against specific risks such as settlement risk, operational risk and business risk and to protect the financial and operational stability of the payment system'.[41] In 2015,

[38] Commission decision of 24 July 2002, OJEC [2002] L318/17 (thereafter, VISA 2002).

[39] VISA 2002, § 79.

[40] European Parliament and the Council, Regulation (EU) n 751 of 2015 on interchange fee on card-based payment transactions, OJEU [2015] L123/1. With regard to the interaction between antitrust enforcement and regulation, see: See V. Falce, Il mercato integrato dei sistemi di pagamento a dettaglio tra cooperazione e concorrenza (Primi appunti ricostruttivi), in Banca e borsa 2008, vol. 61(5), I, 558–584.

[41] Parliament and the Council, Directive (EU) n 64 of 2007 on payment services in the internal market amending Directives 97/7/EC, 2002/65/EC, 2005/60/EC and 2006/48/EC and repealing Directive 97/5/EC, OJEC [2007] L319/1. In Article 28 as well as throughout the PSD1 the concept of payment system means 'a funds transfer system

the PSD1 was replaced by the PSD2[42] and Article 28 was renumbered as Article 35. Both Payment Services Directives left open the issue of whether or not the payment system might be considered an essential facility in the provision of payment services. On this point, the Court of Justice had already given a hint in its ruling on the Groupment Cartes Bancaires *v* Commission.[43] Indeed, the Third Chamber of the Court held that the multilateral agreement setting the card issuing/acquisition of merchants ratio may not be considered a restriction of competition by object since any measures should be analyzed with regard to 'the nature of the services at issue, as well as the real conditions of the functioning and structure of the markets—of the economic or legal context in which that coordination takes place'. As for network industries or multi-sided markets, interactions between sides in the system must be analyzed by antitrust and judicial authorities in terms of their own effects.[44]

Something that pricing and non-pricing arrangements have in common is the critical role of card platforms, namely VISA—a privately-owned for-profit corporation—, acting as matchmakers in order to internalize the indirect and two-sided network externalities exhibited by payment services. Indeed, the platform is set up as a common meeting place (virtual or real platform) with a view to facilitating interactions between the two sides of the market and minimizing transaction costs.[45] However, the platform, through its governing council, may deliberate membership

with formal and standardised arrangements and common rules for the processing, clearing and/or settlement of payment transactions'. The VISA-card network may be subsumed under the definition of payment system.

42 Parliament and the Council, Directive (EU) n 2366 of 2015 on payment services in the internal market, amending Directives 2002/65/EC, 2009/110/EC and 2013/36/EU and Regulation (EU) No 1093/2010, and repealing Directive 2007/64/EC, OJEU [2015] L337/35.

43 Judgment of the European Court of Justice of 11 September 2014, Case C-67/13 P (hereafter, 2014 Cartes Bancaires). More specifically: J. Ruiz Calzado & A. Scordamaglia-Tousis, Groupement des Cartes Bancaires v Commission: shedding light on what is not a 'by object' restriction of competition, in Journal of European Competition Law & Practice 2015, 1–3.

44 2014 Cartes Bancaires, § 86.

45 See D. S. Evans & R. Schmalensee, Markets with two-sided platforms, in 1 Issues in Competition Law and Policy 667 (ABA Section of Antitrust Law 2008), 674 ff.

conditions and fees as well as MIF structure and level.[46] Both of these may influence the features and costs of services provided to final users and the efficiency of the market as a whole. Indeed, such agreements may become a way of impairing access to new products or services as well as for new members, but they may also influence the trade-off between incumbents and newcomers, raising the issue of the trade-off between intra- and inter-system competition.

In the context outlined above, the point is whether FinTech may replace the platform-based coordination model dealing with the competition concerns raised by the role of the VISA-like matchmaker. Thinking of decentralized ledger technology (DLT)—at least public DLT[47]—, FinTech may supersede traditional matchmakers whose task is to get both sides of the market—issuers and acquirers, cardholders and merchants—on board in order to operate payment services. Indeed, in public and permissionless DLT, every node in the network is entitled to read the information and to validate the exchanges by solving an algorithm; this feature may replace most of the tasks performed by matchmakers like VISA such as the exchange of payment information, the activity of clearing and the settlement of payment transactions. Furthermore, all forms of DLT feature immutability and 'resistance to tampering' in the sense that '-[their] data are externally verifiable and all data are immutable'. But what happens from the inside?

DLTs are forms of network-based governance, and as such they bring about informal cooperation structures. More specifically, the actors cooperate for mutual advantage as long as they maintain mutually beneficial links, and to this extent, the actors refrain from acting opportunistically by way of acting opportunistically.[48] The point is that there is a complex ecosystem of actors in the shadows, ranging from software developers,

[46] 'The platform can affect the volume of transactions by charging more to one side of the market and reducing the price paid by the other side by an equal amount': J. C. Rochet & J. Tirole, Two-sided markets: a progress report, November 29, 2005. Available at: https://www.tse-fr.eu/sites/default/files/medias/doc/by/rochet/rochet_tirole.pdf.

[47] The DLT is a data ledger that may be public, private or hybrid. In a public DLT, every node of the network is empowered to read and validate transactions over the ledger by means of a proof-of-work mechanism; in the fully private ledger there is a central-decision maker who releases write-permissions, while read-permissions may be public or restricted; in the middle, there are the hybrid cases. More details in: M. Pilkington.

[48] See M. Bevir, Governance. A very short story, Oxford University Press: Oxford, 2012, 26 ff.

validators or record keepers to exchanges. Indeed, it has been critically underscored that in permissionless blockchains (subsumable within the broader category of DLT), the decentralization feature is very fluid because it constantly changes over time with no control.[49] In the future, we may learn from the ongoing experience of the pilot regime on DLT market infrastructures for tokenized financial instruments.[50]

4 Collecting and Sharing Credit Data

The 2007 Competition Sector Inquiry also focused on the lack of open and affordable access to good quality credit data, which would seem to be a prerequisite for any commercial banks wishing to provide lending products. It seems—according to the Report—that widespread credit data are not available in several Member States because credit data markets are underdeveloped and the operation of credit data registers among commercial banks is deemed to be not compliant with competition law, at least in some Member States.

Since 2007, regulatory steps forward have mainly concerned the supervisory relationship between on the one hand, deposit-taking institutions, financial corporations and asset-management vehicles engaged in lending activity on a significant basis, and on the other hand, central banks (and the European Central Bank). Anacredit,[51] for example, is a common granular analytical credit database[52] that, like other central credit registers, is operated by central banks and serves purposes of banking supervision.

By contrast, as for the contractual relationship between the consumer/borrower and the lender/commercial bank, there is still a regulatory gap

[49] See A. Walch, Deconstructing "decentralization," in Chris Brummer (ed), Cryptoassets. Legal, regulatory, and monetary perspectives, Oxford University Press: Oxford, 2019, 39–68.

[50] European Parliament and the Council, Regulation (EU) n 858 of 2022 on a pilot regime on market infrastructure based on distributed ledger technology, OJ [2022] L151/1.

[51] Jean-Marc Israël, Violetta Damia, Riccardo Bonci & Gibran Watfe, The analytical credit dataset. A magnifying glass for analysig credit in the euro area, ECB Occasional Paper Series no. 187.

[52] European Central Bank, Regulation (EU) n 867/2016 of 18 May 2016 on the collection of granular credit and credit risk data, OJEU [2016] L144/44; Guidelines of the European Central Bank of 23 November 2017 on the procedures for the collection of granular credit and credit risk data.

that may be filled by an Artificial Intelligence (AI) system. This is defined in the regulation proposal as a 'software that is developed with one or more techniques and approaches listed in the Annex I and can, for a given set of human-defined objectives, generate outputs such as contents, predictions, recommendations, or decisions influencing the environments they interact with'.[53] However, the use of AI is allowed only as long as it does not go beyond the boundaries established by the GDPR. Indeed, Article 22 (1),[54] subject to the exceptions established in the following paragraph,[55] aims to protect the data subject (namely, the natural person holding the data) from the dangers of any decision-making process based exclusively on automation without any evaluation by a human being.

This legal background may explain the *Schufa* case, a preliminary ruling still pending before the European Court of Justice.[56] Schufa is a private German credit information agency that provides its contractual partners (for example, credit or financial institutions) with information on the creditworthiness of third parties (the data subject). Schufa provided a score based on mathematical statistical methods and the third party refused to enter a loan contract with the data subject. This case raises at least three questions on the limits of AI systems applied to the creditworthiness of prospective borrowers: (i) whether scoring is a type of processing activity; (ii) whether the establishment of the score amounts to a decision because it seems that the GDPR draws a conceptual distinction between scoring and decision-making; (iii) to what extent the right of the data subject to obtain from the controller (in this case Schufa), consistently with Article 14 GDPR, information about the existence of

[53] COM (2021) 206 final.

[54] Article 22 (1) GDPR provides that 'The data subject shall have the right not to be subject to a decision based solely on automated processing, including profiling, which produces legal effects concerning him or her or similarly significantly affects him or her'.

[55] Article 22 (2) GDPR laid down that 'Paragraph 1 shall not apply if the decision: (1) is necessary for entering into, or performance of, a contract between the data subject and a data controller; (2) is authorised by Union or Member State law to which the controller is subject and which also lays down suitable measures to safeguard the data subject's rights and freedoms and legitimate interests; or (3) is based on the data subject's explicit consent'.

[56] Case C- 634/21, OQ v Land Hessen, Joined Party: SCHUFA Holding AG.

an automated decision-making process and the logic involved meets the limits of commercial and industrial secrecy.

The idea that the assessment of consumers' credit risk should not be left to the AI system is also central to the regulation proposal mentioned above, which emphasizes the high level of danger of any AI system that may impair consumers' access to financial resources or essential services such as housing, electricity and telecommunication services because it can 'perpetuate historical patterns of discrimination, for example based on racial or ethnic origins, disabilities, age, sexual orientation, or create new forms of discriminatory impacts'.[57]

5 Conclusions

This paper analyzes competition concerns in the banking sector taking cues from the 2007 Commission Sector Inquiry in order to assess whether FinTech applications may in some ways deal with them. The aim of this chapter was not to analyze or explain FinTech innovation, but to examine the state of (banking and competition) law with which FinTech innovations are going to engage.

The legal analysis is based on EU antitrust enforcement and the positive harmonization process for banking and payments; its first step was to establish whether the banking business is, due to the social importance of the credit intermediation function, in any way to be considered a service of general economic interest and, if so, exempted from the application of competition law. The answer is no: legislative coordination—both in times of growth and of crisis—and European case law has always encouraged the liberalization process. trying to eliminate regulatory fragmentation along national lines; it has provided that the operation of taking-up funds from the public to extend credit is an economic activity and, as such, subject to EU competition rules and regulations, but the Züchner case and the 1998 Commission Report to the Council of Ministers about the banking sector leave some room for formally considering one or the other bank activity as a SGEI. However, the most interesting element here concerns

[57] COM (2021) 206 final, 26.

the role of CBDC in the process of financial inclusion. Indeed, more or less according to the legal framework and the business model, the digital euro might ease the financial inclusion process. Waiting for the establishment of the digital euro, the legal analysis emphasizes how the role of payment service providers in the onboarding process may deal with the risk of disintermediation, but some nagging doubts remain as to whether a payment account is the proper mechanism to reach out to unbanked consumers.

Section III deals with the primary antitrust concern: price and non-price competition issues in the debit and credit card industry. The main point here is the role of two-sided platforms as matchmakers: permissionless and public DLT infrastructures may replace a VISA-like system but at the same time they are difficult to reconcile with the idea of being legally accountable for market conduct as well as with the need for transparent governance structures in the financial institution-supervisory authority relationship. Finally, Section IV pointed to credit risk data and the lack of good quality credit data, which may impair lending activity to consumers. The AI system may serve to tackle this issue, but a clear-cut policy-making choice is needed to set a balance between individual and automated assessment of creditworthiness, examining what makes the two different despite the general lack of trust in any form of middle-man, agent or institution that gradually grew during the last financial crises.[58]

[58] This paper is updated to May 2023

CHAPTER 4

Prudential Regulation Policy Responses to Financial Technological Innovations: The Future for Banks and Crypto-Finance?

Iris H. Y. Chiu

1 Introduction

Mainstream commercial banks are being confronted with a new era of digital challenges, from fintech entities that utilise mobile application and platform technologies to reach markets[1] to decentralised forms of financial services carried out on peer-to-peer permissionless blockchains such

[1] See generally I. H.-Y. Chiu and G. Deipenbrock (eds), The Routledge Handbook of Financial Technology and Law (Oxford: Routledge 2021).

I. H. Y. Chiu (✉)
UCL Faculty of Law, London, England
e-mail: hse-yu.chiu@ucl.ac.uk

M. Bodellini et al. (eds.), *Commercial Banking in Transition*, Palgrave Macmillan Studies in Banking and Financial Institutions,
https://doi.org/10.1007/978-3-031-45289-5_4

as Ethereum.[2] Machine learning technology is also increasingly transforming certain functions in banks.[3] Against this backdrop, the chapter discusses the scope for prudential regulation policy to respond to market opportunities for banks in relation to crypto-finance. Crypto-finance may broadly be defined as the universe of innovations and services that relate to assets that are privately and digitally generated, such assets are usually transferred via protocols that involve cryptography that entails the dispensation of a centrally trusted authority to finalise or validate such transfers. Crypto-finance may thus be regarded as essentially facilitating disintermediated forms of financial activity and distinguishes from the centralised and comprehensive forms of intermediation banks often undertake.[4] However, the universe of crypto-finance is not possible without certain forms of centralisation that provide network effects,[5] or market credibility and operational smoothness,[6] leading some commentators to opine that 'Decentralised Finance' (DeFi) is 'fake' to an extent.[7] In this manner, it is not farfetched to consider the market opportunities for commercial banks in the world of crypto-finance.

Section A provides a primer on the disincentives for commercial banks to be entangled with crypto-finance based on the Basel Committee's prudential policy recommendation. We address the legitimate concerns

[2] Conveniently called 'DeFi', see Wulf A. Kaal, Digital Asset Market Evolution, 2021, 46 J Corp L, 909; Fabian Schär, Decentralized Finance: On Blockchain- and Smart Contract-Based Financial Markets, 2021, 103(2) Federal Reserve Bank of St. Louis Review, 153–174.

[3] See G. Hertig, Relying on AI for Financial Compliance and Supervision, Oxford Business Law Blog (16 Feb 2022), https://www.law.ox.ac.uk/business-law-blog/blog/2022/02/relying-ai-financial-compliance-and-supervision, Bank of England and FCA, Artificial Intelligence: Public–Private Forum Report (Feb 2022), https://www.bankofengland.co.uk/-/media/boe/files/fintech/ai-public-private-forum-final-report.pdf?la=en&hash=F432B83794DDF3F580AC5A454F7DFF433D091AA5.

[4] On banks' full or direct intermediation role, see 'Introduction', ch1, John Armour et al., Principles of Financial Regulation (Oxford: OUP 2019).

[5] Crypto-exchanges like Coinbase, Binance etc.

[6] Such as writers and maintainers of automated protocols, or those with governance rights over automated protocols, 15–18, Financial Stability Board, Assessment of Risks to Financial Stability from Crypto-assets (16 Feb 2022), https://www.fsb.org/wp-content/uploads/P160222.pdf.

[7] See L.-A. Sørensen and D. Zetzsche, From Centralized to Decentralized Finance: The Issue of 'Fake-DeFi' (2021), https://papers.ssrn.com/sol3/papers.cfm?abstract_id=3978815.

and drawbacks of the disincentivising approach and consider what business lines in crypto-finance can there be opportunities for mainstream commercial banks. Due to space constraints, this chapter will only select to discuss one potential key business line for banks in the realm of crypto-finance. Section B discusses commercial bank lending that can be secured by crypto collateral, and what may be needed in terms of legal and regulatory support in that regard. This Section suggests that an 'experimental' prudential policy can be explored for commercial banks venturing into these opportunities. Section C briefly concludes.

2 New Market Opportunities for Mainstream Commercial Banks in Crypto-Finance?

Policy-makers observe the increasing entanglement of mainstream finance with crypto-finance,[8] such as the exposure of crypto-finance to mainstream financial instruments,[9] as well as investment exposures by mainstream investors, both retail and institutions (mainly hedge funds). Nevertheless, policy-makers are at the moment risk averse regarding mainstream commercial banks' exploration of business opportunities in crypto-finance. This is understandable given that crypto-assets, previously thought to be uncorrelated with conventional assets for risk diversification, seem now to be affected by movements in conventional asset markets. The Basel Committee's policy recommendations,[10] which are generally highly persuasive if not practically adopted in many jurisdictions' bank regulation regimes, arguably disincentivise banks from holding crypto-assets whether as part of credit or market-based business.

[8] FSB (2022).

[9] Which is the design of many popular stablecoins, pegged against a fiat currency, such as one tether pegged to one US dollar, based on reserves managed by Tether to enable it to honour the peg, see https://tether.to/en/. Tether however was accused by the US authorities of not maintaining sufficient reserves hence misleading investors, leading to a settlement with the NY Attorney-General in USD$18.5 million, see 'Cryptocurrency firms Tether and Bitfinex agree to pay $18.5 million fine to end New York probe' (CNBC, 23 Feb 2021), https://www.cnbc.com/2021/02/23/tether-bitfinex-reach-settlement-with-new-york-attorney-general.html; with the Commodity and Futures Trading Commission in USD $42.5 million, see https://www.cftc.gov/PressRoom/PressReleases/8450-21.

[10] TBC final recommendations.

The Basel Committee's Prudential Policy for Crypto-Assets

The Basel Committee acknowledges that the technologies of tokenisation, i.e. the digital representation of a financial asset as a token that can be issued, offered, traded and generally dealt with in technologically empowered manners, has given rise to 'crypto-assets' that require clarification for treatment in prudential regulation applicable to banking institutions. The Committee categorises three groups of 'crypto-assets', i.e. in Groups 1a, 1b, 2a and 2b for differential prudential treatment,[11] seeking to achieve a simple categorisation system that reflects the same regulatory treatment for similar risks.

Group 1a crypto-assets are essentially digitalised and tokenised versions of traditional assets[12] or based on such assets or a pool of such assets. They would be treated similarly to the prudential treatment afforded to exposures to the equivalent traditional assets if the following conditions are met, but subject to whether (a) novel market risks arise if there are changes in terms of market structures where the crypto-asset is traded and (b) whether novel operational risks arise due to changes in technological operations. Group 1a assets should be consistent with traditional assets in terms of how ownership rights are framed in law and recognised and how other rights such as dealing or redemption are documented and recognised for enforceability. Group 1a assets should also be documented, and capable of transfer and settlement finality. They should be capable of being transacted in a manner that achieves the same compliance with settlement, anti-money laundering, operational resilience and risk governance rules applicable to traditional assets whether on similar or different types of networks (such as distributed ledger platforms).

Group 1b assets refer to stablecoins where a digitalised token references traditional assets in order to maintain stability in value. Banks' risk to such exposures stems from market value deterioration in relation to redemption, and where the vehicle that holds the pool of referenced assets is not bankruptcy remote from the issuer. The Basel Committee recommends

[11] Basel Committee on Banking Supervision, 'Prudential Treatment of Cryptoasset Exposures: Consultation Document' (July 2021), https://www.bis.org/bcbs/publ/d519.pdf; 'Prudential Treatment of Cryptoasset Exposures: Second Consultation' (June 2022), https://www.bis.org/bcbs/publ/d533.htm.

[12] Defined as bonds, loans, securities, commodities or cash, ibid.

that the prudential treatment for exposures to bankruptcy remote stablecoin vehicles should be the same as the treatment for direct market risk exposure to the underlying assets. Bankruptcy remoteness should however be supported by robust legal opinion. Where bankruptcy remoteness is not applicable, the market risk treatment of direct exposure to the underlying assets would be multiplied by the credit risk exposure of the bank to an unsecured creditor, such risk to be adjustable depending on the exact obligations of the bank, such as commitment to buy, in relation to the exposure. It is arguable that such prudential treatment is not exactly deterring, as being similar to banks' exposures to interests in managed collective investments. The above treatment applies only where (a) the referenced assets are traditional assets; (b) the stabilisation mechanism is fully robust and effective at all times; (c) the stabilisation mechanism is transparent and accountable based on sound data and risk management and (d) the other requirements for Group 1a crypto-assets are satisfied. If any of these requirements are not met, banks' exposures to stablecoins would be risk -weighted at 1250%, a punitive risk weighting that would entail a high cost in bank capital to engage in such exposures.

Although Group 1 crypto-assets are likely to be technologically framed iterations of assets that resemble conventional financial assets, increased prudential provision is recommended for special infrastructure risks such as those associated with unknown risks involving distributed ledger structures.[13]

For Group 2 crypto-assets, these refer to crypto-assets that do not meet the requirements for Group 1 crypto-assets discussed above. These potentially include cryptocurrency such as bitcoin and ether, used as native currency in the transfer protocols of their respective permissionless blockchains; crypto-assets such as digital tokens issued by developers of applications in fund-raising rounds, known as 'initial coin offerings'[14];

[13] At 2.5% of exposure in market value, see the Basel Committee's second consultation, note 11.

[14] See S. Adhami et al., Why do Businesses Go Crypto? An Empirical Analysis of Initial Coin Offerings, 2018, 100 Journal of Economics and Business, 64; the debates in characterising the nature of ICOs and their pre-sold tokens can be found in J. Rohr and A. Wright, Blockchain-based Token Sales, Initial Coin Offerings, and the Democratization of Public Capital Markets, 2019, 70 Hastings Law Journal, 463; T. L. Hazen, Tulips, Oranges, Worms, and Coins—Virtual, Digital, or Crypto Currency and the Securities Laws, 2019, 20 North Carolina Journal of Law and Technology, 493; P. Maume and M. Fromberger, Regulation of Initial Coin Offerings: Reconciling U.S. and E.U. Securities

non-fungible tokens representing property rights in a unique underlying asset[15]; and fungible tokens that can be fractionalised out of non-fungible tokens.[16] The Basel Committee initially recommended that Group 2 crypto-assets be risk-weighted at 1250% of the net positions held by banks, with no difference in treatment between credit or market risk, and that such assets are not eligible for credit risk mitigation. This prudential regulatory treatment seems punitive for banks whether in terms of accepting crypto-assets as collateral against lending or holding such assets, their derivatives or interests related to such assets in the trading book. The risk weight assumes the maximum and catastrophic losses banks can suffer.

Upon extensive industry representation, the Basel Committee in its second consultation proposed to treat a group of crypto-assets that fall within its defined 'Group 2a' category differently. Group 2a assets are direct holdings or cash-settled derivatives of cryptoassets that have found their way into mainstream regulated trading. This includes direct holdings of crypto-assets traded in regulated exchange-traded products as well as cash-settled derivatives based on a reference rate for the cryptoasset as published by a regulated exchange. Such crypto-assets must satisfy conditions of capitalisation and trading liquidity, as well as having regular observable data for price. However, with the mid-2022 crypto

Laws, 2019, 19 Chicago Journal of International Law, 548; A. Collomb, P. de Fillippi and K. Sok, Blockchain Technology and Financial Regulation: A Risk-Based Approach to the Regulation of ICOs, 2019, 10 European Journal of Risk Regulation, 263; Y. Guseva, A Conceptual Framework for Digital-Asset Securities: Tokens and Coins as Debt and Equity, 2020, 80 Md L Rev, 166.

[15] Debates on what property rights are conferred in non-fungible tokens, see J. Fairfield, Tokenized: The Law of Non-Fungible Tokens and Unique Digital Property, 2021 Indiana Law Journal, https://ssrn.com/abstract=3821102; J. M. Moringello and C. K. Odinet, The Property Law of Tokens, 2022 Florida Law Review, forthcoming, https://ssrn.com/abstract=3928901; J. Marinotti, Tangibility as Technology, 2021, 37 Ga St U L Rev 671.

[16] This process derives fungible tokens out of a non-fungible token to disperse ownership and enable trading and liquidity in smaller values. *Fractional.art* provides a platform for artists to fractionalise their NFTs by locking the NFT as collateral in a smart contract and converting into fungible tokens in the artist's wallet. See also Nftfy, L. Carvalho, The Decentralised Fraction (6 Nov 2020), https://medium.com/nftfy/the-decentralized-securitization-48b62c12d114; L. Carvalho, 'Nftfy User Guide' (9 Nov 2020), https://medium.com/nftfy/nftfy-users-guide-83c72e1b5b21, Niftex, https://landing.niftex.com/.

crash[17] and dramatic declines of market capitalisation of many cryptoassets including Dogecoin, fluctuating value thresholds may pose a risk to banks with crypto-asset portfolios, in terms of their prudential compliance. Group 2a crypto-assets benefit from a modified version of risk weighting for standardised approaches to credit and market risk but the application of an internal models approach to risk weighting is not permitted.

The above treatment of crypto-assets may not deter banks excessively from exposure to popular crypto-assets but it is queried if such an approach is arbitrary, and needs revisiting in light of market developments. Further, it remains unclear how bank lending secured on crypto-collateral should be treated. It may be argued that such lending would not attract the punitive prudential treatment as the borrower's credit risk would determine risk weighting and crypto-collateral would not raise the borrower's credit risk to 1250% risk weighting as such.[18] The collateral would just not benefit from recognised credit risk mitigation.[19]

Further, it is questioned if the Basel Committee's distinction between Group 2a and 2b assets is warranted in light of the incoming European regulation for crypto-assets generally. If regulatory support as well as liquid/developed market conditions are conditions for treating crypto-assets less punitively in terms of prudential compliance, then should new European regulation for crypto-assets influence prudential policy for them?

One should be cognisant of market-building regulations such as the European Markets in Crypto-assets Regulation (MiCA),[20] which is likely to be the first significant regulatory template for crypto-finance.[21] Under

[17] Douglas W. Arner, Dirk A. Zetzsche, Ross P. Buckley and Jamieson M. Kirkwood, 'The Financialization of Crypto: Lessons from FTX and the Crypto Winter of 2022–2023' (2023), https://papers.ssrn.com/sol3/papers.cfm?abstract_id=4372516.

[18] Art 193(1), EU Capital Requirements Regulation 575/2013.

[19] Arts 194, 197–200, ibid.

[20] European Commission, Proposal for a Regulation of the European Parliament and of the Council on Markets in Crypto-assets, and amending Directive (EU) 2019/1937 (2020), https://eur-lex.europa.eu/legal-content/EN/TXT/?uri=CELEX%3A52020PC0593.

[21] Though not without criticism see I. H.-Y. Chiu, Regulating the Crypto-economy (Oxford: Hart Publishing 2021), chs 5, 6; also D. A. Zetzsche, F. Annunziata, D. W. Arner and R. P. Buckley, The Markets in Crypto-Assets regulation (MiCA) and the EU Digital Finance Strategy, 2021, 16 Capital Markets Law Journal, 203.

the MiCA, asset-referenced crypto-assets, which are the equivalent of stablecoins discussed above, would be marketable across the European Economic Area if regulated under MiCA. MiCA crucially addresses the issues of robust stabilisation, or reserve management of the referenced assets, as well as risk governance, transparency, clarity of holders' rights including dispute resolution, and conduct duties on the part of stablecoin issuers. However, MiCA does not demand that the reserve assets for stablecoins be of any particular type, such as traditional assets, as long as they are appropriately disclosed and selected for proper risk management to meet holders' expectations in relation to their rights. Hence, it is queried whether regulated stablecoins under MiCA should fall within Group 1b of the Basel Committee's categorisation?

Further, it is also queried if crypto-assets (not asset-referenced or electronic money cryptoassets) that can be offered in the EEA under MiCA should be subject to a 1250% risk weight for banks' credit or market risk exposures. These would not fall within Group 1 crypto-assets as currently defined by the Basel Committee, but they would be different from unregulated crypto-assets in the markets to date as they would benefit from MiCA's regulation. On the other hand, there is arguably justification for treating them as Group 2 crypto-assets. The regulation MiCA provides is in terms of their offer to EEA markets based on a rather broadly framed white paper. Although issuers are subject to broadly framed duties of conduct to investors such as the need to act fairly, honestly and professionally, to communicate in a fair and non-misleading manner and to prevent, identify, manage and disclose conflicts of interest, it is arguable that these are not sufficient to deal with the financial risk in these assets that are of concern to prudential regulators. Unless and until these cryptoassets reach the trading, capitalisation and liquidity thresholds specified for Group 2a, their financial risk should be conservatively managed by banks. In this manner, the maximum risk-averse treatment of a 1250% risk weight is not inconsistent with the Basel Committee's application to assets that may be complex, novel or lack transparency, affecting the liquidity and prospects of value realisation when needed.[22]

[22] See https://www.bis.org/basel_framework/chapter/CRE/42.htm.

The Contest of Regulatory Objectives

There remains a need to reconcile policy objectives between supporting innovation which involves risk-taking and prudential provision which is seen as the foundation for micro stability at banks and financial institutions. The former also involves forms of financial inclusion or mobilisation for borrowers with different profiles.[23]

There are potential benefits for banks and mainstream financial institutions in crypto-finance. New profit-making opportunities from secured lending against crypto-collateral can be attractive[24] although new forms of due diligence, processes of control over security and enforcement for value realisation would be needed for banks to maximise their opportunities in this area.[25] Volatility in crypto value can also pose challenges for security valuation, but it can be argued that volatility exists for other asset classes too and it is a matter of sufficient market learning over time to be able to price such risks. Further, there is a role for mainstream banks and financial institutions to offer innovation upon their established skills in competing with DeFi interfaces. DeFi applications are algorithmically programmed and can be rigid, while mainstream banks' relationship-based intermediation expertise can allow banks to explore more interactions between conventional and crypto-finance for risk management. New competition between mainstream financial institutions and DeFi can feed upon each other and spur new forms of learning and innovation. Although financial sector innovation is not unequivocally productive of social good,[26] regulators should consider the needs of market choice, especially for mobilising the younger generation who often cannot benefit from getting onto the property ladder sufficiently early, market participants' protection alongside micro and macroprudential policy. Macroprudential policy in particular has only been weakly explored

[23] 'Why Gen Z Could Turn to DeFi Mortgages to Build Real Estate Wealth' (9 May 2022), https://forkast.news/defi-mortgages-help-gen-z-real-estate-wealth/.

[24] 'Crypto Loans Unlock Cash, but They Carry Risks' (Nerdwallet, 14 Oct 2021).

[25] Sect B.

[26] See I. H.-Y. Chiu, A Rational Regulatory Strategy for Governing Financial Innovation, 2017, 8 European Journal of Risk Regulation, 743.

in the decade since the global financial crisis 2007–2009.[27] As MiCA and other regulatory regimes for crypto-assets are being developed for their legitimation and market-building, regulators should holistically consider these reforms alongside the Basel Committee's prudential policy recommendations, in order to map out risks and priorities regarding supporting innovation, consumer protection and financial stability monitoring.

Further, it is queried whether exposure to crypto-assets is useful for risk diversification. Financial stability can arguably be better safeguarded if risk interconnections are not concentrated and dispersed.[28] At the moment, the 'financialisation' of crypto-assets is largely taking place in unregulated peer-to-peer DeFi spaces. Crypto-asset holders may be able to lend to each other secured by crypto collateral, via automated protocols that lock-up security, manage collateral value top-ups and redemption,[29] participate in pools that facilitate lending and liquidity transformations[30] or join in automated management of 'investment' interests by protocols that are programmed to select investment opportunities,[31] hedging opportunities or prediction betting markets.[32] This universe has been perceived to be quite 'separate' from mainstream finance and may entail less risk of loss contagion to mainstream financial institutions. If so, regulators

[27] B. Stellinga, The Rise and Stall of EU Macro-Prudential Policy. An Empirical Analysis of Policy Conflicts over Financial Stability, Market Integration, and National Discretion, 2021, 59 Journal of Common Market Studies, 1438.

[28] M. Dijkman, A Framework for Assessing Systemic Risk, April 2010, World Bank Policy Research Working Paper, 5282, http://elibrary.worldbank.org/content/workingpaper/10.1596/1813-9450-5282; F. Allen, A. Babus and E. Carletti, Financial Connections and Systemic Risk, July 2010, NBER Working Paper No 16177, http://www.nber.org/papers/w16177; M. Beville, Financial Pollution: Systemic Risk and Market Stability, 2010, 36 Florida State University Law Review, 245.

[29] 'Crypto Lending Platforms: The Ultimate List' on centralised, exchange-based lending platforms to which cryptocurrency users can lend or obtain loans, e.g. Binance, BlockFi, and decentralised protocol-based lending networks such as Compound, see https://101blockchains.com/crypto-lending-platforms/.

[30] Such as Uniswap, Sushiswap, Curve etc., see 'What Are Liquidity Pools in DeFi and How Do They Work?' (14 Dec 2020), https://academy.binance.com/en/articles/what-are-liquidity-pools-in-defi.

[31] Such as DAOInvest, https://daoinvest.org/.

[32] Such as Augur, Polymarket, see 'How Crypto Transforms Prediction Markets' (Coindesk, 18 Feb 2021), https://www.coindesk.com/tech/2021/02/18/how-crypto-transforms-prediction-markets/.

need not take an excessively disincentivising approach to banks as financial stability risks are not prominent. However, more recent observations of correlations between crypto-asset losses and conventional asset price declines[33] suggest that crypto diversification may be more hazardous than beneficial. This is because financial institutions have increasingly participated in DeFi and brought about growth and asset price appreciation in crypto-financial markets. Hedge funds already allocate parts of their portfolio to crypto-assets,[34] and mainstream institutions seek exposure to crypto-exchange-traded funds, whose offerings have increased amongst listed exchanges in many jurisdictions.[35] Stablecoin issuers hold mainstream financial assets in order to manage their pegs for stability,[36] and retail investors increasingly access crypto-currency and crypto-assets directly,[37] not to mention that non-fungible tokens, many of which emanate from gaming worlds, are starting to be both consumed by retail purchasers[38] and financialised by opportunities in DeFi.[39] Since financial intermediaries adapt and shift with agility towards profit-making opportunities, partitions between crypto-finance and mainstream finance are

[33] 'Bitcoin Plummets in Weekend after Stock Rout, Breaching Support Level to Around $34,000' (Fortune, 9 May 2022), https://fortune.com/2022/05/08/bitcoin-falls-over-weekend-after-stock-rout/.

[34] 'Hedge Funds Expect to Hold 7% of Assets in Crypto within Five Years' (Financial Times, 15 June 2021), https://www.ft.com/content/4f8044bf-8f0f-46b4-9fb7-6d0eba723017.

[35] 'Bitcoin Exchange Traded Fund Debuts on Wall Street' (Financial Times, 20 Oct 2021), https://www.ft.com/content/7bad0235-9fdd-4e0c-8d20-35a6c41696e0; 'Fidelity Enters Crypto Space with Europe's Cheapest Physical Bitcoin ETP' (15 Feb 2022), https://etfstream.com/news/fidelity-enters-crypto-space-with-europe-s-cheapest-bitcoin-etp/.

[36] Discussed in pp. 15–18, FSB (2022); D. Bullman, J. Klemm and A. Pinna, In Search for Stability in Crypto-Assets: Are Stablecoins the Solution?, ECB Occasional Paper, 2019.

[37] E.g. FCA, 'Cryptoasset Consumer Research 2021' (June 2021), https://www.fca.org.uk/publications/research/research-note-cryptoasset-consumer-research-2021; '16% of Americans Say They Have Ever Invested in, Traded or Used Cryptocurrency' (11 Nov 2021), https://www.pewresearch.org/fact-tank/2021/11/11/16-of-americans-say-they-have-ever-invested-in-traded-or-used-cryptocurrency/.

[38] '5 NFT-Based Blockchain Games that Could Soar in 2022' (8 Jan 2022), https://cointelegraph.com/news/5-nft-based-blockchain-games-that-could-soar-in-2022.

[39] Discussed in I. H.-Y. Chiu and J. G. Allen, Exploring the Assetisation and Financialisation of Non-fungible Tokens (NFTs): Opportunities and Regulatory Implications, 2022, 37 Banking and Finance Law Review, 401.

artificial and unlikely to be maintained. The correlation now seems to be accepted, as price crashes in cryptocurrency in mid-2022 are consistent with conventional asset routes such as in stocks and shares.[40] The Basel Committee's prudential treatment of crypto-assets is not only timely but also warranted.

What Potential Business Lines in Crypto-Finance for Banks?

This chapter suggests that there are three potential business lines banks may explore in engaging with crypto-finance, which are related to their present expertise. This does not foreclose other opportunities such as in fund management and collective investment. First, banks may expand into crypto-based secured lending, whether in relationship-based lending or transformation into capital-market credit products. Second, banks may consider offering custodial and payment services intermediation for crypto-finance. Third, banks may consider offering dealing services in crypto-assets such as cryptocurrency, similar to market-making for foreign exchange. In Section B we focus on the first due to space constraints, arguably also the most attractive for banks. We discuss briefly below that the second is fraught with unresolved policy concerns and the third is likely unattractive for banks.

It may be thought that banks have a natural advantage in offering custodial and payment services for cryptocurrency. Banks have a long history of offering store-of-value services in the deposit and other savings accounts and are extensively regulated[41] in relation to onboarding customers, carrying out conduct duties regarding expediency and settlement of payments and taking responsibility for unauthorised transfers and even push payment fraud in the UK.[42] In this manner, regulatory institutions support social confidence in banks' custodial and payment

40 'Why is Crypto Crashing? Analysts List the Key Reasons Behind this Week's Implosion' (Fortune, 14 May 2022), https://fortune.com/2022/05/13/why-is-crypto-crashing-bitcoin-ethereum-tech-stocks/.

41 EU Payment Services Directive (EU) 2015/2366.

42 Payment Services Regulator, 'Authorised Push Payment (APP) Scams Consultation Paper' (Nov 2021), https://www.psr.org.uk/publications/consultations/cp21-10-authorised-push-payment-app-scams-consultation-paper/.

services, which can benefit cryptocurrency users, including merchants,[43] corporations,[44] and institutional[45] and retail users. BNY Mellon in the US, for example, has started offering crypto custodial services mainly to support institutional investors' increasing portfolio diversification into crypto-finance.[46]

However, such a foray may be unattractive for both banks and policy-makers. For banks, the infrastructure for mainstream payment services is either maintained by the central bank[47] or by network operators supervised by central banks and financial regulators.[48] Such infrastructures are separate and not interoperable with permissionless blockchains such as Bitcoin and Ethereum. Indeed permissionless blockchains are written on different protocols and even different computing languages and are in competition with each other.[49] The decentralised systems of transaction validation and ledger maintenance on permissionless blockchains pose

[43] 'Retailers to Drive Crypto Payments Adoption: Survey' (23 Dec 2021), https://cointelegraph.com/news/retailers-to-drive-crypto-payments-adoption-survey.

[44] E.g. 'Tesla Says It Held Nearly $2 Billion Worth of Bitcoin at the End of 2021' (CNBC News, 7 Feb 2022), https://www.cnbc.com/2022/02/07/tesla-held-nearly-2-billion-worth-of-bitcoin-at-the-end-of-2021.html; Deloitte & Touche, Corporate Investing in Crypto (2021), https://www2.deloitte.com/content/dam/Deloitte/us/Documents/audit/corporates-investing-in-crypto-microstrategy.pdf.

[45] 'Institutional Money is Pouring Into the Crypto Market and Its Only Going to Grow' (Forbes, 12 Aug 2021), https://www.forbes.com/sites/lawrencewintermeyer/2021/08/12/institutional-money-is-pouring-into-the-crypto-market-and-its-only-going-to-grow/.

[46] 'BNY Mellon Announces Crypto Custody and Spies Integrated Services' (11 Feb 2021), https://www.coindesk.com/business/2021/02/11/bny-mellon-announces-crypto-custody-and-spies-integrated-services/.

[47] 'Real-time Gross Settlement Systems Such as Maintained by the Bank of England', https://www.bankofengland.co.uk/-/media/boe/files/payments/rtgs-chaps-brief-intro.pdf; 'Target2 Maintained by the European Central Bank', https://www.ecb.europa.eu/paym/target/target2/html/index.en.html; and 'The Fedwire Maintained by the US Federal Reserve Board', https://www.federalreserve.gov/paymentsystems/fedfunds_about.htm.

[48] 'Usually for Retail Payments Such as Pay.UK Which is Overseen by the Payment Services Regulator', https://www.wearepay.uk/.

[49] 'Ethereum Dominates among Developers, But Competitors are Growing Faster' (6 Jan 2022), https://cointelegraph.com/news/ethereum-dominates-among-developers-but-competitors-growing-faster.

challenges for regulatory supervision[50] and mining capacity is dispersed throughout the globe.[51] In this manner, banks are not able to offer customers any better promise in relation to the quality and efficiency of payment and settlement on permissionless blockchains. Banks may participate in the competitive landscape by offering wallet services, but account-based services may be unattractive to users. Many wallet applications for cryptocurrency do not purport to maintain control and access to users' crypto-assets.[52] They can be downloaded onto a smartphone and users are provided with private keys and recovery seed phrases. Account-based services such as with a bank are arguably more cumbersome in terms of banks' knowledge of and control over users' data and transactions.[53]

It may be argued that banks as custodial and payment service providers would not be servicing users on permissionless blockchains. Rather they could provide services for the mainstream economy so that cryptocurrency can be transferred in conventional retail and wholesale payments interfaces. This may be welcomed by merchants, corporations, institutions and retail users who wish to mobilise the mainstream potential of cryptocurrency.[54] However, policy-makers may frown upon the role of banks in mobilising cryptocurrency for the mainstream. This is because banks would be performing the role of facilitating competition between private

[50] P. Hacker, I. Lianos, G. Dimitropoulos and S. Eich, 'Introduction' and Jonathan Rohr and Aaron Wright, 'Blockchains, Private Ordering, and the Future of Governance'; P. Hacker, I. Lianos, G. Dimitropoulos and S. Eich (eds), Regulating Blockchain (Oxford: OUP 2019).

[51] Why Geographical Distribution of Bitcoin and Ethereum Nodes Matter' (7 Jan 2020), https://crypto-current.co/why-geographical-distribution-bitcoin-ethereum-nodes-matter/.

[52] E.g. Coinomi, myEtherWallet, Metamask.

[53] K. Thrasher, The Privacy Cost of Currency, 2021, 42 Michigan Journal of International Law, 403.

[54] A. Bechtel, A. Ferreira, J. Gross and P. Sandner, The Future of Payments in a DLT-based European Economy: A Roadmap, 2020, https://ssrn.com/abstract=3751204; McKinsey & Co, 'New Trends in US Consumer Digital Payments' (Oct 2021), https://www.mckinsey.com/~/media/mckinsey/industries/financial%20services/banking%20blog/new%20trends%20in%20us%20consumer%20digital%20payments/new-trends-in-us-consumer-digital-payments%20-%20final.pdf.

cryptocurrencies and the sovereign's fiat currency.[55] Users could migrate to a store of value in cryptocurrency, benefiting from potential 'investment returns' from cryptocurrency price changes. Adoption by the private sector of cryptocurrency as a medium of exchange or unit of account could undermine monetary sovereignty and weaken central banks' monetary policy effectiveness. At worst mainstream investment opportunities denominated in sovereigns' currency may be substituted by crypto-assets, and this may adversely affect issues of sovereign debt which have knock-on effects upon fiscal policies and ultimately, the strength of states.

It is likely that central banks and financial regulators would disincentivise banks from mobilising cryptocurrency custodial and payment services by imposing prudential regulatory costs, such as in relation to new areas of operational risk, as well as conservative accounting treatment for banks' liabilities for cryptocurrency to their users. This development is likely fraught with policy challenges as policy-makers cannot fully control how banks may respond to profit-making opportunities. But threats to the effectiveness of monetary and ultimately fiscal policies are likely to entail guarded responses from central banks and states.

Next, we also opine that banks are unlikely to extend their dealer expertise in markets such as foreign exchange to cryptocurrency. Banks have become established market-makers and dealers in the foreign exchange market,[56] much of which is unregulated and takes place over-the-counter,[57] with London being the pre-eminent market.[58] It is queried whether banks may be able to act in a similar manner in relation to cryptocurrency, therefore also making cryptocurrency widely accessible to retail consumers. We argue here that existing market structures for cryptocurrency are less attractive than the market structures favourable to banks as forex dealers at present. The forex market features sociologically

[55] R. M Lastra and J. G. Allen, Virtual Currencies in the Eurosystem: Challenges Ahead, 2019, 52 International Lawyer, 177; C. Zimmermann, Monetary Policy in the Digital Age, Lianos et al. (eds), Regulating Blockchain, 2019, ch5.

[56] C. Becker, The Liquidity Mechanics of Dealer Banks in the Market-Based Credit System, 2021, 105 Economic Modelling, 105648.

[57] P. Lysandrou, A. A. Nesvetailova and R. Palan, The Best of Both Worlds: Scale Economies and Discriminatory Policies in London's Global Financial Centre, 2017, 46 Economy and Society, 159.

[58] Ibid., also Bank of England, 'The Foreign Exchange and Over-The-Counter Interest Rate Derivatives Market in the United Kingdom' (Qaurterly Bulletin, Q4, 2019).

significant features of a closely knit group of large international dealer banks whose micro-incentives shape market prices.[59] Over-the-counter trading comprises significant volumes of trades, reflecting the bilateral interactions needed for the market.[60] Further, there is a lack of regulatory intervention[61] or oversight as market players are sophisticated 'peers' vis a vis each other, therefore allowing the market to operate based on implicit understandings and trust.[62] Dealer bank domination of the forex market is arguably a necessary condition for its unregulated but smooth working and liquidity conditions.

The cryptocurrency market structures are radically different from dealer banks' cosy forex markets. Bitcoin and ether feature high concentrated holdings amongst several large 'whales' who are not financial sector figures.[63] Mainstream banks are too late to gain a dominant foothold in those markets. Further, cryptocurrency holdings correspond to mining capacity, which is geographically dispersed, but it is observed that Asia has a higher mining concentration for Ethereum while the US and Europe have a higher mining concentration for Bitcoin.[64] Market-making in cryptocurrency is rare and few specialists undertake this.[65] This is likely because the open permissionless blockchains of Bitcoin and Ethereum promote good levels of liquidity brokered by an effective landscape of crypto-exchanges such as Coinbase, Binance, Kraken etc. Crypto-exchanges such as Binance, Bitfinex, Okex and Huobi also carry out mining and offer mining pool membership for their members,[66] therefore

[59] G. Høidal Bjønnes and D. Rime, Dealer Behavior and Trading Systems in Foreign Exchange Markets, 2005, 75 Journal of Financial Economics, 571.

[60] Lysandrou et al. (2017).

[61] Ibid., but see the need for a peer-based Financial Markets Standards Board after the forex manipulation scandal, see 'How the Forex Scandal Happened' (BBC News, 20 May 2015), https://www.bbc.co.uk/news/business-30003693, and the BIS Global FX Code which is soft law holding forex trading to internationally convergent standards, https://fmsb.com/publication/publication-170525-fmsb-statement-on-bis-global-fx-code/.

[62] Lysandrou et al. (2017).

[63] 'Morgan Stanley says Ethereum Less Decentralized, Ether More Volatile Compared to Bitcoin' (16 Feb 2022), https://www.binance.com/en/news/top/6984003.

[64] Ibid.

[65] 'Mapping the Crypto Market Maker Landscape: List of 34 Market Makers' (10 Feb 2020), https://hummingbot.io/en/blog/2020-02-crypto-market-marker-list/.

[66] E.g. https://pool.binance.com/en; https://www.okx.com/en-in/pool/okex.

contributing to cryptocurrency supply and enhancing the liquidity effects on their exchanges. These market structures have over time become established and in this light, there may be no special benefits for banks to foray into dealing opportunities for cryptocurrency.

We turn to opportunities in relation to crypto-based lending in the next Section.

3 Secured Crypto Lending by Banks?

There are potential profit-making business opportunities for banks in relation to secured lending based on crypto collateral.[67] Customers with crypto wealth may not be of the same demographics or profiles as customers with conventional assets.[68] If banks foray into providing services for customers with crypto wealth, they are potentially tapping into a new market, largely comprising of younger, tech-savvy customers. Income from relationship-based lending secured against crypto collateral can be a new source of revenue, and other services may be desired by such customers too in relation to wealth management. Further, banks can innovate upon securitised products based on crypto-secured loans, generating fee income.

It may be argued that there is little incentive for holders of crypto wealth to engage in mainstream fiat loans. If crypto holders wish to make financial returns, they can participate in DeFi using their crypto wealth, gaining leverage and exploiting opportunities for yield without engaging with the fiat financial economy. Aave or Compound, for example, allows crypto holders to make short unsecured flash loans so that a crypto-asset can be borrowed for a short period of time within a set parameter determined by the platform's protocol. The borrowed crypto-asset can be used for a quick arbitrage to earn the borrower financial returns and is

[67] A preliminary question of whether crypto-assets are property is almost definitively resolved in UK Jurisdiction Taskforce, Legal Statement on Crypto-assets and Smart Contracts (Nov 2019), https://35z8e83m1ih83drye280o9d1-wpengine.netdna-ssl.com/wp-content/uploads/2019/11/6.6056_JO_Cryptocurrencies_Statement_FINAL_WEB_111119-1.pdf, paras 60–84, although the issues relating to security were brief and unresolved, paras 100–106.

[68] 'Millennial Millionaires Have a Large Share of Their Wealth in Crypto, CNBC Survey Says' (10 June 2021), https://www.cnbc.com/2021/06/10/millennial-millionaires-have-large-share-of-wealth-in-crypto-cnbc-survey-.html.

returned to the platform within the same transaction, or else the transaction is automatically rolled back. However, there is demand for crypto to fiat loans, which used to be serviced by specialist lenders such as BlockFi or Celsius,[69] and even crypto-exchanges are diversifying into such business. These early movers tried to establish standards in the market regarding loan-to-value standards, managing the risks of crypto volatility by having collateral top-up provisions within a certain amount of time as well as repayment and enforcement standards. However, during the crypto crash of mid-2022, the potential elimination of poorly risk-managed crypto-lenders could turn borrowers back to conventional financial institutions.

There are comparative advantages for conventional banks. Where crypto wealth holders need to meet economic needs in the mainstream economy, such as buying real estate,[70] paying for high-value assets and services like education and business and trade finance, they may still turn to banks as established financial intermediaries. However, a drawback for these borrowers is that conventional financial institutions may apply haircuts to crypto-collateral in excess of what crypto-lenders would have done, especially if the mood of risk aversion sets in. It can be argued that crypto holders who need cash to purchase a high-value asset, for example, should prefer to liquidate the crypto holdings rather than turn to conventional secured lending in fiat backed by crypto. It is arguable that crypto holders may not wish to liquidate their crypto holdings to purchase in cash, as they may wish to hold onto crypto for longer-term appreciation, especially during times of market volatility.[71] Moreover,

[69] At the time of writing, these popular lenders against crypto-collateral have suffered significant financial losses due to the crash in prices of major cryptocurrencies, affecting the value of collateral as well as borrowers' default risk, see 'How Crypto Lender Celsius Stumbled on Risky Bank-Like Investments' (Reuters, 15 June 2022), https://www.reuters.com/business/finance/how-crypto-lender-celsius-stumbled-risky-bank-like-investments-2022-06-15/; BlockFi has been purchased by FTX at a steep discount in the midst of it financial woes, see 'FTX Agrees Deal with Option to Buy BlockFi for Up to $240 mn' (Financial Times, 2 July 2022), https://www.ft.com/content/fa95d027-8afd-43f1-b9b1-ee8c204435c7.

[70] 'Crypto Mortgage Product Allows Borrowers to Post Bitcoin as Collateral' (American Banker, New York, 20 Jan 2022).

[71] 'LoanPlus.io Launches New Platform That Offers Anonymous Loans By Using Crypto Portfolio as Collateral without the Need of Selling Crypto Holdings' (M2 Presswire, 2 Apr 2019).

capital gains tax may be applied to crypto holders when they liquidate their holdings, diminishing the realised cash for their purchase or intended economic purposes. Where crypto holders need financial mobilisation in the conventional economy such as to purchase a high-value asset, or fund business needs and expansion, it is not inconceivable for there to be a market demand for crypto wealth to be usable in the conventional financial economy.[72]

Banks need to weigh up the potential profits from such new opportunities against price volatility risk, as demonstrated during the crypto-winter of mid-2022. Financial regulators may also be risk averse in relation to banks' financial stability risks, pushing back against incentives for banks to explore new profit-making opportunities. However, should price volatility as such be a reason as such to refrain from engaging with novel collateral? Even conventional collateral such as real estate suffers from volatility. Further, even highly illiquid personal property can be susceptible to collateralisation.[73] It can be argued that the long-term value of crypto-assets, such as well-capitalised cryptocurrency, crypto-assets based on innovation that can be deployed on Web 3 or the metaverse, as well as certain limited edition non-fungible tokens, may all enjoy some long-term value and should not be quickly dismissed.[74] In relatively benign times, the major cryptocurrencies are arguably relatively liquid, and empirical research on the price volatility of major cryptocurrencies shows that lenders are quite well protected at a 50% loan-to-value ratio.[75] Lenders should consider a balance between accepting novel forms of collateral, benefiting financial inclusion and mobilisation for younger and technologically interested borrowers, while prudentially managing risks by instituting policies such as a loan-to-value ratio that reflects the borrowers' risks and not just the

[72] 'Crypto-Backed Loans: How Banks Are Working to Capitalise on Cryptocurrency Mania' (CNBC, 9 Dec 2021), https://www.cnbctv18.com/cryptocurrency/crypto-backed-loans-how-banks-are-working-to-capitalise-on-cryptocurrency-mania-11745422.htm.

[73] L. N. Coordes, All Bark and No Bite? Pets as Collateral for Secured Loans, 2019, 14 ABI Journal, 64; M. A. H. Dempster, Bond Flotation with Exotic Commodity Collateral, 2020, 20 Quantitative Finance, 1903.

[74] 'Bitcoin Recovers Losses while Crypto Lender Now Accepts NFTs as Collateral' (1 Feb 2022), https://www.proactiveinvestors.co.uk/companies/news/972754/bitcoin-recovers-losses-while-crypto-lender-now-accepts-nfts-as-collateral-972754.html.

[75] J. J. Masilela, R. B. van Wyk and N. Marwa, Assessing the Variability of Crypto Collateral Assets in Secured Lending on the Blockchain, 2021, Development Southern Africa, https://doi.org/10.1080/0376835X.2021.1906630.

collateral risk, and provide for collateral top-up calls within certain parameters of collateral value loss. This broader question in terms of competing regulatory objectives ultimately looms large in the design of prudential and other related regulatory policies.

We turn to issues that need clarification and/or reform for crypto-collateral to be taken in a manner that meets lenders' expectations. There are two areas of law/policy reform that can be enabling for banks foraying into relationship-based lending secured against crypto collateral. First, legal/regulatory standards would be helpful for clarifying how crypto-collateral can effectively be taken as security, and we argue that such law and policy can be considered in tandem with giving the status of financial collateral to crypto collateral. Second, law and policy in the first respect above can assist policy-makers in giving fair prudential regulatory treatment to crypto-collateral, but such a reform should be carefully shaped bearing in mind banks' incentives.

Law and Policy Reform for Security Aspects of Crypto Collateral

First, lenders would benefit from standardisation and guidance in terms of how crypto-assets can effectively be taken as collateral in order to protect their interests in terms of having sufficient 'control' over such assets so that the quality of the security is eligible for clear status in terms of priority and enforcement.

Crypto-assets are intangible in nature and can be stored in wallets held by centralised operators such as crypto-exchanges, or in non-custodial manners, such as by a wallet application not controlled by a centralised operator, or on a physical device storing the digital information of the crypto-assets offline.[76] Centralised operators such as exchanges often have 'ownership' rights of the crypto-assets in the accounts they provide, and users' relationships with exchanges can be framed differently depending on exchanges' terms of use.[77] Where crypto-assets are held in a non-custodial digital wallet, the crypto-asset holder controls the private keys

[76] See ch6, Chiu (2022).

[77] Ibid.

to the wallet, but there is no centralised operator to have recourse to in the event of loss of keys and access to crypto-assets.[78]

Where crypto-assets are held in an exchange's digital wallet, this could be framed as a claim that the crypto-asset holder has against the exchange, and security is in theory to be taken of the claim. It is arguable that a statutory assignment under s136 of the Law of Property Act may work for the lender, but there are uncertainties that arise from the novelties of crypto-exchange arrangements. First, it is uncertain what the nature of the 'claim' is for a statutory assignment to be made. Coinbase, for example, holds itself as a custodial agent for users in relation to users' monies and crypto-assets, in both the EU[79] and the US,[80] hence it can be argued that there is sufficient certainty in those claims resembling a claim against financial custodial agents who hold assets on behalf of clients under a statutory trust.[81] However, Binance and Bitfinex grant their users a licence under contract to use their services including trading, financing and wallet services and reserve extensive rights to access wallets, terminate services etc. under contract.[82] There are extensive disclaimers of liability against users and exclusive uses of arbitration clauses in the event of disputes.[83] Hence, users' rights over crypto-assets held with certain exchanges are subject to much greater uncertainty and this is exacerbated by the lack of clarity in terms of the jurisdictions in which these exchanges are based for the purposes of legal characterisation. Indeed both aforementioned exchanges do not stipulate choice of law clauses and rely on arbitration only for dispute resolution.[84]

[78] Ibid., but see Quadriga CX issue where the exchange's cold wallets are accessed only by private keys stored on the CEO's encrypted computer, and the sudden death of the CEO meant that the encrypted computer cannot be accessed and the private keys to the cold wallets lost to users.

[79] Clause 5.18, https://www.coinbase.com/legal/user_agreement/payments_europe.

[80] Clause 2.6, https://www.coinbase.com/legal/user_agreement/united_states.

[81] Art 16(8), Markets in Financial Instruments Directive 2014/65/EU.

[82] Clauses 2, 5, 6–9, 20, Bitfinex user agreement, https://www.bitfinex.com/legal/exchange/terms; Clauses II.3.d, III.1.a, Binance user agreement, https://www.binance.com/en/terms.

[83] Sections IV, VI, Binance user agreement, https://www.binance.com/en/terms; Clause 20, especially 20.9 in relation to no liability for unauthorised loss of tokens, https://www.bitfinex.com/legal/exchange/terms.

[84] E.g. dispute resolution is by binding private arbitration, Clause 12.4, https://www.bitfinex.com/legal/exchange/terms; Clause X.2, https://www.binance.com/en/terms.

Next, statutory assignments are not effective with notice to a crypto-exchange whose terms do not allow users to deal with the assets in storage. Crypto-exchanges differ in their acceptance of users' freedom to deal with their crypto-assets in the exchange's wallet. Binance, for example, refuses to allow crypto-asset holders who use its Bitfinity wallet to assign rights over the assets to third parties,[85] but assignment seems to be allowed by Coinbase which defers to users' instructions.[86] Bitfinex reserves its right to provide consent for assignments by their users.[87] Banks would need to undertake new forms of diligence[88] regarding exchanges' terms to see if the assignment can proceed. It may be argued that this area of law can only be clarified in tandem with the regulation of crypto-exchanges, such as under MiCA. MiCAR provides for crypto-asset service providers, including exchanges, to safeguard the ownership rights of clients, not dissimilar in wording from the Markets in Financial Instruments Directive applicable to investment firms.[89] This has been held to give rise to a statutory trust in favour of the client.[90] Such clarity in exchanges' relationship with their customers in relation to the holding of crypto-assets can provide the necessary foundations for personal property security law to develop in relation to these assets.

Commentators[91] have opined that it would be preferable for banks to take security over crypto-assets where they are able to bargain for rights of control, such as in a physical device handed over to the bank, subject to a right of return upon redemption, or in a non-custodial wallet so that lenders are not affected by the interposition of complex rights of crypto-asset exchanges. Nevertheless, agreements between lenders and borrowers where borrowers retain control over their crypto-assets, such as

[85] Clause 20.2, https://www.binance.com/en/support/faq/f0559f6cb2c4406cb82ae7b48ee3d405, also Clause XI.6, https://www.binance.com/en/terms.

[86] Clause 2.6.1, 2.6.2, https://www.coinbase.com/legal/user_agreement/united_states.

[87] Clause 24, https://www.bitfinex.com/legal/exchange/terms.

[88] X.r Foccroulle Ménard, Cryptocurrency: Collateral for Secured Transactions?, 2018, 34 Banking and Financial Law Review, 347.

[89] Art 16(8).

[90] Lehman Brothers International (Europe) (in administration) v CRC Credit Fund Ltd and others [2010] EWCA Civ 917.

[91] Ibid.; T. Bierer, Hashing It Out: Problems and Solutions concerning Cryptocurrency Used as Article 9 Collateral, 2016, 7 Case W Res JL Tech & Internet, 79.

in non-custodial wallets, are disadvantageous to lenders, as this is akin to a floating charge which must crystallise upon an event of default. Although crypto-asset holders retain their freedoms to deal with the assets, for example, in profitable options such as staking or lending,[92] lenders risk the dissipation of these assets without recourse. If crypto-assets subject to a floating charge are staked in a liquidity pool and are seized by the application of automated protocols, it is uncertain how lenders can assert their rights as new questions arise regarding whether crystallisation has taken place and priority issues. Lenders could take fixed charges over crypto-assets by having control over the private keys to the relevant wallet, similar to the *Re Brumark* bank account.[93] However, as private keys to non-custodial wallets cannot be verified by a centralised operator,[94] lenders run into the hazard of receiving false keys by rogues.[95] In the alternative, an outright transfer of private keys to lenders subject to conditions of repurchase may be considered, allowing lenders the rights to verify and deal with the crypto-assets too, such as in DeFi, discussed below.

Irrespective of legal classification, lenders could consider emulating DeFi practices in providing automated protocols for collateral lock-up, so that collateral can be released upon redemption. Automated seizure or top-ups can also be managed by the protocols.[96] This is likely to bring the arrangements closer to a *Brumark* fixed charge. However, would the cost of such technological investment be worthwhile compared to the potential profits for lenders? Arguably, lenders can band together, perhaps with the engagement of the Loan Market Association, to invest in a platform protocol that is standardised for all lenders. This increases the economies of scale while opening up the sector to crypto-based secured lending.

Next, legal or policy clarification should be undertaken, perhaps by the Law Commission, in relation to lenders' security rights, i.e. the characterisation of security, whether this amounts to a fixed charge or title transfer

[92] S. Kim, New Crypto-Secured Lending System with a Two-Way Collateral Function, 2021, 6 Ledger 1–16, https://doi.org/10.5915/LEDGER.2021.215.

[93] Re Brumark Investments Ltd [2001] UKPC 28.

[94] Third party verification is often indispensable to lenders in terms of securing the validity of their rights, see T. Chapoto and A. Q. Q. Aboagye, African Innovations in Harnessing Farmer Assets as Collateral, 2017, 8 African Journal of Economic and Management Studies, 66.

[95] Foccroulle Ménard (2018).

[96] Similar to dai, https://makerdao.com/en/.

with repurchase rights or a new category of security altogether, and how enforcement should take place.[97] Thirdly, lenders need to consider the competition in the crypto-financial space, as the locking up of crypto-collateral generally entails some return of remuneration for crypto-asset holders foregoing profitable opportunities during the 'lock-up'. In order to maximise the financial opportunities connected with the collateral, lenders holding onto crypto-collateral could participate in DeFi activities themselves.[98] DeFi activities are of course not without risk, and novel arrangements need to be considered in terms of risk/reward sharing with borrowers who allow the lock-up of their crypto collateral. These arrangements would be novel and unprecedented in security arrangements and would benefit from industry standardisation and clear legal footing.

Recognition as Financial Collateral

The second area of reform in law and policy that could be considered to support bank lending secured by crypto-collateral is the inclusion of certain crypto-collateral within the treatment of financial collateral for enforcement and priority purposes. Under the EU Financial Collateral Directive 2002 (FCD)[99] which is transposed in the UK, regulated financial institutions such as banks can benefit from priority and easier enforcement against financial collateral provided to them under title transfer or security collateral arrangements. 'Financial collateral' is defined as cash and 'financial instruments' broadly.[100] The inclusion of certain crypto-collateral within the scope of financial collateral allows banks to enjoy enforcement convenience and priorities that banks are familiar with, and this may be superior to crafting a set of enforcement and priority rules from scratch. Even if the means of taking collateral as discussed above raises issues of legal characterisation that need resolving, the broad scope

[97] Granted that a model law is an ongoing project, see Spyridon V. Bazinas, The UNCITRAL Legislative Guide on Secured Transactions and the Draft UNCITRAL Model Law on Secured Transactions compared, in Louise Gullifer and Orkun Akseli (eds), Secured Transactions Law Reform: Principles, Policies and Practice (Oxford: Hart Publishing 2016), 481–502.

[98] Such as Kim (2021).

[99] Directive 2002/47/EC.

[100] Art 1(4)(a), ibid.

of 'title transfer' or 'security' arrangements in the Directive could functionally cover the range of arrangements applicable to crypto-collateral. Further, the rights of use or dealing conferred under the FCD to collateral takers[101] would be consistent with banks' interest in maximising the financial potential of collateral in DeFi, as discussed above.

However, the question would be whether crypto-collateral meets the expectations underlying 'financial instruments' within the scope of the Directive. The ease of enforcement is largely due to the nature of financial instruments being tradeable or liquid, benefitting from reasonably clear valuation for the purposes of setting off, or appropriation and liquidation. It is arguable that Group 2a cryptoassets, which are already defined to meet the Basel Committee's conditions of market capitalisation, liquidity and price observability, should qualify as financial collateral. For Group 2b cryptoassets, it can be argued that with MiCA's regulatory regime for crypto-assets, the rise of markets for regulated crypto-assets could improve tradeability and liquidity and help elevate many crypto-assets to the status of 'financial instruments' within the FCD's scope. This scope can potentially be wider than the thresholds defined for Group 2a assets. However, it can be argued that although the FCD definition pertains to security enforcement while the Group 2a/b distinction pertains to prudential treatment, enforceability of collateral and realisation of value is connected to prudential protection, hence the thresholds for Group 2a and FCD qualification should arguably be the same. Nevertheless, a counter-argument can be made for widening the FCD scope for crypto-assets. As Group 2b cryptoassets, even if they do not fall within Group 2a, can be relatively liquid and traded at many crypto-exchanges, the ability for banks to treat such assets as financial collateral and liquidate them quickly can be important for prudential protection.

The width of scope in the FCD may incentivise banks to accept them as collateral hence there is a broader issue of whether such incentives should be created. This harks back to a broader question regarding the balance of objectives between supporting innovation and financial mobilisation for borrowers with different profiles, versus the maintenance of conservative status quo in risk aversion against financial stability risks. This ultimate larger question needs to be debated in regulatory policy.

[101] Arts 5, 6, ibid.

Reform in Prudential Treatment for Risk Mitigation

Finally, it is arguable that banks' relationship-based lending secured on crypto-collateral can benefit from prudential recognition in credit risk mitigation. Financial forms of collateral benefit from prudential regulatory treatment as 'credit risk mitigation' techniques under the European Capital Requirements Regulation, based on certain conditions. These relate to being recognised forms of tradeable and liquid financial instruments such as sovereign and corporate debt and equity securities, securitised assets, units in collective investment schemes and gold. Securities instruments must enjoy good credit risk treatment and be included in an Index or traded on a recognised exchange, and all the financial instruments within scope must be sufficiently liquid, such as the units in collective investment schemes benefiting from daily public price quotes.[102] In this manner, it is queried whether the Basel Committee should clarify whether the differentiated Group 2a assets treatment should extend to credit risk mitigation. Further, financial collateral that benefits from credit risk mitigation treatment in prudential regulation must benefit from sufficiently clear legal footing in relation to their enforceability under applicable law, as well as operational procedures to ensure sufficient control over collateral, including in third parties' custody, and the regular verification of their market value.[103] Prudential recognition in credit risk mitigation crucially depends on what can be achieved in reforms in the law and policy regarding the security aspects of crypto-collateral.

At a broader level, the rationales for improved prudential treatment of crypto-collateral as 'credit risk mitigation' should be considered in terms of whether a financial inclusion or mobilisation issue arises for certain borrowers. It is possible that many young and technologically savvy borrowers have cryptoassets in their digital wallets but have not been able to accumulate traditional assets such as residential property.[104] Although competing for market share could stoke banks' perverse incentives and excessive risk-taking, there is a need to consider how policy

[102] Art 197, EU Capital Requirements Regulation 575/2013.

[103] Arts 194, 207, ibid.

[104] 'Most Millennial and Gen Z Investors Say Crypto Is Part of Their Retirement Strategy' (21 Jan 2022), https://money.com/gen-z-millennials-invest-crypto-retirement/; 'Why Gen Z Could Turn to DeFi Mortgages to Build Real Estate Wealth' (9 May 2022), https://forkast.news/defi-mortgages-help-gen-z-real-estate-wealth/.

introduced in this area balances the provision for new needs and the preservation of bank and financial stability. In this manner, implications for macroprudential supervision may need to be considered.

4 Conclusion

This chapter discusses the rise of crypto-assets in their potential interfaces with the banking business and the challenges posed to prudential regulatory policy. Prudential regulatory policy has after the global financial crisis become more conservative but also dependent on recognised characteristics of mainstream financial assets in order to map financial risks. Hence, existing prudential regulation does not optimally accommodate crypto-instruments brought about by new techniques in technological and financial revolutions, reflected in the Basel Committee's risk-averse approach to banks' direct exposures. The chapter suggests there are new business opportunities for banks that can be explored, and the engagement between crypto and conventional finance cannot be prevented. In exploring the responses needed in law and regulation, the key area selected for discussion is how crypto-collateralised secured lending as a potential new business line for banks would require the support of legal and regulatory clarifications and reform.

CHAPTER 5

Digitalizing the Commercial Banking Business Model: Vanishing Bank Branches and the Risks of Financial Exclusion of the Elderly

Anne-Marie Weber, Anne-Christin Mittwoch, Weronika Herbet-Homenda, and Weronika Stefaniuk

1 Introduction

A key element of what is commonly referred to as the fourth industrial revolution or "Industry 4.0" is the transformation of how commercial services are delivered.[1] In search of efficiency savings and broader

[1] See Morrar et al., The Fourth Industrial Revolution (Industry 4.0): A Social Innovation Perspective, Technology Innovation Management Review, 2017, 7(11), 12, 15.

A.-M. Weber (✉) · W. Herbet-Homenda · W. Stefaniuk
University of Warsaw, Warsaw, Poland
e-mail: a.weber@wpia.uw.edu.pl

W. Herbet-Homenda
e-mail: w.herbet@uw.edu.pl

M. Bodellini et al. (eds.), *Commercial Banking in Transition*, Palgrave Macmillan Studies in Banking and Financial Institutions,
https://doi.org/10.1007/978-3-031-45289-5_5

customer pools, businesses are moving their activity inexorably online.[2] Participation in the digital world is often no longer a result of conscious choices.[3] In many areas, including essential daily transactions, traditional person-to-person services are not an available option anymore, coercing consumers towards a change in habits.[4]

Along with other sectors of the economy, the digital revolution is rapidly paving its way into financial services and transforming commercial banking business models.[5] An obvious empirical indicator for the ongoing transition from personal on-site service to the digital space can be found in the continuously decreasing number of physical bank branches.[6] Many types of commercial banking services can be executed via computer or smartphone and Fintech innovations are becoming the key drivers of the transition.[7] With the increasing potential to reduce commercial banks' operating costs, physical bank branches have become redundant. Consequently, empirical data derived across Europe proves that bank branches

W. Stefaniuk
e-mail: w.stefaniuk@student.uw.edu.pl

A.-C. Mittwoch
Martin Luther University Halle-Wittenberg, Halle, Germany
e-mail: anne-christin.mittwoch@jura.uni-halle.de

[2] See E. Avgouleas, Regulating Financial Innovation, in: N. Moloney, E. Ferran, J. Payne (eds.), The Oxford Handbook of Financial Regulation, Oxford, 2015, 659–660.

[3] Which is against the assumptions of rational choice as default of rational choice (in economics) about individual decision—making process; see F. Gómez Pomar, M. Artigot Golobardes, Rational Choice and Behavioural Approaches to Consumer Issues, in: H.W. Micklitz, A.L. Sibony, F. Esposito (eds.), Research Methods in Consumer Law, 119, 124.

[4] See E. Hilgendorf, Introduction: Digitization and the Law—A European Perspective, in: E. Hilgendorf, J. Feldle (eds.), Digitization and the Law, 2018, 9.

[5] E.g.: Capgemini/Efma, World Retail Banking Report 2022, https://www.worldretailbankingreport.com; compare with: D. Kingsford Smith, O. Dixon, The Consumer Interest and the Financial Markets, in: N. Moloney, E. Ferran, J. Payne (eds.), The Oxford Handbook of Financial Regulation, Oxford, 2015, 695–735. U. Blaurock, Einführung, in: U. Blaurock, F. Maultzsch (eds.), Vertrauensschutz im digitalen Zeitalter, 9, 10.

[6] See O. Bennet, Bank Branches: Why Are they Closing and What is the Impact?, Report 2020.

[7] See D.W. Arner et al., Sustainability, Fintech and Financial Inclusion, European Business Organization Review, 2020, 21, 7, 9; D.A. Zetzsche, D.W. Arner, R.P. Buckley, Sustainability, Financial Inclusion and Efficiency: A Trilemma or a Trifecta for the Regulation of Digital Finance?, Banking & Financing Law Review 2023, 39 (3), 44.

are steadily vanishing.[8] As an example, according to statistics published by the Polish Financial Supervision Authority, at the end of 2017, a total of 10,418 bank branches were operational in Poland.[9] According to data for December 2021, the number of banking outlets had dropped to 7961.

Similarly, in Germany, the total amount of bank branches in 2019 was 28,384 and dropped to 25,779 in one year. This means that it decreased by 20%.[10] According to some projections, as many as 25% of bank branches in Europe will close within the next three years.[11] Certainly, the COVID-19 pandemic has significantly expedited this tendency.[12] The restrictions around the world regarding personal "live" contact and provision of services have forced the financial sector to adapt its business models and thus additionally accelerated digital innovation. Similarly, on the customer side, the use of digital financial services—and especially the need for contactless financial products and services—has increased significantly during the pandemic.[13]

While the online shift is naturally inevitable, we claim that its fallout requires more scrupulous academic attention. The current legal research and literature on the digitalization of commercial banking business

[8] Ibid., 7–35.

[9] Including traditional branches, expositories and other customer service outlets; compare: statistics data published on the Polish Supervision Authority, https://www.knf.gov.pl/?articleId=56224&p_id=18, all online sources were last accessed on 08 January 2023.

[10] See German Federal Bank, Bank office report 2020. Development of the bank office network in 2020, https://www.bundesbank.de/resource/blob/623012/4e62983a8010d54b2168e051bde2430b/mL/bankstellenbericht-2020-data.pdf.

[11] See the graph showing the decrease of commercial bank branches in EU in the last made by The World Bank, https://www.data.worldbank.org/indicator/FB.CBK.BRCH.P5?end=2020&locations=EU&start=2004; Bank Branches and COVID-19: Where are Banks Closing Branches during the Pandemic?

By Kimberly Kreiss, https://www.federalreserve.gov/ecoNres/notes/feds-notes/bank-branches-and-covid-19-where-are-banks-closing-branches-during-the-pandemic-20211217.htm.

[12] See interview with President of the European Banking Federation as of 16 April 2022, https://www.bankingsupervision.europa.eu/press/publications/newsletter/2022/html/ssm.nl220216.en.html.

[13] Se: World Bank, The impact of Covid-19 on digital financial inclusion, report for the Italian presidency of the G20 for the Global Partnership for Financial Inclusion (GPFI), 2021, https://www.gpfi.org/sites/gpfi/files/sites/default/files/5_WB%20Report_The%20impact%20of%20COVID-19%20on%20digital%20financial%20inclusion.pdf.

models primarily focus on the challenges that arise for the active participants in this process[14]—both on the financial institutions' and the digitized customers' side.[15] The forward-looking enthusiasm about the digital revolution provokes assumptions as regards the banks' customers' adjustment abilities. This chapter seeks to redirect the focus on those bank customers who are affected by the digital revolution in commercial banking yet fail to become its active participants.[16] Against the background of existing research, we identified older people as a group of consumers particularly prone to digital exclusion.[17] Consequently, we aim to assess the risks of financial exclusion of the elderly that stem from the unfolding transition of commercial banking.[18] To that extent, this chapter reflects the growing necessity to assess the implications of an ageing society in the social sciences.[19] Our focus on older people as a

[14] See High-Level Expert Group, Building the European Information Society for Us All: Final Policy Report of the High-Level Expert Group 15, 32, 48 (1997), https://www.op.europa.eu/s/orbo.

[15] See S. Carbó et al., Financial Exclusion, 6.

[16] See Report by Richard Berry, Older People and the Internet. Towards a "System Map" of Digital Exclusion, https://ilcuk.org.uk/older-people-and-the-internet/; G. Helleringer, A Behavioural Perspective on Consumer Finance, in: E. Hilgendorf and J. Feldle (eds.), Digitization and the Law, Würzburg, 2018, 334, 335; EU structural financial indicators: https://www.ecb.europa.eu/press/pr/date/2020/html/ecb.pr200608_ssi_table~3054d55051.en.pdf.

[17] See, i.e., OECD (2020), OECD/INFE 2020 International Survey of Adult Financial Literacy, https://www.oecd.org/financial/education/launchoftheoecdinfeglobalfinancialliteracysurveyreport.html, 60. The authors are aware of the fact that there are other vulnerable groups in this respect, however, the reasons for vulnerability and respective remedies are divers and are addressed elsewhere, see: World Bank, The impact of Covid-19 on digital financial inclusion, report for the Italian presidency of the G20 for the Global Partnership for Financial Inclusion (GPFI), 2021; D. McKillop, J. Wilson, Public Money & Management, 2007, 27(1), 9.

[18] See P. Kossecki, A. Borcuch, Digital, Social and Financial Exclusion Among Elderly People, 9.

[19] See E. Hilgendorf, Introduction: Digitization and the law—A European Perspective, 9, 10; D.W. Arner et al., EBOR, 2020, 21, 7, 12; S. Frerichs, What is the 'Social' in Behavioural Economics? The Methodological Underpinnings of Governance by Nudges, in: H.W. Micklitz, A.L. Sibony, F. Esposito (eds.), Research Methods in Consumer Law, 399, 439; S. Grundmann, European Contract Law in the Digital Age, 6.

distinct category of bank customers follows the approaches that stress the heterogeneity of consumers.[20]

Taking the empirical evidence on the phenomenon of vanishing bank branches as a point of departure, we first outline how the digitalization of commercial banking business models translates into the accessibility of financial services for older people (Sect. 2). We then proceed to characterize the risks of the digital exclusion of the elderly (Sect. 3) and investigate whether there is a case for legislative intervention, in particular against the backdrop of changing societal expectations as to the role of banks in a new economic and social reality (Sect. 4). Subsequently, we delineate potential legislative strategies which could address the digital exclusion of the elderly from financial services (Sect. 5). In our concluding remarks, we summarize how risks associated with the digital exclusion of the elderly could impact the future of commercial banking business models in forthcoming years (Sect. 6).

2 Access to Financial Services by the Elderly

In general, the digital transition in commercial banking is being marketed by the sector as beneficial for customers, which is understandable given the backdrop of banks' cost-cutting and profit-increasing purposes of these processes.[21] From the customer's perspective, the constant access to new products, faster service at any time and place, as well as the reduction of the number of documents can be identified as important advantages of online banking.[22] As a result, the switch from on-site to digital services

[20] See M. Nagatsu, M. Małecka, How Behavioural Research has Informed Consumer Law: The Many Faces of Behavioural Research, 357, 368; F. Möslein, Behavioural Analysis and Socio-Legal Research: Is Everything Architecture?, 441, 446; F. Gómez Pomar, M. Artigot Golobardes, Raptional Choice and Behavioural Approaches to Consumer Issues, 119, 128, all in: H.W. Micklitz, A.L. Sibony, F. Esposito (eds.), Research Methods in Consumer Law.

[21] See the Report 'New Rules for an Old Game: Banks in the Changing World of Financial Intermediation', https://www.mckinsey.com/pl/~/media/ClientLink/New%20rules%20for%20an%20old%20game%20Banks%20in%20the%20changing%20world%20of%20financial%20intermediation/Banks-in-the-changing-world-of-financial-intermediation-GBAR.pdf; F. Mubarak, R. Suomi, Elderly Forgotten? Digital Exclusion in the Information Age and the Rising Grey Digital Divide, 2022, 3.

[22] See E. Avgouleas, Regulating Financial Innovation, 659–660; E. Hilgendorf, Introduction: Digitization and the Law—A European Perspective, 9.

certainly increases the overall accessibility of financial services for the average consumer. However, as stated above, this narrative erodes when examining the access to financial services in reference to specific customer groups,[23] which raises the alarm of potential discrimination.[24]

Market behaviour, preferences, and, most importantly, cognitive abilities of seniors suggest that the digitalization of commercial banking could actually significantly limit their access to financial services.[25] Due to these characteristics, the elderly value personal contact with customer service staff at a bank branch.[26] In addition, the basic expectation for this group of consumers is clarity, transparency (both linguistic and graphical), and immutability of the terms and conditions of the agreements concluded.[27] An essential factor that determines the choice of a provider of banking services amongst older people is naturally the proximity of the branch. In this matter, the costs of maintaining an account or fees for cash withdrawal are only of secondary importance.

Older people are less confident in using online banking due to a lack of trust in financial operations via the Internet[28] because the use of online banking requires a basic proficiency in the use of electronic devices and essential knowledge regarding the nature of the financial services rendered.[29] This is confirmed by existing research suggesting that digital

[23] See P. Vassilakopoulou, E. Hustad, Inf Syst Front, 2021, 5, https://doi.org/10.1007/s10796-020-10096-3; N. Reich et al., European Consumer Law, 45–46.

[24] See A. Numhauser-Henning, Ageism, Age Discrimination and Employment Law in the EU, in: I. Doron, N. Georganzi (eds.), Ageing, Ageism and the Law: European Perspectives on the Rights of Older Persons, 98–115.

[25] See C.K. Sanders, E. Scanlon, J. Hum. Rights Soc., 2021, 6(2), 130, 137; Svensson et al., The Capabilities Approach and the Concepts of Self-Determination, Legal Competence and Human Dignity in Social Services for Older People, in: H.F. Erhag et al. (eds.), A Multidisciplinary Approach to Capability in Age and Ageing, 175–176.

[26] See the Report 'What Does a Bank for the Elderly Look Like?', https://www.scb.co.th/en/personal-banking/stories/elder-banking.html; A. Kesby, Hum Rights Rev, 2017, 18(4), 371–382.

[27] See S. Grundmann, European Contract Law in the Digital Age, 6; P. Kossecki, A. Borcuch, Digital, Social and Financial Exclusion Among Elderly People, 16.

[28] See T. Greenham, F. Travers-Smith, Cashing Out. The hidden costs and consequences of moving to cashless society. RSA Action and Research Center, 2019, 20; F. Asmi, T. Ishaya, Understanding the Behavior of the Elderly towards Internet Banking in the UK, SOTICS, 2012, 104.

[29] See N. Moloney, Financial Market Governance and Consumer Protection in the EU, in: E. Faia et al. (eds.), Financial Regulation. A Transatlantic Perspective, 221–224.

skills and financial literacy are lower amongst the elderly than in other age groups.[30] In particular, studies show that the deteriorating cognitive abilities that come with ageing have a substantial effect on the decline of the financial literacy index, especially in people over 60[31] (the age of 60 as the conventional limit of old age is proposed by the World Health Organization and the OECD). Additionally, seniors often lack experience using new technologies that were simply non-existent a few years or decades ago.[32] Therefore ironically, in the field of financial services, it will often be those most in need of assistance who are least able to navigate a digital route to accessing them.[33]

A vital barrier limiting the active participation of seniors in digitalized financial services also stems from their low level of income (mainly pensions), which limits access to digital devices, and high health expenses.[34] This may cause practical problems—e.g., the inability to purchase a digital device that would enable the use of online banking services or the Internet connection itself.[35]

[30] See F. Asmi, T. Ishaya, Understanding the Behavior of the Elderly towards Internet Banking in the UK, SOTICS, 2012; A. Oehler, S. Wendt, J Consum Policy, 2017, 40(2), 179–191; M.S. Finke, J.S. Howe, S.J. Huston, Management Science, 2017, 63(1), 213–230.

[31] See WHO, https://www.who.int/news-room/fact-sheets/detail/ageing-and-health; OECD, Financial Consumer Protection and Ageing Populations, 2020, https://www.oecd.org/finance/Financial-consumer-protection-and-ageing-populations.pdf.

[32] Report by Richard Berry, Older People and the Internet. Towards a "System Map" of Digital Exclusion, https://ilcuk.org.uk/older-people-and-the-internet/.

[33] EU Consumer Protection 2.0 Structural asymmetries in digital consumer markets. A joint report from research conducted under the EUCP2.0 project, https://www.beuc.eu/sites/default/files/publications/beuc-x-2021-018_eu_consumer_protection.0_0.pdf; L. Georgieva, Digital Inclusion and the Elderly: The Case of Online Banking, in: I. Schuurman, L. Sevens, V. Yaneva, J.O'Flaherty (eds.), Proceedings of the LREC, 2018, 8, 9.

[34] See, i.e. OECD (2020), Financial Consumer Protection and Ageing Populations, https://www.oecd.org/finance/Financial-consumer-protection-and-ageing-populations.pdf.

[35] See A. Lusardi, Financial Literacy and Financial Decision-Making in Older Adults, Generations: Journal of the American Society on Aging, 2012, 36(2), 25.

3 The Risks of Financial Exclusion of the Elderly

The digital exclusion of seniors caused by the ongoing digital transformation of commercial banking translates into their financial exclusion.[36] The limitations and difficulties in accessing services and products offered by commercial banks can be associated with several risks that can be of a strictly financial but also social nature.[37]

Financially excluded people are exposed not only to the loss of direct benefits associated with access to certain services and products, including in particular essential services (e.g., cash withdrawal).[38] Most importantly, the financial exclusion of seniors may affect their quality of life, lead to social marginalization, and lower the individual's self-esteem due to the need for outside help in order to complete daily tasks.[39] In addition, financial exclusion of specific social groups affects the economy as a whole, including suboptimal market functioning, inadequate allocation of capital, increased burdens on the social welfare system, and slower economic growth.[40] Financial exclusion affects key socio-economic factors, i.e., inflation, national income, unemployment, supply, demand, and components related to the quality of life.[41]

[36] See P. Kossecki, A. Borcuch, Digital, Social and Financial Exclusion Among Elderly People, 9; D. McKillop, J. Wilson, Public Money & Management, 2007, 27(1), 9.

[37] See V. Gallistl et al., Journal of Aging Studies, 2021, 71; S.J. Czaja, C.C. Lee, Information Technology and Older Adults, in: J.A. Jacko, A. Sears (eds.), The Human–Computer Interaction Handbook, 2nd ed., 777–792; N. Charness, W.R. Boot, Aging and Information Technology Use: Potential and Barriers, 2009.

[38] See F. Mubarak, R. Suomi, Elderly Forgotten? Digital Exclusion in the Information Age and the Rising Grey Digital Divide, 2022, 4; P. Kossecki, A. Borcuch, Digital, Social and Financial Exclusion Among Elderly People, 6; T.N. Friemel T.N., New Media & Society, 18(2), 313–331.

[39] See T.E. Metherell et al., Digital Exclusion Predicts Worse Mental Health Among Adolescents during COVID-19, 2022; K. Walsh, T. Scharf, N. Keating, Eur J Ageing, 2017, 14(1), 81–98.

[40] See Research note 3/2010 Financial exclusion in the EU. New evidence from the EU-SILC special module, https://ec.europa.eu/social/BlobServlet?docId=9816.

[41] See OECD, Financial Consumer Protection and Ageing Populations, 2020, https://www.oecd.org/finance/Financial-consumer-protection-and-ageing-populations.pdf; Impact of access to financial services, including by highlighting remittances on development: Economic empowerment of women and youth, https://www.unctad.org/system/files/official-document/ciem6d2_en.pdf; L. Ayalon, International Psychogeriatrics, 2020, 32(10),

In terms of the category of lending services, limited access to financial services provided by commercial banks pushes seniors towards the tentacles of illicit, fraudulent, and unsupervised providers of such services. These providers often design their business models with full awareness of the elderly's preferences and resulting vulnerabilities and offer, for example, in-person visits at home.[42] The elderly's exclusion from commercial banking services thus puts them at a greater risk of being victims of fraud, scams, or excessively overpriced services.[43]

The abovementioned risks related to financial exclusion are particularly important given the demographic structure of European societies, which have been experiencing significant transformations commonly referred to as population ageing or greying. This process is expressed by an increase in the percentage of older people within society while the share of people of working age in the total population decreases. The direct causes of the ageing of European societies are primarily attributed to the steady rise in the population's life expectancy, declining birth rates, declining fertility rates, and migration. It is projected that by 2100, the population of EU countries over 65 years of age will increase dynamically from 20.2% in 2019 and will account for nearly 31.3% of the total population of the European Union, while the percentage of the oldest population, i.e., over 80 years of age, will increase from 5.8% to 14.6%.[44] The share of people aged 80 years or above in the EU's population is projected to increase between 2021 and 2100 from 6.0% to 14.6%.[45]

1–4; D. Goodwin et al., Debt, Money Management and Access To Financial Services, 1999, 42.

[42] See Report: Fighting Fraud: Senate Aging Committee Identifies Top 5 Scams Targeting Our Nation's Seniors Since 2015, https://www.aging.senate.gov/imo/media/doc/Fraud%20Book%202021.pdf.

[43] See Report by Richard Berry, Older People and the Internet. Towards a "System Map" of Digital Exclusion, https://www.ilcuk.org.uk/older-people-and-the-internet/; F. Mubarak, R. Suomi, Elderly forgotten? Digital Exclusion in the Information Age and the Rising Grey Digital Divide, 2022, 4.

[44] https://www.ec.europa.eu/eurostat/statistics-explained/index.php?title=Population_structure_and_ageing, see: Aging Europe. Looking at the lives of older people in the EU, https://www.ec.europa.eu/eurostat/documents/3217494/11478057/KS-02-20-655-EN-N.pdf.

[45] Eurostat 2021, https://www.ec.europa.eu/eurostat/statisticsexplained/index.php?title=Population_structure_and_ageing.

The effective integration of the elderly in our society is incrementally being recognized as a pivotal component of "successful aging" that feeds into the creation of a harmonious social fabric.[46] The well-being of older people is embedded in goal No. 3 of the 17 Sustainable Development Goals constituted by the UN Agenda 2030.[47] Social integration of older people also spotlights "upwards solidarity", the often less-prevalent factor of the demand for intra-generational responsibility, in this case, the responsibility of the younger for the older. While the effects of digitalization marginalize the elderly in multiple ways, the implications of digital exclusion regarding financial services seem to be of peculiar significance.[48] Financial inclusion, in particular, the capacity to execute payments for goods and services, is instrumental to any activity of the elderly aimed at satisfying their needs. Consequently, financial exclusion affects all areas of the elderly's societal involvement. Whereas the progressing digitalization in the distribution of goods and the rendering of other non-financial services still did not extinguish their viable "traditional" alternatives, the proceeding digital transition in commercial banking often discards these alternatives permanently and abruptly. Further, the digitalization of financial services runs at a higher level of complexity than the digital revolution in the elderly's other day-to-day situations (e.g., purchasing an online bus ticket) and thus requires greater technical capacities.

4 The Current State of EU Law: The Case for Legislative Intervention

It is said that the growing population of seniors in Europe benefits from historically well-established human rights tradition and the widely perceived need for special protection of the elderly.[49] Manifestations

[46] See F. Esposito, Conceptual Foundations for a European Consumer Law and Behavioural Sciences Scholarship, in: H.W. Micklitz, A.L. Sibony, F. Esposito (eds.), Research Methods in Consumer Law, 38–76.

[47] See: https://www.sdgs.un.org/goals.

[48] See P. Vassilakopoulou, E. Hustad, Inf Syst Front, 2021, 1, https://doi.org/10.1007/s10796-020-10096-3.

[49] European Law Institute (2020). The Protection of Adults in International Situations, https://www.europeanlawinstitute.eu/fileadmin/user_upload/p_eli/Publications/ELI_Protection_of_Adults_in_International_Situations.pdf; Office of Deputy Prime Minister (2006). The Social Exclusion of Older People: Evidence from the First Wave

of such awareness can be found in EU legislation and various social policies aimed at safeguarding the essentials for the eldest part of European society. However, the question arises as to whether the current state of the law and the measures adopted thereunder are sufficient to ensure adequate protection of the seniors' rights against the risk of financial exclusion associated with increasing digitalization and the consistent reduction of bank branches.

Primary EU law stipulates fundamental rights of seniors, i.e., the right to live with dignity and independence and the right to participate in social and cultural life (Article 25 of the EChFR). Nonetheless, there is no universal and comprehensive regulation that would further detail these general standards and thus ensure their effective protection. As a result, the actual enforcement of the elderly's rights has so far mainly mirrored the general principle of non-discrimination, primarily provided in Article 18 of the TFEU (in terms of discrimination based on nationality) and then centrally located in Article 21 of the EChFR, prohibiting unjustified unequal treatment based on other characteristics, including, i.e., gender, religion or belief, disability, sexual orientation, and—importantly—age.

Age discrimination is assumed to violate the fundamental right to respect for human dignity, equality of treatment, and respect.[50] As a consequence, the adoption of legislation that prohibits unjustified forms of age discrimination and provides its victims with effective remedies is recognized as a key element of an effective equality strategy and one of the EU priorities.[51] At the same time, despite the general nature of the problem, age discrimination and its negative social implications are

of the English Longitudinal Study of Ageing (ELSA), https://www.ifs.org.uk/publications/social-exclusion-older-people-evidence-first-wave-english-longitudinal-study-ageing; A. Kesby, Hum Rights Rev, 2017, 18(4), 371–393; Hammarberg T., Human Rights of Older Persons: Participation, Equality and Dignity, 2011; S. Mapp, S.G. Gabel, J. Hum. Rights Soc. Work, 2017, 2(4), 107; B. Lewis, K. Purser, K. Mackie, The Human Rights of Older Persons. A Human Rights-Based Approach to Elder Law; C. Martin, D. Rodgriguez-Pinzón, B. Brown, Human Rights of Older People—Universal and Regional Legal Perspectives.

[50] Fredman S., The Age of Equality, in: S. Fredman, S. Spencer (eds.), Age as an Equality Issue: Legal and Policy Perspectives, 21–70.

[51] EC (2005), Age Discrimination and European Law, https://www.ec.europa.eu/social/BlobServlet?docId=1691, 5.

marked mainly in terms of employment and addressed by specific regulations of EU labour law.[52] In this respect, the general prohibition of both direct and indirect discrimination is further specified in Article 2 of Council Directive 2000/78/EC of 27.11.2000, the so-called Employment Equality Directive, which establishes a general framework for equal treatment in employment and occupation. This minimum standard has, in general, led to positive reforms at the national level and helped to challenge structural inequalities in the labour market. The ECJ has referred primarily to this directive and its framework for equal treatment since the famous Mangold case when deriving a general principle of non-discrimination on the grounds of age from the fact that this principle was laid down in various international instruments and in the constitutional traditions common to the Member States.[53] Since the EChFR entered into force in 2009, the ECJ has based this unwritten principle of EU primary law also on Art. 21 EChFR.[54] In 2018, the Court finally applied Art. 21 EChFR directly between the private parties of an employment relationship, stating that the prohibition of discrimination was mandatory as a general principle of EU law and that Art. 21 EChFR was sufficient in itself to confer on individuals a right where they may rely on as such in any dispute between private actors, as long as the respective field was covered by EL law.[55] These findings are important for the future development of EU law as regards the digital exclusion of the elderly from

[52] See also EC (2005), Age Discrimination and European Law; EC (2011), Age and Employment, https://www.op.europa.eu/en/publication-detail/-/publication/dd16da05-dc71-4c65-b2bd-6c48cde3c5ee; AGE Platform Europe (2021). The Right to Work in Old Age. How the EU Employment Framework Directive still leaves older workers behind, https://www.social.un.org/ageing-working-group/documents/AGE%20Platform%20Europe_The%20right%20to%20work%20in%20old%20age.pdf; M. Freeland, L. Vickers, Age discrimination and EU labour rights law, in: A. Bogg, C. Costello, A.C.L. Davies (eds.), Research Handbook on EU Labour Law, 527–546; Numhauser-Henning A., Ageism, Age Discrimination and Employment Law in the EU, 98–115; M. Rönnmar, A. Numhauser-Henning, Age Discrimination and the Labour Law—Comparative and Conceptual Perspectives in the EU and Beyond.

[53] ECJ case 144/04 Mangold [2005] ECR I-9981 (para. 74 et passim).

[54] ECJ case 555/07 Kücükdeveci [2010] ECLI:EU:C:2010:21; confirmed by ECJ case 447/09 Prigge [2011] ECLI:EU:C:2011:573 and ECJ case 441/14 *DI* [2016] ECLI:EU:C:2016:278.

[55] ECJ case 414/16 Egenberger [2018] ECLI:EU:C:2018:257 (para 76); ECJ case 68/17 IR/JQ [2018] ECLI:EU:C:2018:696 (para 69); both cases dealt with the prohibition of discrimination on grounds of religion or belief, their findings however, apply equally

financial services, as the market participants concerned in this respect are typically of a private law nature. But Art. 21 EChFR alone will not create an effective standard of protection, as it does not provide a detailed legal framework for the respective issues that may arise. For this purpose, more specific acts of EU secondary law are required.

Related instruments of protection from age discrimination have not yet been introduced outside the field of employment.[56] In 2008, the European Commission drafted a proposal for a Council Directive on implementing the principle of equal treatment irrespective of religion, belief, disability, age, and sexual orientation, justifying that discrimination based on these criteria, unlike the one related to gender, race or ethnic origin, "is prohibited only in employment, occupation, and vocational training".[57] In terms of equal access to the financial sector, the proposed regulations, which were, however, never adopted, provided that age, as well as disability, can be an essential element of the assessment of risk for certain products and the price, provided that such assessment is based on "accurate data and statistics" (Article 2). According to some authors, this and other exemptions indicated in the presented proposal were susceptible to abuse and reinforcement of certain age-related stereotypes.[58]

Given the above, age discrimination in terms of access to financial products and services is currently governed mainly by the general prohibition of discrimination, particularly in the form of Art. 21 EChFR as interpreted by the ECJ, which, due to its vagueness, turns out to be an inefficient measure for the protection of the elderly facing the consequences of commercial banking digitalization represented mainly by the vanishing bank branches phenomenon. Therefore, seeking other legal instruments to mitigate the aforementioned related risk of exclusion seems appropriate.

In this context, it is worth considering a legal framework for the protection of older people as consumers, including in particular: the

to the prohibition of discrimination on grounds of age, as age is equivalent ground for discrimination.

[56] See N. Georgantzi, The European Union's approach towards Ageism, in: L. Ayalon, C. Tesch-Römer (eds.), Contemporary Perspectives on Ageism, 341, 346.

[57] EC, COM (2008) 426 final, https://www.eur-lex.europa.eu/legal-content/EN/TXT/HTML/?uri=CELEX:52008PC0426.

[58] See N. Georgantzi, The European Union's Approach towards Ageism, 341, 347.

Consumer Rights Directive,[59] the Unfair Commercial Practices Directive[60] and the Consumer Credit Directive,[61] but also the recent Directives on the sale of goods[62] and the supply of digital content and services.[63] The vast body of consumer protection law therein encompasses instruments aimed to provide the safety of products, certain tools designed to ensure that consumers are provided with clear and correct information, as well as mechanisms protecting consumers from unfair commercial practices.[64] In general, to determine the appropriate level of protection, all of these measures refer to the average consumer, who is deemed reasonably well-informed, reasonably observant, and circumspect.[65] On the other hand, some regulations introduce occasional references to the concept of a ***vulnerable consumer***, which might also apply to the elderly.[66]

The distinction between "average" and "vulnerable" consumers is established in the Unfair Commercial Practices Directive. According to Article 5(2) of the directive, commercial practices are considered unfair

[59] Directive 2011/83/EU of 25 October 2011 on consumer rights, amending Council Directive 93/13/EEC and Directive 1999/44/EC of the European Parliament and the Council and repealing Council Directive 85/77/EEC and Directive 97/7/EC of the European Parliament and of the Council [2011] O.J.L304/64.

[60] Directive 2005/29/EC of 11 May 2005 concerning unfair business-to-consumer commercial practices in the internal market and amending Council Directive 84/450/EEC, Directives 97/7/EC, 98/27/EC and 2002/65/EC of the European Parliament and of the Council and Regulation (EC) No 2006/2004 of the European Parliament and of the Council.

[61] Directive 2008/48/EC of the European Parliament and of the Council of 23 April 2008 of credit agreements for consumers and repealing Council Directive 87/102/EEC; see also the proposal for an updated version: COM (2021) 347 final of 30 June 2021.

[62] Directive (EU) 2019/771 of the European Parliament and of the Council of 20 May 2019 on certain aspects concerning contracts for the sale of goods, amending Regulation (EU) 2017/2394 and Directive 2009/22/EC, and repealing Directive 1999/44/EC.

[63] Directive (EU) 2019/770 of the European Parliament and of the Council of 20 May 2019 on certain aspects concerning contracts for the supply of digital content and digital services.

[64] See N. Reich et al., European Consumer Law, 36; L. Waddington, Reflections of the Protection of 'Vulnerable' Consumers under EU Law, Maastricht Faculty of Law Working Paper No. 2013–2.

[65] In terms of the average consumer test see e.g. the CJEU case C-210/96 Gut Springerheide, EU:C:1998:369, para 1; F. Esposito, Conceptual Foundations for a European Consumer Law and Behavioural Sciences Scholarship, 38, 68–70.

[66] See N. Reich et al., European Consumer Law, 45–46.

if they fail to comply with the requirement of professional diligence and materially distort the economic behaviour of the *average consumer*. At the same time, the directive aims at preventing abuses against the *particularly vulnerable consumers*. Therefore, pursuant to Article 5(3) of the directive, commercial practices which are likely to materially distort the economic behaviour only of a clearly identifiable group of consumers who are particularly vulnerable to the practice or the underlying product because of their mental or physical infirmity, age or credulity in a way which the trader could reasonably be expected to foresee, shall be assessed from the perspective of the average member of that group.

Even though, given the above definition, older people are amongst the group of vulnerable consumers, regardless of the concerns raised by the definition of vulnerability,[67] it appears that the measures for protection against unfair commercial practices do not adequately address the risk of financial inclusion posed by the vanishing of bank branches. As indicated above, the relocation of commercial banking to the digital environment and the consequent reduction of on-site personal service is motivated by the banks' business decisions, which, however, can hardly be characterized as unfair. It therefore seems that the negative consequences suffered by non-digitized consumers are only a "side-effect" and not the overall intent of the described process.

Further, a reference to *particularly vulnerable* consumers can be found in the Consumer Rights Directive that harmonizes the common aspects of distance and off-premises contracts with regard to, i.e., consumer information and the right to withdrawal from such agreements. According to Recital 34, in providing clear and comprehensible information to the consumer prior to the completion of any contract, the trader should take into account the specific needs of consumers who are particularly vulnerable due to the same criteria as those listed in Article 5(3) of the Unfair Commercial Practices Directive (Sirena 2020, p. 10). Analogous regulations have been implemented in Directive 2008/48/EC on credit agreements for consumers (Article 4(2), Recital 9).[68]

[67] See J. Stuyck, The Notion of the Empowered and Informed Consumer in Consumer Policy and How to Protect the Vulnerable under Such a Regime, in: G. Howells et al. (eds.), The Yearbook of Consumer Law, London, 2007, 167, 178–179.

[68] Directive 2008/48/EC of 23 April 2008 on credit agreements for consumers and repealing Council Directive 87/102/EEC [2008] O.J.L133/66.

In light of the abovementioned fragmented regulations, it should be agreed that EU law does not provide a clear vision or policy for protecting vulnerable consumers, including the elderly.[69] At the same time, the need for special treatment of vulnerable consumers is often recognized, e.g., by the Committee on the Internal Market and Consumer Protection of the European Parliament[70] or by the European Commission.[71]

Specific needs of specific consumer groups were one of the five priority areas distinguished by the Commission in the New Consumer Agenda 2020–2025, including (1) ecological transformation, (2) digital transformation, (3) redressability and enforcement of consumer rights, (4) specific needs of specific consumer groups, (5) international cooperation. As noted in the Agenda: "*The elderly and people with disabilities have special consumption needs. It is important to ensure easy access to clear and consumer-friendly information both online and offline in accordance with EU requirements for accessibility of products and services. A fair and non-discriminatory approach to digital transformation should take into account the needs of older consumers, consumers with disabilities, and offline users in general, who may be less familiar with digital tools*". Although the Commission has aptly identified the need to protect seniors both through education and by providing specific mechanisms to counter exclusion due to the dynamic digitalization of commerce, no legislative initiatives have yet been taken in this regard.

Similarly, no normative solutions to the problem of financial exclusion of the elderly are provided by the sector-specific regulations governing digital financial services.[72] The Digital Finance Strategy presented by the European Commission on 24 September 2020, as well as the legislative actions taken against its background, are intensely focused on e-banking

[69] See L. Waddington, Reflections of the Protection of 'Vulnerable' Consumers under EU Law, Maastricht Faculty of Law Working Paper No. 2013–2, 35.

[70] Committee on the Internal Market and Consumer Protection (2012). Report on Strategy for Strengthening the Rights of Vulnerable Consumers, https://www.europarl.europa.eu/doceo/document/A-7-2012-0155_EN.html.

[71] Communication from the Commission to the European Parliament and the Council (2020). New Consumer Agenda. Strengthening Consumer Resilience for Sustainable Recovery, COM/2020/696 final, https://www.eur-lex.europa.eu/legal-content/EN/TXT/?uri=CELEX%3A52020DC0696.

[72] See D. Szilágyi, Vulnerable Consumers and Financial Services in the European Union: The Position of the EU Court of Justice, Public Goods and Governance, 2020, 5(1), 30, 34.

safeguards and thus overlook the issues related to access to banking for non-digitalized consumers.

In view of the above, as the rapid ageing European population interlocks with the digital revolution in commercial banking, a significant social challenge for European policymakers emerges. The COVID-19 pandemic has underscored the pressing nature of this challenge as the tragic consequences of the pandemic in terms of the elderly's vulnerability and the systemic healthcare failures in institutional care have reminded Europeans about the necessity to address the needs of the older part of our societies with the same diligence that is being devoted to problems faced by the younger ones. The need to seek instruments to restore and preserve the ability of seniors to participate effectively in commercial banking appears urgent.

The case for legislative intervention regarding the financial exclusion of the elderly is supported by the growing tendency to view access to the financial market (the right to financial inclusion) as a human right.[73] Another argument supporting the call for legislative intervention regarding the discussed problem lies in the changing societal expectations regarding the role of banks in a new economic and social reality. Key importance for the consideration of legal reform thus lies in the assumption that financial institutions carry a particular social responsibility.[74] This allows arguing that banks are obliged to address and prevent the financial exclusion of seniors. As a consequence, a limitation of commercial banks' freedom to shape their business models would appear justified.

It follows from the above that the current legal regime at the EU level does not address the digital exclusion of the elderly from financial services in an explicit or sufficient manner. Although the digitalization of economic transactions with consumers' participation is undoubtedly and rightfully treated as a key area of challenge for consumer policies,

[73] See UN Environment Programme (2016). Human Rights and Sustainable Finance. Exploring the Relationship, Inquiry Working Paper 16/01, https://www.ihrb.org/uploads/reports/IHRB_UNEP_Human_Rights_Sustainable_Finance_Feb2016.pdf; B.P. Kumar, Munich Personal RePEc Archive Paper No. 80336, 2014, 13.

[74] See C. Mayer, Prosperity: Better Business Makes the Greater Good, 22; C. Lenter, K. Szegedi, T. Tatay, Corporate Social Responsibility in the Banking Sector, Public Finance Quarterly, 2015, 60(1), 95–103.

no adequate policy discourse has emerged on the digital exclusion of the elderly from financial services so far.

5 Potential Legislative Strategies

Measures aimed at preventing financial exclusion and bringing excluded people back into the financial system are referred to as financial inclusion instruments.[75] We propose that future academic and policy efforts, in particular, explore the following potential legislative strategies:

A. Identification of Seniors as a Special Group of Consumers

The analysis of the specific conditions and market behaviour of seniors justifies consideration of their normative distinction as a specific consumer "subgroup" of vulnerable consumers. Such legislative intervention would create a starting point for reflection on the protective instruments dedicated to seniors. To that end, it would be necessary to assess whether the distinction of seniors as special consumers would be justified with regard to the entire spectrum of their participation as consumers in economic life or whether only their presence in the financial market requires such a procedure.[76]

B. Obligatory On-Site Service Maintenance

It is necessary to consider the permissibility and scope to oblige commercial banks to provide personal customer service. Various possible forms of such an obligation could be subject to consideration. In particular, one could debate the obligation to operate stationary service points, provide mobile service points or other infrastructure, or introduce specific communication channels.[77] Potential solutions regarding the addressees of such an obligation must be carefully reviewed. In particular, the situation of banks that have historically served customers in branches and are now, with a significant number of non-digital seniors in their customer

[75] See D.W. Arner et al., Sustainability, Fintech and Financial Inclusion, 7–9.

[76] See H.W. Micklitz, A.L. Sibony, F. Esposito, The Bright and Adventurous Future of Consumer Law Research, in: H.W. Micklitz, A.L. Sibony, F. Esposito (eds.), Research Methods in Consumer Law, 1, 35.

[77] See L. Georgieva, Digital Inclusion and the Elderly: The Case of Online Banking, 8–11.

portfolio, withdrawing from this business model would have to be assessed differently from the situation of banks that, when entering the market, did not envisage an outpost-based customer service model. As an example of creating obligations on the side of financial institutions to counter financial exclusion, the enactment of legislation on access to a basic payment account should be mentioned. Thus, there are already examples of financial inclusion instruments to be found in the EU legal framework, which oblige banks to enter into agreements, thus limiting their freedom of operation.

C. Disclosure Obligations

In the context of the problem of vanishing bank branches, consideration should be given to the information obligations of banks regarding the planned branch closure. The idea would be to construct a mechanism for informing customers well in advance of a branch closure and indicating alternatives to personal service at the closing bank branch. The bottom-up initiative of banks in the UK, titled *The Access to Banking Standard*, under which the implementation of the obligations of banks, adopted as soft law, is externally supervised by designated state authorities, may serve as a model for analysis. One of the obligations formulated as part of this document narrows down to identifying which customers may be particularly vulnerable to foreclosure or require additional assistance and, consequently, contacting them. In doing so, the analysis would have to take into account the current state of the debate in consumer law, from which doubts about the effectiveness of information obligations towards consumers as an effective mechanism for their protection are increasingly resounding.[78]

D. Institutional Solutions

In the context of providing seniors with access to digital financial services, possible mechanisms of an institutional nature could also be considered. In particular, the legitimacy of creating dedicated units within the activities of the institutional gatekeepers of the financial market should be examined. In this regard, it would also

[78] See F. Esposito, Conceptual Foundations for a European Consumer Law and Behavioural Sciences Scholarship, 38, 63–66; F. Gómez Pomar, M. Artigot Golobardes, Raptional Choice and Behavioural Approaches to Consumer Issues, 119, 120; A. Oehler, S. Wendt, Good Consumer Information: The Information Paradigm at its (Dead) End?, J Consum Policy, 2017, 40(2), 179–191.

be appropriate to reflect on the idea of equipping these institutions with competencies that would promote the actual enforcement of the elderly's rights related to access to the financial market.

E. Financial Education

The possibility of burdening banks with the obligation to undertake financial education activities for seniors needs to be investigated.[79] In particular, this includes measures to improve the digital skills of senior citizens. It would be necessary to analyse the possible forms of such an obligation, which requires, first of all, taking into account the methodological currents based on the conclusions of behavioural sciences and against this background—the limited cognitive capabilities and enthusiasm of this age group. In particular, the model of direct implementation of the educational obligation by the banks and the indirect model, in which the banks, within the framework of a structured, common fund, financially contribute to the educational initiatives of seniors carried out at the national or alternatively, local level, should be analysed. Of particular interest seems to be the question to what extent the private sector (commercial banks) should be burdened with the cost of raising the digital competence of seniors.

6 Conclusion

The above analysis indicates that the digital transition in commercial banking business models should be identified as an important driver of the elderly's financial exclusion. In particular, the abandonment of the traditional means of rendering basic financial services is emblematically reflected in the empirical data on the steady decrease in the number of bank branches across Europe. Seniors' preferences regarding person-to-person interactions, lower digital skills, and cognitive barriers to obtaining them effectively limit this group of customers' access to financial services. This problem seems particularly urgent in light of the ageing of European societies and forecasts of further transformations of the demographic structure in the coming years. It requires stressing that the diagnosed

[79] See J.A. Pachis, K.L.M. Zonneveld, Comparison of Prompting Procedures to Teach Internet Skills to Older Adults, Journal of Applied Behaviour Analysis, 2019, 52(1), 173–187.

digital exclusion of the elderly from financial services is not of ***interim*** character. Though the general advancement of digital skills in our society may be projected, the pace of technological development will always edge out the rate of seniors' learning processes. At the same time, the current legal regime at the EU level does not provide the elderly with adequate protection against financial exclusion. Therefore, a legislative intervention on the EU level appears mandated. However, further research and policy work needs to be conducted to evaluate the different yet not necessarily conflicting potential legislative strategies for the financial inclusion of the elderly. In light of the heated debate on the social obligations of banks, fundamental questions will revolve around the issue of how far banks can be burdened with the responsibility of actively safeguarding the elderly's access to financial services. To this end, the financial inclusion of seniors may crucially influence the execution of digitalization-driven business models which banks increasingly pursue. While such development is naturally not going to stop or significantly slow down the observable transition in commercial banking, the strain of compliance with new regulatory burdens and the associated costs could alter the scope of banks' efficiency gains that result from the digitalization of their services.

CHAPTER 6

The 'Game Changer' in the Euro Area: Banking Union and Commercial Banking

Lucia Quaglia

1 Introduction

Banking Union, which was an important response of the European Union (EU)—to be precise, the euro area—to the sovereign crisis in the euro area periphery, has far-reaching implications for commercial banking in Europe, as it transformed banking supervision and resolution in the euro

L. Quaglia (✉)
Department of Political Science, University of Bologna, Bologna, Italy
e-mail: lucia.quaglia@unibo.it

M. Bodellini et al. (eds.), *Commercial Banking in Transition*, Palgrave Macmillan Studies in Banking and Financial Institutions,
https://doi.org/10.1007/978-3-031-45289-5_6

area[1] The main goals of Banking Union were not only to break the 'doom loop'[2] between ailing banks and fiscally weak sovereigns, but also to contribute to the completion of Economic and Monetary Union (EMU). Thus, Banking Union, as initially conceived, was to be based on three pillars: single banking supervision, single banking resolution, and a common deposit guarantee scheme. Moreover, a common fiscal backstop was to be set up.[3]

This paper explains the establishment of Banking Union, its functioning over the first decade and how it has withstood the test of the covid-related economic crisis. It is argued that the Banking Union that

[1] S. Donnelly, Power Politics and the Undersupply of Financial Stability in Europe, *Review of International Political Economy*, 2014, 21 (4), 980–1005; S. De Rynck, Banking on a Union: The Politics of Changing Eurozone Banking Supervision, *Journal of European Public Policy*, 2015, 23 (1), 119–135; R. Epstein, and M. Rhodes, The Political Dynamics behind Europe's New Banking Union, *West European Politics*, 2016, 39 (30), 415–437; G. Glöckler, J. Lindner, and M. Salines, Explaining the Sudden Creation of a Banking Supervisor for the Euro Area, *Journal of European Public Policy*, 2016, 24 (8), 1135–1153; D. Howarth, and L. Quaglia, The Political Economy of Banking Union, Oxford: Oxford University Press, 2016; D. Howarth, and L. Quaglia, Internationalized Banking and National Preferences on European Central Bank Supervision, *West European Politics*, 2016, 39 (3), 438–461; B. Nielsen, and S. Smeets, The Role of the EU Institutions in Establishing the Banking Union. Collaborative Leadership in the EMU Reform Process, *Journal of European Public Policy*, http://dx.doi.org/10.1080/13501763.2017.1285342; D. Schaffer, A Banking Union of Ideas? The Impact of Ordoliberalism and the Vicious Circle on the EU Banking Union, *Journal of Common Market Studies*, 2016, 54 (4): 961–980; F. Schimmelfennig, A Differentiated Leap Forward: Spillover, Path-dependency, and Graded Membership in European Banking Regulation, *West European Politics*, 2016, 39 (30), 483–502; M. Skuodis, Playing the Creation of the European Banking Union: What Union for Which Member States, *Journal of European Integration*, 2017, http://dx.doi.org/10.1080/07036337.2017.1404056.

[2] The doom loop, which came to the fore during the sovereign debt crisis, was a vicious link between ailing banks and fiscally weak sovereigns in the euro area periphery. In fact, the deterioration in the market for government bonds of countries hit by the sovereign debt crisis weakened the capital position of their domestic banks because the latter had been accumulating a significant amount of national government bonds on their balance sheets. At the same time, the increasing fragility of banks in the Eurozone periphery put a drag on the government's fiscal position by raising the prospect of a government intervention to rescue ailing banks, W. Schelkle (2017) The Political Economy of Monetary Solidarity: Understanding the Euro Experiment, Oxford: Oxford University Press.

[3] The single rule-book is often considered as a further pillar of Banking Union. However, the rule-book applies to the entire EU, not only the euro area, and was established prior to Banking Union in the context of the single market in finance.

was eventually set up was rather different from the one initially envisaged, notably: bank resolution partly remained at the national level, a common deposit guarantee scheme was not established, and the common backstop was set in place as late as 2020. In turn, the functioning of this 'incomplete' Banking Union has produced 'asymmetric' effects: it has promoted the harmonisation of banking supervision, especially for the banks under the direct supervision of the European Central Bank (ECB); whereas the harmonisation of resolution has been limited because the national authorities have been inclined to apply the 'Sinatra doctrine' by dealing with ailing banks in 'their own ways'. That said, in response to the covid pandemic, the ECB-centric Single Supervisory Mechanism (SSM) has taken important measures to mitigate the economic fallout caused by the pandemic.

This paper is organised as follows. Section 2 discusses the establishment of Banking Union, while Sect. 3 examines its functioning over the first decade. Section 4 discusses how Banking Union dealt with the covid-related economic crisis, in particular the measures taken by the ECB-SSM to respond to the economic and financial fallouts caused by the pandemic and what this entailed for the euro area banking system.

2 The Establishment of Banking Union

Against the background of the sovereign debt crisis in the euro area, the President of the European Council, the President of the Eurogroup, the President of the Commission and the President of the ECB presented an interim report titled 'Towards a Genuine Economic and Monetary Union' in June 2012. The Van Rompuy (2012) report, which was also known as the 'Four Presidents Report', proposed what later became known as Banking Union, namely 'an integrated financial framework to ensure financial stability in particular in the euro area and minimise the cost of bank failures to European citizens. Such a framework elevates responsibility for supervision to the European level, and provides for common mechanisms to resolve banks and guarantee customer deposits'. The project of Banking Union was subsequently endorsed by the European Council and euro area summit in June 2012. It was to include all the countries in the euro area as well as the countries that decided and were able to opt in.

The main objective of Banking Union was to break the 'vicious circle' between ailing banks and struggling sovereigns by providing financial assistance to countries and banks hit by the crisis. The sovereign debt-bank doom loop arose in the context of the sovereign debt crisis because of the flight of foreign investors from euro periphery member states. Banks headquartered in these countries came to hold an increasing amount of debt issued by governments—measured both as a percentage of total debt issued and as a percentage of total bank assets. The threat of default on this debt undermined confidence in the solvency of a number of euro periphery banks, including some that had escaped the 2008 international financial crisis largely unscathed. Confidence in the solvency of euro periphery governments, already facing a heavy and rising debt burden, was further undermined by the prospect of further bank bail-outs.[4]

More generally, Banking Union was intended to address the 'financial trilemma' identified by Dirk Schoenmaker (2013) and consists of financial stability, international banking and national financial policies. In the trilemma, any two of the three objectives can be combined but not all of them: one has to give. The single currency made the trilemma more acute in the euro area not only by increasing cross-border banking in the euro area, but also by undermining national financial policies, because the function of lender of last resort could no longer be performed by the national authorities. Furthermore, national resolution powers were limited by fiscal rules in the euro area (prior to their relaxation in the context of the covid-related economic crisis). Consequently, the safeguard of financial stability could only be achieved at the euro area level.[5]

For these reasons, euro area member state governments agreed (in some cases with great reluctance) to set up Banking Union, which shifts policies for supervision and resolution from the national level to the Banking Union level. The UK, which was not part of the single currency and had a very internationalised rather than 'Europeanised' banking system, lacked an incentive to join Banking Union. Central and Eastern European member states of the EU that had banking systems dominated by foreign (mostly euro area) owned banks had an incentive to

[4] D. Howarth, and L. Quaglia, The Political Economy of Banking Union, Oxford: Oxford University Press, 2016.

[5] Ibid.

join Banking Union because they were not in a position to safeguard financial stability domestically.[6] The euro area countries that faced the trilemma had however different preferences on the various elements of Banking Union, depending on the concern of national policy-makers for moral hazard and the configuration of their national financial systems. Hence, the negotiations of certain components of Banking Union were time-consuming[7] and a 'light' version of Banking Union was agreed upon in the end.

The first component of the Banking Union to be set up was the Single Supervisory Mechanism (SSM).[8] The final agreement on the SSM, which was reached by the European Council in December 2012, foresaw that the ECB would be responsible for the overall effective functioning of the SSM and would have direct oversight of euro area banks. This supervision, however, would be differentiated and the ECB would carry it out in close cooperation with national supervisory authorities. The regulation establishing the SSM also permitted the ECB to step in, if necessary, and supervise any of the 6000 banks in the euro area. The SSM applied only to the euro area member states and to the non-euro area member states that decided to join the Banking Union.

The establishment of the SSM involved a compromise concerning the distribution of supervisory powers between the ECB and the national competent authorities. Direct ECB supervision, through joint supervisory teams, was to cover only those banks with assets exceeding €30 billion or those having assets representing at least 20 per cent of their home country's annual GDP. The thousands of smaller, *less significant* banks headquartered in the euro area would continue to be under the

[6] A. Spendzharova (2014). Banking Union under Construction: The Impact of Foreign Ownership and Domestic Bank Internationalization on European Union Member-States' Regulatory Preferences in Banking Supervision, Review of International Political Economy, 21 (4), 949–979.

[7] See: S. De Rynck, Banking on a Union: The Politics of Changing Eurozone Banking Supervision, *Journal of European Public Policy*, 2015, 23 (1), 119–135; S. Donnelly, Power Politics and the Undersupply of Financial Stability in Europe, *Review of International Political Economy*, 2014, 21 (4), 980–1005; R. Epstein, and M. Rhodes, The Political Dynamics behind Europe's New Banking Union, *West European Politics*, 2016, 39 (30), 415–437.

[8] G. Glöckler, J. Lindner, and M. Salines, Explaining the Sudden Creation of a Banking Supervisor for the Euro Area, *Journal of European Public Policy*, 2016, 24 (8), 1135–1153.

direct supervision of the competent national authorities, but according to harmonised rules and practices. This compromise of two-level supervision reflected, above all, the demands of the German government, which opposed transferring supervisory responsibilities of the country's regional public savings banks (Sparkassen) and cooperatives to the ECB.[9]

The second component of Banking Union to be set up was the Single Resolution Mechanism (SRM). In July 2013, the Commission proposed the establishment of the SRM, designed to complement the SSM. Most of the intergovernmental negotiations concerned the decision-making process in the SSM and the establishment of the Single Resolution Fund (SRF) financed by bank levies, which were raised at the national level. The Commission, supported by French, Spanish and Italian policy-makers, wanted to be given the final power to decide whether to place a bank into resolution and determine the application of resolution tools. However, German policy-makers argued that the Single Resolution Board (SRB) should be given this power, and insisted on setting up the SRF through an intergovernmental agreement among the participating member states.[10]

In March 2014, an intergovernmental agreement was reached on the establishment of the SRM. As advocated by German policy-makers, the SRB would be responsible for the planning and the resolution of cross-border banks, as well as those directly supervised by the ECB. National resolution authorities would be responsible for all other banks, except banks that required access to the SRF. Moreover, the SRF, financed by bank levies raised at the national level, would initially consist of national compartments that would be gradually merged over eight years. The Regulation on the Single Resolution Mechanism (SRM) was adopted in conjunction with the Bank Recovery and Resolution Directive (BRRD), which harmonised resolution instruments and powers in the EU. The BRRD and the SRM Regulation introduced a new instrument in bank resolution, the bail-in, which substantially reduced the need for public funding to bail out banks.[11] Thus, the SRM would be fiscally neutral.

[9] D. Howarth, and L. Quaglia, Internationalized Banking and National Preferences on European Central Bank Supervision, *West European Politics*, 2016, 39 (3), 438–461.

[10] D. Howarth, and L. Quaglia, The Political Economy of Banking Union, Oxford: Oxford University Press, 2016.

[11] B. Nielsen, and S. Smeets, The Role of the EU Institutions in Establishing the Banking Union. Collaborative Leadership in the EMU Reform Process, *Journal of European Public Policy*, http://dx.doi.org/10.1080/13501763.2017.1285342.

The instrument of the bail-in was to enable banks to withstand financial stress by imposing losses on creditors (bail-in), without resorting to state-funded recapitalisation (bail-out).

The third missing component of the Banking Union was what later became to be known as the European Deposit Insurance Scheme (EDIS).[12] In June 2012, the interim Van Rompuy Report (a.k.a. Four Presidents' Report) report mentioned the need to set up an EDIS. The Commission had prepared a draft proposing a new agency, the European Deposit Insurance and Resolution Authority (EDIRA), which would control a new European Deposit Guarantee and Resolution Fund. Due to German opposition, the proposal for the EDIRA was removed and the final Commission document *A Roadmap Towards Banking Union* was released. Thus, the final Van Rompuy Report issued in December 2012 only made reference to an *Agreement on the Harmonization of National Resolution and Deposit Guarantee Frameworks*. German policy-makers criticised the EDIS as an unacceptable step towards debt mutualisation. In contrast, policy-makers in France and in the euro area periphery regarded the EDIS as the final pillar of the Banking Union, being necessary to severe the doom loop between banks and sovereigns. The ECB regarded the EDIS as an important component of the Banking Union, but one that could be implemented at a later date.[13]

The issue came back to the policy agenda in June 2015, when supranational actors, including ECB president Mario Draghi and Commission President Jean-Claude Juncker, endorsed the creation of the EDIS in the *Five Presidents' Report* on the future of the euro. In the autumn of 2015, the Commission proposed the EDIS for bank deposits in the euro area as the third pillar of Banking Union. The Commission's proposal would, as a first step, involve the establishment of 'a mandatory reinsurance scheme that would contribute under certain conditions when national deposit guarantee schemes are called upon'. It would, in effect, act as a backstop to national deposit guarantee schemes. This initiative took place despite explicit German opposition. As in the case of the creation of the SRF, the

[12] Donnelly, S. 2018. Power Politics, Banking Union and EMU, London: Routledge. D. Howarth, and L. Quaglia. (2018). The Difficult Construction of the European Deposit Insurance Scheme: A Step Too Far in Banking Union, *Journal of Economic Policy Reform*, 21 (3), 190–209.

[13] D. Howarth, and L. Quaglia, The Political Economy of Banking Union, Oxford: Oxford University Press, 2016.

intergovernmental discussion on the creation of the EDIS pitted countries' interests against each other. On one hand, there were the interests of the countries expected to make net contributions to common rescue funds, either coming from taxpayers or banks. On the other hand, there were the interests of the countries that were expected to be the principal recipients. Negotiations are ongoing at the time of writing.

Finally, the credibility of the SRM/SRF and the EDIS was linked to the possibility of accessing a common fiscal backstop. Given the fact that the use of the ESM was subject to unanimity, German policy-makers enjoyed a veto on any decision to engage in direct bank recapitalisation. Under the rules established for the direct recapitalisation of banks, euro area member states agreed that a bank's creditors should absorb 'appropriate' losses before ESM funds could be accessed. These appropriate losses were defined by the BRRD's rules on the bail-in. Moreover, ESM rules required a bank's home government to initially contribute at least twenty per cent of the recapitalisation and then ten per cent from 2017 onward. German policy-makers, joined by Austrian, Dutch and Finnish policy-makers insisted that ESM funds could not be used to cover legacy problems. Hence, the fiscal backstop did not materialise when the Banking Union was set up.[14]

Overall, Banking Union was set up in a timely fashion. However, it was incomplete and asymmetric in three main aspects. First, member state governments retained their vetoes on the mutualisation of national resolution funds and continued to have an important say on the use of the SRF in the SRM. Indeed, a rather complex compromise was reached concerning the resolution process in the SRB. Second, the EDIS was not set up. Third, an agreement to use the European Stability Mechanisms as a common fiscal backstop for the SRF was reached as late as 2020, as explained in the following section. Most of the intergovernmental negotiations on the core components of the Banking Union basically boiled down to distributional conflicts in two dimensions: the centralisation of decision-making, and the allocation of costs via risk-sharing in the Banking Union. The discussions pitted expected net contributors against those expected to be the principal recipients of funding. Thus, compromises between the two coalitions were sought during the negotiations. The institutional design eventually set up for the Banking Union was

[14] Ibid.

closer to the preferences of the German-led coalition, as far as risk-sharing was concerned. However, German policy-makers had to make concessions concerning the transfer of decision-making to the EU/euro area level. The result was an incomplete and asymmetric Banking Union, which was rather different from the one initially envisaged: out of the three pillars initially proposed, only one and a half were set in place (supervision and partly, resolution).

3 The Functioning of an Incomplete Banking Union

This section provides an overview of the first ten years of operation of Banking Union by reviewing the functioning of its main pillars: the SSM, the SRM, and the debate on the missing common deposit guarantee scheme. It is argued that the institutional set up of the SSM favoured the harmonisation of banking supervision, while promoting only limited harmonisation of banking resolution, which remained a 'patchwork' across member states. A common deposit guarantee scheme was discussed but, eventually, not established, whereas in 2020 member states agree to make the ESM the fiscal backstop of the single resolution fund.

In 2014, the SSM began functioning. At the centre of the SSM there was the ECB, which was an independent, well-resourced institution, with a proven capacity to take bold (sometimes, politically controversial) decisions,[15] as suggested, inter alia, by the pledge, at the peak of the sovereign debt crisis, to do 'whatever it takes to save the euro'. Within the SSM, the ECB had clearly assigned regulatory and supervisory competences, granted by the Treaty and the SSM legislation discussed above. It also had substantial financial and human resources to deploy for its new tasks: the ECB hired about nine hundred supervisory officials in less than two years (2014–2016).

In 2014, the ECB published a list of 128 banks subject to direct ECB supervision (the so-called 'significant banks'), which accounted for approximately 80 per cent of the assets of euro area banks.[16] In the

[15] A. Verdun, Political Leadership of the European Central Bank, *Journal of European Integration*, 2017, 39 (2), 207–221.

[16] At the start of 2020, approximately 117 banks were subject to direct ECB supervision (the so-called 'significant banks') (ECB 2019), which accounted for approximately 82% of the assets of euro area banks (Institut Montaigne 2021). Bulgaria and Croatia joined the

same year, the ECB published the SSM Supervisory Manual and a Guide to Banking Supervision.[17] As a way to deal with the 'legacy problems' pointed out by the German-led coalition, the ECB undertook a comprehensive assessment of the banks subject to its direct supervision.[18] The comprehensive assessment consisted of the ECB's assets quality review (AQR) and the stress tests of the European Banking Authority (EBA). The AQR reviewed more than 800 portfolios, amounting to approximately 57 per cent of the risk-weighted assets of the 128 banks examined. Crucially, the AQR significantly improved the transparency and comparability of bank data across the euro area by harmonising the definition of non-performing loans and uncovering hidden losses. In doing so, the ECB found massive shortfalls in the loans that banks and national regulators classified as non-performing (i.e. bad). This figure amounted to 15 per cent more than the total previously announced by the national competent authorities. Amongst the banks that failed the comprehensive assessment, Italian and Greek banks were the most exposed, with, respectively, nine and four failing.[19]

Although the problems of ailing banks resulted from past legacies and would have existed without Banking Union, the ECB-led supervision in the SSM exposed these banking problems more starkly. A clear example was the ECB's comprehensive assessment, which highlighted that several banks suffered from non-performing loans. Whereas in the past, national supervisory forbearance was a common practice, this was no longer possible under the supervision of the ECB in the SSM. In certain cases, such as the Monte dei Paschi di Siena in Italy, the Novo Banco in Portugal and the Banco Popular in Spain, the viability of the banks was at risk. Thus, the harmonisation of banking supervision in Banking Union

SSM in October 2020. Their entry meant that more significant banks were added (five Bulgarian banks and eight Croatian banks).

[17] European Central Bank, Asset Quality Review: Phase 2 Manual, 2014, March, Frankfurt.

[18] European Central Bank, Guide to Banking Supervision, 2014, November, Frankfurt.

[19] See for further details: J. Gren, D. Howarth, and L. Quaglia, Supranational Banking Supervision in Europe: The Construction of a Credible Watchdog, *Journal of Common Market Studies*, 2015, 53 (S1), 181–199.

meant stricter supervision, while constraining the room for manoeuvre of national banking supervisory authorities in the euro area periphery.[20]

Besides promoting the harmonisation of supervision in the euro area, as explained above, the SSM (and within it, the ECB) also promoted the harmonisation of regulation, to be precise the EU banking rule book, so as to secure a level playing field in the euro area. The process started by focusing on significant banks and subsequently extended to less significant banks. In 2015, the ECB issued a (binding) regulation concerning the exercise of so-called 'general options' and national discretions vis-à-vis significant banks directly supervised by the ECB. In 2016, the ECB issued a (non-binding) guideline on the exercise of options and national discretions on 'case-by-case' and a (non-binding) guidance for the assessment of non-performing loans for significant banks. In 2017, the ECB began working on regulatory harmonisation concerning less significant banks, issuing a (non-binding) recommendation on the exercise of options and national discretions.[21]

In 2015, the SRB was set up as an EU agency and the SRM began functioning. The SRM had a rather weak institutional setup, compared to the SSM. It did not have a well-established supranational institution, such as the ECB, as its centre. Unlike the ECB, the SRB was an agency, which limited its independence, decision-making capacity and resources. Only in 2020, euro area member states agreed to use the ESM as a backstop to the SRF. Although the SRM and the BRRD were supposed to harmonise bank resolution in Banking Union, this happened only to a limited extent. The institutional model chosen for the SRM meant that resolution partly remained a national competence for small domestic banks. For banks under direct ECB supervision as well as cross-border banks, resolution was to be managed by the SRB through a convoluted decision-making process[22] and without the backing of a substantial SRF. Consequently, there was considerable national variation in the way in which the national authorities dealt with ailing banks in Banking Union, in particular concerning the important question of 'who pays'. Indeed,

[20] L. Quaglia, The Politics of an 'Incomplete' Banking Union and Its 'Asymmetric' Effects', *Journal of European Integration*, 2019, 41 (8), 955–969.

[21] For a detailed analysis, see J. Gren, Doctoral Thesis, 2017, University of Luxembourg.

[22] Z. Kudrna. Financial Market Regulation: Crisis-Induced Supranationalization. *Journal of European Integration* 38 (3), 2016: 251–264.

the national authorities have been inclined to apply the 'Sinatra doctrine' by dealing with ailing banks in 'their own ways'.[23]

More generally, the institutional design of Banking Union suffers from a major 'disjuncture'. Some legal competences and powers no longer belong to the national authorities, they have been transferred to different authorities at the euro area level and these authorities sometimes act in a poorly coordinated way. In a nutshell, the ECB decides whether a bank under its direct supervision is 'failing or likely to fail'. The SRB is in charge of resolving banks whose resolution is in the 'public interest'. Other failing banks are liquidated by the national authorities according to national law. The Commission monitors the use of state aid, its effects on competition as well as the application of rules on private sector burden-sharing. Yet, the political responsibility and accountability to deal with ailing banks remains at the national level, and so does the fiscal capacity to bail out banks, subject to EU rules. Timely coordination concerning the management of ailing banks is already difficult at the national level because different authorities with different incentives are involved. The process is even more difficult when competences, powers, responsibility and accountability are split across levels of governance.

4 Banking Union at the Test of the Covid Pandemic

This section discusses how Banking Union withstood the test of the covid-related economic and financial crisis, in particular by focusing on the response of the strongest pillar of Banking Union, the ECB-centric SSM. The ECB was crucial in shaping the euro area's response to the crisis as a central bank in charge of monetary policy and as a banking supervisor. On the monetary policy side, which is not discussed in this paper, the ECB adopted conventional and unconventional measures.[24] On the supervisory side, unlike on the monetary policy side, the ECB did not have previous direct crisis experience because before the establishment of Banking Union the ECB did not have any competence concerning

[23] L. Quaglia, The politics of an 'incomplete' Banking Union and its 'asymmetric' effects', *Journal of European Integration*, 2019, 41 (8), 955–969.

[24] For more details see L. Quaglia, and A. Verdun, Explaining the Response of the ECB to the Covid-19 Related Economic Crisis: Inter-crisis and Intra-crisis Learning, Journal of European Public Policy, 2022, 30 (4): 635–654.

banking supervision, which was the sole responsibility of national banking supervisory authorities in the euro area. During the covid crisis, for the first time, the ECB had the opportunity to use instruments both on the monetary policy side and the supervisory side, which could pull in the same direction because both were allocated at the same level, the euro area level. It also meant that whereas in the global financial crisis and the euro crisis, the banks were part of the problem, during the covid pandemic there was an enormous effort made by the ECB to make sure that banks were part of the solution.[25] To this end, the ECB's measures aimed 'to allow banks to keep providing financial support to viable households, small businesses and corporates' hit by the economic fallout.[26]

Moreover, the ECB's supervisory measures should not be considered in isolation. In fact, 'important synergies' existed between these measures and those taken in parallel by the monetary and fiscal authorities. As the central bank of the euro area, the ECB provided banks with cheap funding supplemented by an extraordinary asset purchase programme. As the banking supervisor of the euro area, the ECB eased capital and liquidity constraints to increase the ability of banks to lend and absorb losses. Euro area governments decided to temporarily relieve the difficulties of debtors with payment moratoriums and guarantees on bank loans, and, in response, the ECB increased supervisory flexibility regarding the regulatory treatment of loans receiving such public support.[27]

Let us examine in more detail the three sets of measures taken by the ECB on the supervisory side in reaction to the pandemic. First, the ECB Banking Supervision provided temporary relief of ***bank capital and liquidity buffers*** in March 2020. These buffers were designed with a view to allowing banks to withstand economic stress and the European banking sector had built up a significant amount of these buffers. The ECB allowed banks to operate temporarily below the level of capital defined by the Pillar 2 Guidance, the capital conservation buffer and the liquidity

[25] A. Enria, Flexibility in Supervision: How ECB Banking Supervision is Contributing to Fighting the Economic Fallout from the Coronavirus, 27 March 2020.

[26] Ibid.

[27] A. Enria, Opinion Piece, published in Les Echos, Expansión, Frankfurter Allgemeine Zeitung, Phileleftheros, La Stampa and Ta Nea on 30 March 2020, in Jornal de Negócios on 31 March 2020, in the Times of Malta on 1 April 2020 and in Latvijas Avīze on 3 April 2020.

coverage ratio.[28] Banks were allowed to partially use capital instruments that did not qualify as Common Equity Tier 1 capital, for example, Additional Tier 1 or Tier 2 instruments, to meet the Pillar 2 Requirements. Banks were expected to use the extra capital ensuing from these measures to support the economy and not to increase dividend distributions.

The ECB estimated that the capital relief provided by the possibility to operate below the Pillar 2 Guidance of Pillar 2 and the frontloading of the new rules on the Pillar 2 Requirement composition amounted to €120 billion of CET1 capital. This relief was available for banks to absorb losses without triggering any supervisory actions or to potentially finance up to €1.8 trillion of loans to households and corporates. In April 2020, the ECB reduced bank capital requirements for market risk, and in September 2020, the ECB announced temporary relief on banks' leverage ratio. The main purpose of these measures was to free capital that banks could use to lend to businesses and households.

Second, in late March 2020, the ECB introduced supervisory flexibility regarding *the treatment of non-performing loans (NPLs)*, in particular, to allow banks to benefit from guarantees and moratoriums put in place by public authorities to tackle the economic distress. To begin with, supervisors would exercise flexibility regarding the classification of debtors as 'unlikely to pay' when banks called on public guarantees granted in the context of coronavirus. The supervisor would also exercise flexibility regarding loans under covid-related public moratoriums. Furthermore, loans that became non-performing and were under public guarantees would benefit from preferential prudential treatment in terms of supervisory expectations about loss provisioning. The ECB also allowed the use of transitional arrangements in accounting standards IFRS 9, so as to increase flexibility in accounting for NPLs. The main purpose of these measures was to reduce the losses deriving from NPLs so as not to create holes in the balance sheets of banks, which would then need to raise new capital to deal with these losses.

Third, in late March 2020, the ECB issued recommendations to banks *not to pay dividends or buy back shares* during the pandemic. The ECB expected banks shareholders to join the collective effort to support the economy. These ECB's recommendations were renewed in July 2020 and

[28] A. Enria, Flexibility in Supervision: How ECB Banking Supervision is Contributing to Fighting the Economic Fallout from the Coronavirus, 27 March 2020.

December 2020, when, however, the ECB revised (softened) its recommendations, acknowledging the reduced uncertainty in macroeconomic projections. The ECB expected dividends and share buy-backs to remain below 15 per cent of the cumulated profit for 2019–2020 and not higher than 20 basis points of the Common Equity Tier 1 ratio, whichever was lower. Banks that intended to pay dividends or buy back shares needed to be profitable and have robust capital trajectories.[29] The ECB's recommendations on dividend distribution restrictions were 'intended to keep precious capital resources within the banking system ... to enhance its capacity to lend to the real economy and to support other segments of the financial sector as they come under stress'.[30]

There were however some criticisms concerning the ECB-SSM's supervisory measures in response to the pandemic. First, the possibility of reducing the capital buffer—the extra capital space to lend to businesses—was not taken up by many banks. Banks worried about having to increase capital buffer again after the crisis, thus, they did not reduce these buffers in the first place. At the same time, the fact that banks did not use capital should not be a criticism of the ECB's action, it means that banks were sound and did not need to do so. Second, some banks did not follow the ECB's recommendations on dividend payments. The ECB was criticised for its 'one size fits all approach' for all banks, even those in good health. Pundits argued that the use of 'recommendations' had limitations as they were not legally binding and hence, lacked real bite. Third, the bank-sovereign nexus that Banking Union was designed to tackle was reinforced during the pandemic crisis, even though this was not due to ECB-SSM's supervisory actions. The extension of government guarantees to banks and the payment moratoria for bank customers reinforced the linkages between domestic banking systems and their respective sovereigns (national governments). The ECB-SSM called for close monitoring of the exit from the payment moratoria and loan guarantees that had been extended to banks across Europe, paying attention to banks'

[29] A. Enria, Opinion Piece, published in Les Echos, Expansión, Frankfurter Allgemeine Zeitung, Phileleftheros, La Stampa and Ta Nea on 30 March 2020, in Jornal de Negócios on 31 March 2020, in the Times of Malta on 1 April 2020 and in Latvijas Avīze on 3 April 2020.

[30] A. Enria, Flexibility in Supervision: How ECB Banking Supervision is Contributing to Fighting the Economic Fallout from the Coronavirus, 27 March 2020.

exposures to local or central governments in the context of rising public debts.[31]

Overall, the measures that the ECB took on the supervisory side were unprecedented, both in scale and effectiveness, to contain the economic fallout arising from the pandemic. The pandemics could have triggered further fragmentation in Banking Union, as had happened during the previous crises, but this did not happen. And, in contrast to previous crises, euro area banks remained resilient and capable of supporting the economy. Whereas the policy measures taken during the 2008 international financial crisis primarily aimed to stabilise the euro area banking sector itself, those enacted in response to the pandemic sought to mitigate the broader impact of the pandemic on the euro area real economy. In this respect, the banking sector was a key conduit, given its critical role in lending to firms and households. While the total amount of state guarantees announced by euro area governments during the pandemic was comparable to that during the great financial crisis (16 per cent of euro area GDP in 2020 versus 18 per cent then), during the pandemic such guarantees targeted non-financial corporations rather than banks themselves. Thus, unlike during the great financial crisis, governments did not have to intervene to directly support euro area banks as a result of the pandemic itself.[32]

The resilience of the euro area banking sector had two sources. The first was the policy response from different authorities—monetary, supervisory, regulatory and fiscal. The second factor contributing to banks' resilience during the pandemic was that the euro area banking system as a whole was in a much better position in the run-up to the pandemic than it had been in the past. The ECB-SSM had promoted the application of stricter and more harmonised banking regulation in the euro area and the development of stringent common supervisory standards. Thus, the ECB's banking supervision has increased the resilience of banks enabling them to withstand severe crises, such as the pandemic.[33] 'As

[31] K. af Jochnick, COVID-19: Recovery and Regulatory Response, the IIF 7th Annual European Banking Union Colloquium, 17 November 2020.

[32] K. af Jochnick, Speech at the Financial Stability Conference 2021, Berlin, 19 November 2021.

[33] K. af Jochnick, COVID-19: Recovery and Regulatory Response, the IIF 7th Annual European Banking Union Colloquium, 17 November 2020.

supervisor, the ECB deserves credit for bringing the entire system to a higher common standard'.[34]

Banking Union and, the ECB-SSM within it, withstood well the test of the pandemic crisis.[35] It was the first time that there was a 'completely unified European supervisory response'—a 'single banking supervisor rolled out a relief package for banks across the euro area'—supervisory decisions were taken quickly, in close coordination with monetary policy measures.[36] The 'fast and unified supervisory response' at the euro area level 'would not have been thinkable' during the 2008 international financial crisis.[37] 'Banking union has worked well in the current crisis. European banking supervision was able to react very fast and in a fully unified manner. Compared with 2008, this is a huge improvement! So, if anything, the current crisis is a wake-up call: it shows that we need European solutions for European problems'.[38] Yet, the ECB urged to complete Banking Union by establishing a European deposit insurance scheme.[39] Moreover, the ECB pointed out the need to improve and harmonise the toolbox for dealing with crises in small and medium-sized banks and the need to make the financial sector more resilient to country-specific shocks.[40]

[34] K. af Jochnick, Speech at the Financial Stability Conference 2021, Berlin, 19 November 2021.

[35] L. Quaglia, and A. Verdun, The European Central Bank, the Single Supervisory Mechanism and the Covid 19 Related Economic Crisis: A Neofunctionalist Analysis, *Journal of European Integration*, 2023.

[36] A. Enria, Opinion Piece, published in Les Echos, Expansión, Frankfurter Allgemeine Zeitung, Phileleftheros, La Stampa and Ta Nea on 30 March 2020, in Jornal de Negócios on 31 March 2020, in the Times of Malta on 1 April 2020 and in Latvijas Avīze on 3 April 2020.

[37] A. Enria, Flexibility in Supervision: How ECB Banking Supervision is Contributing to Fighting the Economic Fallout from the Coronavirus, 27 March 2020.

[38] A. Enria, Interview with Andrea Enria, Chair of the Supervisory Board of the ECB, Supervision Newsletter, 13 May 2020.

[39] A. Enria, Interview with Andrea Enria, Chair of the Supervisory Board of the ECB, Supervision Newsletter, 13 May 2020; K. af Jochnick, COVID-19: Recovery and Regulatory Response, the IIF 7th Annual European Banking Union Colloquium, 17 November 2020.

[40] Ibid.

5 Conclusion

Overall, Banking Union and within it the ECB-SSM performed well in the first decade after their establishment. It also coped relatively well with the pandemic-related economic crisis. For the first time, the ECB was able to use simultaneously and in a coordinated way its monetary policy arm and its banking supervisory arm. Although the ECB's response on the supervisory side was less bold than on the monetary side, the ECB's supervisory response was quick and effective. It was also unprecedented because the ECB did not have supervisory responsibilities when previous crises came to light. By and large, there were three broad areas in which the ECB as a banking supervisor sought to offset the worst impact of the crisis on the banking sector: temporary relief of capital and liquidity buffers; supervisory flexibility regarding the treatment of non-performing loans (NPLs), recommendations to banks not to pay dividends or buy back shares during the pandemic. On the one hand, the ECB's supervisory actions in the run-up to and during the Covid-19-related economic contributed to ensuring that banks coped with the shock and remained in business. Hence, they strengthened the resilience of the banking system in the euro area. On the other hand, the national measures taken by governments, notably, state guarantees and financial support to businesses and households were also important in helping banks and the economy in general to cope with the crisis. Moreover, there were important fiscal measures adopted at the EU level, notably, the Next Generation EU.[41]

[41] D. Howarth, and L. Quaglia, Failing Forward in Economic and Monetary Union: Explaining Weak Eurozone Financial Support Mechanisms, *Journal of European Public Policy*, 2021, 28 (10), 1555–1572.

CHAPTER 7

The Financing of Problem Banks: Critical Issues and Challenges Ahead

Marco Bodellini

1 Introduction

In dealing with problem banks, this chapter discusses two of the main sources of financing that such institutions can benefit from, namely emergency liquidity assistance (ELA) and deposit guarantee schemes (DGSs) support. Accordingly, this chapter analyses the most relevant legal provisions of the legal framework currently in force in the European Union (EU) by focusing on their main shortcomings.

Problem banks are understood as those facing a crisis. This definition is broad enough so as to include banks undergoing both (in)solvency crises and (il)liquidity crises as well as banks still facing an early stage crisis and banks that have already met the triggers to be placed into a crisis management procedure. Irrespective of the nature of the crisis concerned, in order for banks to stand its negative impact some form of external support is often needed. The legal framework provides different alternatives concerning how to finance a problem bank depending on the stage

M. Bodellini (✉)
Luxembourg, Luxembourg

M. Bodellini et al. (eds.), *Commercial Banking in Transition*, Palgrave Macmillan Studies in Banking and Financial Institutions,
https://doi.org/10.1007/978-3-031-45289-5_7

of the crisis, its seriousness, the objective of the intervention, the size of the bank concerned and the availability of external funding.

By looking at the European regime on ELA and DGSs, this chapter addresses some of the main issues at stake with a view to contributing to the debate on the enhancement of the legal framework. In particular, with regard to ELA, the script outlines the inconsistency between making the European Central Bank (ECB) the supervisor for the Banking Union's significant banks while leaving the provision of ELA a prerogative of national central banks (NCBs). On this basis, a reinterpretation of the legal provisions in force is supported with a view to tasking the ECB with ELA provision functions. With regard to DGSs' contribution in assisting problem banks, this chapter backs the argument in favour of expanding the DGSs mandate by enabling them to carry out also the so-called optional measures.

2 Emergency Liquidity Assistance: Definition and Requirements

ELA is one of the tools that central banks are empowered to deploy in performing their function as lenders of last resort (LOLR).[1] Lending of last resort is the central bank's assistance which can be either provided to avoid contagious effects that would endanger the overall financial stability of the banking system or granted to help out individual banks experiencing liquidity issues.[2] On these grounds, there are two approaches that are relevant for LOLR: (1) the so-called monetary approach, and (2) the so-called credit approach.[3]

[1] On lending of last resort and ELA, see C. Hofmann, Reconsidering Central Bank Lending of Last Resort, European Business Organization Law Review, 2018, *passim*; A. Steinbach, The Lender of Last Resort in the Eurozone, Common Market Law Review, 2016, 53, 361–384; L. Garicano and R. Lastra, Towards a New Architecture for Financial Stability: Seven Principles, Journal of International Economic Law, 2013, 13, 3, 597–621.

[2] See S. Dietz, The ECB as Lender of Last Resort in the Eurozone? An Analysis of an Optimal Institutional Design of Emergency Liquidity Assistance competence within the Context of the Banking Union, Maastricht Journal of European and Comparative Law, 2019, XX, 1–41.

[3] See P. Praet, The ECB and Its Role as Lender of Last Resort during the Crisis, European Central Bank, 2016, https://www.ecb.europa.eu/press/key/date/2016/html/sp160210.en.html.

The monetary approach refers to the supply of liquidity by central banks to the financial system as a whole. It can take the form of general market liquidity assistance via ordinary open market operations and via extraordinary or unconventional measures in case of a general liquidity shortage, that potentially affects the liquidity situation of all financial institutions.[4] This approach relates to the monetary policy measures implemented by central banks in order to maintain price stability.[5] During the global financial crisis of 2007–2009 and during the COVID-19 pandemic, the ECB acted as a LOLR by providing money through its conventional operations,[6] but it also deeply committed to deter a contraction in the stock of bank-created money through unconventional measures.[7]

On the other hand, the credit approach refers to the supply of liquidity to individual banks; this type of central bank's intervention is commonly known as ELA.[8] ELA is one of the most important instruments at central banks' disposal to fight liquidity shortage and emergency situations at the individual level and was extensively used in the EU during the global financial crisis, mainly in order to keep financial stability.[9] It constitutes a lending function of central banks in cases where institutions can no longer raise funding from the market. Therefore, it is one of the first lines of defence in a crisis. ELA is granted to individual financial institutions, that

[4] See R. Lastra, International Financial and Monetary Law, Oxford, 2015, 377.

[5] See M. Bodellini and D. Singh, Monetary Policy in the Face of the Covid-19 Crisis: The Interesting Case of the United Kingdom, Open Review of Management, Banking and Finance, 2020, 2, *passim*.

[6] See M. Bodellini, La politica monetaria della Bank of England davanti all'emergenza Covid-19: spunti di riflessione per una (ri)lettura critica del Trattato sul funzionamento dell'Unione europea, Rivista Trimestrale di Diritto dell'Economia, 2021, 1, 98–135.

[7] See D. Domanski, R. Moessner and W. Nelson, Central Banks as Lenders of Last Resort: Experiences during the 2007–10 Crisis and Lessons for the Future, BIS Papers No. 79, 2014, 51, https://www.bis.org/publ/bppdf/bispap79c_rh.pdf.

[8] See P. Tucker, The Lender of Last Resort and Modern Central Banking: Principles and Reconstruction, BIS Papers No. 79, 2014, 15, https://www.bis.org/publ/bppdf/bispap79b_rh.pdf.

[9] See S. Dietz, The ECB as Lender of Last Resort in the Eurozone? An Analysis of an Optimal Institutional Design of Emergency Liquidity Assistance Competence within the Context of the Banking Union, Maastricht Journal of European and Comparative Law, 2019, XX, 1–41.

face temporary liquidity problems, which might spread to other market participants and constitute a cause for contagion.

In order for ELA to be granted by the central bank, however, a number of conditions have to be met. According to the so-called Bagehot model,[10] the requirements for receiving ELA are:

1. banks must be solvent, despite facing liquidity issues;
2. illiquid banks must give adequate collateral to the central bank;
3. interest rates are typically (although not necessarily) higher than those of monetary policy operations;
4. liquidity is to be provided on a case-by-case basis only to specific institutions;
5. liquidity assistance is to be given on a temporary basis; and
6. the central bank needs to be given discretion in deciding on whether to extend liquidity or not (so-called principle of constructive ambiguity).[11]

These requirements aim at achieving two main goals, namely protecting the central bank from losses and mitigating moral hazard.[12]

On the one hand, limiting access to ELA to solvent institutions makes sure that only those institutions which have more assets than liabilities and that still comply with capital requirements can be helped by the central bank. Those banks are regarded as able, at least in principle, to pay back the loan to the central bank also in that they have assets to offer to the central bank as collateral. These two elements should protect the central bank from the risk of suffering losses resulting from the bank's inability to repay the loan. In addition, insofar as the central bank charges interest rates which are higher than those of monetary policy operations, it can

[10] On the so-called Bagehot model see R. Lastra, International Financial and Monetary Law, Oxford, 2015, 151.

[11] See P. Tucker, The Lender of Last Resort and Modern Central Banking: Principles and Reconstruction, BIS Papers No. 79, 2014, 15, https://www.bis.org/publ/bppdf/bispap79b_rh.pdf.

[12] See P. Krugman, The Return of Depression Economics and the Crisis of 2008, New York, 2009, 63, who defines moral hazard as 'any situation in which one person makes the decision about how much risk to take, while someone else bears the cost if things go badly'.

record a profit which in turn would further enhance the central bank's capital solidity.

On the other hand, allowing the central bank to decide on whether to grant ELA on a case-by-case basis, giving it full discretion in this regard and ensuring that the support can be given only temporarily are key elements to contrast the risk of moral hazard. If those elements were missing, banks could base their lending operations on the expectation that should they face liquidity tensions they would be able to rely unconditionally upon the central bank's support. This certainty would affect banks' risk management policies as they would have an incentive to exploit the maturity mismatch between their assets and liabilities with a view to increasing their profits. This would arise from longer-term assets being typically more remunerative than short-term assets. However, irrespective of the long-term assets' ability to generate higher profits, liquidity risks (ontologically embedded in the maturity mismatch featuring commercial banking) need to be carefully managed by banks to avoid ending up facing a run scenario, whereby the institution cannot meet depositors' withdrawals in that its assets are illiquid and thus hard to sell. Under the Bagehot model, therefore, the terms for exercising the power to act as lender of last resort are not usually set out explicitly in regulatory provisions. According to the principle of 'constructive ambiguity' in the context of ELA provision, hence the central bank must have full discretion in order to be in a position to appropriately assess the risks and act accordingly in each single case. On the contrary, the existence of an explicit regulatory provision would put the stability of the financial system at risk as a result of greater exposure of banks to moral hazard and thus ultimately to insolvency; as a consequence, this might render necessary the imposition of stricter micro-prudential regulations than generally required, with a view to preventing banks' exposure to risks undertaken in their conduct of business.

Critical Aspects of ELA and the Rationale for Vesting Central Banks with ELA Functions

Against this backdrop, one of the most critical aspects in providing ELA relates to the difficulty in distinguishing between (in)solvency and (il)liquidity. The dividing line between (in)solvency and (il)liquidity in the banking sector can be very thin and often it is just a time line.[13] While in corporate law, solvency is typically referred to as the situation where a firm has more assets than liabilities (insolvency test), in banking, solvency typically refers to the bank's compliance with the capital requirements set out in the domestic regulation.[14] Liquidity, on the other hand, is typically referred to as the capability to pay debts as they fall due. Still, in banking, liquidity has peculiar connotations in that banks perform a key function in maturity transformation, which makes liquidity tensions rather common, despite often being only temporary and thus manageable.

By matching (in)solvency and (il)liquidity, a bank can end up in four different situations:

1. a bank that is solvent and liquid;
2. a bank that is solvent but illiquid;
3. a bank that is insolvent but still liquid; and
4. a bank that is insolvent and illiquid.

In the first scenario (bank solvent and liquid), the bank is sound and does not need any assistance. The second scenario (bank solvent but illiquid) is the typical situation where ELA plays a significant function in allowing such a bank to face its temporary liquidity issues. The third scenario (bank insolvent but still liquid) is rather uncommon in practice as it would need the bank to have short-term assets and long-term liabilities, which is exactly the opposite of what a commercial bank balance sheet typically looks like. The fourth scenario (bank both insolvent and illiquid) is when ELA is no longer enough and either a recapitalization takes place, or the bank has to be submitted to either resolution or liquidation.

Even if in theory illiquidity and insolvency are different concepts, in practice often a bank that is illiquid sooner or later might end up being also insolvent. This can happen due to the fact that a bank that needs to meet significant withdrawals might have to fire-sell its assets,

[13] See R. Lastra, C. Russo and M. Bodellini, Stock Take of the SRB's Activities Over the Past Years: What to Improve and Focus On? Study Requested by the ECOM Committee of the European Parliament, 2019, 11, <https://www.europarl.europa.eu/RegData/etudes/STUD/2019/634392/IPOL_STU(2019)634392_EN.pdf>.

[14] See M. Bodellini, The Long 'Journey' of Banks from Basel I to Basel IV: Has the Banking System Become More Sound and Resilient than it Used to Be? ERA Forum, 2019, 20, 81–97.

thereby suffering proportional losses. Such losses can in turn cause it to become insolvent. That is the reason why ELA is so important to prevent banks from fire-selling their assets and central banks play a pivotal role in keeping solvent but illiquid banks alive.

On the other hand, the rationale for providing central banks with the function and associated powers to provide ELA to illiquid banks lies in the synergies existing between exercising such a task and safeguarding the stability of both the payment system and the financial system as a whole. Last-resort lending is incorporated in the instruments used to satisfy the policy objective of safeguarding financial stability. Also, central banks have typically the power of printing money, therefore by definition they are in a position to be always able to provide banks with the liquidity they need to face a temporary crisis.

Central Banking in the Euro-Area and ELA Provision in the Banking Union

The European System of Central Banks (ESCB) has the task of defining, conducting and implementing the monetary policy of the Eurozone and has 'price stability' as its primary objective according to the Treaty on the Functioning of the European Union (TFEU).[15] The ESCB is comprised of the ECB and the NCBs.[16]

The decision-making process is centralized at the Euro-Area level within the ECB bodies. In the adoption of monetary policy measures, NCBs are included indirectly as part of the ECB bodies and thereby take part in the decision-making process. Implementation is decentralized with the NCBs executing the monetary policy measures adopted by the ESCB. NCBs, as the national authorities, implement the ESCB's policies. NCBs have a double function: (1) they act as agents within the ESCB fulfilling tasks at the European level and according to EU law and, (2) they act

[15] See Amtenbrink, Central Bank Challenges in the Global Economy, in Herrmann and Terhechte (eds.), European Yearbook of International Economic Law 2011, Berlin 2011, 21, where it is said that 'a clear monetary policy objective geared towards the combating of inflation has become the dominant feature of central banks'.

[16] See Hinarejos, Economic and Monetary Union, in Barnard and Peers (eds.), European Union Law (Oxford University Press, 2013); Fabbrini, Economic governance in Europe: Comparative Paradoxes and Constitutional Challenges (Oxford University Press, 2016), 203.

in their capacity as national authorities, within their own responsibility according to national law.

Given that neither the Treaties (Treaty of the European Union (TEU) and TFEU) nor the ESCB Statute contain any explicit provisions on last resort lending two alternative views have emerged as to how to perform such a function. While the first view is the so-called decentralized approach under which this task should be carried out by the NCBs, the second view is the so-called centralized approach under which the ECB should be in charge to provide ELA.[17]

On the basis of Article 14.4. of the ESCB Statute, the decentralized approach has been backed by the ECB. Article 14.4. of the ESCB Statute states that 'National central banks may perform functions other than those specified in this Statute unless the Governing Council finds, by a majority of two thirds of the votes cast, that these interfere with the objectives and tasks of the ESCB. Such functions shall be performed on the responsibility and liability of national central banks and shall not be regarded as being part of the functions of the ESCB'. The ECB has so far provided a restrictive interpretation of article 14.4 of the ESCB Statute according to which ELA provision is a task to be fulfilled by NCBs. The main reason for such a restrictive interpretation seems to be connected to the fact that ELA is considered a tool aimed at maintaining financial stability. Financial stability in turn is not the first objective that the ECB/ESCB is meant to achieve, this being price stability under article 127(1) TFEU (exclusive competence). Accordingly, the financial stability mandate in the setting of the Treaties is only a secondary objective under article 127(5) TFEU (contributory competence).

This position has also been grounded in article 123 TFEU on the prohibition of monetary financing. The provision of ELA by the ECB might violate Article 123 TFEU in the event that the bank concerned used the received liquidity to buy bonds issued by the government of the country where it is based. Similarly, a violation of article 123 TFEU would occur even in the event of ELA granted by the ECB to insolvent banks as the central bank would de facto take over a state's function.

[17] On the two opposite views see S. Dietz, The ECB as Lender of Last Resort in the Eurozone? An Analysis of an Optimal Institutional Design of Emergency Liquidity Assistance Competence within the Context of the Banking Union, Maastricht Journal of European and Comparative Law, 2019, XX, 1–41.

The ECB restrictive interpretation of article 14.4 has been reaffirmed in the ELA Agreement 2017 that sets out the procedure to provide ELA, even though the latter is not a legally binding act. According to the ELA Agreement 2017, ELA occurs when '(a) a Eurosystem NCB provides central bank money and/or (b) any other assistance that may lead to an increase in central bank money to a financial institution or a group of financial institutions facing liquidity problems, where, in either case, such operation is not part of the single monetary policy'. ELA is thus provided under the main responsibility of the NCB concerned. As a result, the provision of such assistance is at the sole discretion of NCBs, on the condition that the ECB has not prohibited it. Hence, it is not the ECB itself that provides ELA and the eventual losses arising from the bank defaulting on paying back the credit line will appear on the NCB's balance sheet. As a result, ELA remains the responsibility of the NCBs, at their own cost, but with the necessary authorization of the ECB that has a veto power.[18]

In order to benefit from ELA, banks facing liquidity tension, have to be assessed as solvent. Interestingly, now such an evaluation is to be made by the ECB for significant banks. The ELA Agreement 2017 provides explicitly that a credit institution is considered solvent for ELA purposes if either of the following conditions is met:

a. Its Common Equity Tier 1, Tier 1 and total capital ratios, as reported under the CRR on an individual and consolidated basis, comply with the minimum regulatory capital levels (namely 4.5%, 6% or 8%, respectively).
b. If the above condition is not met, there is a credible prospect of recapitalization by which the above minimum regulatory capital levels would be restored within 24 weeks after the end of the reference quarter of the data that showed that the bank does not comply with these standards; in duly justified, exceptional cases the GC may decide to prolong the above-mentioned 'grace period'.

[18] For example, in 2013 the ECB decided that emergency liquidity assistance to credit institutions in Cyprus could only be considered if an EU/IMF programme was in place to ensure the solvency of the concerned credit institutions.

About the duration, the ELA Agreement 2017 stipulates that the provision of ELA may only exceed twelve (12) months following a non-objection by the Governing Council requested by the Governor of the NCB concerned at the latest once the provision of ELA exceeds ten (10) months. If any provision of ELA exceeds 12 months, the Governor of the NCB concerned must justify the further provision of ELA in a letter to the President of the ECB on a monthly basis, and the Governing Council may impose additional requirements and conditions.

In order to ensure that ELA operations do not interfere with the single monetary policy of the Eurosystem, the ECB would have to be informed or consulted. This information is to be provided by the NCB and should allow a smooth sterilization of any undesired liquidity effects and an assessment of any systemic implications.

ELA to credit institutions established in euro area member states was repeatedly activated during the Global Financial Crisis. In the 2010–2013 period, ELA was provided in Ireland, Greece and Cyprus. In 2014, ELA was provided in Portugal. In 2015, ELA was provided again in Greece. In 2017, ELA was provided in Spain.[19]

However, the ECB also exercised its veto power under article 14.4 of the ESCB Statute in June 2015 when the economic and financial situation in Greece was escalating, because the Eurogroup decided not to prolong the existing rescue program after the announcement of a bailout referendum. The Greek banks were in urgent need of liquidity, but the ECB objected to increasing the ELA ceiling.[20]

The Inconsistencies of the Framework Currently in Place

Before the creation of the Banking Union, prudential supervision was conducted at the national level; in that context, it was allegedly coherent to assume that national authorities had adequate expertise and information to assess the problems of banks within their jurisdictions. It was

[19] See S. Dietz, The ECB as Lender of Last Resort in the Eurozone? An Analysis of an Optimal Institutional Design of Emergency Liquidity Assistance competence within the Context of the Banking Union, Maastricht Journal of European and Comparative Law, 2019, XX, 1–41.

[20] See Bank of Greece, 'Press Releases', Bank of Greece (2019), https://www.bankofgreece.gr/pages/en/bank/news/pressreleases/DispItem.aspx?Item_ID.5055&List_ID.1af869f3-57fb-4de6-b9ae-bdfd83c66c95&Filter_by.DT.

therefore understandable that ELA was a function to be performed by NCBs on the basis of the adage that assistance on a rainy day requires supervision on a sunny day.[21]

However, as supervision has been centralized at the European level and the ECB has become the main banking supervisor within the so-called Single Supervisory Mechanism (SSM), *i.e.* the first pillar of the Banking Union, the current ELA framework presents a number of shortcomings and should be reconsidered. On these grounds it has been defined as the fourth missing pillar of the Banking Union,[22] and it has been pointed out that the ECB should be at all effects the lender of last resort for all those institutions under its supervision.[23] By so doing ELA would link monetary policy and supervision.

This position has been grounded in a number of legal considerations. Firstly, granting the ECB a clear LOLR function would not require a Treaty change. A mere reinterpretation of Article 14.4 of the ESCB Statute would be sufficient in light of the rationale under Article 18.1 of the ESCB Statute (general liquidity provision) and of new circumstances (namely the creation of the Banking Union). This reading of the TFEU would also be aligned with the principle of subsidiarity. Importantly, times have changed and now financial stability has become in practice a key objective for the ECB/ESCB, even though the Treaties have remained unaltered.[24] At the very least such a (re)interpretation of TFEU would be required for significant institutions.

[21] See M. Hallerberg and R. Lastra, The Single Monetary Policy and Decentralisation: An Assessment, In-Depth Analysis—European Parliament—Directorate General for Internal Policies Policy, September 2017, 8.

[22] See R. Lastra, Reflections on Banking Union, Lender of Last Resort and Supervisory Discretion, From Monetary Union to Banking Union, on the Way to Capital Markets Union New opportunities for European integration, ECB Legal Conference 2015, December 2015, 154.

[23] See S. Dietz, The ECB as Lender of Last Resort in the Eurozone? An Analysis of an Optimal Institutional Design of Emergency Liquidity Assistance Competence within the Context of the Banking Union, Maastricht Journal of European and Comparative Law, 2019, XX, 1–41.

[24] See R. Lastra—K. Alexander, The ECB Mandate: Perspectives on Sustainability and Solidarity, In-Depth Analysis Requested by the ECON Committee of the European Parliament, Monetary Dialogue Papers, June 2020, 8.

3 Deposit Guarantee Schemes

In view of the costs resulting from a credit institution's failure, its impact on the economy as a whole and on the confidence of depositors, which could in turn trigger financial instability, it is crucial to have mechanisms in place for promptly reimbursing failed banks' depositors. This task is undertaken by DGSs. Thus, DGSs represent one of the major players within the banking system safety net.[25] Their main function consists of protecting covered depositors in the event of their bank being placed into liquidation and closed down. When that is the case, by quickly paying out covered depositors, DGSs ensure that the stability of the system is preserved, thereby avoiding the crisis of one bank is transmitted to other institutions, which could give rise to a number of other failures.[26]

The paramount importance of this function arises from the natural vulnerability of banks, which can face crises at any point in time.[27] Such a risk is embedded in the banks' business model and way of operating, as they take deposits from the public and use them to extend loans. While deposits are withdrawable on demand, loans have typically longer-term maturity. Such a timing difference creates the so-called maturity mismatch between assets and liabilities, which can prompt liquidity issues, should several depositors decide to withdraw their deposits at the same time. This in turn results from the bank typically having invested deposits to make loans, with the consequence that the latter no longer has those funds available and therefore will need to sell its (liquid and illiquid) assets to meet depositors' requests. Whereas the sale of liquid assets is usually easy and fast, the sale of illiquid assets is not always feasible and sometimes can only take place at discounted prices, thereby causing losses to the bank, which can even affect its capital position. In this way, liquidity crises can easily turn into solvency crises. In addition, banks are also

[25] See International Association of Deposit Insurers, Public Policy Objectives for Deposit Insurance Systems—Guidance Paper, 2020, 3, where it is outlined that 'A deposit insurance system may not be effective if it does not have clear, relevant and well-defined objectives that point to the broad functions it serves within the safety-net framework'.

[26] See accordingly A. Arda and M. Dobler, The Role for Deposit Insurance in Dealing with Failing Banks in the European Union, IMF Working Paper, 2022, 22/2.

[27] See M. Bodellini, The Optional Measures of Deposit Guarantee Schemes: Towards a New Bank Crisis Management Paradigm? European Journal of Legal Studies, 2021, 1, 342.

prone to (in)solvency issues which can manifest in the event of a considerable number of borrowers defaulting on the loans they were given. Several defaults would cause proportionally high losses that can wipe out the bank's capital, thereby making the institution in question insolvent. Against this background, the presence of DGSs is meant to reassure depositors about getting their covered deposits back even in the event of their bank ending up in a crisis and being liquidated. This awareness should hence refrain depositors from running on their bank. The reimbursement of covered depositors is known as the pay-box function and in the EU the coverage level is EUR 100.000 per depositor per bank.

On these grounds, each credit institution must be part of a DGS, thereby ensuring a high level of depositor protection and a level playing field between credit institutions. For the same reasons, DGSs are funded by banks, which are requested to pay contributions to their schemes.

The pay-box function is clearly fundamental to prevent, or at least mitigate, the impact of banking crises and, as such, needs to be included in the bank crisis management legal framework. Nevertheless, the so-called optional functions (i.e. the implementation of alternative measures aimed at preventing a bank's failure and the provision of financial means in the context of liquidation aimed at preserving access of depositors to covered deposits), that DGSs can be empowered to perform pursuant to Article 11, paragraphs 3 and 6 of the Deposit Guarantee Schemes Directive (DGSD), might end up being even more effective, from a system-wide perspective, to maintain financial stability and to reduce the destruction of value potentially resulting from an atomistic (or piecemeal) liquidation with depositors pay-out.[28]

The following paragraphs will discuss these two DGSs' optional measures. This chapter will refer to the DGSs measures regulated under Article 11 paragraphs 3 and 6 of the DGSD as optional or alternative measure(s), optional or alternative intervention(s) or optional or alternative function(s), interchangeably.

DGSs Optional Measures to Prevent a Bank's Failure

The intervention of a DGS at the first symptoms of a bank's crisis can be particularly effective in preventing the latter from escalating and getting

[28] The terms atomistic liquidation and piecemeal liquidation are used interchangeably throughout this chapter.

out of control. In fact, many banking crises, still at an early stage, can be more efficiently solved thanks to the ability of DGSs to help restructure the institutions concerned. Such a preventive intervention, in addition, can be seen as beneficial for the whole system that otherwise could be negatively affected both in reputational and economic terms. Indeed, in the context of bank crises, there is always a special public interest to take into account, that is to safeguard depositors. Safeguarding depositors in turn is instrumental to keeping the stability of the system. In some cases, this goal can be more successfully achieved through preventive action.

Yet, DGSs are expected to conduct a cost–benefit analysis before performing preventive interventions. The benchmark to consider in conducting such an assessment is the hypothetical cost that they should pay to reimburse covered depositors in the event that the bank in crisis ended up being liquidated without the deposits being transferred to another bank. If such an assessment shows that the cost of depositors' pay-out is higher than the cost of the preventive intervention, then the latter should take place. Still, the cost of depositors' pay-out is to be calculated also in light of the amount that the DGS expects to recover from the insolvency proceeding after subrogating the depositors' rights, although, from this perspective, the extension of depositors' super priority to DGSs represents a possible obstacle.

Experience has shown that preventive measures are generally less costly than the reimbursement of depositors.[29] Nevertheless, there might also be cases where a bank collects only a limited amount of covered deposits, but at the same time performs crucial functions for its group. The failure of such a bank could have terrible effects on the other group members and possibly on financial stability. In such a case, however, the cost of preventive measures might exceed the cost of paying out covered depositors, thereby preventing their application.

On these grounds, DGSs can be seen as reactive system-wide tools, funded directly by banks, to be employed at the early stages of a crisis, on the assumption that it is in the interest of the whole banking system to prevent (or at least mitigate) its negative effects. Accordingly, their task should be to play a central role in preventing banking crises by disbursing, at an early stage, the resources provided by other banks.

[29] See European Forum of Deposit Insurers, EFDI State of Play and Non-Binding Guidance Paper. Guarantee Schemes Alternative Measures to Pay-out for Effective Banking Crisis Solution, 2019, 29.

DGSs Optional Measures in the Context of a Bank's Liquidation

The ability of DGSs to provide financial support in the context of a bank's winding up is particularly important for the latter to be orderly, as requested by the BRRD, and effective. According to Article 32(b) of the BRRD, indeed, Member States shall ensure that a FOLF institution in relation to which the resolution authority considers that all the conditions for resolution are met, except for the resolution action being in the public interest, shall be wound up in an orderly manner in accordance with the applicable national law.

The final objectives of the winding up procedure are the liquidation of the assets and the payment of creditors, which are to be carried out by the liquidators. This means that the creditors' interest to be repaid should drive the action of both the authorities and the liquidators. Nevertheless, a number of other extremely relevant interests should be taken into due consideration in running the procedure in order for it to be orderly and effective. Chief among them are the stability of the system, the confidence of depositors and investors and the safeguarding of the going concern value of the failing bank.

To this end, normal corporate insolvency proceedings, (typically run by law courts), which apply to non-financial firms, are often considered inadequate for banks.[30] This results from such proceedings being usually lengthy and slow and primarily aimed at liquidating the assets. The proceeds arising from the sale of the assets are then used to pay creditors. As a consequence, the continuation of the FOLF bank's activities would not be guaranteed, possibly provoking the destruction of value.[31] The interruption of the activities in turn can have a potential destabilizing impact on the bank's counterparties and, more broadly, on the banking

[30] See T. Huertas, The Case for Bail-ins, in A. Dombret and P. Kenadjian (eds.), *The Bank Recovery and Resolution Directive. Europe's Solution for 'Too Big to Fail'*? (De Gruyter 2013) 167–168; R. Guynn, 'Are Bailouts Inevitable?' (2012) 29 Yale Journal on Regulation 121, 137–140; W.-G. Ringe, 'Bail-in between Liquidity and Solvency', (2006) University of Oxford Legal Research Paper Series No. 33/2006, 6, <https://papers.ssrn.com/sol3/papers.cfm?abstract_id=2782457> accessed 30 August 2020.

[31] See R. Lastra, C. Russo and M. Bodellini, Stock Take of the SRB's Activities over the Past Years: What to Improve and Focus On? Study Requested by the ECOM Committee of the European Parliament, 2019, 11, <https://www.europarl.europa.eu/RegData/etudes/STUD/2019/634392/IPOL_STU(2019)634392_EN.pdf>.

and financial system as well as, sometimes, on its geographical areas of operation.

Accordingly, even though the final objective of the winding up procedure is the assets' liquidation and the payment of the bank's creditors, still atomistic liquidation with depositors' pay-out is seldom considered an effective and efficient crisis management procedure for failing banks, mostly because it does not ensure the continuation of critical functions, thereby potentially affecting the bank's counterparties. This in turn might end up destroying the going concern value of the good parts of the bank in crisis and therefore can be detrimental for both the bank's creditors and the system as a whole.

To avoid these negative outcomes, the liquidation procedure should then take forms resembling—to a certain extent—the resolution procedure. This can be achieved through the use of legal instruments similar to the resolution tools now regulated by the BRRD. Thus, the main tool to use in the winding up procedure with a view to continuing (at least some of) the FOLF bank's critical functions would be an instrument similar to the sale of business tool.[32] The latter would allow to transfer both assets and liabilities (including deposits) of the bank under liquidation to another bank at market prices (which are expected to be higher than liquidation prices), thereby allowing for the continuation of (at least some of) the activities of the failing bank through the purchasing institution and safeguarding in this way the going concern value of the failing entity.

In this way, the winding up could become a means to allow for the continuation of (some of) the failing bank's activities through a different bank, thereby merging together the dissolving function of the liquidation procedure with the business continuity character of the sale of business tool. The outcomes which could be achieved through the application of the'sale of business-like tool' in a winding up procedure would be the following: (1) deposits could be moved to the purchasing bank and depositors, therefore, would be fully protected, thereby avoiding runs on other banks and possibly systemic risk; (2) borrowers would keep on

[32] Pursuant to Article 2, paragraph 1, number 58 of the BRRD, the sale of business tool is 'the mechanism for effecting a transfer by a resolution authority of shares or other instruments of ownership issued by an institution under resolution, or assets, rights or liabilities, of an institution under resolution to a purchaser that is not a bridge institution …'. According to Article 38 paragraph 1 of the BRRD, 'Member States shall ensure that resolution authorities have the power to transfer to a purchaser that is not a bridge institution … (b) all or any assets, rights or liabilities of an institution under resolution'.

accessing financial means provided by the purchasing bank, avoiding to negatively affect the real economy; (3) assets and liabilities (or at least some of them) would be transferred to the purchasing bank, thereby allowing for the continuation of the business activity and maintaining the going concern value.

Yet, even if liquidators manage to find another institution willing to purchase all (or a part of) the assets and liabilities of the bank under liquidation, the value of the liabilities to transfer to the purchasing bank would still, fairly obviously, exceed the value of the assets. In such a scenario, DGSs can play a pivotal role in successfully help run the liquidation procedure. Indeed, they might provide funds to be used to compensate the purchasing bank for taking on such a negative balance between assets and liabilities (primarily deposits). Nonetheless, such an intervention is to take place only if the amount of resources to provide is estimated to be lesser than the amount that the DGS should pay to covered depositors in the event of an atomistic liquidation without the transfer of deposits to another bank. In this regard, the European Forum of Deposit Insurers (EFDI) has taken the view that the least cost evaluation should consider a comprehensive range of elements, including the direct (financial, operational, etc.) and indirect costs (missing return on liquidity, increasing cost of funding, etc.) of pay-out, adequate haircuts on the expected recovery side, and also contagion and reputation risks which may lead to further reimbursements; on the other side, the costs of 'interventions in liquidation' for the DGS, entailing refundable or recoverable disbursements and guarantees, are proposed to be calculated to the extent of expected losses estimated at the date of the intervention.[33]

Against this background, the application of the 'sale of business-like tool' during the winding up procedure can be seen as an alternative to the bank's atomistic liquidation with depositors' pay-out. The choice between these two alternatives (i.e. atomistic liquidation *vis-à-vis* application of the 'sale of business-like tool') should be based on a comparative assessment. Accordingly, the authorities should run a counterfactual scenario on the basis of which the liquidation strategy is to be informed.

In developing this counterfactual scenario, it should be assumed that in the event of a piecemeal liquidation with depositors' pay-out: (1) the

[33] See European Forum of Deposit Insurers, EFDI State of Play and Non-Binding Guidance Paper. Guarantee Schemes Alternative Measures to Pay-out for Effective Banking Crisis Solution, 2019, *passim*.

assets will be sold at discounted prices over a relatively long period of time; (2) the bank's activities will be immediately interrupted; (3) the pledged performing assets will be seized and enforced by the secured creditors; (4) the DGS will have to step in to protect covered depositors; (5) the contractual relationships will be immediately terminated with liquidators calling back all the loans and credit lines previously extended to the bank's borrowers.

In practical terms, this would cause enterprises and households to be obliged to pay back their loans to the liquidators overnight. This, in turn, could create a domino effect triggering a significant number of failures affecting many more counterparties. Uninsured depositors and unsecured creditors would have to wait for the winding up procedure timeframe to try and get (likely, only a part of) their money back. The DGS should immediately reimburse the covered depositors and after that it could exercise the subrogation right to the depositors' rights in the liquidation procedure. Nevertheless, due to the limited amount of immediately available resources, in some cases, the DGS will likely have to ask its member banks for extra contributions. Also, the guarantees released by guarantors, if any, would be immediately enforced. As a consequence, the guarantors would have to pay immediately the guarantee-holders before being able to exercise the ensuing subrogation right in the liquidation procedure.

For all these reasons the application of the 'sale of business-like tool' is often considered more efficient than a piecemeal liquidation with depositors' pay-out, since it can allow, on the one hand, for the continuation of the bank's most critical functions and, on the other hand, for the protection of the FOLF bank's going concern value. Consequently, the atomistic liquidation with the DGS reimbursement of covered depositors should be activated only in those cases in which the sudden interruption of the bank's activities and the destruction of the going concern value are not considered to negatively affect the system.

Legal Obstacles to the Implementation of the DGSs' Optional Measures

While the Court of Justice of the European Union decision in the Tercas case has put an end to the contrasts concerning the qualification of DGSs' optional measures as state aid provision, (at least for those DGSs the decision-making of which is not imputable to the state),[34] the depositor preference extended to DGSs subrogating to depositors' rights in the insolvency proceedings might still be an obstacle to the implementation of such measures.[35] Such a rule, coupled with a narrow reading of the 'least cost principle', could end up making every DGS optional intervention very difficult, if not impossible. The granting of this super priority to DGSs impacts the optional interventions in that they are allowed only to the extent that the DGS does not end up spending more money than the amount it would have had to pay in order to reimburse covered depositors in the context of a piecemeal liquidation according to the 'least cost principle'. The critical aspect is that, due to the super priority, it is unlikely that the DGS will be called on to bear relevant losses.

By only focusing on a single crisis, the DGS might seem to be better off as it will recover all (or a relevant part of) the resources provided to reimburse the affected covered depositors, due to the extension of the depositor preference. Nonetheless, this is not necessarily the best possible outcome for the system,[36] which would be the overall cheapest and safest solution, also taking into account the interests of taxpayers.[37]

Moving from this assumption, the 'least cost principle' should be rethought in light of the overarching interest of the system and without just considering the cost paid by the DGS in performing optional measures in the crisis concerned.[38] Therefore, the amount to be paid

[34] See Court of Justice of the European Union, Judgment in Case C-425/19 P Commission v Italy, Fondo interbancario di tutela dei depositi, Banca d'Italia et Banca Popolare di Bari SCpA, 2 March 2021.

[35] See M. Bodellini, The Optional Measures of Deposit Guarantee Schemes: Towards a New Bank Crisis Management Paradigm? European Journal of Legal Studies, 2021, 1, 342.

[36] See A. De Aldisio and others, Towards a Framework for Orderly Liquidation of Banks in the EU, Notes on Financial Stability and Supervision of Banca d'Italia 2019, 6, who use an example to demonstrate that even when an optional measure implemented by the DGS ends up being more expensive for it than depositors pay-out, such a strategy is typically more effective from a system-wide perspective.

[37] See European Forum of Deposit Insurers, EFDI State of Play and Non-Binding Guidance Paper. Guarantee Schemes Alternative Measures to Pay-out for Effective Banking Crisis Solution, 2019, *passim*.

[38] On this see European Banking Authority (n 45), 81, stating that 'There is a need to provide more clarity on how to assess that: the costs of the measures do not exceed the costs of fulfilling the statutory or contractual mandate of the DGS (as per Article 11(3)); the costs borne by the DGS do not exceed the net amount of compensating

should be compared to the sum of direct and indirect costs for the banking system—and potentially for the real economy—arising from an atomistic liquidation. In other words, disregarding the 'indirect costs' for the system would lead to a partial result which is not able to point out the best possible solution.[39]

This reading of the rules, in turn, is in line with the rationale behind the DGSD, which clearly provides the possibility for DGSs to intervene by carrying out optional measures.[40] It would be irrational to provide such a possibility and then to introduce other rules in different legislative acts substantially hindering the performance of such measures. Furthermore, this is the very essence of the Financial Stability Board's 'Key Attributes of Effective Resolution Regimes' that require authorities to resolve FOLF banks without using public money, while avoiding the creation of negative systemic effects. Given that the resources of a DGS are those provided by the banks, their use in handling crises should be facilitated on the grounds that otherwise the whole system, and thereby the public, could be negatively affected.

Accordingly, the scope of the least cost principle should be enlarged in order to enable the performance of system-wide driven solutions based on the DGSs' optional interventions. For this proposal to properly work without creating legal uncertainties, article 11, paragraph 3 and article 11, paragraph 6 of the DGSD should be amended by clearly spelling out how such a revised principle should be applied in practice, namely by stating which (direct and indirect) costs should be taken into account and compared with the amount of depositor pay-out.

The counterargument to this line of reasoning could be that a system-wide interpretation of the least cost principle would be either arbitrary and inaccurate or practically impossible. Nevertheless, in this regard, it has

covered depositors at the credit institution concerned' (as per Article 11(6)). There is also a need for more clarity on what kind of costs should be taken into account in the abovementioned assessments (only direct or also indirect costs—and what costs constitute indirect costs), particularly because the current lack of clarity poses the risk that different authorities will take different approaches to the least cost assessment; such clarifications should be made in a legal product that provides sufficient legal certainty for DGSs'.

[39] See M. Bodellini, The Optional Measures of Deposit Guarantee Schemes: Towards a New Bank Crisis Management Paradigm? European Journal of Legal Studies, 2021, 1, 342.

[40] See M. Bodellini, International Bank Crisis Management—A Transatlantic Perspective, Oxford, 2022, *passim*.

been stated that even though the calculation of indirect costs would not be easy, still according to previous experiences these costs can be material. Therefore, a methodology to calculate them could be developed.[41]

In any case, if such a different and broader application of the 'least cost principle', aimed at taking into account the overarching interest of the system, was to be considered as practically impossible, then a more radical solution would be the abolition *sic et simpliciter* of the extension to the DGSs of the super priority in the exercise of their subrogation rights within the insolvency proceedings. In substantive terms, the result would be the same, as DGSs would be allowed to also perform the optional measures under article 11, paragraphs 3 and 6 of the DGSD. Given that the interests of the banking system and the interests of DGSs are equivalent, the latter should not raise any opposition to such a legislative amendment, which, in turn, would align the EU regime with the US one.

4 Concluding Remarks

No financing tool supporting problem banks is effective in every case. Each of them has pros and cons and their efficient use mainly depends upon the characteristics of the crisis to manage. Yet, a sensible legal framework provides the authorities with a large toolkit, allowing them to pick the most effective instrument after a case-by-case assessment. To do so, authorities need to be given some discretion in their choices. Yet, such discretion needs in turn to be counterbalanced with proportional accountability.

This chapter has discussed two of the main sources of financing for problem banks, namely ELA and DGS support, which are very important and accordingly should be included in the legal framework of every jurisdiction. Both of them indeed can be effective tools depending on the situation concerned. While ELA is an emergency and temporary measure applied with a view to enabling solvent banks to tackle liquidity issues,

[41] In this regard see A. De Aldisio and others, Towards a Framework for Orderly Liquidation of Banks in the EU, Notes on Financial Stability and Supervision of Banca d'Italia 2019, 6, arguing that 'even if it is more difficult to quantify these costs than it is to quantify direct costs, experience shows that they can indeed be material, as the history of crises is full of contagion episodes. It would not be overly difficult to identify a methodology to estimate these additional costs'.

DGS support through optional measures might be helpful in several scenarios. In the early stages of a crisis, preventive action can avoid an escalation bound to lead to insolvency, whereas, in the context of a liquidation procedure, DGS support can minimize value destruction and avoid a negative impact on the stability of the system.

CHAPTER 8

The Review of the EU Bank Crisis Management and Deposit Insurance Framework

Johannes Langthaler

1 Introduction

After the Global Financial Crisis in 2008, the G-20 rushed to endorse reforms to solve that banks can become *too-big-to-fail*. The underlying idea behind the new rules was to end bailouts by the public and allow for the bail-in of shareholders and creditors. Newly established resolution authorities are supposed to put ailing banks under resolution, using their now powerful tools and solutions at its hand to stabilize a bank in

The opinions expressed in this book chapter are those of the author and do not necessarily reflect those of the Raiffeisen Bank International AG or other institutions.

J. Langthaler (✉)
Raiffeisen Bank International AG, Vienna, Austria
e-mail: johannes.langthaler@rbinternational.com

M. Bodellini et al. (eds.), *Commercial Banking in Transition*, Palgrave Macmillan Studies in Banking and Financial Institutions,
https://doi.org/10.1007/978-3-031-45289-5_8

resolution and restructure it once stabilized, so the bank can exit resolution safely. As of today, jurisdictions worldwide are still in the process of implementing these G-20 bank resolution standards, including the European Union (EU). The Financial Stability Board (FSB) in Basel, reporting to the G-20, only recently outlined that significant progress in terms of implementation among FSB jurisdictions has been achieved over the past decade, including the establishment of resolution frameworks, higher loss-absorbing capacities, and enhanced supervision. At the same time, some gaps still need to be closed in the areas of obstacles to resolvability, continued state support, and data availability and reporting.[1]

Supervisory and resolution authorities have fundamentally different objectives. The supervisory authority ensures, among other tasks, that capital requirements are adequately calibrated to mitigate risks. The resolution authority instead solely focuses on the resolvability of a bank to make it restructure-able (resolvable) in the event of its failure but does not focus on risk and probabilities. The major objective of the resolution authority is to ensure the feasibility and credibility of the application of its resolution powers during the resolution weekend. According to the international FSB standards, the resolution tools at the hands of the resolution authority are the Bail-In instrument, the Transfer of assets and liabilities, and the Bridge institution solution.[2] With these tools, the bank resolution framework shall make banks allow to fail (make banks *safe to fail*), instead of making banks *fail-safe*, something which would require the built-up of excessive capital requirements that would negatively distort the bank's overall profitability and competitiveness.

This idea of bank resolution striving towards making banks resolvable for ending the *too-big-too-fail* dilemma is discussed in the literature controversially and not shared unanimously. Avgouleas and Goodhart (2011) perceive the Bail-In instrument as weak unless the failure of a

[1] FSB jurisdictions: Argentina, Australia, Brazil, Canada, China, France, Germany, Hong Kong, India, Indonesia, Italy, Japan, Korea, Mexico, Netherlands, Russia, Saudi Arabia, Singapore, South Africa, Spain, Switzerland, Turkey, United Kingdom, United States. See Financial Stability Board, Evaluation of the Effects of Too-big-to-fail Reforms: Final Report, 2021, https://www.fsb.org/wp-content/uploads/P010421-1.pdf.

[2] See Financial Stability Board, Key Attributes of Effective Resolution Regimes for Financial Institutions, Chapter 3: Resolution Powers, 2011, https://www.fsb.org/wp-content/uploads/r_111104cc.pdf.

bank is clearly idiosyncratic.[3] Persaud (2014) argues that bail-in securities not only would encourage excessive lending, but even shift the burden of bank failure to retail clients such as pensioners and lead to a further escalation of a crisis.[4] During public discussions, market participants and representatives from authorities are regularly raising their doubts about whether resolution would work for a cross-border global systemically important bank (G-SIB) or in a market-wide crisis. As of today, the Bail-In instrument has not been applied and tested during a real-life resolution case, as mainly bail-in led resolution actions have not occurred so far and its operationalization and efficacy thus can only be assessed once a major bank fails in the future.

Accordingly, the FSB recognized the lack of implementation progress of the bail-in instrument in most of its jurisdictions worldwide, indicating the desire to move from bail-out to bail-in might not be evenly shared and supported across all jurisdictions.[5] This, however, does not preempt that the absence of the bail-in instrument implies these jurisdictions are not able to achieve effective resolution, or vice versa, the availability of Bail-in in a jurisdiction necessarily means resolution will be effective.[6] IMF (2016) assesses that because of the complexity of implementing Bail-in, authorities consider easier ways of increasing loss absorbency capacity, for example increasing banks' minimum capital adequacy requirements.[7] All FSB jurisdictions have been committing to resolution instruments other than bail-in instead, and for example, faithfully implemented the Transfer of assets and liabilities instrument, and with the exception for South Africa and Turkey where the respective legislative proposals are under way, also the Resolution planning for systemic firms.[8]

[3] See Emilios Avgouleas and Charles Goodhart, Critical Reflections on Bank Bail-ins, Journal of Financial Regulation, 2011.

[4] See A. D. Persaud, Why Bail-In Securities Are Fool's Gold, PIIE Policy Briefs 14–23, 2014.

[5] See Financial Stability Board, Key Attributes of Effective Resolution Regimes for Financial Institutions, Chapter 3: Resolution Powers, 2011, 26–28, https://www.fsb.org/wp-content/uploads/r_111104cc.pdf.

[6] Ibid., 26–27, footnote 2.

[7] See International Monetary Fund, FSAP Russian Federation on Bank Resolution and Crisis Management Framework, 2016, 20 para 25, https://www.imf.org/external/pubs/ft/scr/2016/cr16308.pdf.

[8] Ibid.

2 Bank Resolution in the EU and the United States

After the shock in 2008, EU legislators proposed three different sets of reforms to strengthen the banking system: (i) higher capital buffers, implementing the international FSB Basel III—standards, (ii) the already mentioned bank resolution framework, and (iii) the so-called bank structural reform. While all EU jurisdictions have been implementing the first two reforms during the past years or are in the process of its implementation, the bank structural reform package lacked political will and has been suspended by EU legislators during the legislative process.

EU legislators have been implementing the bank resolution framework in 2014, which comprises of the Bank Recovery and Resolution Directive, the Single Resolution Mechanism Regulation, and the Deposit Guarantee Schemes Directive. The EU created a new supranational body, the Single Resolution Board (SRB), acting as the responsible resolution authority for the Euro Area in 21 of the EU's 27 Member States, and which is in charge not only for G-SIBs but all significant institutions domiciled within the Euro Area, and even very small institutions with certain eligible cross-border activities. The new rules require all these credit institutions to improve their resolvability and issue and maintain sufficient loss-absorbing capacity to ensure the bail-in instrument would work if needed. For this, EU legislators introduced the Minimum Requirement of Eligible Liabilities and Own Funds (MREL) which implements the international FSB Standard on Total Loss Absorbing Capacity (TLAC).

Noteworthy, EU legislators have implemented MREL going far beyond what would have been required under the international TLAC standard—something which is referred to as "EU gold-plating". While the TLAC standard is applicable only to G-SIBs, the EU legislators decided to apply MREL in principle to all EU-domiciled credit institutions. It introduces several additional elements and layers of discretion for MREL that were not existent under TLAC. Except for Pillar 1 MREL for G-SIBs and for the newly introduced category of "Top-Tier Banks" with total assets greater than EUR 100 bn, all credit institutions are subject to individually calibrated MREL requirements set by the resolution authorities. Unfortunately, this approach suffers greatly from a lack of transparency, as the resolution authorities are not disclosing important criteria for the calibration at the individual level, for example on determining the level of the subordination requirement, on the duration of the transitional period for building up MREL capacity, or on the applicable measures to address the breach of the MREL requirement. On top of that, each of the 27 Member States pursues own policies for MREL setting, further contributing to a fragmented landscape of different MREL policies in place within the EU. Not surprisingly, market participants perceive the EU MREL framework as complex and over-detailed. The divergent application of MREL across the EU creates ambiguity for banks and investors, even for banks under the remit of the same resolution authority, on what are the applicable requirements and how to meet them.

Two key rationales for an effective bank resolution framework are enhanced market transparency for investors to value bail-in debt and predictable sector involvement. Along these lines, Tröger (2020) assesses the EU framework "*that complicating already complex specifications of the FSB for TLAC by implementing MREL with more detailed and case-specific amendments and an exorbitant emphasis on proportionality and technical fine-tuning for MREL (..) makes it barely conceivable that the pricing of MREL instruments reflects the accurate risk assessment of investments because of so many discretionary choices a multitude of agencies are supposed to make in the administration of the EU regime*" and "*a highly detailed and discretionary design (..) fails to fully alleviate the predicament of investors in bail-in debt*".[9]

The bank resolution framework in the United States (U.S.) is set up very differently than the one in EU. In the U.S., the bank resolution agenda is split between the Federal Reserve (FED), who oversees resolution for the seven G-SIBs in its jurisdiction, and the Federal Deposit Insurance Corporation (FDIC), who is responsible for the rest, the small and medium-sized banks in the U.S. Contrary to the EU, the U.S. legislators implemented the international FSB TLAC only for G-SIBs and do not apply it to any other bank.[10] The FDIC refrained from introducing a Public-Interest-Test at all, that is an analysis whether the resolution of a particular ailing bank is justified by a public interest which

[9] See T. Tröger, Why MREL Won't Help Much, Journal of Banking Regulation Vol. 20, 2019, and Nikos Maragopoulos, The MREL Framework under the Banking Reform Package, European Banking Institute Working Paper Series 2020—no. 72, 2020.

[10] One could argue, however, that the contributions to the Deposit Insurance Fund (DIF) in the U.S. system are some sort of equivalent to the EU MREL standard.

at the same represents an important condition for resolution in the EU framework. The FDIC acts already since the 1930s as a centralized and all-encompassing framework and combines a Deposit Guarantee Scheme (DGS), a resolution authority and a financial supervisor all in one. Since the crisis in 2008, the FDIC resolved (restructured) over 500 small and medium-sized U.S. banks under its framework, where the payout of secured deposits has been the exception rather than the rule during that period.

The U.S. framework requires every G-SIB to prepare and disclose its own resolution plan, which details the resolution strategy for every respective individual bank. In the EU it is for the resolution authority to draft a resolution plan,[11] another element which is criticized from market participants, since the resolution authority does not disclose the full content of the resolution plan and keeps important elements confidential. Bodellini and Groen (2021) argue that the EU framework should require resolution authorities to publish a non-confidential and abridged version of the resolution plan to increase overall transparency around resolution planning and allow different stakeholders to enhance their preparation for potential bank failures.[12]

3 Building up MREL Capacity

Recent data published by EU authorities show that the largest EU banks have been issuing substantial amounts of MREL capacity, which certainly makes the bail-in instrument more credible and feasible for these institutions.[13] Still, because of the rigorous implementation of TLAC in the EU, in many cases EU-domiciled credit institutions are required to meet onerous MREL requirements, including some banks with a business model not supporting the issuance of MREL capacity at all, or banks

[11] The SRB alone drafted approximately 115 resolution plans for banks under its remit, on top of the resolution plans drafted by 21 national resolution authorities within the Banking Union. See Banks under the SRB's remit, https://www.srb.europa.eu/en/content/banks-under-srbs-remit.

[12] See M. Bodellini, W. P. De Groen, Impediments to Resolvability—What is the Status Quo? EGOV, 2021.

[13] See Single Resolution Board, MREL Dashboard, Q1.2022, https://www.srb.europa.eu/system/files/media/document/2022-07-26_MREL-Dashboard-Q1-2022.pdf.

operating in countries with shallow capital markets, which are not deep and liquid enough for such MREL issuances.

At year-end 2021, 50% of small and medium-sized EU banks face challenges with the build-up of their final MREL Targets until 1 January 2024 and they are required to fill a remaining cumulative shortfall of around EUR 4.2 bn or 4.5% TREA until that period.[14] The banks with a balance sheet smaller than EUR 100 bn remain the entities with the highest proportion of MREL shortfall.[15]

Some of these small and medium-sized banks are mostly funded by equity and deposits with no or limited experience in accessing capital markets for external funding, and the question arises whether requiring such institutions to issue MREL would be sustainable in the long term, especially against the background of fragile profitability and capability to roll-over instruments of these banks in the short-term and the more in times of economic crisis. At year-end 2021, the outstanding MREL stock of these banks is composed of Common Equity Tier 1 (53%), Senior unsecured liabilities (23%), and non-covered non-preferred deposits (12%); in some Member States, CET1 was even the only sources of MREL-eligible instruments and accounted for 100% of the available stock.[16] Restoy (2021) assesses that within the Euro Area 70% of institutions directly supervised by the European Central Bank (ECB) "*are not listed on markets, almost 60% have never issued convertible instruments and almost one quarter do not finance themselves with subordinated debt*".[17]

Banks with limited access to capital markets will meet their MREL to a significant part with their own funds, which most likely will be heavily depleted at the point of failing-or-likely-to-fail and thus would require a

[14] The average final target for the represented 24.7% of the Total Risk Exposure Amount (TREA) including the Capital Buffers. See Single Resolution Board, Resolvability Assessment 2021, 2022, 40, https://www.srb.europa.eu/system/files/media/document/2022-07-13_SRB-Resolvability-Assessment.pdf.

[15] European Parliament, Public Hearing with Elke König, ECON on 13 July 2022, 2022, 5, https://www.europarl.europa.eu/RegData/etudes/BRIE/2022/699515/IPOL_BRI(2022)699515_EN.pdf.

[16] See Single Resolution Board, Resolvability Assessment, 2022, 41, https://www.srb.europa.eu/system/files/media/document/2022-07-13_SRB-Resolvability-Assessment.pdf.

[17] See Fernando Restoy, Speech: How to Improve Funding of Bank Resolution in the Banking Union—The Role of Deposit Insurance, 2021, https://www.bis.org/speeches/sp210511.htm.

bail-in of uncovered deposits in the event of resolution.[18] While the international TLAC standard addresses this issue by requiring banks to meet the TLAC requirement with at least one-third of debt instruments, the so-called debt allowance, the EU MREL framework does not allow for such a precaution and the cases, where banks meet their MREL mainly with own funds, cannot be avoided. At the same time would the significant build-up of equity for meeting the MREL requirement make debt financing via MREL cheaper because of the lower risk premium and thus could organically contribute to a more balanced funding profile. Nevertheless, these banks most probably would have to change their business model, which would from a system-wide perspective, run counter to the intention of the supervisory authorities, including the European Central Bank, towards a diverse set of business models within the EU, which is being assessed as a "*form of risk diversification that increases the ability to absorb shocks*".[19] The application of MREL requirements on small and medium-sized banks could also speed up consolidation of the banking market, as it happened for example in the U.S. It seems however, that the European Central Bank has preferences for alternative solutions in the bank resolution framework, more specifically the enforced operationalization of the transfer strategy, which would "*allow their orderly exit from the banking market while ensuring the protection of depositors*".[20]

There are other banks that in principle would have the size for accessing capital markets for building up MREL capacity, and those banks may be even systemic in the jurisdiction they operate. However, the jurisdictions these banks are operating in lack deep and liquid enough capital markets, for example in Central, Eastern, and Southeastern Europe.

[18] See P. Machado, Speech: The Challenges of Resolving Mid-sized Banks, 2021, https://www.srb.europa.eu/en/content/challenges-resolving-mid-sized-banks-pedro-machado-frs.

[19] See European Central Bank, ECB Contribution to the European Commission's Targeted Consultation on the Review of the Crisis Management and Deposit Insurance Framework, 2021, 10, https://www.ecb.europa.eu/pub/pdf/other/ecb.consultation_on_crisis_management_deposit_insurance_202105~98c4301b09.en.pdf.

[20] Ibid.

4 Review of the Crisis Management and Deposit Insurance Framework

The EU resolution authorities request banks to build up significant amounts of MREL capacities and to have reached steady-state resolvability by 2024. At the same time, there is a broad consensus about the dysfunction of the current EU bank resolution framework. EU legislators are about to publish a legislative proposal during the first quarter of 2023, which is expected to address several dysfunctionalities in the existing bank resolution framework, the so-called Review of the Bank Crisis Management and Deposit Insurance Framework (CMDI Review).[21]

First, the proposal most likely will include a clarified and harmonized public interest assessment. The public interest assessment is a key policy in the EU resolution framework and assesses whether the failure of a particular bank would impact the public interest and if positive, the bank would be resolved under the bank resolution framework, or if negative, alternatively would undergo national insolvency procedures. In the current setup, most small and medium-sized banks would not enter resolution due to a negative outcome of the public interest test. First experiences in some EU countries under the current framework have proven that a sample of banks are assessed as too small for resolution and too big for insolvency proceedings, or put differently, the previous *too big to fail* was rather replaced by "too small to survive". The current framework also provides for differences in the triggers for several key policies across EU Member States, including for the public interest test, but also the failing-or-likely-to-fail assessment or for entering insolvency proceedings. Some EU banks have been declared failing-or-likely-to-fail during the past years but could neither enter resolution nor insolvency proceedings and were stuck in a so-called limbo situation. For other cases, mainly small and medium-sized banks, instruments similar to the ones available in resolution have been applied under national insolvency proceedings, creating incentives to avoid resolution for such banks at all.[22]

[21] See European Commission, Banking Union—Review of the Bank Crisis Management & Deposit Insurance Framework, 2020, https://ec.europa.eu/info/law/better-regulation/have-your-say/initiatives/12737-Banking-Union-review-of-the-bank-crisis-management-deposit-insurance-framework-DGSD-review-_en.

[22] For example, ABLV Bank in Luxembourg, or Sberbank Europe AG in Austria. For an overview of EU resolution cases see Single Resolution Board, Resolution Cases, 2022, https://www.srb.europa.eu/en/cases.

Second, the application of resolution instruments is expected to be broadened for smaller and medium-sized banks at both European and national level. More specifically, the EU intends to mirror the already existing purchase and assumption transactions for small and medium-sized banks in the U.S. framework under the responsibilities of the FDIC and facilitate the use of transfer strategies for this category of banks in the EU framework. The SRB is expected to receive more powers and act as a centralized decision-taker for the increased sample of banks under its remit. The DGS would support the funding of the transfer of assets and liabilities under the "least cost principle" which serves as an alternative to the payout of deposits. For such purchase and assumption transactions to work, the creditor ranking in national insolvency laws will need to be further harmonized across the EU. The public interest test would need to be removed for these small and medium-sized banks, given resolution proceedings would apply to these institutions. Noteworthy, the public interest test is similarly implicit in the U.S. framework given there are two resolution regimes, one for G-SIBs under the remit of the FED and one for small and medium-sized banks run by the FDIC.[23]

Any changes to national insolvency laws and the public interest test are politically difficult and require time. As an interim solution, and for gradual implementation of the new framework, the regime could be implemented as a start first at the national level via national manuals for ensuring a uniform approach as much as possible. A combination of funds from the DGS and the Single Resolution Fund (SRF)[24] could provide funding for such purchase and assumption transactions. In the final stage, the resolution of smaller and medium-sized banks could become centralized at Euro Area level. The U.S. FDIC model however cannot simply be copied and applied in the EU as these two jurisdictions are different. The EU banking market, for example, is much less consolidated as compared to the U.S. and MREL requirements will most likely not be fully removed for small and medium-sized institutions, but rather be redefined. Restoy (2021) sketches first ideas in this direction, for example, subordinated

[23] See Boersenzeitung, Interview with Elke König, 2021, https://www.boersen-zeitung.de/banken-finanzen/unfortunately-we-are-not-making-any-progress-at-all-on-this-issue-4ab478bc-46fb-11ec-bf4a-dccaf4fffe05.

[24] In the EU, the SRF can support the resolution of banks if certain conditions are met. The fund is built up over 8 years and will reach 1% of covered deposits of credit institutions in the Euro Area—Approximately EUR 80 bn—Until 2024.

MREL on pre-resolution balance sheet could be liquidated and support purchase and assumption transactions "*where the accounting value of the assets required by the acquirer would be larger, despite the DGS support, than that of transferred liabilities*".[25]

Third, further harmonization of the use of national DGS for crisis management is expected, including a harmonized least-cost test to govern its use outside payout to covered depositors. In the current setup, the role of DGS in insolvency and resolution proceedings is not harmonized yet across the EU. While in countries such as Italy or Denmark the DGS could reduce potential losses (similar as in the FDIC model), in most EU countries the DGS has a rather passive role and could not support the funding of the transfer of asset and liabilities to other institutions. Certainly, this maintains an uneven level playing field for banks and depositors across the Euro Area and increases fragmentation of the banking sector across national borders which further amplifies the nexus between sovereigns and banks. National DGS funds and decisions at local level could provide incentives to avoid resolution and try for national solutions, if access to DGS is easier and requires lower burden-sharing requirements as compared to the SRF. For the DGS to support funding of purchase and assumption transactions and the subsequent exit of market of an ailing small and medium-sized banks, and for ensuring harmonization, the current DGS super priority in the creditor hierarchy would need to be removed and the "least cost principle" reviewed.

Fourth, harmonization of targeted features of national bank insolvency laws. This includes the work on an EU-wide general depositor preference covering all deposits that benefit from the same ranking, which would facilitate the DGS funding of a purchase and assumption transaction. Some EU Member States have already granted a legal preference in insolvency to a broader category of deposits, such as deposits of large corporates for the part exceeding the coverage level of the DGS. In the U.S., such a general depositor preference is in place and DGS funds are being (successfully) used for bank resolution.[26]

[25] See F. Restoy, Speech: How to Improve Funding of Bank Resolution in the Banking Union—The Role of Deposit Insurance, 2021, https://www.bis.org/speeches/sp210511.htm.

[26] See Single Resolution Board, Replies Target Consultation Document, 2021, 47, https://www.srb.europa.eu/system/files/media/document/2021-04-20_srb_replies_consultation_cmdi_review.pdf.

Fifth, several supranational EU institutions strongly believe in a common DGS at EU level as the preferred solution, a European Deposit Insurance Scheme (EDIS). Both, the ECB and the SRB, loudly proclaim that EDIS would help to overcome national ring-fencing and facilitate the free flow of capital and liquidity within the EU, thereby increasing private loss absorption.[27] EDIS would remove the "*vulnerabilities associated with the remaining links between bank risks and the availability of domestic funds to address them*".[28] Still, similar to changes in the national insolvency law, EDIS will be most likely not yet politically feasible. In June 2022, the EU political leaders could not reach an agreement on a timeline and work plan for the introduction of EDIS.[29] Noteworthy, also in the U.S. the introduction of a common DGS in 1933 underwent a political burdensome process and was preceded by 150 proposals over more than 50 years. As a transitional solution, the EU legislators are expected to try to reach faster reforms for strengthening existing possibilities such as the use of national DGS and SRF and the provision of liquidity until 2024[30] and decide on a fully-fledged EDIS including loss sharing later.

Lastly, to avoid cases in the past, where banks did not enter resolution proceedings, but received state aid from the public budget and benefitted from DGS alternative measures under national insolvency proceedings,[31] the European Commission launched a separate public consultation on the evaluation of banks' State aid rules in March 2022. The proposal targets to harmonize the EU 2013 Communication on Banks State Aid with the EU resolution framework in order to avoid such "bail-out in disguise".[32]

[27] Ibid.

[28] See F. Restoy, Speech: How to Improve Funding of Bank Resolution in the Banking Union—The Role of Deposit Insurance, 2021, https://www.bis.org/speeches/sp210511.htm.

[29] See Boersenzeitung, Interview with Elke König, 2021, https://www.boersen-zeitung.de/banken-finanzen/unfortunately-we-are-not-making-any-progress-at-all-on-this-issue-4ab478bc-46fb-11ec-bf4a-dccaf4fffe05.

[30] See Euro Group, Press Statement Published on 16 June, 2022, https://www.consilium.europa.eu/de/press/press-releases/2022/06/16/eurogroup-statement-on-the-future-of-the-banking-union-of-16-june-2022/.

[31] E.g. Nord/LB in Germany, Banca Monte dei Paschi in Italy.

[32] See Single Resolution Board, Elke König's Speech at the ECON Committee, 2021, https://www.srb.europa.eu/en/content/srb-chair-elke-konigs-speech-econ-committee.

5 Cooperative and Savings Banks

The CMDI Review will most likely also address Cooperative and Savings Banks more explicitly in the bank resolution framework. European political leaders clarified the upcoming CMDI proposal will "*take due account of the specificities in the national banking sectors, including by preserving a functioning framework for institutional protection schemes to implement preventive measures*".[33] Cooperative and Savings Banks are highly important in the EU banking landscape and have a long history in some EU countries, such as Germany, Austria, Italy, Poland, or Spain. Usually, the structure of these banks has in common that it is related to an Institutional Protection Scheme (IPS). Haselmann et al. (2022) describe the IPS as "*a set of mutual support promises among institutions that are members of the same scheme*".[34] For example, in Germany, banks with such a structure hold more than 80% of all deposits from non-banks in the country, with overall increasing market shares. In all these countries, IPS-related institutions have a large market share, especially in retail banking, savings, and residential real estate loans. Due to mutual support promises, "*a depositor of a bank that is a member of an IPS is promised to receive additional protection in case of the bank's non-viability*".[35]

It needs to be seen what will be proposed as part of the CMDI Review. For example, mutual funding schemes from IPS-related models could be accounted towards MREL, for smaller banks at least. MREL requirements could be adjusted downwards subject to a subset of IPS-related measures laid down in the recovery plan, which may be actionable immediately in resolution and would be implemented quickly, having a positive impact on any loss scenario. Resolution authorities will be required to test their availability, timeliness, and independence in all scenarios, as such IPS-related measures would form part of the resolution strategy. For such measures to work, the responsibilities of the IPS and the bank owners would need

[33] See Euro Group, Press Statement, 2022, https://www.consilium.europa.eu/de/press/press-releases/2022/06/16/eurogroup-statement-on-the-future-of-the-banking-union-of-16-june-2022/.

[34] See R. Haselmann, J. P. Krahnen, T. H. Tröger, M. Wahrenburg, Institutional Protection Schemes: What are their Differences, Strengths, Weaknesses, and Track Records? ECON Committee, 2022.

[35] Ibid.

to be clarified, and clear triggers for support to be defined when the IPS is supposed to act.

Haselmann et al. (2022) describe the IPS-related structure, which provides a guarantee to the individual bank, as the "*backbone of any group governance. It carries out the day-to-day monitoring of its members, initiates early interventions in case of emergence of risks, and it implements the reorganization in times of crisis*".[36] Therefore, in the case of an ailing individual member bank, it could be taken over by a dedicated neighbor member of the IPS using a purchase and assumption transaction as outlined above. This approach would have the advantages that intensive monitoring of individual local banks and overall system compatibility is already in place. The reorganization would be initiated and completed at the level of the bank and under certain conditions the IPS could facilitate the transfer.

6 Why the Completion of the EU Capital Markets Union Matters

A significant number of Euro Area banking groups, including Austria, France, and Italy, operate large subsidiary networks in Central, Eastern, and Southeastern Europe.[37] Lehmann (2019) describes the markets in the region "*to have turned out to be consistently profitable and have generated steady asset growth since the global financial crisis, more than their euro-area home markets and subsidiaries are typically significant within host markets and are often also significant individually within the respective banking groups*".[38] Over the last 30 years, these Euro Area banking groups and their deep involvement were perceived as important facilitators of European Integration and promotors of the EU single market

[36] Ibid.

[37] Central, Eastern and Southeastern Europe refers to the three Baltic countries, Poland, Hungary, the Czech Republic, Slovakia, Slovenia, Croatia, Bulgaria, Romania, Albania, Bosnia & Herzegovina, Kosovo, FYR Macedonia, Montenegro, Serbia, Belarus, Moldova, Russian Federation and Ukraine.

[38] See Alexander Lehmann, Crisis Management for Euro-area Banks in Central Europe, Alexander Lehmann, Bruegel Policy Contribution, Issue n°14, 2019.

in Central, Eastern, and Southeastern Europe.[39] Their significant cross-border investments contributed to the creation of jobs, higher gross domestic product growth in those countries, and more inward foreign direct investment flows from (other) EU countries.

The banking sector today in the region is assessed as strong, with a solid return on equity and high capital coverage. Joint public–private initiatives such as the Vienna Initiative[40] founded after the global financial crisis in January 2009 supported such a development. While the funding model of the subsidiaries operating before 2009 relied on wholesale markets and parent-bank liquidity, the Vienna Initiative succeeded in making the subsidiaries to rely stronger on local deposits and, where possible, on local debt markets, thereby reducing the overall risk and strengthening the resilience of the subsidiaries.

Lehmann (2019) assesses the benefits that Euro-Area banks brought to the region as "*valuable not only in risk management and transfer of skills*".[41] Indeed, the local subsidiaries support the development of local capital markets and thus overall, the proper functioning of the EU single market. In some of these countries, no deep and liquid capital markets existed at all a priori due to the small size of the local banking sectors and the limited absorption capacity of local capital markets. Furthermore, according to Lehmann (2019) the decentralized funding made these subsidiaries amenable for local Multiple-Point-of-Entry (MPE) resolution

[39] Whether the Central, Eastern and Southeastern Europe financial markets have become more or less integrated with the rest of the euro is disputed and depends on the empirical measures used. For a discussion of related literature, see Alexander Lehmann, Crisis Management for Euro-area Banks in Central Europe, Bruegel Policy Contribution, Issue n°14 | November 2019.

[40] The Vienna Initiative was established at the height of the 2008/2009 global financial crisis as a private and public sector platform to ensure that Western banking groups provided sufficient capital and liquidity to their subsidiaries in Central, Eastern and Southeastern Europe during the crisis. The founders and driving forces of the initiative are the EIB, the European Commission, the European Bank for Reconstruction and Development, the International Monetary Fund and the World Bank. In January 2012, the initiative was relaunched under the name "Vienna 2.0" as renewed risks to the region had emerged from the Euro Area crisis. Its focus is now on strengthening the coordination of authorities in banks' home and host countries to stabilize cross-border activities. For more information, See European Investment Bank, Vienna Initiative: New Working Group on Capital Markets Union for CESEE region, 2017, https://www.eib.org/de/press/all/2017-054-vienna-initiative-new-working-group-on-capital-markets-union-for-cesee-region.

[41] See A. Lehmann, Developing Resilient Bail-in Capital, 2019, https://www.bruegel.org/blog-post/developing-resilient-bail-capital.

schemes and facilitated the separation from the parent entity, at least in financial terms.[42] As of today, several subsidiaries of Euro Area banking groups operating in the region follow the MPE resolution strategy, which requires them to issue and maintain local MREL capacity. The financing under market conditions in host jurisdictions under the MPE model ensures a level playing field with respect to national institutions in these host jurisdictions.

The development of a common capital market remains a key priority for the EU and the functioning of the EU's internal market. The Capital Market Union (CMU), an umbrella term for a set of new regulations and reforms brought up by EU legislators over the past years, has the aim to increase investment by investors across national boundaries. The implementation of crisis management regulation, including the issuance of local MREL debt, and achieving the objectives of the CMU must be aligned and benefit from each other.

The CMDI review should address the existing differences in local frameworks for dealing with bank failures and remove regulatory barriers to make investing in other EU member states equally attractive than investing in the domestic market—which fits the idea of the EU's internal market. Further harmonization of bank insolvency rules and uniform protection of the same category of investors and depositors across EU Member States under the CMDI review would strengthen the CMU, as "*investors would have more certainty when investing cross-border*".[43] For example, no matter if investors invest in a medium-sized bank that then grows and falls under the remit of the SRB, or suddenly has its home in another state, "*the rules (and thus the risk) in regulation terms remain the same*".[44] Furthermore, improving cooperation with third country resolution authorities and broadening the narrow-qualified investor base for MREL bonds would benefit the objectives of CMU.

42 Ibid.

43 See Single Resolution Board, The Crisis Management Framework for Banks in the EU: What Can Be Done with Small and Medium-sized Banks? 2021, https://www.srb.europa.eu/en/content/crisis-management-framework-banks-eu-what-can-be-done-small-and-medium-sized-banks and European Central Bank, ECB Contribution to the European Commission's Targeted Consultation on the Review of the Crisis Management and Deposit Insurance Framework, 2021, https://www.ecb.europa.eu/pub/pdf/other/ecb.consultation_on_crisis_management_deposit_insurance_202105~98c4301b09.en.pdf.

44 Ibid.

Vice versa could the completion of CMU also benefit the EU crisis management framework. Updated CMU regulation needs to support EU banks to meet their MREL capacities on deep and liquid capital markets in EUR denominated debt (and not only in U.S. dollar). Where not sufficiently deep and liquid markets exist yet, the issuance and marketability of local subordinated debt could be developed with support from supranational investors, such as the International Finance Corporation and European Bank for Reconstruction and Development. These bodies must continue to support MREL issuances of banks in the Central, Eastern, and Southeastern Europe as anchor investors for this new asset class but further clarity on their regulatory treatment is needed. Lehmann (2019) points out that the European Investment Bank does not have a clear policy mandate to develop capital markets and has concerns regarding the use of public money which could be subject to the bail-in instrument in a potential banking resolution.[45] The World Bank (2018) stepped up to recognize bank resolution becoming a global occupation and increased its training activities,[46] but at the same time ascertains some risk that an "*increased bank bond issuance induced by regulatory measures such as MREL might counteract efforts to develop and deepen the corporate bond market*" and related crowding-out effects.[47]

Still, independent local subsidiaries having their own MPE resolution scheme must "*be backed up by local investor class that shelters host-country taxpayers from the risks of bank failure*".[48] Lehmann (2019) suggests the CMU regulation to better encourage and facilitate MREL exposures of long-term institutional investors.[49] Once an individual bank approaches resolution, short-term investors such as hedge funds may flee the MREL, which would further deteriorate the funding costs of the bank. Smaller banks with similar business model and exposures towards private-sector debt or government bond holdings might sell of increasing

[45] See A. Lehmann, Crisis Management for Euro-area Banks in central Europe, Bruegel Policy Contribution Issue n°14, 2019.

[46] Ibid.

[47] See World Bank Group, Report on Capital Markets Union, 2018, https://vienna-initiative.com/resources/themes/vienna/wp-content/uploads/2018/03/VI-CMU-Working-Group-Final-Report-March-2018.pdf.

[48] See A. Lehmann, Crisis Management for Euro-area Banks in Central Europe, Bruegel Policy Contribution Issue n°14, 2019.

[49] Ibid.

amounts of the MREL as well, and could therefore set-off contagion, from the one bank close to resolution, to others where similar risks are perceived, caused by short-term investors flight from bail-in able securities and MREL bonds in individual jurisdictions. As outlined above, bank resolution frameworks deal mostly with idiosyncratic bank failures, but inherently fail to deal with a systemic crisis. According to Lehmann (2019), long-term investors, such as pension and insurance funds, should be encouraged by CMU regulation to take on more significant exposures, for example "*through requirements for capital coverage and asset valuation in the regulation of insurance funds. As financial system risks have been reduced, and risks have become less correlated between institutions, bail-in securities could become a more established asset class*".[50]

A dedicated working group on CMU established in 2017 by the Vienna Initiative network committed to analyzing structural obstacles and regulatory gaps that slow down the development of capital markets in Central, Eastern, and Southeastern Europe and to develop solutions at the national and regional level. Such initiatives are in line with the EU's push to strengthen capital markets, which will have a significant impact on financing investment and sustainable growth in the region.

7 Cooperation Is Key for Success in Resolution Planning

Cross-border resolution planning for banking groups will only work if the authorities where the parent and its subsidiaries operate cooperate closely. Up to date, post-crisis ring-fencing and a lack of trust and cooperation between home and host authorities still prevail in banking markets.

Again Central, Eastern, and Southeastern European countries must be a geographical focus area also in the context of cooperation. The SRB and the resolution authorities outside the Euro Area meet once a year in resolution colleges, where they agree on a joint decision on the resolution strategy. This process is relatively new, but unfortunately less transparent as compared to supervisory colleges, which also meet more often. What further complicates the cooperation for bank resolution is that every resolution authority outside the Euro Area has set its own MREL requirements based on its individual MREL policy. While these national MREL

[50] Ibid.

policies in principle converge towards the MREL policy published by the SRB, they still differ from each other in terms of calibration and timing and contain discretionary elements that are not transparently disclosed.

Improving the transparency would improve the credibility of resolution plans as well. Lehmann (2019) suggests the SRB could provide "*early and full access to bank recovery and resolution plans*" during Resolution Colleges and take the lead on a credible group-resolution plan for the entire group, which would ensure that bail-in capital is converted once necessary by the local authority in the host country, with SRF access to be sued for banking sector risks outside the Euro Area.[51] At the same time the SRB will need to prepare that host countries outside the Euro Area will implement independent resolution planning (and even resolution action, if necessary). The recent resolution of Sberbank Europe AG, a banking group headquartered in the Euro Area but its subsidiaries operating in the Euro Area, EU, and non-EU countries has proven that banks are international in life, but national in death.[52]

It will remain a particular challenge how the SRB assesses the separability of local subsidiaries in host countries and how it would address impediments to separability in host countries where financial markets and infrastructure are less developed.[53] World Bank (2019) raises that "*the full set of resolution tools may not be feasible in some jurisdictions, with the practical approach mostly likely being a purchase and assumption operation and possibly a bridge bank operation. The main challenge for the first is the choice of acquiring bank and the implications for the market. The biggest challenge for a bridge bank is the limited capacity in most countries to run such an operation and the risk that it will last longer than expected. Discussions on MREL/TLAC would be premature in this context as bail-in could be difficult, if not impossible, because there are few non-deposit liabilities and debt markets yet to be developed. This situation is the*

[51] Ibid.

[52] See S&P Ratings, The Failure of Sberbank Europe: International in Life, National in Death, 2022, https://www.spglobal.com/ratings/en/research/articles/220304-the-failure-of-sberbank-europe-international-in-life-national-in-death-12300778.

[53] See A. Lehmann, Impediments to Resolvability of Banks, EGOV, 2019, https://www.bruegel.org/sites/default/files/wp-content/uploads/2019/12/IPOL_IDA2019634360_EN.pdf.

same in many other developing countries across the globe".[54] But the World Bank also recognizes benefits for non-EU hosts from increased cooperation with EU authorities, as it fosters regulatory convergence in the field of bank resolution. Non-EU hosts should participate in EU resolution colleges and EU authorities should support non-EU host countries to adapt EU regulation and fit it to their national circumstances.[55]

8 Concluding Remarks

The progress in implementing bank resolution regimes differs worldwide not only across FSB jurisdictions but also within FSB jurisdictions for individual banks. Larger banks are assessed to be closer to becoming resolvable than smaller and medium-sized banks which rather face structural resolvability issues foremost but not limited to the building up of MREL capacity. The EU legislator is expected to publish until the first quarter of 2023 its CMDI Review proposal which should provide for reform, particularly for the resolution of small- and medium-sized banks.

The CMDI Review is expected to better align the resolution framework with IPS-related banking models, such as cooperative and savings banks. For example, mutual funding schemes from IPS-related models could be accounted towards MREL, for smaller banks at least, or MREL requirements could be adjusted downwards subject to a subset of IPS-related measures laid down in the recovery plan. Due to a lack of political agreement of European leaders, the EU legislator will first try to strengthen national DGS and the provision of liquidity, which should be ready for publication by 2024, and decide further on a fully-fledged EDIS including loss sharing at a later stage.

The development of the EU crisis management framework and the CMU must be viewed together and benefit from each other. The upcoming CMDI review will address and harmonize existing differences in local resolution frameworks and remove regulatory barriers to make

[54] See I. Ahmad, T. Beck, K. D'Hulster, P. Lintner, and F. D. Unsal, Banking Supervision and Resolution in the EU—Effects on Small Host Countries in Central, Eastern and South Eastern Europe, World Bank FinSAC, 2019, 47 https://thedocs.worldbank.org/en/doc/589991557325278014-0130022019/original/FinSACBREffectsonSmallHostCountriesEurope.pdf.

[55] Ibid., 43.

cross-border investing more attractive in Central, Eastern, and South-eastern Europe, while vice versa the CMU regulation can encourage and facilitate MREL exposures of long-term institutional investors. Closer and improved cooperation with non-Euro Area countries, within and outside the EU, is a prerequisite to make cross-border resolution work.

CHAPTER 9

Sustainable Commercial Banking in European Union Law: A Renewed Mandate for Commercial Banks?

Pablo Iglesias-Rodríguez

1 Introduction

The relationship between commercial banks[1] and sustainability[2] has two core dimensions which reflect an inward-outward dynamic. On the one side, commercial banks are affected by sustainability factors. On the other

[1] This chapter uses a definition of a 'commercial bank' as "a deposit-taking institution, whose primary activity has been that of giving loans"—see D.s N. Chorafas, Handbook of Commercial Banking: Strategic Planning for Growth and Survival in the New Decade, Houndmills, Palgrave, 1999, 52.

[2] In this chapter, the term 'sustainability' is used to refer to the quality of positively

I am very grateful to both the Max Planck Institute for Comparative and International Private Law and the University of Foggia for financing research that led to this chapter. Its contents reflect the law as of 1 November 2022.

P. Iglesias-Rodríguez (✉)
School of Law, Politics and Sociology, University of Sussex, Brighton, UK
e-mail: P.Iglesias-Rodriguez@sussex.ac.uk

M. Bodellini et al. (eds.), *Commercial Banking in Transition*, Palgrave Macmillan Studies in Banking and Financial Institutions,
https://doi.org/10.1007/978-3-031-45289-5_9

side, commercial banks are actors whose actions have a major impact on sustainability.

As regards the first dimension, commercial banks are affected by sustainability risk(s). The Federation of European Risk Management Associations (FERMA) defines the latter as an "uncertain social or environmental event or condition that, if it occurs, can cause significant negative impact on the company".[3] The two main categories of sustainability risks are physical risks and transition risks.

The term 'physical risk' is normally used to refer to risks sourcing from climate variability-related events—e.g., droughts, heatwaves, or floodings—which have an adverse impact on society and the economy.[4] Commercial banks may be highly exposed to these types of risks. For example, farmers and/or agricultural companies affected by physical climate risks may experience major losses and this may affect their ability to repay loans to commercial banks from which they borrowed.[5] This, in turn, increases credit risks for the commercial banks concerned.[6] A study published by Deloitte The Netherlands in the year 2021 examined the relationship between mortgage loan default rates and flood insurance

contributing to the environment, social and employee welfare, the protection of human rights, anti-corruption, and anti-bribery. This definition largely embraces the notion of sustainability underlying article 2(24) of the Sustainable Finance Disclosure Regulation (SFDR)—Regulation (EU) 2019/2088 of the European Parliament and of the Council of 27 November 2019 on sustainability-related disclosures in the financial services sector OJ L 317/1.

[3] Federation of European Risk Management Associations, People, Planet & Performance: The Contribution of Enterprise Risk Management to Sustainability, Brussels, Federation of European Risk Management Associations, 2021, 7, https://www.ferma.eu/app/uploads/2021/03/Ferma-sustainability_2021_final.pdf.

[4] See e.g., Basel Committee on Banking Supervision, Climate-related Risk Drivers and Their Transmission Channels, Basel, Bank for International Settlements, 2021, v, 6–7, https://www.bis.org/bcbs/publ/d517.pdf.

[5] Network for Greening the Financial System, Physical Climate Risk Assessment: Practical Lessons for the Development of Climate Scenarios with Extreme Weather Events from Emerging Markets and Developing Economies, Technical Document, (September 2022), 19, 28, https://www.ngfs.net/sites/default/files/media/2022/09/02/ngfs_physical_climate_risk_assessment.pdf.

[6] On the links between climate risks and credit risks see e.g., P. Monnin, Integrating Climate Risks into Credit Risk Assessment. Current Methodologies and the Case of Central Banks Corporate Bond Purchases, 2018, Council on Economic Policies Discussion Note 2018/4, 3–4, https://www.cepweb.org/wp-content/uploads/2019/02/CEP-DN-Integrating-climate-risks-into-credit-risk-analysis.pdf.

claims across the United States (US) in the period 2000–2019; the results showed that the risk of floods of a mortgaged residential property is a statistically relevant driver of mortgage loan defaults in 46 out of 50 US states[7]; this supports the idea that there is a strong link between physical sustainability risks and commercial banks' credit risk.

'Transition risk' is a concept that, similarly to physical risk, is used primarily in relation to the environment and refers to risks that emerge because of changes linked to the process of shift towards a less carbon-dependent economy; these changes are often driven by regulation or consumer choices.[8] For example, in recent years European Union (EU) policy makers have adopted several regulatory measures aimed at furthering compliance with net-zero targets; examples of this are the EU bans of certain single-use plastics from July 2021[9] or the EU prohibitions concerning the sale of new cars with combustion engines from 2035 onwards.[10] Likewise, purchasing trends show that globally consumers are increasingly concerned about sustainability, and this is reflected in their product choices.[11] This may ultimately have a detrimental impact on less sustainable businesses and, indirectly, on commercial banks which provide funding to them. A joint report published by the European Central Bank (ECB) and the European Systemic Risk Board (ESRB)

[7] See R. Walles, R. Jansen and M. Folpmers, Climate Change Related Credit Risk. Case Study for U.S. Mortgage Loans, Amsterdam, Deloitte, 2021, https://www2.deloitte.com/content/dam/Deloitte/nl/Documents/financial-services/deloitte-nl-fsi-climate-related-risk-full-article.pdf.

[8] See e.g., Basel Committee on Banking Supervision, Climate-related Financial Risks—Measurement Methodologies, Basel, Bank for International Settlements, 2021, vi, https://www.bis.org/bcbs/publ/d518.pdf.

[9] Arts. 5 and 17 Directive (EU) 2019/904 of the European Parliament and of the Council of 5 June 2019 on the reduction of the impact of certain plastic products on the environment OJ L 155/1.

[10] Council of the European Union, First 'Fit for 55' proposal agreed: the EU strengthens targets for CO2 emissions for new cars and vans (Press Release, 27 October 2022), https://www.consilium.europa.eu/en/press/press-releases/2022/10/27/first-fit-for-55-proposal-agreed-the-eu-strengthens-targets-for-co2-emissions-for-new-cars-and-vans/.

[11] See e.g., A. Emmert, The Rise of the Eco-friendly Consumer, 2021, 104 Strategy+Business (8 July 2021), https://www.strategy-business.com/article/The-rise-of-the-eco-friendly-consumer.

in July 2021[12] showed that approximately 30% of credit exposures to non-financial corporations of the euro area banking system are to firms that are subject to high or growing physical risks—e.g., floods, heat stress, water stress.[13] As regards transition risks, the same report indicated that, approximately, 50% of euro area bank loan exposures to non-financial corporations is to firms in so-called climate policy-relevant sectors, namely, sectors vulnerable to transition risks.[14]

When it comes to the second dimension, commercial banks and, notably, their lending behavior may have a major impact on sustainability. For instance, by funding polluting enterprises, commercial banks contribute indirectly to the degradation of the environment.[15] Conversely, by favoring access to credit to sustainable activities, commercial banks may contribute to firms engaging in more sustainable activities which give them easier and less costly access to debt financing.[16] While banks' lending behavior in Europe varies substantially, research shows that, in 2021 the largest 25 European commercial banks lent almost USD 55 billion to the oil and gas industry.[17]

The concerns about the impact of sustainability on commercial banks and of the latter on the former has led policy makers both at the international and national levels to develop various policy and regulatory proposals and actions aimed at guaranteeing that banks take stock of and disclose information about sustainability issues.[18] In the EU, the

[12] European Central Bank and European Systemic Risk Board, Climate-related Risk and Financial Stability (July 2021), https://www.ecb.europa.eu/pub/pdf/other/ecb.climateriskfinancialstability202107~87822fae81.en.pdf

[13] European Central Bank and European Systemic Risk Board (2021), 15.

[14] European Central Bank and European Systemic Risk Board (2021), 24.

[15] See e.g., CDP, The Time to Green Finance. CDP Financial Services Disclosure Report 2020, 2020, 33, https://cdn.cdp.net/cdp-production/cms/reports/documents/000/005/741/original/CDP-Financial-Services-Disclosure-Report-2020.pdf?1619537981.

[16] See e.g., L. Bernick, Can Sustainable Companies Get a Lower Cost of Capital? (GreenBiz, 4 March 2019), https://www.greenbiz.com/article/can-sustainable-companies-get-lower-cost-capital.

[17] ShareAction, Oil & Gas Expansion A Lose-Lose Bet for Banks and their Investors (February 2022), 32, https://api.shareaction.org/resources/reports/Oil-Gas-Expansion-lose-lose.pdf.

[18] See e.g., Organisation for Economic Co-operation and Development, OECD Business and Finance Outlook 2020: Sustainable and Resilient Finance, Paris, OECD

European Commission (Commission) has published various documents, largely inspired by the Paris Agreement[19] and the United Nations 2030 Agenda and its 17 sustainable development goals,[20] which acknowledge both the threats that sustainability risks pose to the financial system and the importance of building a financial system that fosters sustainability. Notable examples of this are the Action Plan on Financing Sustainable Growth,[21] and the European Green Deal (Green Deal).[22] These initiatives proposed the adoption of actions aimed at ensuring that firms: (a) embed the pursuance of sustainability and long-term objectives into their corporate governance; (b) enhance their disclosure about sustainability-related issues; and (c) take stock of sustainability risks.[23] This, in turn, has led to the proposal and adoption of EU laws and administrative rules which tackle specifically commercial banks or that have an impact on them and which, in different ways, embrace these sustainability-related targets. Some examples are the Taxonomy Regulation,[24] the Proposal for a Corporate Sustainability Reporting Directive

Publishing, 2020, 133–134, https://www.oecd.org/daf/Sustainable-and-Resilient-Finance.pdf.

[19] Paris Agreement to the United Nations Framework Convention on Climate Change, December 12, 2015, T.I.A.S. No. 16-1104.

[20] United Nations, Transforming Our World: The 2030 Agenda for Sustainable Development, New York: UN Publishing, 2015, https://sdgs.un.org/sites/default/files/publications/21252030%20Agenda%20for%20Sustainable%20Development%20web.pdf.

[21] Communication from the Commission to the European Parliament, the European Council, the Council, the European Central Bank, the European Economic and Social Committee and the Committee of the Regions. Action Plan: Financing Sustainable Growth (COM (2018) 97 final).

[22] Communication from the Commission to the European Parliament, the European Council, the Council, the European Economic and Social Committee and the Committee of the Regions. The European Green Deal (COM (2019) 640 final).

[23] Action Plan on Financing Sustainable Growth, 2018, 2–4, 9–11; and Green Deal (2019), 17.

[24] Regulation (EU) 2020/852 of the European Parliament and of the Council of 18 June 2020 on the Establishment of a Framework to Facilitate Sustainable Investment, and Amending Regulation (EU) 2019/2088 OJ L 198/13.

(CSRD Proposal),[25] the Proposal for a Capital Requirements Regulation III (CRR III Proposal),[26] the Proposal for a Capital Requirements Directive VI (CRD VI Proposal),[27] or the Proposal for a Corporate Sustainability Due Diligence Directive (CSDD Proposal).[28]

There are two key concepts that underlie these policy actions, reforms, and proposals for reform. The first is the notion that agency relationships and problems in firms, including in commercial banks, go beyond the traditional categories which focus on the relationships between directors and shareholders, between different types of shareholders, or between firms and their contracting parties.[29] Instead, by putting sustainability at the center of corporate governance, EU policymakers implicitly acknowledge an agency relationship between firms that offer products and services—e.g., commercial banks—, as agents, and all members of society affected by sustainability or with an interest in sustainability, as principals. The second, which is closely linked to the first, is the idea that firms in general and commercial banks in particular must consider, in their decision-making, the interests of those parties affected by or with an interest in sustainability; this, in turn, has significant potential implications for the definition of the corporate objective of commercial banks and for the answer to the question of: on whose interests should commercial banks be run?

[25] Proposal for a Directive of the European Parliament and of the Council Amending Directive 2013/34/EU, Directive 2004/109/EC, Directive 2006/43/EC and Regulation (EU) No 537/2014, as regards Corporate Sustainability Reporting (COM (2021) 189 final).

[26] Proposal for a Regulation of the European Parliament and of the Council Amending Regulation (EU) No 575/2013 as regards requirements for credit risk, credit valuation adjustment risk, operational risk, market risk and the output floor (COM (2021) 664 final).

[27] Proposal for a Directive of the European Parliament and of the Council amending Directive 2013/36/EU as regards supervisory powers, sanctions, third-country branches, and environmental, social and governance risks, and amending Directive 2014/59/EU (COM (2021) 663 final).

[28] Proposal for a Directive of the European Parliament and of the Council on Corporate Sustainability Due Diligence and amending Directive (EU) 2019/1937 (COM (2022) 71 final).

[29] For an analysis of these agency relationships and problems see e.g., J. Armour, H. Hansmann, and R. Kraakman, Agency Problems, Legal Strategies and Enforcement, 2009, John M. Olin Center for Law, Economics, and Business Discussion Paper No. 644, http://www.law.harvard.edu/programs/olin_center/papers/pdf/Kraakman_644.pdf.

This chapter analyzes selected key EU policy actions, legal reforms, and proposals for reform with an impact on the commercial banks' sustainability reporting duties (Sect. 2) and on their obligations to take stock of sustainability risks and impacts (Sect. 3), with a focus on the following questions: Are these policy actions and reforms effective in fostering sustainability?; Do they mitigate agency problems between commercial banks and stakeholders affected by or with an interest in sustainability?; To what extent are they leading to a redefinition of the corporate objective of commercial banks and of the duties of their directors?

2 Sustainability as an Object of Disclosure: Commercial Banks' Sustainability Reporting

EU sustainability policies give substantial weight to sustainability transparency and reporting as instruments for the accomplishment of a more sustainable economy. The underlying policy rationale for a sound sustainability reporting framework is twofold. First, it allows investors concerned with sustainability to make informed decisions and allocate capital to sustainable activities.[30] Second, it exposes the sustainability practices of firms and hence increases the ability of stakeholders to hold them to account for them; this, in turn, increases firms' incentives to take into account sustainability concerns in their operations.[31] As put by the Action Plan on Financing Sustainable Growth: "transparency on sustainability will not only inform market participants, but also help to steer companies in a more sustainable and long-term direction".[32]

The Non-Financial Reporting Directive (NFRD),[33] which amended the Accounting Directive,[34] provided the first EU framework on corporate sustainability reporting. It applies to certain large firms in the EU,

[30] See H. B. Christensen, L. Hail, and C. Leuz, Mandatory CSR and Sustainability Reporting: Economic Analysis and Literature Review, 2021, 26 Review of Accounting Studies, 1176–1248, 1203.

[31] Christensen, Hail, and Leuz, 2021, 1203.

[32] Action Plan on Financing Sustainable Growth, 2018, 3.

[33] Directive 2014/95/EU of the European Parliament and of the Council of 22 October 2014 amending Directive 2013/34/EU as regards disclosure of non-financial and diversity information by certain large undertakings and groups OJ L 330/1.

[34] Directive 2013/34/EU of the European Parliament and of the Council of 26 June 2013 on the annual financial statements, consolidated financial statements and related

including commercial banks.[35] The NFRD embraces the principle of double materiality whereby firms must report on both the impact that sustainability has on them and their own impact on sustainability.[36] While the adoption of the NFRD meant an important shift towards a more unified system of sustainability reporting in the EU, it suffered from various weaknesses which hindered the accomplishment of its targets.[37] Over the years, EU legal and regulatory developments have complemented the NFRD disclosure regime or have proposed amendments to it in areas that have an impact on the content and scope of sustainability reporting by commercial banks; some notable examples of these developments are the Taxonomy Regulation, the CSRD Proposal, and the CRR III Proposal.[38]

This section examines these and other key EU legal and regulatory developments on or with an impact on sustainability reporting by commercial banks with a view to ascertaining the implications that they may have on their sustainability reporting obligations as well as on the overall notion of the commercial banks' objectives. In order to do so, the analysis focuses on three aspects, namely the commercial banks subject to sustainability reporting, the substantive scope of the commercial banks' sustainability reporting obligations, and the strategies aimed at guaranteeing compliance with sustainability reporting by commercial banks.

reports of certain types of undertakings, amending Directive 2006/43/EC of the European Parliament and of the Council and repealing Council Directives 78/660/EEC and 83/349/EEC OJ L 182/19.

[35] Art. 19(a)(1) Accounting Directive, introduced by art. 1(1) NFRD.

[36] On the notion of double materiality see e.g., R. Gourdel, I. Monasterolo, N. Dunz, A. Mazzocchetti, and L. Parisi, The Double Materiality of Climate Physical and Transition Risks in the Euro Area, 2022, ECB Working Paper Series No. 2665, 6–7.

[37] For a discussion on this see P. Iglesias-Rodríguez, The disclosure of corporate social responsibility in the EU after Directive 2014/95, 2016, 37(10), The Company Lawyer, 319–326.

[38] The Disclosures Regulation—Regulation (EU) 2019/2088 of the European Parliament and of the Council of 27 November 2019 on sustainability-related disclosures in the financial services sector OJ L 317/1—contains a comprehensive regime regarding sustainability reporting that also applies to credit institutions that provide portfolio management. However, the focus of the Disclosures Regulation is on investments and financial products and, hence, it falls beyond the scope of this chapter's analysis, which relates to commercial banks and their core activities.

Commercial Banks Subject to Sustainability Reporting: Towards an Expanded Subjective Scope

The NFRD's sustainability reporting obligations apply to limited liability companies that comply concurrently with three criteria, namely being large, of public interest, and with over 500 employees.[39] While all commercial banks are deemed as public-interest entities,[40] not all of them are necessarily large companies[41] or have more than 500 employees. More generally, not all credit institutions that provide commercial banking-like services are limited liability companies. The CSRD Proposal expands the scope of application of sustainability reporting duties of the Accounting Directive to a broader set of entities. Notably, it eliminates the requirements of being a public-interest company, and of having more than 500 employees and, instead, it proposes a system where sustainability reporting applies to companies that are either large, or listed in the EU—with the exception of micro-companies—or both.[42] In addition, when it comes to credit institutions, the CSRD Proposal determines that sustainability reporting obligations apply to them regardless of their specific legal form, including to those that are not limited liability companies—e.g., certain mutual and cooperative banks.[43] Despite these proposed changes, which according to the Commission would almost quadruplicate the number of entities covered by sustainability reporting obligations,[44] it is unclear the extent to which this may ultimately have a major impact on the number of commercial banks that would be under the remit of the CSRD Proposal. Notably, if a commercial bank is not large, the sustainability reporting duties would apply to it only if it is listed in the EU, and the vast majority of banks in the EU—more than 90%—are not

[39] Arts. 1(1) and 19(a)(1) Accounting Directive, introduced by art. 1(1) NFRD.

[40] Art. 2(1)(b) Accounting Directive.

[41] According to art. 3(4) of the Accounting Directive, these are those fulfilling at least two criteria among the following: (1) a balance sheet exceeding €20,000,000; (2) a net turnover over €40,000,000; (3) more than 250 employees.

[42] Art. 1(3) CSRD (as agreed by the Council and the Parliament on 30 June 2022), amending art. 19(a) of the Accounting Directive.

[43] Explanatory Memorandum, recital 23 and art. 1(1)—amending art. 1 of the Accounting Directive—CSRD Proposal.

[44] From the current 11,600 companies subject to the NFRD reporting obligations, to approximately 49,000 companies—see CSRD Proposal, 10.

listed.[45] Likewise, while the inclusion of mutual and cooperative banks within the scope of application of the CSRD Proposal broadens the types of credit institutions that must report on sustainability, these do not suit the definition of commercial banks. A more ambitious approach by the CSRD Proposal could have included within its scope of application all credit institutions. However, this option was not truly considered by EU policy makers and, some key stakeholders, such as the European Banking Federation, as well as the ECB opposed a move in such direction.[46] The agreement between the Council and the European Parliament of 30 June 2022[47] introduced a phased-in implementation approach whereby small and non-complex credit institutions[48] would be subject to sustainability reporting from 1 January 2026 onwards.[49] However, this would not imply a substantial change in the scope of application of the CSRD because small and non-complex credit institutions would still be outside the scope of sustainability reporting obligations, unless they are large or listed entities—excluding micro-undertakings.[50] The CSRD Proposal's approach and its lack of embracement of the whole spectrum of credit institutions within its scope of application contrasts with the approach followed by the Commission in its CRR III Proposal of 27 October 2021, which proposes that all credit institutions, regardless of their size, complexity, or listing status must disclose information on environmental,

[45] European Commission, Study on the Non-Financial Reporting Directive. Final report (November 2020), 42.

[46] European Banking Federation, Position of the European Banking Federation on the Corporate Sustainability Reporting Directive (September 2021), 4, https://www.ebf.eu/wp-content/uploads/2021/09/EBF_CSRD_Final.pdf; Opinion of the European Central Bank of 7 September 2021 on a proposal for a directive amending Directive 2013/34/EU, Directive 2004/109/EC, Directive 2006/43/EC and Regulation (EU) No 537/2014, as regards corporate sustainability reporting (CON/2021/27) OJ C 446/02, para 4.4.

[47] Council of the European Union, Dossier interinstitutionnel: 2021/0104(COD), 10835/22 (Brussels, 30 June 2022).

[48] As defined by art. 4(1)(145) CRR.

[49] Art. 5 CSRD (as agreed by the Council and the Parliament on 30 June 2022)—see Council of the European Union, Dossier interinstitutionnel: 2021/0104(COD), 10835/22 (Brussels, 30 June 2022).

[50] Art. 5 CSRD (as agreed by the Council and the Parliament on 30 June 2022)—see Council of the European Union, Dossier interinstitutionnel: 2021/0104(COD), 10,835/22 (Brussels, 30 June 2022).

social and governance (ESG)[51] risks to which they are exposed, including physical risks and transition risks.[52] Such an expanded scope of application to all credit institutions signifies an important change compared to the CRR II regime, which imposes ESG risks' disclosure obligations only to credit institutions that are both large and listed in the EU.[53] In the view of the Commission, the underlying rationale for this policy shift lies in the limited effectiveness of the CRR II regime, which excludes a number of credit institutions from the obligations regarding the disclosure of ESG risks[54] and hence hinders the ability of markets and financial supervisors to properly assess the ESG risks to which credit institutions are exposed.[55] Likewise, both the Commission and the ECB noted that the degree of exposure of a credit institution to ESG risks is not by all means proportional to its complexity or size and, therefore, all credit institutions should be required to disclose those risks regardless of their specific features.[56] The approach followed by the CRR III Proposal also evidences that an expansive scope of application is not incompatible with the notion of proportionality. For example, while the CRR regulatory regime encompasses the idea of double materiality as regards ESG risks' reporting,[57] the CRR III Proposal determines that for small and non-complex credit institutions, disclosure requirements must be limited to

[51] Some of the EU legal developments discussed in this chapter specifically use the term 'ESG risks', which refers to sustainability risks—see CRR III Proposal, 30.

[52] Art. 1 CRR III Proposal amending art. 449a of the CRR.

[53] Art. 449a CRR.

[54] CRR III Proposal, 32.

[55] Recital 40 CRR III Proposal.

[56] Recital 40 CRR III Proposal and Opinion of the European Central Bank of 24 March 2022 on a proposal for amendments to Regulation (EU) No. 575/2013 of the European Parliament and of the Council as regards requirements for credit risk, credit valuation adjustment risk, operational risk, market risk and the output floor (CON/2022/11) 2022, OJ C 233/02, para 8.3.

[57] Art. 434a of the CRR delegates to the European Banking Authority (EBA) the development of draft implementing technical standards that define, among others, the rules applicable to ESG risks' disclosures by credit institutions. EBA's draft implementing technical standards determine that credit institutions must disclose both the ESG risks to which they are exposed and how their own actions contribute to the mitigation of ESG risks—see European Banking Authority, Final Report. Final draft implementing technical standards on prudential disclosures on ESG risks in accordance with Article 449a CRR (EBA/ITS/2022/01, 24 January 2022), recitals 3 and 15.

information about their exposure to ESG risks.[58] Proportionality is also embraced in the rules on the periodicity of the ESG risks' reporting, which is annual for small and non-complex credit institutions—compared to the default regime, which requires semi-annual reporting.[59]

EU Binding Common Reporting Standards and the Limits to Commercial Banks' Sustainability Reporting Discretion

The CSRD Proposal introduces both greater detail and harmonization regarding the content of sustainability reporting.[60] The provisions of the NFRD concerning the latter are rather vague and give companies substantial freedom in the choice of both what sustainability-related information to disclose and how to do so,[61] hence bringing the risk of lack of comparability, consistency, and relevance of sustainability information.[62] The Commission noted that the NFRD's framework indeed suffers from important weaknesses, as evidenced by the failure of companies to report on all relevant sustainability information and by problems in the reliability and comparability of the information that they disclose.[63] Although in the years 2017 and 2019 the Commission led some harmonization efforts through the issuance of non-binding guidelines on the methodology regarding the reporting of non-financial information,[64] these measures were insufficient to effectively address the caveats of the NFRD's reporting framework and, in the view of the Commission, this justified legislative intervention and a shift towards a system of EU

[58] Art. 1 CRR III Proposal amending art. 449a of the CRR.

[59] Art. 1 CRR III Proposal amending art. 449a of the CRR.

[60] Notably, through the new content of art. 19(a).

[61] Iglesias-Rodríguez, 2016, 322–323.

[62] Iglesias-Rodríguez, 2016, 324.

[63] European Commission, Commission Staff Working Document: Fitness Check on the EU framework for public reporting by companies, *Accompanying the document* Report from the Commission to the European Parliament, the Council and the European Economic and Social Committee on the review clauses in Directives 2013/34/EU, 2014/95/EU, and 2013/50/EU (Brussels, 21 April 2021, SWD (2021) 81 final), 6.

[64] Communication from the Commission—Guidelines on non-financial reporting (methodology for reporting non-financial information) C/2017/4234, OJ C 215/1; and Communication from the Commission—Guidelines on non-financial reporting: Supplement on reporting climate-related information C/2019/4490, OJ C 209/1.

binding common reporting standards.[65] Under the proposed system, the Commission would play a key role through the development, by way of delegated acts, of common European sustainability reporting standards to be applied by companies in their sustainability reporting.[66] This regulatory model largely builds on the one embraced by the Taxonomy Regulation, which delegates to the Commission the development of the content and methodology of the companies' reporting concerning the environmental sustainability of their activities.[67] Through such delegation the Commission has supplemented the content of the Taxonomy Regulation[68] and has specified reporting rules applicable to the main activities of commercial banks.[69] For example, the Taxonomy Regulation Delegated Act determines that commercial banks must disclose their Green Asset Ratio (GAR), which shows the proportion of their assets—e.g. loans and debt securities—that finance or are invested in environmentally sustainable economic activities.[70]

Besides the direct impact on the commercial banks' sustainability reporting, the expanded subjective and substantive scope of sustainability reporting obligations under the Taxonomy Regulation and the CSRD Proposal may also have an indirect positive effect on the quality of the commercial banks' reporting; with a greater number of companies with which commercial banks interact being subject to a more detailed and harmonized sustainability reporting framework, banks should be able to

[65] Recital 32 CSRD Proposal.

[66] Art. 1(4) CSRD (as agreed by the Council and the Parliament on 30 June 2022), introducing Articles 19b, 19c, and 19d in the Accounting Directive, and art. 1(7b) CSRD (as agreed by the Council and the Parliament on 30 June 2022).

[67] Under the Taxonomy Regulation, undertakings subject to the NFRD's sustainability reporting duties are required to disclose how and the extent to which their activities are environmentally sustainable—art. 8 Taxonomy Regulation.

[68] Commission Delegated Regulation (EU) 2021/2178 of 6 July 2021 supplementing Regulation (EU) 2020/852 of the European Parliament and of the Council by specifying the content and presentation of information to be disclosed by undertakings subject to Articles 19a or 29a of Directive 2013/34/EU concerning environmentally sustainable economic activities, and specifying the methodology to comply with that disclosure obligation OJ L 443/9 (Taxonomy Regulation Delegated Act).

[69] Recital 1, art. 4, and annex 5 Taxonomy Regulation Delegated Act.

[70] Section 1.2.1 annex 5 Taxonomy Regulation Delegated Act.

offer a more accurate portrayal of their sustainability risks and impacts in their own reporting.[71]

The Potential of Trusteeship Strategies on the Quality of Commercial Banks' Sustainability Reporting

The NFRD excludes sustainability information from the audit regime applicable to financial information[72] and envisages a very limited role for auditors as regards the former, whereby they must merely check that companies provide the statements or reports with the relevant sustainability information.[73] However, there is not a requirement to audit and verify the content of the sustainability information provided. This, in turn, brings about the risk that companies subject to sustainability reporting under the NFRD lack incentives to disclose sustainability risks and impacts accurately and consistently.[74] Indeed, research on the quality of mandatory non-financial reporting by banks shows that this is rather low.[75] Similarly, a report published by the ECB in March 2022[76] that examined a sample of 109 banks showed that circa 75% of them did not report whether climate and environmental risks have an impact on their risk profile,[77] and 57% did not explain how climate and environmental

[71] For instance, the European Banking Federation acknowledged that "standardised disclosures from non-financial corporates will be a key enabler in ensuring that banks [...] are able to assess the sustainability profile of their portfolios"—see European Banking Federation (2021).

[72] Art. 34(3) Accounting Directive, introduced by art. 1(5) NFRD.

[73] Art. 19(a)(5) Accounting Directive, introduced by art. 1(1) NFRD; and art. 29(a)(5) Accounting Directive, introduced by art. 1(3) NFRD.

[74] See e.g., Iglesias-Rodríguez, 2016, 325.

[75] P. Schröder, Mandatory non-financial reporting in the banking industry: assessing reporting quality and determinants, 2022, 9(1) Cogent Business & Management, 1–24, 14. The study focused on mandatory non-financial reporting in the period 2017–2019 by the 100 largest banking institutions operating in Germany.

[76] European Central Bank, Supervisory assessment of institutions' climate-related and environmental risks disclosures. ECB report on banks' progress towards transparent disclosure of their climate-related and environmental risk profiles (March 2022), https://www.bankingsupervision.europa.eu/ecb/pub/pdf/ssm.ECB_Report_on_climate_and_environmental_disclosures_202203~4ae33f2a70.en.pdf.

[77] European Central Bank, 2022, 16.

risks may potentially influence their strategy.[78] The CSRD regime determines that auditing must extend to the actual content of sustainability information[79] and, in doing so, to some extent it blurs the dividing lines between the auditing of financial reporting and the auditing of sustainability reporting. The CSRD sustainability reporting audit rules would have an expansive effect as they would also apply to taxonomy-related disclosures.[80] Under the proposed regime, auditors[81] would just provide a limited assurance audit,[82] which is less exhaustive than a reasonable assurance audit.[83] However, despite the relatively limited scope of the proposed auditing requirement, it would mean an important shift from a sustainability reporting system where compliance is pursued primarily through regulatory strategies based on reporting rules and standards[84] towards a system that gives greater preeminence to trusteeship

[78] European Central Bank, 2022, 19.

[79] Art. 1(10) CSRD (as agreed by the Council and the Parliament on 30 June 2022), amending art. 34 of the Accounting Directive.

[80] Art. 8 Taxonomy Regulation.

[81] The CSRD rules also encompass the possibility, subject to conditionality, that independent assurance services providers carry out the assurance of the sustainability reporting—see e.g., Art. 1(10) CSRD (as agreed by the Council and the Parliament on 30 June 2022), amending art. 34 of the Accounting Directive.

[82] Art. 1(10) CSRD (as agreed by the Council and the Parliament on 30 June 2022), amending art. 34 of the Accounting Directive.

[83] Limited assurance audits provide a negative opinion to the effect that nothing in the information appears to be not properly reported. In contrast, a reasonable assurance audit offers a positive opinion indicating that the information is properly reported—A. M. Brockett and Z. Rezaee, Corporate Sustainability: Integrating Performance and Reporting, Hoboken, New Jersey, John Wiley and Sons, 2012, 292.

[84] Regulatory strategies are aimed at constraining the behavior of the agent, for example through rules and standards—see R. Kraakman, J. Armour, P. Davies, L. Enriques, H. B. Hansmann, G. Hertig, K. J. Hopt, H. Kanda, and E. B. Rock, The Anatomy of Corporate Law: A Comparative and Functional Approach, 2nd ed., Oxford, Oxford University Press, 2009, 38–40.

governance strategies[85] that put at their center auditors as corporate gatekeepers[86] whose role is to mitigate potential agency problems between the entities providing sustainability reporting and the parties to whom the sustainability information is addressed.

The introduction of the enhanced auditing requirement by the CSRD Proposal fosters the external control over sustainability reporting and hence increases the ex-ante incentives of commercial banks to properly assess information on their sustainability exposures and impacts and to report such information in an accurate and consistent manner that complies with applicable reporting rules.[87] Besides the potential negative reputational impact[88] that low-quality reporting may have on a commercial bank, non-compliant sustainability disclosures may also expose directors of commercial banks to an increased risk of liability. In this respect, both the NFRD and the CSRD Proposal determine that "the members of the administrative, management and supervisory bodies" of the entities subject to sustainability reporting obligations are collectively responsible for guaranteeing that the sustainability information is drafted

[85] Governance strategies are aimed at facilitating the control of the agent's behavior by the principal; one of such strategies is the trusteeship strategy whose target is to mitigate the agents' conflicts of interest and their incentives to behave in ways that are detrimental to their principals—see Kraakman, Armour, Davies, Enriques, Hansmann, Hertig, Hopt, Kanda, and Rock, 2009, 38–39, 42–44.

[86] On the role and limitations of auditors as gatekeepers see e.g., J. C. Coffee Jr., The Acquiescent Gatekeeper: Reputational Intermediaries, Auditor Independence and the Governance of Accounting, 2001, Columbia Law & Economics Working Paper No. 191, https://scholarship.law.columbia.edu/faculty_scholarship/1249.

[87] On the potential of third-party independent assurance in fostering the quality of sustainability reporting see e.g., N. Dando and T. Swift, Transparency and Assurance Minding the Credibility Gap, 2003, 44 Journal of Business Ethics, 195–200.

[88] On the links between sustainability reporting and banks' reputation see e.g., R. Bischof, N. Bourdier, P. Gassmann, P. Wackerbeck, and S. Marek, European Bank Transformation: Why Banks Can No Longer Ignore ESG (Strategy&, 7 December 2021), https://www.strategyand.pwc.com/de/en/industries/financial-services/transforming-eu-banks/esg.html. More generally, on the links between the degree of sustainability of a credit institutions' activities and reputation see European Central Bank, Guide on climate-related and environmental risks. Supervisory expectations relating to risk management and disclosure (November 2020), 39–40, https://www.bankingsupervision.europa.eu/ecb/pub/pdf/ssm.202011finalguideonclimate-relatedandenvironmentalrisks~58213f6564.en.pdf.

and published in accordance with the applicable EU statutory sustainability reporting framework, and that they may be liable for the failure to do so.[89]

The EU law developments examined in this section show a trend towards a regulatory model where banks' discretion as regards the scope and content of their sustainability reporting is more limited. This, by way of an expansion of the subjective scope of sustainability reporting obligations, a greater centralization of rulemaking responsibilities in respect of sustainability reporting duties at the EU legislative and administrative levels, and a strengthening of trusteeship strategies that grant greater weight to auditors as gatekeepers of commercial banks' sustainability reporting. While these mechanisms suffer from some potential limitations, they nonetheless have the potential to enhance the quality of commercial banks' sustainability reporting and hence, to diminish agency problems between commercial banks and stakeholders targeted by or with an interest in sustainability reporting. At the same time, while these developments in the field of sustainability reporting do not impose actual obligations on commercial banks to pursue sustainability, one of their core underlying policy rationales is to foster sustainability. Hence, from this point of view, it could be argued that they embrace a shift towards a model where non-shareholder stakeholder interests are given greater weight in the corporate objective of commercial banks.

3 Sustainability as an Objective to be Considered (and Pursued?) by Commercial Banks

The concept of the company's interest, which largely determines the company's objective, is interpreted differently across jurisdictions, but most approaches fall into two main categories. The first is the shareholder value approach model, which identifies the interest of the company with the interest of its shareholders. Consequently, under this model, directors are expected to act in a way that promotes and maximizes the interest of the company understood as the interest of its owners.[90]

[89] Art. 33 Accounting Directive, art.1(4) NFRD amending art. 33(1) of the Accounting Directive, and art. 1(9) CSRD (as agreed by the Council and the Parliament on 30 June 2022), amending art. 33(1) of the Accounting Directive.

[90] For a thorough discussion on the shareholder value approach see e.g., A. Keay, The Corporate Objective, Cheltenham: Edward Elgar, 2011, 40–113.

The second is the stakeholder value approach, which proposes that the interest of the company includes, not only the interests of its shareholders but also those of non-shareholder stakeholders who are affected directly or indirectly by the actions or omissions of a company. Hence, according to this model, when directors take decisions they are expected to consider and pursue the interests of a wider set of constituencies than in the shareholder value approach.[91] In addition, there are hybrid models that combine elements of both the shareholder value approach and the stakeholder value approach, such as the enlightened shareholder value approach, which postulates that directors must pursue the interest of the company for the benefit of its owners but, in doing so, they must consider the interest of other non-shareholder stakeholders.[92]

EU law has traditionally been reluctant to define the notion of the company's objective and the substantive scope of the directors' general duties. However, the focus of EU policies in the field of company law and corporate governance has primarily been on the promotion of the internal market[93] through policies that largely favor shareholders' interests[94]; this, in turn, has resulted in a legal and regulatory framework that generally embraces the shareholder value approach.[95]

In recent years, EU law has started to acknowledge, albeit timidly, the importance that companies consider stakeholders' interests and sustainability in their decision-making. For example, according to the Long-Term Shareholder Engagement Directive,[96] stakeholder engagement in corporate governance is instrumental to companies pursuing longer-term

[91] For a comprehensive overview of the stakeholder value approach see e.g., Keay, 2011, 114–172.

[92] On the see e.g., D. Millon, Enlightened Shareholder Value, Social Responsibility and the Redefinition of Corporate Purpose Without Law, in P.M. Vasudev, and S. Watson (eds.) Corporate Genlightened shareholder value approachovernance after the Financial Crisis, Cheltenham, Edward Elgar, 2012, 68–100.

[93] See Ernst & Young, Study on directors' duties and sustainable corporate governance. Final Report, Brussels, European Commission, 2020, 43.

[94] CFA Institute, Corporate Governance Policy in the European Union Through an Investor's Lens, Charlottesville, VA, CFA Institute, 2016, 7.

[95] CFA Institute, 2016, 27.

[96] Directive (EU) 2017/828 of the European Parliament and of the Council of 17 May 2017 amending Directive 2007/36/EC as regards the encouragement of long-term shareholder engagement OJ L 132/1.

interests and hence, it should be encouraged.[97] In the banking field, the Capital Requirements Directive IV (CRD IV)[98] explicitly recognizes the value of credit institutions' responsibility towards stakeholders and society as an instrument for regaining the trust of the latter in the financial sector in the aftermath of the global financial crisis.[99] Despite this, the definition of the corporate objective and of the role of directors in its pursuit has largely been left to the discretion of the Member States; this has resulted in a fragmented system where companies are subject to different regimes, some of which rely on ineffective self-regulation.[100] The CRD VI Proposal and the CSDD Proposal have proposed reforms that address, among others, the problems of fragmentation[101] through new binding rules that would reshape the way in which banks across the EU should consider sustainability in their activities. The remainder of this section examines these two legislative proposals and offers and assessment on whether and how they would redefine the duties of commercial banks' directors and the corporate objective of commercial banks.

The CRD VI Proposal: Inward-looking Sustainability and Directors' Duty of Care in Commercial Banks

The CRD VI Proposal acknowledges the prudential implications of ESG risks and requires that credit institutions put in place and periodically review governance and risk management strategies, policies, and processes to identify, oversee, manage, report, and mitigate ESG physical and transition risks and exposures.[102] This involves, inter alia, the performance of tests to measure their resilience vis-à-vis long-term negative ESG impacts[103] and the adoption of decisions concerning the type, amount,

[97] Recital 14 Long-Term Shareholder Engagement Directive.

[98] Directive 2013/36/EU of the European Parliament and of the Council of 26 June 2013 on access to the activity of credit institutions and the prudential supervision of credit institutions and investment firms, amending Directive 2002/87/EC and repealing Directives 2006/48/EC and 2006/49/EC OJ L 176/338.

[99] Recital 52 CRD IV.

[100] CSDD Proposal, 2, 10, 11.

[101] CRD VI Proposal, 11; and CSDD Proposal, 3.

[102] Art. 1(12), (13), (14) CRD VI Proposal amending arts. 73, 74(1), 76(1), (2) of CRD IV, respectively.

[103] Art. 1(17) CRD VI Proposal inserting art. 87a(3) in CRD IV.

and allocation of capital to deal with ESG risks.[104] Conversely, the CRD VI Proposal requires competent authorities of the Member States to assess, monitor, review, and test the robustness, proportionality and appropriateness of the credit institutions' framework and actions aimed at addressing ESG risks.[105]

The CRD VI Proposal somewhat contributes to reshaping the objective standard of the duty of care, skill and diligence applicable to directors of credit institutions by requiring that "the management body shall possess collective knowledge, skills and experience to be able to adequately understand...the associated risks it is exposed to, in the short, medium and long term, taking into account the environmental, social and governance factors".[106] Consequently, the overall knowledge, skill, and experience that is reasonably expected of the board of directors of a commercial bank would include ESG risks and their potential impact. The wording of the CRD VI Proposal establishes a collective—rather than an individual—qualified objective standard of the duty of care and, therefore, according to it, not all the directors of a commercial bank would be expected to have expertise on and knowledge about ESG risks. However, in terms of liability, the reach of this provision is potentially pervasive because it may lead to liability of all the members of the management body of a commercial bank for breaches of the duty of care, skill, and diligence in relation to actions or omissions with regards to or with an impact on ESG risks.

When it comes to the exercise of administrative powers in relation to the governance and risk management strategies, policies, and processes put in place by credit institutions to address ESG risks, the CRD VI Proposal establishes a two-level allocation of powers. On the one side, competent authorities of the Member States are given, primarily, supervisory powers in relation to those strategies, policies, and processes.[107] The CRD VI Proposal acknowledges the relevance of enforcement powers in relation to ESG risks by including, among the list of minimum supervisory powers of Member State competent authorities, the power to require

[104] Art. 1(12) CRD VI Proposal amending art. 73 of CRD IV.

[105] Art. 1(17) CRD VI Proposal inserting art. 87a(1), (2), (4) in CRD IV and amending arts. 98 and 100 of CRD IV.

[106] Art. 1(19) CRD VI Proposal amending art. 91 of CRD IV.

[107] See e.g., art. 1(17) CRD VI Proposal inserting art. 87a(1)–(4) in CRD IV.

credit institutions to adjust their risk management, governance, and business models to address ESG transition risks.[108] On the other side, EU level authorities are entrusted with rulemaking responsibilities aimed at guaranteeing the consistency of the regulatory and supervisory measures and practices put in place by the competent authorities of the Member States; for example, the European Banking Authority (EBA), the European Securities and Markets Authority (ESMA) and the European Insurance and Occupational Pensions Authority (EIOPA) are delegated the joint development of guidelines that guarantee consistency in the stress tests of ESG risks carried out by competent authorities of the Member States.[109] This decentralized model allows Member State competent authorities to tailor supervision to domestic conditions. However, at the same time, it brings about a potential risk of supervisory inconsistency in the application of the CRD VI Proposal rules. In this respect, while one of the objectives of the CRD VI Proposal is to foster the consistency of the supervisory practices of Member State competent authorities in relation to ESG risks that affect credit institutions,[110] those authorities may not necessarily have strong incentives to enforce ESG risk rules actively and strongly against domestic commercial banks, for example if this puts them in a less favorable position vis-à-vis commercial banks of other Member States.[111] Under the proposed system, the EBA would receive extensive delegations to issue both guidelines on criteria and methodologies relevant to the supervision of commercial banks' governance and risk management strategies, policies, and processes regarding ESG risks,[112] and guidelines addressed to Member State competent authorities aimed at guaranteeing their independence and preventing conflicts of interests in their functioning.[113] Hence, the quality of EBA's guidelines and their degree of acceptance among domestic competent authorities would be

[108] Art. 1(26) CRD VI Proposal amending art. 104 of CRD IV.

[109] Art. 1(25) CRD VI Proposal amending art. 100 of CRD IV.

[110] Recital 35 CRD VI Proposal.

[111] On the issue of supervisory race to the bottom in the EU see e.g., N. Véron, The Wirecard Debacle Calls for a Rethink of EU, not just German, Financial Reporting Supervision (Peterson Institute for International Economics, 30 June 2020), https://www.piie.com/blogs/realtime-economic-issues-watch/wirecard-debacle-calls-rethink-eu-not-just-german-financial.

[112] See e.g., art. 1(17) CRD VI Proposal inserting art. 87a(5) in CRD IV.

[113] See e.g., art. 1(2) CRD VI Proposal amending art. 4(4) of CRD IV.

critical factors in deterring the latter from engaging in potentially biased supervisory behaviors that would hinder the accomplishment of the CRD VI Proposal's objectives.

The CSDD Proposal: Outward-looking Sustainability, Directors' Duties and the Emergence of an EU-Wide Corporate Objective for Commercial Banks

The CSDD Proposal institutes two duties that bind directors of commercial banks[114] to take stock of sustainability factors in their decision-making. The first is a duty of care—as defined by the CSDD Proposal—which requires that "when fulfilling their duty to act in the best interest of the company, directors [...] take into account the consequences of their decisions for sustainability matters, including, where applicable, human rights, climate change and environmental consequences, including in the short, medium and long term".[115] The second is a duty of due diligence whereby directors must institute, carry out, and monitor due diligence in relation to human rights and the environment[116]; this due diligence duty imposes, among others, a requirement for directors to identify, prevent, mitigate, or eliminate negative impacts of their companies on human rights and the environment.[117]

As regards the first duty, the CSDD Proposal's characterization of the duty "to act in the best interest of the company" as a duty of care raises some questions about the scope of potential liability of commercial banks' directors for breach of such duty and the latter's effectiveness as an instrument to direct the behavior of directors towards sustainable choices. In this respect, traditionally the duty to act in the best interest of the company has not been regarded as a duty of care but rather as a duty of loyalty that binds directors to do what is best for the company.[118] Consequently, judicial tests aimed at ascertaining whether directors have

[114] The CSDD rules would apply to companies, including credit institutions, which comply with certain criteria regarding number of employees and net turnover—see arts. 2–3CSDD Proposal.

[115] Art. 25(1) CSDD Proposal.

[116] Arts. 4–11, and 26(1) CSDD Proposal.

[117] Art. 4(1)(b)–(c) CSDD Proposal.

[118] See e.g., S. Rousseau, E. Mackaay, P. Larouche, and A. Parent, Business Law and Economics for Civil Law Systems, Cheltenham, Edward Elgar, 2021, 214.

complied with such duty tend to focus on whether they acted in good faith and, notably, whether directors reasonably believed that they were pursuing the best interest of the company.[119] In contrast, judicial tests of compliance with the duty of care generally focus on the assessment of whether directors are acting with the standard of conduct expected of a reasonable business person.[120] This approach of the CSDD Proposal has some limitations in terms of creating the proper incentives for directors of commercial banks to act in a way that fosters sustainability. In this respect, the CSDD Proposal may lead to a system where failures of directors of commercial banks to "take into account the consequences of their decisions for sustainability matters" would not be deemed to be in breach of the duty to act in the best interest of a commercial bank as long as the directors concerned are able to show mere compliance with the requirements of the duty of care, which relate primarily to proper acquisition of information and its due assessment[121] rather than to broader considerations about good faith. Hence, under the proposed system, directors of commercial banks may have strong incentives to carefully collect and assess information on sustainability impacts (e.g., in relation to the credit activities of their banks), but they may not necessarily have strong incentives to take decisions that actually embrace sustainability or mitigate potential adverse sustainability impacts.

More generally, the regime encompassed by article 25 of the CSDD Proposal is one that does not require directors of commercial banks to act in a way that promotes sustainability or to mitigate potential negative impacts on sustainability but rather one where directors are merely required to take into consideration the effects of their decisions on sustainability. In this regard, the CSDD Proposal advocates a model with some similarities to the UK's enlightened shareholder value approach[122]

[119] See e.g., R. McCorquodale and S. Neely, Directors Duties and Human Rights Impacts: A Comparative Approach, 2022, 22(2), Journal of Corporate Law Studies, 605–639, 614–615.

[120] See e.g. T. Klauberg, General Case on Directors' Duties, in M. Siems and D. Cabrelli (eds.), Comparative Company Law: A Case-Based Approach, 2nd ed., Oxford, Hart Publishing, 2018, 68.

[121] See e.g., E. Banks, Corporate Governance: Financial Responsibility, Controls and Ethics, Houndmills, Palgrave, 2004, 40.

[122] The enlightened shareholder value approach is enshrined in Section 172 of the Companies Act 2006.

but tailored to the corporate governance system encompassed by each Member State, in the sense that, unlike the UK's model, it does not give preeminence to the maximization of the interest of shareholders but, instead, it requires that regardless of the system followed in a given Member State, directors take stock of sustainability concerns in their decision-making. Research has shown that the enlightened shareholder value approach has a rather limited effect in fostering directors' embracement of non-shareholder stakeholders' interests[123]; in addition, according to some research, the banking sector is one where directors are particularly dismissive of the principles embodied by the enlightened shareholder value approach.[124] Consequently, it is highly unlikely that article 25 of the CSDD Proposal in itself would lead to directors of commercial banks in the EU being proner to the adoption of more sustainable policies and decisions.

Compared to the duty of care, the duty of due diligence, contemplated in article 26 of the CSDD Proposal, shows, in principle, greater potential for advancing the behavior of commercial banks' directors towards more sustainable choices. The CSDD Proposal's due diligence regime requires companies to, among other things, embrace due diligence in their policies, and to identify, prevent, mitigate, or eliminate adverse impacts on human rights and the environment that source directly or indirectly from their operations.[125] Directors are responsible for setting up and monitoring all these due diligence actions and policies and for inputting potential or actual adverse impacts on human rights or the environment into their company's strategy.[126] Hence, the due diligence duty requires directors of commercial banks, not only to consider sustainability issues but also to take specific actions to integrate sustainability in their decision-making.

The regime envisaged by the CSDD Proposal is far reaching as it binds companies subject to it, including commercial banks, to address due diligence not only in relation to their own operations, but also in relation to those of their subsidiaries as well as "the value chain operations

[123] See e.g., A. Keay and T. Iqbal, The Impact of Enlightened Shareholder Value, 2019, 4 Journal of Business Law, 304–327.

[124] See e.g., N. Grier, Enlightened shareholder value: did directors deliver? 2014, 2 Juridical Review, 95–111.

[125] Art. 4 CSDD Proposal.

[126] Art. 26 CSDD Proposal.

carried out by entities with whom the company has an established business relationship".[127] When it comes to credit institutions in their role as providers of financial services, the CSDD Proposal determines that such value chain refers only to the activities and operations of the credit institutions' professional or business clients that are receiving a credit, loan or, more generally, financial services from them.[128] The implications of this regime for commercial banks are pervasive. First, according to it, they are required to monitor the activities of pertinent clients with a view to ascertaining whether these bring about potential or actual adverse impacts on human rights and/or the environment.[129] Moreover, according to the provisions of the CSDD Proposal, as a general rule, if a commercial bank cannot prevent, properly mitigate, minimize, or bring to an end adverse impacts sourcing from the operations of a relevant client, it must not extend existing or start new commercial relations with it.[130] In addition, if the law applicable to the contract(s) with the client allows it, the commercial bank must either temporarily suspend existing commercial relationships with the client or, when the adverse impact is severe, terminate the relevant commercial relationship(s) with it.[131] The consequences resulting from a breach of these rules are extensive as any consequential damage may lead to civil liability of a commercial bank.[132] Likewise, these rules have a significant potential impact on the behavior of banks' clients as they may strongly deter them from engaging in activities with adverse sustainability impacts. Notwithstanding, the CSDD Proposal envisages a special regime for companies providing financial services, such as commercial banks, that somewhat waters down the scope of the due diligence obligations that bind them and their directors.

Firstly, the CSDD Proposal excludes from the value chain of commercial banks SMEs that are receiving funding or insurance from them.[133] Bank loans constitute a major source of financing for SMEs in the Euro

[127] Art. 1(1)(a) CSDD Proposal; see also arts. 6(1), 7(1), and 8(1) CSDD Proposal.

[128] Recital 19 and art. 3(g) CSDD Proposal.

[129] Art. 6 CSDD Proposal.

[130] Arts. 7(5) and 8(6) CSDD Proposal.

[131] Arts. 7(5) and 8(6) CSDD Proposal.

[132] Art. 22 CSDD Proposal.

[133] Art. 3(g) CSDD Proposal.

area[134] and, hence, their exclusion limits substantially the sample of companies whose actions with a negative impact on sustainability may preclude them from receiving funding or even trigger a loan contract termination by a commercial bank.

Secondly, according to the CSDD Proposal, in cases where commercial banks cannot prevent, properly mitigate, minimize, or eliminate severe adverse impacts sourcing from the activities of a client, they are not required to terminate financial services contracts with such client—including loan and credit contracts—if that contractual termination "can be reasonably expected to cause substantial prejudice to the entity to whom that service is being provided".[135] While, under the CSDD Proposal commercial banks would still have the power to terminate those contracts, even when there is a substantial prejudice for the client, it is unclear whether they may have a strong incentive to do so, due to two main reasons. First, the early termination of a credit or loan contract would likely cause financial prejudice to both the client/debtor and the commercial bank/creditor; the CSDD Proposal does not define what a 'substantial prejudice' for a client means, and, hence, the determination of whether this occurs in a given case is left to the discretion of a commercial bank, which consequently enjoys considerable leeway in making such determination; as early termination may involve important direct economic costs for the commercial bank,[136] the latter may have an incentive to interpret the notion of 'substantial prejudice' in a way that is beneficial for the client, even in cases where the latter's activities may lead to severe adverse impacts for human rights and/or the environment. Second, even though the CSDD Proposal stipulates that "Member States shall provide for the availability of an option to terminate the business relationship in contracts governed by their laws",[137] such contractual termination may be contentious, particularly when the commercial bank

[134] See e.g., European Central Bank, Survey on the Access to Finance of Enterprises in the euro area. April to September 2021 (November 2021), 18, https://www.ecb.europa.eu/stats/accesstofinancesofenterprises/pdf/ecb.safe202111~0380b0c0a2.en.pdf.

[135] Arts. 7(6) and 8(7) CSDD Proposal.

[136] On the risks of early redemption of loan contracts for banks see e.g., Basel Committee on Banking Supervision, Standards. Interest rate risk in the banking book, Basel, Bank for International Settlements, 2016, https://www.bis.org/bcbs/publ/d368.pdf.

[137] Arts. 7(5) and 8(6) CSDD Proposal.

justifies it on the grounds of the occurrence of an unresolved 'severe adverse impact'. The CSDD Proposal defines this concept in rather vague terms[138] and, as a result, the responsibility for determining the occurrence of a severe adverse impact largely falls in the discretion of a commercial bank, which in order to avoid potential litigation with a client affected by the termination may have an incentive to avoid characterizing an adverse impact as severe.

Thirdly, the scope of due diligence monitoring duties is more lenient for companies that provide financial services than for other companies in the sense that the former is required to identify potential or actual adverse impacts only prior to the provision of the financial service to the client.[139] Consequently, commercial banks would not be required to develop a system of ongoing monitoring of their clients' activities and hence the likelihood of an identification of clients' post-contract activities that bring about potential or actual adverse impacts would be low.

4 Summary and Concluding Remarks

This chapter has examined policy actions, legal proposals, and reforms regarding or with an impact on commercial banks' sustainability-related obligations. The main findings of the chapter as regards the questions formulated in the introduction are the following.

When it comes to the question of whether these policy actions, proposals, and reforms may be effective in fostering sustainability, the analysis has shown that despite their limitations, they show promise in increasing sustainable behavior by both commercial banks and firms that interact with them. On the one side, by giving greater public exposure to commercial banks' approaches and practices in relation to sustainability, and by expanding the substantive scope of their sustainability-related obligations, they may increase the incentives of commercial banks to further embrace sustainability. On the other side, by imposing on commercial banks sustainability-related obligations in relation to the activities of their

[138] Art. 3(l) of the CSDD Proposal defines 'severe adverse impact' as: "an adverse environmental impact or an adverse human rights impact that is especially significant by its nature, or affects a large number of persons or a large area of the environment, or which is irreversible, or is particularly difficult to remedy as a result of the measures necessary to restore the situation prevailing prior to the impact".

[139] Art. 6(3) CSDD Proposal.

clients, the EU sustainability regime has potential implications on the behavior of banks' clients and may discourage their engagement in activities with negative sustainability impacts that may hinder their access to credit.

The chapter also examined whether the assessed EU policy actions, proposals, and reforms may mitigate agency problems between commercial banks and stakeholders affected by or with an interest in sustainability. The expanded scope of sustainability reporting, the strengthening of trusteeship strategies in relation to it, and the institution of a series of duties that require commercial banks' directors to take stock of sustainability in their decision-making, limit the ability of commercial banks, as agents, to engage in unsustainable practices or, more generally, to disregard sustainability factors. At the same time, these measures help principals—i.e., stakeholders affected by or with an interest in sustainability—to monitor the behavior of commercial banks vis-à-vis sustainability and to hold them to account.

A key question examined in this chapter is the extent to which the EU policy actions, proposals, and reforms in the area of corporate and financial sustainability are leading to a redefinition of the corporate objective of commercial banks and of the duties of their directors. The analysis shows that relevant EU policy and legal developments expand substantially the catalog and scope of commercial banks' directors' duties in relation to sustainability, even though, in some respects, their design does not foster the incentives of commercial banks and their directors to pursue sustainability or to mitigate adverse sustainability impacts. As regards the corporate objective, the model embraced by the relevant EU legal developments in the field of corporate and financial sustainability is one that requires commercial banks' directors to consider sustainability aspects in their decision-making but it falls short of imposing an actual duty to pursue sustainability. Hence, from this perspective, this model resembles an enlightened shareholder value approach, rather than a stakeholder value approach. Nonetheless, this still represents an important policy shift in respect of the existing and prevailing system at the EU level, which primarily embraces the shareholder value approach.

An important policy question that is relevant for future reforms in this area, is the extent to which it would be appropriate to further move the commercial banks' corporate objective towards a stakeholder value approach, in a way that sustainability, as such, becomes an objective to be pursued by commercial banks' directors in their decision-making. While, undoubtedly, there are several benefits associated with a system where commercial banks actively pursue sustainability, we should also be mindful of the impact that a full shift towards a stakeholder value model—and the pace at which it takes place—might have on policy objectives different from sustainability but equally important. Commercial banks play a key role in the economy by channeling funds to business activities; hence, their willingness and ability to provide financing to certain sectors and activities may have a critical impact on the ability of the latter to produce and supply goods and services. The adoption of EU legal reforms whereby commercial banks would operate under a stakeholder value approach largely built around the concept of sustainability could dramatically limit their incentives and ability to provide financing to activities that may not be deemed as sustainable but that may be essential for society. This, in turn, could lead to a scenario of disorderly green transition where there is a mismatch between sustainability requirements imposed by law and regulation on the one side and the readiness of the economy to supply essential goods and services that comply with such sustainability criteria, on the other side.[140] The COVID-19 Pandemic and Russia's unlawful attack and invasion of Ukraine are reminders of the relevance that products that are not deemed as sustainable may have in guaranteeing health and/ or safety in critical situations, for the time being.[141] Any future reforms

[140] On the risks of a disorderly transition to net zero see e.g., O. Wyman, Decarbonisation and Disruption. Understanding the Financial Risks of a Disorderly Transition using Climate Scenarios, Geneva, United Nations Environment Programme, 2021, https://www.unepfi.org/wordpress/wp-content/uploads/2021/02/UNEP-FI-Decarbonisation-and-disruption.pdf.

[141] The COVID-19 Pandemic has led to a major increase in the demand, both by the medical sector and individuals, of plastic-made personal protective equipment essential for the protection of health, such as face masks—see e.g., European Environment Agency, Impacts of COVID-19 on single-use plastic in Europe's environment (Briefing no. 4/2021), https://www.eea.europa.eu/publications/impacts-of-covid-19-on. Russia's unlawful attack and invasion of Ukraine and the ensuing impact on the supply of energy towards Europe has led some EU countries, notably those highly dependent on Russia, such as Germany, to return to coal so as to guarantee that their own energy needs are met—see e.g., Germany reactivates coal power plants amid Russian gas supply threats (Euractiv, 9 March 2022), https://www.euractiv.com/section/energy/news/germany-reactivates-coal-power-plants-amid-russian-gas-supply-threats/.

with an impact on the corporate objective and the duties of directors of commercial banks should take stock of these considerations and go hand in hand with broader reforms of the productive system in the EU so as to avoid scenarios where there is a trade-off between the accomplishment of sustainability and the guaranteeing of critical societal objectives.

CHAPTER 10

Commercial Banks and Competition Concerns—SDG Policy Priorities

Lela Mélon and Alenka Recelj Mercina

1 Introduction

In today's world, banks are not limited to accumulating financial resources: their functions vary from accumulating temporarily free funds of individuals and legal persons and their placement, mediation in payments, transactions in the stock and foreign exchange markets, settlement and cash services, acquiring, virtual pooling, etc.[1] Furthermore, they are now expected to ensure continuous movement of funds in a

[1] See N. Semenova and A. Vasilkina, The Fundamental Goals and Principles of Sustainable Development of a Commercial Bank, Proceedings of the International Scientific and Practical Conference on Sustainable Development of Regional Infrastructure (ISSDRI 2021), 2021, 345, ISBN: 978–989-758–519-7.

L. Mélon (✉)
Pompeu Fabra University, Faculty of Law, Barcelona, Spain
e-mail: lela.melon@upf.edu

A. R. Mercina
Head of Sustainability, Nova Ljubljanska Banka (NLB), Ljubljana, Slovenia
e-mail: Alenka.recelj@nlb.si

M. Bodellini et al. (eds.), *Commercial Banking in Transition*, Palgrave Macmillan Studies in Banking and Financial Institutions,
https://doi.org/10.1007/978-3-031-45289-5_10

way that meaningfully contributes to the sustainable development of the economy by addressing environmental and social challenges.[2] The so-called "climate transition finance," understood as the extent to which an issuer's financing program supports the implementation of its climate change strategy, should clearly communicate how the issuer intends to adapt its business model to make a positive contribution to the transition to a low-carbon economy. Corporate climate change strategies should respond to stakeholder expectations by purposefully and explicitly seeking to play a positive role in achieving the goals of the Paris Agreement.[3] Disclosures regarding corporate strategies may be aligned with recognized reporting frameworks such as the recommendations of the Task Force on Climate-Related Financial Disclosures (TCFD) or similar frameworks.

The way banks have been approaching this new role was mainly through an attempt to reduce the negative impact of environmental and climate-related factors on sustainable development by reallocating financial resources in favor of green sectors of the economy,[4] while simultaneously being aware of their own risks related to external and internal environment, which can lead to the loss of stability of the bank as an organization.[5] The NLB Group took a different road and took responsible banking as its starting point: instead of a cherry-picking approach to the challenges of sustainability, it embarked on an ambitious path of a holistic change of their strategy and set responsible banking as a top priority, and its experience can provide insights for other institutions embarking on a similar path as well as for policymakers as to which aspects of the existing and upcoming legislation are adding and which subtracting from an efficient transition towards a model of sustainable banking.

[2] See e.g. R. A. Bespalov and S. V. Antonenko, Creation of a "Green" Bank in the Context of "Digitalization" of the Economy, 2 Bulletin of the Bryansk State University, 2019, 143–151.

[3] United Nations, Framework Convention on Climate Change (2015) Adoption of the Paris Agreement, 21st Conference of the Parties, Paris: United Nations. AN OFFICIAL PUBLICATION. Bell, E., Cullen, J.

[4] See M. D. Miah, S. M. Rahman and M. Mamoon, Green Banking: The Case of Commercial Banking Sector in Oman, 2020, 23 Environment, Development and Sustainability, 2681–2697.

[5] See I. K. Bitkina, The Influence of Macroeconomic Factors on the Deposit Operations of Commercial Banks, 2018, 1 Bulletin of the Moscow Humanitarian and Economic Institute, 33–39.

The NLB Group is a universal bank, operating in a geographical niche with fragmented smaller markets in South-Eastern European region, represents the most influential commercial bank in that particular geographical field, and has been setting responsible banking as their top priority as frontrunners in the region. It receives limited attention from large, global banks which gives it the opportunity to operate with economies of scale and scope and flexibility and options for bespoke solutions, tailored to client's need. It's market position (above 10% market share on each market and being number one on the domestic market) puts it into a comfortable position where they can choose the most advantageous approach for growth (e.g. either organic, through mergers and acquisitions or price/volume) while proving the prudent and measured risk approach through the cycle of profitable business operations. In 2021 it published the NLB Group Sustainability Framework,[6] which aligns its business model with the UN's Sustainable Development Goals in all three pillars (contribution to society, sustainable finance, and sustainable operations). NLB performed an impact analysis as a consequence of its commitment to the UN Principles for Responsible banking and published regional sustainability targets.[7] As regards the environmental dimension of ESG, it has been addressed by upgrading its climate-related and environmental risk management, integration of EU Taxonomy regulation, and measuring the carbon footprint of the Group's own operations in 2021, and supported by the social dimension through continuous CSR activities as well as the #HelpFrame project. The NLB Group is the first Slovenian bank to commit to coal-related financial exclusion as of 2021 (and will not provide any new financing to thermal coal mining or coal-fired electricity generation capacity in any way, including eventual transitional enhancements). It is simultaneously the first financial institution in Slovenia to join UNEP FI—Principles of responsible banking (in September 2020) and Net-Zero banking Alliance (May 2022) and the first bank in Slovenia to announce sustainability-related targets (through the impact areas of climate, resource efficiency, healthy and inclusive economies).

The NLB Group has a strategic advantage in becoming a regional sustainability champion, mainly due to its internal capabilities in terms

[6] See more at https: //www.nlb.si/nlb-sustainability-framework.pdf.

[7] See more at https://www.nlb.si/sustainability_report_2021.pdf.

of highly motivated and dedicated employees to developing and implementing sustainability agenda; its strong presence and understanding of the South-Eastern European region and sustainability opportunities stemming from its geographic position; and last but not least its profound understanding the business environment and culture of the region. With the efforts and investment put in the knowledge, skills, and well-being of its employees through numerous educational programs (provided either by its own Educational Centre with almost half a century of experience and other sources, including conferences and external educational programs), they are building on internal know-how to allow them to follow significant and rapid legislative changes in the field. What can be highlighted in that regard is the NLB Group's ESG training program, that has been developed in 2021 and has ever since been continuously upgraded with the latest sustainability contents. In fact, sustainability became a strong part of employees' on-boarding process (as it is included in training sessions and workshops) and a substantial part of internal communication (e.g. direct CEO address, internal news, events with ESG components, etc.). What is more, to comprehensively address sustainability due to its horizontal role in the bank, a sustainability training framework is being developed, which will encompass the whole ecosystem of sustainability-related topics (sustainable governance, climate, environmental, social, and ESG topics), made readily available to new and existing employees.

The approach of the NLB Group towards their sustainability transition has been holistic, one fueled with the awareness that it supposes engagement in sustainable banking (responsible financing, financial inclusion, and sustainable products and services), responsible organization (green and safe workplace, workplace culture and sustainable supply chain) and community impact (social engagement and environmental engagement). While such an approach is to be applauded, the process has been a challenging one especially due to this ambitious goal of an overarching change. The chapter outlays the path taken by the NLB Group, providing an insight and suggestions for future approaches of policymakers to aid such a transition being a smoother task.

The present chapter is structured as follows: Sect. 2 presents the path of transition of the NLB Group and its challenges, Sect. 3 continues with the outcomes of this transition, and concludes with a summary and recommendations for amelioration of the legislative framework supporting or mandating such a transition.

2 The Ambition and the Struggles: The "How to" Towards Sustainable Commercial Banking

General Considerations—Internal Challenges

The NLB Group started its journey towards a more sustainable banking model with the awareness that sustainability represented a complete novelty for the financial industry, especially in the geographic area where the bank is present and as such merits a treatment of change management, as it necessarily entails a significant change to its business model and corporate culture. The main concern related to the change of business model is one of lack of financing and lending opportunities, which is true only to a certain extent, when looking through the prism of trying to fit sustainability-related risks into the traditional financial risks framework. The legislative sustainability-related tsunami at the EU level brought about a substantial demand for financing of transition to net zero by 2050 and with it new opportunities. The downside of such a heightened demand in a short timeframe though is the demand for adaptation and building of new knowledge, capabilities, and culture among internal teams, which requires getting familiarized with non-financial and non-banking topics, where CO_2 in particular becomes the new currency. What proved crucial in this respect is the adaptability of the NLB Group's employees and their willingness to engage in continuous learning, to be able to successfully implement sustainability-related concerns across the bank's functions.

While the change of the bank's business model has been a significant challenge, it has not been the only one: the change of banks' products and services offered to their clients has been accompanied with a significant change of bank's goals, internal and external stakeholders' expectations and processes such as data gathering and digitalization. This presupposes whole new sets of data to be monitored and followed for the reporting to be disclosed in line with regulatory requirements as well as investors' expectations. Sustainability also influences bank's operations: the change towards responsible organization requires focus and change as regards the use of electricity and heating, revision of the space demand and possible improvements in commuting, etc. These changes have been implemented and discussed in parallel with the implementation of sustainable banking, which has been challenging but at the same time eye-opening, as it allowed the whole team to understand the challenges their corporate clients are changing in their own sustainable transition journey. A change in NLB Group's culture and its values occurred through these actions and it influenced every department in the bank due to this holistic approach, which was seen as the only possible approach to provide truly sustainable banking services to its clients in the long run.

What is indisputable is the fact that the transition to a sustainable banking model represents a "learning by doing" process, which provides the best results if implemented early on. There is a first mover's advantage for any organization that embarks on the sustainability journey, especially given the speed of legislative changes related to sustainability requirements in diverse interconnected and interrelated sectors. One of the main success factors at the NLB Group has been the active engagement and leadership of the board members and executives which resulted in an efficient setting and the communication of NLB's sustainability vision and strategy throughout the organization. The recognition of the top management of sustainability being a crucial focal point, and not a mere trend, has been the driving force of the sustainable transition in the NLB. Accompanied with a clear definition of sustainability's effect on bank's strategy, vision, and value, as well as a clear plan of implementation in the bank's operations, the employees have been appropriately informed and engaged in the transition early on, and this sense of joint direction has significantly contributed to a smooth implementation of the plan of transition. Regular communication between colleagues allowed for early detection of possible hurdles in the process of transition, and resulted in an efficient cascading of sustainability-related KPIs and their systematic incentivization through upgraded remuneration policy.

The initial plan has been supported with a more extensive implementation of ESG factors, and the NLB Group chose as its guiding framework the Principles of Responsible Banking (PRB), when it became a signatory of United Nations Environment Programme Finance Initiative (UNEP FI) in September 2020. A compass was needed for the transition itself, and the UNEP FI presented a great map for paving NLB Group's sustainable path for the future. Identifying the lack of expertise on the matter inside the NLB Group, initially external advisors have been involved, to enable NLB's employees to obtain the required knowledge as well as additional employees have been hired to create an internal sustainability department. This allowed the bank to build an internal bank of knowledge and further raise awareness of the critical points of sustainability transition through internal workshops. Internally the implementation of

PRB required the inclusion of colleagues from a very broad sphere of departments given the extent of impact areas. This has been beneficial not only for the introduction of the PRB, but has also served as an example what the implementation of sustainability actually entails, which is a continuous cross-sectoral cooperation and regular discussions with a very broad audience, as sustainability represents a horizontal topic. In that regard and related to performing impact analysis, fruitful discussions were held in terms of what truly is material for NLB Group and where it has significant influence, what are the key factors influencing its operations, business strategy, and development. This allowed for the identification of other aspects related to sustainable transition which have not been identified beforehand. Once all the required steps have been performed, the first targets were set and the self-assessment report has been filled out. At this stage, the NLB Group comprehended the extent of PRB requirements and the push for the sustainable transition they represent. What has proven to be especially fruitful were the one-on-one meetings on receiving feedback after the submission of self-assessment report, providing valuable insights, and setting the direction for the future.

While the implementation of the PRB has been a success, two main challenges can be highlighted: getting on board the broad internal audience and the harmonization of targets. As joining the PRB happened at the beginning of the NLB's sustainability path, the core sustainability team received numerous questions and had to resolve numerous doubts as to who PRB is relevant and how does it fit in the NLB strategy and operations. It has been very time-consuming, especially as many working groups have been established internally, which required an extensive amount of coordination, but it has proved extremely beneficial in the implementation of the set sustainability strategy. Of significant aid to that effect were internal workshops held simultaneously with the performance of impact analysis, which started the dialogue which did away with the existing fears and doubts. As regards the harmonization of targets, while NLB Group previously publicly disclosed some of its targets, it has for the first time explicitly set guidelines and targets. The commitment this implies caused a process of a few rounds of harmonization and numerous discussions which were pivotal in aligning expectations of all internal stakeholders. Looking back, this was one of the most important steps of NLB's PRB implementation path, as targets are crucial in terms of external communication and proof of corporate commitment in terms of its sustainability-related ambitions.[8] This process has also facilitated a significant expansion of NLB's relevant ESG KPIs that are being internally monitored. The process, in a very simplified form, can be described as follows: at the onset basic sustainability-related targets were set, with the awareness that much is yet to be done in the upcoming years in terms of the further development of these targets and their upgrade by following methodology of the Science Based Targets Initiative.[9] The need for cascading systems of KPIs has been identified in order to efficiently support the targets. To support the transition, a lot of attention has been put to data capturing, collecting, collating as well as facing the significant challenge of aggregate reporting, which requires process changes, IT developments, and additional investments. These challenges have proved to be very constructive and helped the NLB Group to build knowledge and raise internal awareness on sustainability transition of the organization as a whole. Now the question remains if every institution will have the opportunity (in terms of time available to them) to combine the top-down and bottom-up approach, or the test-and-try approach was a privilege of first-movers?

Specific Challenges with ESG Disclosures and Standardization of Sustainability Reporting—The Multitude of Regulative Sources

The past few years a significant growing interest by financial market participants and other stakeholders in more relevant, reliable, and comparable disclosures could be observed, related to the ESG factors (referred to as "non-financial information" or "sustainability reporting").[10] From 2021, the European Union regulates financial disclosure of sustainable

[8] See NLB 2021 Sustainability Report, available at: https://www.nlb.si/sustainability_report_2021.pdf (last accessed on 29.08.2022).

[9] See more at https://sciencebasedtargets.org/.

[10] Noted also by the European Commission, see e.g. the Communication from the Commission to the European Parliament, the Council, the European Economic and Social Committee and the Committee of the Regions, EU Taxonomy, Corporate Sustainability Reporting, Sustainability Preferences and Fiduciary Duties: Directing finance towards the European Green Deal COM/2021/188 final, 8–11.

investments with a special SFDR regulation,[11] while the US will regulate greenwashing from 2022, and other countries following the trend. The SFRD regulation lays down sustainability disclosure obligations for issuers of financial products and financial advisers towards end-investors in relation to the integration of sustainability risks by financial market participants (i.e. asset managers, institutional investors, insurance companies, pension funds, etc.) and financial advisers in all investment processes and for financial products that pursue the objective of sustainable investment. The emphasis is on the effects of business on the climate, protection of biodiversity, and respect for human rights in supply chains. While in the early 2000s the European Commission saw corporate social responsibility as a voluntary exercise, allowing companies to engage in socially (and environmentally) beneficial activities, in the framework of shareholder primacy with a slight stakeholder orientation. That changed with the EU Directive on non-financial reporting[12] which mandated reporting from large undertakings in the EU on non-financial matters, and has been transposed in Slovene legislation through amendment of Article 70 c of ZGD-1J.[13] The latter has been obliging publicly traded companies, credit and insurance companies, pension finds as well as medium-sized and large companies with more than 500 employees. The Article 70 c of the ZGD-J has been the most relevant for the NLB Group, as well as the guidance provided by the Global Reporting Initiative (GRI) as a long-standing standard-setter in the field of sustainable finance, now serving as a basis for the development of European Financial Reporting Advisory Group's (EFRAG) sustainability reporting standards.[14] European legislation in the area of sustainable finance in particular has provided a significant stimulus to the market demand for sustainability reporting. Subject to the acceptance of the proposal of the Corporate Sustainability Reporting

[11] Regulation (EU) 2019/2088 of the European Parliament and of the Council of 27 November 2019 on sustainability-related disclosures in the financial services sector PE/87/2019/REV/1 OJ L 317.

[12] Directive 2014/95/EU of the European Parliament and of the Council of 22 October 2014 amending Directive 2013/34/EU as regards disclosure of non-financial and diversity information by certain large undertakings and groups OJ L 330.

[13] https://www.uradni-list.si/glasilo-uradni-list-rs/vsebina?urlurid=2017730.

[14] See e.g. EFRAG [Draft] European Sustainability Reporting Standard P1 Sustainability Statements, available at: https://www.efrag.org/Assets/Download?assetUrl=%2Fsites%2Fwebpublishing%2FSiteAssets%2FESRS%2520P1%2520on%2520Sustainability%2520Statements.pdf (last accessed on 29.08.2022).

Directive (CSRD),[15] amending the existing reporting requirements of the Non-Financial Reporting Directive (NFRD),[16] steps have been taken to provide a comprehensive set of European Sustainability Reporting Standards (ESRS), addressing the heightened demand for common standards while acknowledging some key specificities of the European context, such as (1) the need to cover the entire spectrum of ESG topics; (2) the importance of the "double materiality" principle, as well as (3) the need to be consistent with major pieces of sustainable finance legislation, such as the Taxonomy Regulation,[17] the Regulation on sustainability-related disclosures in the financial services sector (also referred to as "SFDR")[18] and the Regulation on sustainability indices used as benchmarks in financial instruments and financial contracts or to measure the performance of investment funds (also referred to as "Benchmarks Regulation").[19] CSRD extends the scope to all large companies and all companies listed on regulated markets (except listed micro-enterprises); it requires an audit of reported information, introduces overall more detailed reporting requirements; it requires companies to digitally "tag" the reported information, so it is machine readable and feeds into the European single access point envisaged in the capital markets union action plan. The reports under CSRD are to be compiled and audited to account for 2024 financial year for companies, subject to NFRD; for 2025 financial year for other large

[15] Proposal for a Directive of the European Parliament and of the Council amending Directive 2013/34/EU, Directive 2004/109/EC, Directive 2006/43/EC and Regulation (EU) No 537/2014, as regards corporate sustainability reporting COM/2021/189 final.

[16] Directive 2014/95/EU of the European Parliament and of the Council of 22 October 2014 amending Directive 2013/34/EU as regards disclosure of non-financial and diversity information by certain large undertakings and groups OJ L 330.

[17] Regulation (EU) 2020/852 of the European Parliament and of the Council of 18 June 2020 on the establishment of a framework to facilitate sustainable investment, and amending Regulation (EU) 2019/2088 (Text with EEA relevance) PE/20/2020/INIT OJ L 198.

[18] Regulation (EU) 2019/2088 of the European Parliament and of the Council of 27 November 2019 on sustainability-related disclosures in the financial services sector (Text with EEA relevance) PE/87/2019/REV/1 OJ L 317.

[19] Regulation (EU) 2016/1011 of the European Parliament and of the Council of 8 June 2016 on indices used as benchmarks in financial instruments and financial contracts or to measure the performance of investment funds and amending Directives 2008/48/EC and 2014/17/EU and Regulation (EU) No 596/2014 OJ L 171.

firms and two years later for the remaining qualifying SMEs with a 2-year opt-out.

The developments in terms of corporate sustainability reporting in the EU have been and are especially pertinent in terms of the speed of sustainability transition in the corporate world in general, and the Proposal of the CSRD frames the actions required and expected also from banking institutions. The general aim of this instrument is aiding in achieving sustainable and inclusive growth, managing financial risks stemming from climate change, biodiversity loss, environmental degradation, and social challenges, stimulating transparency and long-term orientation of financial and corporate activities and disclosing environmental, social, and governance-related risks. Article 19 the proposal for CSRD determines the minimum content of the corporate sustainability report, and the work of EFRAG further fills in the details. This particular development (as acknowledged also by the application timeline of this new instrument) highlights the importance of early engagement in sustainability transition: while, by way of example, much of the (now required) work has already been done by the NLB Group previously to this instrument, the adaptation will be less demanding than in the case of companies and banks that have yet to embark on the path of sustainability transition.

To facilitate meaningful sustainable transformation of organizations, active in the EU, another instrument has been issued, which will transform significantly the corporate landscape in the EU: the key new sustainability governance proposal, Draft Directive on Corporate Sustainability Due Diligence (CSDDD).[20] CSDDD is a broad-based reform, establishing a corporate due diligence duty for companies to identify, prevent, end, or mitigate negative impacts of their operations on people and the environment. Its purpose is to "foster sustainable and responsible corporate behavior and to anchor human rights and environmental considerations" in companies' activities and within their corporate governance structures. To comply with the corporate due diligence duty, companies must integrate due diligence into corporate policies, identify actual or potential adverse human rights and environmental impacts, prevent or mitigate potential impacts, establish and maintain a complaints procedure, monitor the effectiveness of due diligence policies and measures and

[20] Proposal for a DIRECTIVE OF THE EUROPEAN PARLIAMENT AND OF THE COUNCIL on Corporate Sustainability Due Diligence and amending Directive (EU) 2019/1937 COM/2022/71 final.

publicly communicate on due diligence implementation. The CSDDD will apply to company's own operations, its subsidiaries, and their supply chains, including direct and indirect business relationships. It introduces duties for directors to set up and oversee the implementation of due diligence processes and integrate due diligence into official corporate strategy.

What the NLB Group's experience showed is that regional standardization, most notably in Europe, and international efforts need to go hand-in-hand to support the sustainable transition of commercial banking. If regional and global standardization efforts do not coincide, that actually impedes the wished-for transition as it creates an unclear and loose framework for the transition. Both regional and global efforts should enable a target scenario where issuers can rely on high-quality reporting standards which are consistent, interoperable, and global to the largest extent possible (and where necessary also region- or jurisdiction-specific). In the year 2022 European Securities and Market Authority (ESMA) welcomed the International Financial Reporting Standards (IFRS) Foundation's initiative to consolidate some of the existing standard-setting and framework initiatives and strongly supports the work of the International Sustainability Standards Board (ISSB) to reach a common set of internationally accepted high-quality sustainability reporting standards which could serve as a global baseline.

The need for setting up such a comprehensive baseline in the interest of investors is simple and intuitive: the risk of greenwashing in the sustainable investment chain largely stems from claims that often have to do with alleged societal and environmental positive impacts of certain financial products or entities. To that effect, a general feeling has developed in the NLB Group that a convergence of the ISSB proposed reporting requirements with the draft European Sustainability Reporting Standards (ESRS) developed by EFRAG (currently under development), should be reached, to provide a common denominator and a fruitful and sturdy framework for sustainable transition of commercial banking and financial services in general. A comprehensive and truly interoperable standard-setting solution for sustainability reporting is needed. In the absence of such a development, the commercial banking sector faces the risk of a continued fragmentation of the sustainability reporting landscape with not only increasing costs but also increasing risks for the investment community and issuers operating internationally, as well as difficulties in implementing efficient and timely sustainability transition. The latter is seen also in the light of comparability among peers, where benchmarking is impossible as well as an objective assessment of where we stand in terms of sustainability transition. These arguments are further supported by the intentions of the International Banking Federation (IBFed) and Deloitte in the context of the United Nations Conference of Parties 27 (COP27) to publish a report illustrating the banking sector's efforts towards climate neutrality across jurisdictions with the intention of identifying and illustrating best practices, while simultaneously outlining structural differences between jurisdictions as an obstacle to the net-zero transition.

While "setting the stage" with legislation, research on ESG integration into banking practices, practices and guidelines of central banks sounds appropriate and sometimes necessary to ensure or accompany the sustainable transition of banking, the multitude of sources oftentimes slows down the transition due to the lack of clarity of actual requirements for greening commercial banking. By way of example, Bank for International Settlements (BIS) published a report in July 2022 on the topic of integrating ESG factors into risk management systems and international reserve management frameworks by central banks.[21] It acknowledged the societal challenge of managing climate change risks and the role of central banks in the fight against climate change, which through the Network of Central Banks and Supervisors for Greening the Financial System (NGFS) aims to contribute to effective climate-related risk management and the transition to a sustainable economy. While many central banks do not have a formal mandate to incorporate sustainability challenges into their mission, some have noted that doing so is consistent with their existing mandates. These central banks may decide to incorporate climate-related risks into their risk frameworks, and thus improve their decision-making processes given the impact of climate risks on their mission and/or objectives. This freedom of central banks to decide to do so on their own accord (and with the criteria they pick and choose) can indeed prove to be counterproductive if harmonization that facilitates comparability between standards is aimed for. In the case of NLB Group that would mean that the European Central Bank's defined climate risks would need to be observed for its operations in the EU, while for operations in Serbia, Croatia, Bosnia, and Herzegovina etc. another set of climate risks would be observed, severely impeding NLB Group's progress in its transition

[21] BIS Annual Economic Report 2021, available online at https://www.bis.org/publ/arpdf/ar2022e.pdf (last accessed on 29.08.2022).

towards sustainable practices. Indeed, ECB has taken further steps to incorporate climate change into its monetary policy operations to aid the governments and legislators as the main actors in the fight against climate change.[22] The Governing Council of the ECB decided to adjust corporate bond holdings in the Eurosystem's monetary policy portfolios and its collateral framework, to introduce climate-related disclosure requirements and to enhance its risk management practices.[23] These measures have been designed in accordance with the Eurosystem's primary objective of maintaining price stability, while aiming to better consider climate-related financial risk in the Eurosystem balance sheet and with reference to the objective of supporting the green transition of the economy, in line with the EU's climate neutrality objectives. Those measures provide incentives to companies and financial institutions to be more transparent about their carbon emissions and to reduce them.[24] Furthermore, ECB is required to carry out annual stress tests on supervised entities in the context of its Supervisory Review and Evaluation Process. As climate change and the transition to net-zero carbon emissions pose risks to households and firms, they pose risks to the financial sector. Accordingly, exposure to climate-related and environmental risks is among ECB Banking Supervision's strategic priorities for the period of 2022–2024.[25] The 2022 ECB climate-risk stress test should be seen as a joint learning exercise with pioneering characteristics aimed at enhancing both banks' and supervisors' capacity to assess climate risk. In the case of the NLB Group a positive spillover can be noted to the non-EU countries in which it operates, as it is supervised by the ECB due to its incorporation and presence in the EU, which furthers the EU green agenda beyond the borders of the EU.[26]

[22] See more on climate change and the ECB at https://www.ecb.europa.eu/ecb/climate/html/index.en.html (last accessed on 29.08.2022).

[23] See more in ECB Annex: Detailed roadmap of climate change-related actions, available online at https://www.ecb.europa.eu/press/pr/date/2021/html/ecb.pr210708_1_annex~f84ab35968.en.pdf (last accessed on 29.08.2022).

[24] See more on ECB Climate Agenda at https://www.ecb.europa.eu/press/pr/date/2022/html/ecb.pr220704_annex~cb39c2dcbb.en.pdf (last accessed on 29.08.2022).

[25] Ibid.

[26] https://www.bankingsupervision.europa.eu/ecb/pub/pdf/ssm.202011finalguideonclimate-relatedandenvironmentalrisks~58213f6564.en.pdf.

While the activity of ECB in the field of sustainable transition of commercial banking is a necessary and welcome exercise with positive spillover effects, the development and existence of the EU sustainable finance taxonomy[27] sometimes represents a double-edged sword. In the context of the NLB Group sustainable transition, significant usability challenges of the implementation of the EU Taxonomy arose.[28] The main challenges are the following: (1) requiring highly granular data for the technical screening criteria (TSC) purposes, (2) relying on EU legislation and criteria in a global market, (3) inconsistency in the use of estimates and third-party data, (4) no proportional arrangements for smaller companies and projects, (5) certain criteria create the need for retracting to smooth the energy transition over time, (6) using economic activity based classification system (NACE) for complex projects. All of these concerns and challenges are of utmost importance for current and future sustainability-related reporting under the SFDR, CSRD, and the EU Green Bond regulation. Furthermore, a source of additional concern is the recent vote by the European Parliament on the Complementary Delegated Act on climate change mitigation and adaptation, covering certain gas and nuclear activities, which can be seen as an important recognition of the pragmatic and realistic approach in helping Member States on their path towards climate neutrality, yet it is not aligned with the initial ambition of the EU Green Deal[29] and it significantly influenced the first-movers' strategies of transition, given the watered-down ambition it represents in terms of sustainable transition of the EU as a whole. What could offer a remedy for the abovementioned challenges is the following: (1) allowing flexibility in the process of alignment with the "do no significant harm" (DNSH) and minimum safeguard standards, (2) adapting TSC for usability in non-EU jurisdictions, and (3) allowing the use of estimates and third-party sourced data when EU Taxonomy assessments cannot otherwise be obtained.

[27] See n10.

[28] International Capital Market Association, Ensuring the usability of the EU Taxonomy, 2022, available at https://www.icmagroup.org/assets/GreenSocialSustainabilityDb/Ensuring-the-Usability-of-the-EU-Taxonomy-and-Ensuring-the-Usability-of-the-EU-Taxonomy-February-2022.pdf (last accessed on 29.08.2022).

[29] Communication from the Commission to the European Parliament, the European Council, the Council, the European Economic and Social Committee and the Committee of the Regions, The European Green Deal, COM/2019/640 final.

The abovementioned concerns regarding the European regulation of sustainable conduct of organizations in general and commercial banking in particular are partially remedied by EU's next steps, such as the European Commission delegated regulation containing Regulatory Technical Standards (RTS) as a part of the European Supervisory Authorities' (ESA) ongoing efforts to promote a better understanding of the disclosures required under the technical standards of the SFRD ahead of the planned application of the rules on 1 January 2023. Furthermore, the European Commission puts trust in ESA for providing input on how greenwashing can be avoided, by taking actions and developing new tools to ensure adequate monitoring of greenwashing risks, alongside with considering supervisory challenges to enforce new policies. All in all, the EU activity in the field of narrowing down the meaning of what "sustainable" activity is (and for that matter, the global activity) is welcome, but it needs to be reconciled with the need for clarity and simplicity in order to be adequately supporting and incentivizing the sustainable corporate transition in general as well as the sustainable transition of commercial banking in particular.

NLB Sustainability Roadmap 2022–2023: Developing a Climate-Conscious Transition Strategy

The recognition of capital markets having a critical role to play in enabling the climate transition by ensuring the efficient flow of financing from investors to issuers wishing to address climate change risk issuers has been present in the NLB Group for a significant amount of time now. With the aim to fulfill upcoming EU regulatory requirements, stakeholders' expectations (especially investors'), general societal developments, and commitments NLB made with regards to shifting its business model to support decarbonization goals (as a member of UNEP FI—PRB and Net-Zero Banking Alliance (NZBA) initiatives), NLB Group's next step is developing a climate-conscious transition strategy of the bank or in other words the NLB net-zero business strategy. By joining UNEP FI NZBA in May 2022, NLB climate-related and environmental ambitions were significantly strengthened. In line with the NLB's commitment to UNEP FI—NZBA and PBR, NLB Group's goal is to transition all operational and attributable GHG emissions from its lending and investment portfolios to align with pathways to net-zero by mid-century or sooner, including CO_2 emissions reaching net-zero at the latest by 2050, consistent with a maximum temperature rise of 1.5°C above pre-industrial levels by 2100. Following UNEP FI Guidelines for Climate Target Setting for Banks,[30] four key points for the NLB net-zero business strategy must be clearly addressed: (1) the NLB shall set and publicly disclose long-term (2050) and intermediate (2030) targets to support meeting the temperature goals of the Paris Agreement; (2) the NLB shall establish an emissions baseline and annually measure and report the emissions profile of its lending portfolios and investment activities; (3) the NLB shall use widely accepted science-based decarbonization scenarios to set both long-term and intermediate targets that are aligned with the temperature goals of the Paris Agreement; (4) the NLB shall regularly review targets to ensure consistency with current climate science.

The basic elements of the continuous NLB Group sustainable transition can be defined as follows: (1) sustainable business opportunities, (2) climate-related and environmental risk management, and (3) 2022 Sustainability Roadmap. In terms of sustainable business opportunities (1), sustainability is being incorporated in the NLB Group and ESG product portfolio is growing. The bank helps its customers with different financing products in the implementation of sustainability measures in the development of lasting environmental solutions. An ESG-oriented offer includes NLB Green housing loan to finance construction or the purchase of a passive house and finance the purchase of solar panels, heat pumps, and central ventilation. With tailored offers, the banks play their part in transition to a more sustainable future and the NLB Group is fully committed with its strong ESG mission to support and create projects in regional green transformation and well-being. Additional steps were made to complement the ESG offer for legal entities, namely with NLB Green Investment loan for energy efficient business premises with additional benefits included, and NLB Green loan for reducing the carbon footprint offered within the existing range of NLB loans, exclusively for purposes where a sufficient positive impact on the environment was proven. With the addition of green products in its offer the NLB Group promotes sustainability awareness among its clients. In terms of climate-related and environmental risk management (2), the NLB Group engages

[30] UNEP FI Guidelines for Climate Target Setting for Banks, available at https://www.unepfi.org/wordpress/wp-content/uploads/2021/04/UNEP-FI-Guidelines-for-Climate-Change-Target-Setting.pdf (last accessed on 30.08.2022).

in contributing to sustainable finance by incorporating ESG risks into its business strategies, risk management framework, and internal governance arrangements. The management of ESG risks follows the ECB and EBA guidelines with a tendency of their comprehensive integration into all relevant processes. As a systematically important institution, the NLB Group was included in the 2022 ECB Climate Stress Test exercise, assessing how banks are prepared for dealing with financial and economic shocks stemming from climate risk. In terms of 2022 Sustainability Roadmap (3), the NLB Group demonstrated its commitment to a low-carbon economy and financing the transition by joining the UNEP FI Net-Zero Banking Alliance and plans to expand the product portfolio with loans dedicated to supporting energy efficiency and renewable energy production. In 2022 the NLB Group aims to enhance its measurements of CO_2 emissions to full Scope 3 and to start developing its net-zero business strategy. The NLB Group will continue with implementation of climate related and environmental risk management as per the EBA and ECB guidelines, whereas participation in the ECB climate-risk stress test exercise will provide additional valuable insights. Effective integration of sustainability-related regulatory requirements will be important in 2022 for ESG disclosures and reporting (e.g. EU Taxonomy, BASEL Pillar III) and additionally enhanced by meeting the European Bank for Reconstruction and Development (EBRD) and World Bank's Multilateral Investment Guarantee Agency (MIGA) requirements. The NLB Group is also focused on becoming paperless, and on introducing digital-only card. The NLB Group plans to make required steps in the direction of obtaining its first ESG rating for the Bank.

3 Conclusion

The NLB Group experience is most probably not unique, and most plausibly many commercial banks who have identified the need for sustainable reform and embarked on the journey early on have stumbled upon similar challenges with embarking on the path of transition towards sustainability. While the EU legal framework, its policies, and strategies, are aimed at providing sturdy and detailed guidelines as to the content of the "how", they seem to lack the required consistency and clarity, but most importantly coherence to be able to represent efficient guidelines to that effect. The NLB Group, active across the Balkans, represents the most influential commercial bank in that particular geographical area. Designing and implementing its sustainability framework across the group, it has first-hand experienced the benefits and setbacks of the legislation in the field, which did not prevent it from developing and implementing its own Sustainability Pledge 2025. Due to the complexity and at times incoherence of the EU regulation on the matter it based its transition on global standards (namely on the UNEP FI framework), using it as a general framework that was then filled in according to the Group's developed strategy and the existing and upcoming EU regulation. By observing and documenting NLB Group's path towards sustainability, its Sustainability Report 2021[31] gives a notion of the challenges faced in the process of transition towards representing a sustainable financial institution. The present chapter therefore exposed the NLB Group's motivation for a transition towards sustainable commercial banking, the steps taken, and the challenges faced, while analyzing the influence of the existing and upcoming legal frameworks in the geographical areas where the bank is active. Furthermore, market considerations had a significant impact on the speed and content of the revision were noted, informing further the policymaking in the field, allowing for contrasting the EU and non-EU jurisdictions regarding the market attitude towards sustainable commercial banking. The present chapter therefore serves as an empirical account of some of the challenges of the transition towards sustainability, while also providing a limited critical assessment of the quality of the EU legal framework versus the non-EU legal framework. By giving an informed account of the experience of a commercial bank that strategically decide on a holistic transformation of its business model, the present chapter provided insight into the challenges faced when such a transformation is carried out, especially in the cases of divergent legislative frameworks faced by a bank group.

The NLB Group experience shows that more regulation and legislation in the field is welcome, yet what is missing are more tools for implementing the newly set requirements. While the growth of prohibitions and limitations is substantial (as well as in terms of empirical research related to the ESG agenda), the availability of (alternative) tools and activity is not following. While extensive peer cooperation across borders is of some help, there continue to exist significant (also structural) constraints, such as the lack of understanding of financial

[31] Available online at: https://www.nlb.si/sustainability_report_2021.pdf (last accessed on 12.09.2022).

terminology at the core. There is factually no consensus as to what constitutes ESG investing: we might help ourselves with the existing, better-defined ESG analysis (which requires comprehensive research), but in its essence, the term "environmental, social and governance" describes an analytical approach, requiring comprehensive and thorough investment research. This lack of tools for implementation is even more relevant in the light of the developments in terms of banking (a radical change that is brewing in this market), so the use of the "learning by doing" principle, which is costly in terms of financial assets and time, might prove to be contra-productive long-term. While embracing regenerative economic approaches in lieu of expansionist governance is a welcome development, especially in terms of environmental sustainability, the challenges posed by sustainability transition are still substantial. One of those challenges is without a doubt the so-called "just transition", not only in terms of individuals but also in terms of companies who are incapable to compete on these new, sustainable terms. Another challenge is the so-called "data challenge", especially in terms of determining, measuring and managing Scope 3 emissions, as proxies are not allowed and the data provided by companies are nothing more than estimates. The truth of the matter is that a bank cannot be more sustainable than its clients: while the NLB Group can develop and implement a comprehensive net-zero business strategy, it cannot be more successful in its implementation that its clients are. To that effect, the NLB Group plans to continue the open stakeholder communication regarding its financial plans and it has publicly announced it remains committed to meaningful and increased dividend payments, in line with the ambition to grow in a sustainable manner, showing that sustainable growth can be made a reality through a holistic approach towards sustainable organizational transition.

PART II

The Anglo-Saxon Systems

CHAPTER 11

Central Bank Digital Currency and the Agenda of Monetary Devolution

Leonidas Zelmanovitz and Bruno Meyerhof Salama

1 Introduction

Calls for the Federal Reserve (Fed) to adopt a Central Bank Digital Currency (CBDC) that can be used by the public at large—or "retail" CBDCs—have become common in the United States. The idea first gained political attention in 2019 after the release of a white paper by Facebook proposing the creation of a stablecoin called *Libra* (subsequently rebranded as *Diem*, before the project was discontinued). Later, in the context of the response to the COVID-crisis, several proposals were introduced in the U.S. Congress for the creation of "Digital Dollars" and

For helpful comments, we thank Juliana B. Bolzani. All errors are ours.

L. Zelmanovitz
Liberty Fund, Carmel, IN, USA
e-mail: lzelmanovitz@libertyfund.org

B. M. Salama (✉)
UC Berkeley Law School, Berkeley, CA, USA
e-mail: salama@berkeley.edu

M. Bodellini et al. (eds.), *Commercial Banking in Transition*, Palgrave Macmillan Studies in Banking and Financial Institutions,
https://doi.org/10.1007/978-3-031-45289-5_11

"FedAccounts". The proposals failed, but that did not stop the Federal Reserve Bank of Boston from partnering with the *Digital Currency Initiative* at the Massachusetts Institute of Technology to explore the CBDC design space and gain a hands-on understanding of a CBDC's technical challenges and opportunities. Despite occasional pushback from the commercial banking industry[1] and even from within the Fed,[2] CBDCs increasingly look like a question of "when", not of "if".[3]

And yet, create a CBDC with what purpose?

2 The Justifications for Creating a CBDC

The question is daunting even for CBDC enthusiasts, and in the policy space there is no shortage of voices saying that CBDCs are *a solution looking for a problem*. Not that there aren't justifications, which are indeed many: a Fed-issued digital currency is said to be necessary to secure American financial dominance, particularly in light of the impending coming about of China's digital renminbi; to improve monetary policy, particularly in the implementation of stimulative measures; to promote financial inclusion or to address longstanding economic inequalities; to help spurt innovation in ways that the current system cannot; and to avoid fragmenting liquidity or to allow the United States to compete with private-sector money substitutes, specially stablecoins.

Clearly, some of these contentions rest on feebler grounds than others. For example, the idea that a CBDC is needed to increase financial inclusion begs the question of why not using instead simpler solutions that rely on basic commercial accounts, like the FedNow or the "Bank On" accounts initiative promoted by the Fed, or other solutions that have a proven track record, such as those involving telecommunication companies in Africa or payment platforms such as Brazil's PIX.[4] Similarly, the idea that a CBDC is needed to preserve the international status of the US Dollar seems to elevate form over substance and to heavily discount both

[1] See e.g. G. Baer, Central Bank Digital Currencies: Costs, Benefits and Major Implications for the U.S. Economic System, Bank Policy Institute, Staff Working Paper.

[2] R. K. Quarles, Parachute Pants and Central Bank Money, June 28, 2021, Speech delivered at the 113th Annual Utah Bankers Association Convention, Sun Valley, Idaho.

[3] *Financial Times*, June 23, 2021. CBDCs now seem a matter of when not if.

[4] A. Duarte et al., Central Banks, the Monetary System and Public Payment Infrastructures: Lessons from Brazil's Pix, BIS BULLETIN NO. 52, March 23, 2022.

the strengths of the US Dollar—the size of the US economy, the depth of its financial markets, the absence of foreign exchange controls in the US, the country's international military presence, inertia, and so on—as well as the US Dollars vulnerabilities—the US fiscal imbalances and internal political divisions, the reputational damage caused by the repeated use of the Dollar to sanction nations that fall in political disfavor, and, of course, the ascent of China.

To be sure, other justifications for the creation of CBDCs may be more persuasive. For example, a money that is programmable or that expires can in principle be more effective in stimulating demand—if or when such policies are to be pursued, something that is not our concern here. Moreover, it is not inconceivable that condoning (instead of opposing) the technological innovation that is housed within a CBDC could within time help spurt innovation, probably in ways that at this point are not completely foreseeable. And in any case, certain inefficiencies of the commercial banking industry as it stands today should not be ignored. Even in the best case, of course, the adoption of CBDCs is not risk-free. Damage to privacy is a concern that is often remembered (since retail CBDCs can be a tool for the government to directly track people's monetary outlays). Moreover, cyber-security and (especially in the case of retail FedAccounts) administrability also figure prominently.

Discussing the adoption of CBDCs from the perspective of tradeoffs, that is, of pros and cons, is however an incomplete enterprise. The precise risk is that of concealing the political economy that from immemorial times underpins the enterprise of money creation and money regulation. Once we turn to the political economy of money—or perhaps, to the *Law and Macroeconomics* of money, a phraseology that we suggested elsewhere—,[5] a more fundamental interpretation of the creation of CBDCs can be formulated, one that finds a unified meaning in the myriad of policy goals and rationales that are enlisted to support their creation: retail CBDCs represent yet another step towards the devolution of monetary powers from commercial banks to the state. They are, to put it bluntly, a fiscal and monetary tool, and not simply a strategy to reduce transactions costs.

[5] L. Zelmanovitz and B. Meyerhof Salama, LawMacro and the Schism in Law and Economics. Law and Liberty, 2020, available at https://lawliberty.org/how-money-could-revive-law-and-economics/.

We find the agenda of monetary devolution in the simple fact that retail CBDCs displace fractional reserve commercial banking and private money in favor of sovereign money. At the same time, as we explain, there is an alternative route to make use of the technological edge provided by CBDCs without going down the road of monetary devolution. To visualize it we must let go of the idea of adopting a retail CBDCs and focus instead on a CBDC available only to intermediaries. This wholesale CBDC, sometimes referred to as wCBDC, could ground the transition to a crypto-based monetary system where stablecoin issuers would adapt money creation to market needs, complementing and perhaps eventually replacing on-demand deposits. CBDCs would then be used as base money to settle transactions between the stablecoin issuers. The transition would have to be carefully managed, but the result could be one where the United States improves the technological footing of its banking and financial system without running into the problems of capital misallocation that inevitably come about when endogenous money cedes room to sovereign money.

The fiscal and monetary implications of CBDCs, however, mean that the push for monetary devolution—that is, the push for the creation of retail CBDCs and FedAccounts—does not come only from the attraction of the new technologies that underlie CBDCs. Its root cause lies elsewhere, especially in the structural deficits of the United States Treasury that result from a fundamental imbalance between government receipts and expenditures. These structural deficits place the Treasury in a position where it is constantly seeking for additional buyers of government debt—preferably at negative real rates, which is why, incidentally, the inflation that is not so hard to engineer with the current institutional setting comes in handy for the Treasury. Retail CBDCs are then appealing precisely because they increase the ability of the government both to create inflation (engineering the negative interest rates needed to reduce the public debt) and to use such CBDCs to make up for the decreased demand for Treasuries that can come when real interests are negative.

3 The Agenda of Monetary Devolution

Years ago, when we first wrote about the prospects for the adoption of retail CBDCs in the United States, we found that the devolution of monetary powers to the state was CBDCs' "hidden agenda" (we did point out, however, that many among the CBDCs advocates were open about the goal of tilting the current balance between private and sovereign money in favor of the latter).[6] This agenda is now increasingly visible.

The motivations behind the push for sovereign money are many. To refer to only some of them, the strengthening of the ESG platform represents a call for the government to step in to finance the shift to a green economy; international geopolitical competition with China and the outburst of the COVID pandemic have led to renewed calls for industrial policy; political grievances animate calls for the incorporation of state-owned banks; and, last but not least, the deterioration of the United States fiscal situation generates pressure for greater financial repression to facilitate placement of public debt by the Treasury. These and possibly other considerations explain why the base case for the adoption of retail CBDCs in the United States continues to be one of devolution of monetary powers to the state to enable greater financial repression—that is, political allocation of money and credit—and monetary financing of the Treasury.

To see why, the starting point is to understand that CBDCs are a form of sovereign money. At its core, a CBDC is a digital payment instrument, denominated in the national unit of account that is a direct liability of the Fed. Like currency and reserve balances, it is denominated in Dollars and would be considered a part of the monetary base. Moreover, if available to the public, CBDCs would have the same legal tender privileges granted to cash and would be part of the money supply. But unlike currency, a CBDC can only exist in electronic form. The specific electronic form would depend on whether the CBDC is created as a "token" or as an "account". Electronic tokens are designed to mimic paper money. They are like electronic prepaid debit cards or gift cards in that they are not connected to an account-relationship between the depository bank and the token holder. Depending on the institutional design that may be chosen, this depository entity could be the Fed or any other provider of a digital wallet.

Account-based CBDCs can be thought of as universal central bank accounts. They are designed to give retail customers access to online bank accounts directly with the Fed. Like electronic tokens—but unlike

[6] See e.g. Morgan Ricks' testimony before the United States House of Representatives Committee on Financial Services Task Force on Financial Technology, June 11, 2020, available online at https://www.congress.gov/116/meeting/house/110778/witnesses/HHRG-116-BA00-Wstate-RicksM-20200611.pdf.

bank deposits or e-money stored in prepaid cards—these accounts are liabilities of the central bank. They are reserve balances held at the Fed, except that they would be available to everyone, and not only to the 5000 or so depository institutions that maintain accounts at the Fed. Currently, the Fed provides those accounts to banks and governmental entities only. Extending them to individuals would require the enactment of new legislation.

The BIS (Bank of International Settlements), which is heavily involved in developing international standards, has advised countries to prefer account-based instead of toked-based CBDCs.[7] It also recommends including a privacy layer to curb fears of government surveillance.[8] As such, CBDCs would still be a functional substitute for cash, even if operationally the units of Dollars would simply be identity-linked.

The important point, however, is that whether in the form of a token or of a bank account, a CBDC will be a form of money created by the US Federal Government through its monetary authority. This is why we refer to it as "sovereign money". It follows that the proposals to create CBDCs should be accounted in practice for what they are in theory: an attempt to crowd out privately created money—and therefore, an invitation for a greater degree of government-directed credit, money creation, and financial repression (or political allocation of money) than what we already have today.

In addition, by crowding out private money and reducing the number of alternatives for retail payments, CBDCs could indirectly increase the demand for sovereign money. This is not an irrelevant consideration. One should remember that with higher inflation, the United States public debt is currently being placed with negative real interest rates. Thus, in its attempts to keep interests on public debt at bay, the United States may face a problem where the supply exceeds the demand for its securities at the given price.

[7] BIS Annual Economic Report 2021, III. CBDCs—an opportunity for the monetary system, p. 82.

[8] *Id.*, p. 74.

4 Sovereign Money and the Fragility of Private Money

To make sense of the importance of the distinction between private and sovereign money, we have to go back in history. At least for the last three hundred years, in Western societies money has been supplied partly by the state, partly by the market. The state portion of the money supply has historically taken the form of coins and commodity money, and later fiat money with legal tender. The other part of the money supply has been provided by commercial banks: first in the form of banknotes redeemable in government-issued coins, and later in the form of bank credit payable in government-issued paper money—which is why these money-claims issued by banks are also referred to as money "substitutes".

The supply of money by the government first depended on the availability of precious metals. The sovereign was forced to use real resources to invest in the mining of silver and gold or to purchase bullion from which it could mint coins. Except for the old trick of debasing the coinage and reducing its purchasing power, supplying money was costly. Thus, the quantity of coins with the previously expected purchasing power that a sovereign could mint was dependent of the allocation of real wealth. It was only much later that sovereign money was made possible solely on the will of the government (fiat money). In any case, the amount of the money supplied by the government is said to be determined "outside" the market. In this sense, "sovereign money" is also "external" money.

Banks, on the other hand, give credit by creating banknotes or credit bank account balances for their borrowers. The crucial point is that credit is created only when borrowers come with investment propositions that are likely to allow for a profit. Because the amount of money substitutes created by banks depends on the existence of profitable opportunities for lending in the market, that part of the money supply is called "inside money". The beauty of this system is the supply of money adjusts "naturally" to the ever-changing demand for money.

This is the essence of what is now known as "modern finances", that is, fractional reserve banking. This system came about in 1694 with the creation of the Bank of England and then spread worldwide. Instead of using real metal as a medium of exchange, people started to use the Bank's promise to pay gold and silver as the instrument for their private exchanges. This promise was represented on the Bank of England's balance sheet and took the form of banknotes.

The English commercial banks rapidly started to create more money substitutes than the counterpart of the amount of money originally borrowed by the UK Crown or the amount of reserves they kept in their vaults. The banks started to finance credit to commerce and later, farming and industry. These arrangements with "fractional" reserves financed the industrial revolution. They usually worked well when prudently managed under the rules of their creation—especially, that the government could not be financed by the bank with the issuance of banknotes.

However, in situations of emergency, usually because of the need to finance armed conflicts, said arrangements would end up being abused. At that point inflationary war finance would come about. Military crises would therefore reveal the "inherent" fragility of the arrangements under which banks issued more promises to pay in "external" money than the amount of base money in existence. Inflationary war finance would then lay bare the fragility that is inbuilt in fractional reserve banking: basically everywhere (and in fact, until today) banks were organized under a legal framework that allowed the sovereign to exercise its monetary prerogatives to force them to lend to the government in emergency cases.

A focus on this fragility should not obfuscate an underappreciated benefit of this system: it is geared towards directing funding to the most promising investment opportunities. This improves overall economic efficiency both directly and indirectly: directly, because capital is allocated in a productive fashion; and indirectly, by aligning the interests of bankers and depositors, since the search for profit by the former signals to the latter that their savings will be parked in a solvent institution.

This trust-based system can basically be broken in three situations: first, when the sovereign thinks that it is politically expedient to force the banks to lend money to the state (especially to finance war, as explained); second, when, in the absence of adverse clearing, the banks are perceived to have overextended themselves by creating more money substitutes than the amount of money people want to hold (leading to bank runs); and third, when bank lending is politically driven or poorly managed and systematically forgoes the most profitable opportunities. The ensuing evils include bank failures, inflation, and capital misallocation.

Devolution of Monetary Powers as a Response

It is because Western societies have been plagued by these evils for centuries that some politicians, policymakers, and academics have considered abolishing inside money altogether. A well-known example was the monetary reform proposal known as the Chicago Plan, which, in the 1930s, proposed a strict form of monetary devolution called "full reserve" or "narrow banking" where the government would take back the money monopoly. The idea was to separate the credit and monetary functions of the banking system completely by forcing commercial banks to operate under a 100% reserve requirement where deposits and other short-term liabilities would be backstopped with sovereign money on a 1:1 basis. Thus, at the cost of worsening capital allocation, this system would eliminate the risk that taxpayers would have to shoulder the costs of bank runs.

While typically falling short of proposing the complete abolition of inside money along the lines of the Chicago Plan, most CBDC proponents partake in the Chicago Plan authors' concern with bank runs, and perhaps more importantly, they also dispute the ability of the banking system to efficiency allocate capital, whether due to shortsightedness or inability to factor broader societal goals into their decisions to price and extent credit. Hence, their optimism towards CBDCs expected a reduction of the role of inside money.

So far, the Chicago Plan represents the road not taken. In fact, despite private money's fragility, the government actively promotes its creation. For instance, governments worldwide offer or promote "deposit insurance" and "lender of last resort" facilities to entice people to surrender money in exchange for deposits, propping up bank-issued money-claims. Besides that, governments offer the public money that anchors private money and is used to settle the obligations between the banks. These and other measures approximate bank deposits to the risk-free, sovereign money produced by the government.

There is however a flipside: the other side of the bargain is that banks may be forced to help finance the government directly (by having to buy Treasuries) or indirectly (by offering subsidized loans to protected segments). And beyond that, banks will have to lend themselves to extensive regulation. However, in comparison to regulation, retail CBDCs offer a more radical solution to the problem of fractional "fragility": curbing the ability of banks to create money or further regulating its quantity, depending on the particularities of each CBDC scheme. It is a kind of "devolution" to the government of money creation powers that, starting in the late seventeenth century England, were assigned to the private sector.

But to go back to our starting point—to return monetary powers to the government with what purpose? On the one hand, we could say, with the coming about of CBDCs the government will target the fragility of private money head-on by eliminating it. From this viewpoint, CBDCs are nothing but a tech-based variant of previous attacks on inside money such as the "Chicago Plan" or other proposals for full reserve banking. But instead of being simply a tool to deal with the risk of bank runs, retail CBDCs would represent more of the same, since in the end what they would do is make it possible for the government to increase its ability to do something that it already does today—that is, to gain access to real goods without imposing greater taxation in the present. From this viewpoint, retail CBDCs would be nothing but one more stance in which it is advocated that the liquid funds of the community should be politically allocated.

To see why, consider that retail CBDCs will stand in direct competition with bank deposits. Both CBDCs and demand deposits develop the same function and have similar features: they are both digital, they are assets that can be redeemed on demand at face value, and they are both used to make ordinary payments. But while demand deposits are a bank promise to repay the asset in sovereign money, CBDCs are sovereign money itself. From the perspective of the user, all else equal CBDCs are therefore superior in quality to demand deposits. As a result, the issuance of CBDCs tends to displace demand deposits, especially in times of financial stress. Expectedly, therefore, some deposits will be exchanged for CBDCs, a phenomenon often referred to as "disintermediation".

As depositors move from storing liquidity in public rather than private money, demand deposits go down and the ability of commercial banks to further create money diminishes. To avoid a reduction in money supply, the government could set quantitative limits to the ability of depositors to migrate to CBDCs. However, such measure would hardly avoid the crowding out of inside money. It would also be a strange type of measure—if CBDCs are superior to bank deposits, why not allow CBDCs to their fullest extent possible? Besides that, quantitative limits could impose a premium on the circulation of commercial bank deposits, which would reduce their moneyness and potentially hurt financial stability.

Thus, the expected endgame of the coming about of retail CBDCs is one where the government assumes increasing responsibility for lending either directly or by becoming a regular source of funding for the banks.

The expected result would be those that traditionally fall under the rubric of *financial repression*. For one, credit would be allocated to the sorts of projects that the political process deems more worthy of receiving the funds (for example, the United Nations *sustainable development goals*, or SDGs) to a greater extent than today. Moreover, the crowding out of private by sovereign money would also, expectedly at least, assist the government in accelerating debt monetization. The increase in non-bank, or shadow bank, lending would just be another expected, even if unwanted, result.

5 The Mechanics

Let us see how any of that can be accomplished. As a first approximation, we can use the Chicago Plan model to illustrate the mechanics of FedAccounts. Suppose the Fed creates a ledger for all bank accounts in the country directly in its own balance sheet. The Fed then announces that depositors can choose between opening new accounts directly with the Fed or keeping their deposit accounts with their current commercial banks—but in the latter case, under the caveat that each commercial banks must transfer one hundred percent of deposits in real time to corresponding accounts held with the Fed by their customers.

Under such arrangements, the commercial banks will in practice be put in a regime of 100% reserve requirement and will not have money to lend to private borrowers from the floating of the deposits. In turn, the Fed will have as base money (bank reserves with the Fed) the entire liquidity of the country, including the other component of base money, paper currency—assuming, of course, that paper currency will continue to exist, something that some proposals for CBDC do not permit. Thus, all the demand for "cash" (paper money and bank deposits) becomes "Fed-accounts". The money supply becomes a Fed liability, all of it. And the counterpart of those liabilities on the asset side of the Fed's balance sheet are Treasuries and other bonds that are determined based on the Fed credit policies.

Now, under this regime of "full reserve" banking, if the banks wish to lend money, they first need to borrow from the Fed or borrow in the capital markets like any other business. Then, of course, the function of commercial banks changes quite radically. Instead of creating inside money, banks focus on screening consumers, on-boarding, servicing, off-boarding them, as well as watching over and updating the technology platforms. To maintain the level of money supply, the government steps in. It could seem like a regulators' utopia—full devolution of the power to create money—, but the practical outcome can be quite different. The problem is that the repression of financial intermediation by commercial banks expectedly creates market incentives for other nonbank agents to step in and create money-like instruments to satisfy that demand. In other words, new forms of shadow banks will tend to come about.

The devolution of monetary powers to the state that comes up with the creation of retail CBDCs also helps undo the operational independence of central banks and the formal separation between monetary and fiscal policy. This separation was intended by early framers of the Fed and was reinforced in 1933 with the creation of the Federal Open Market Committee (FOMC) and in 1935 with a statutory limitation on monetary financing. Of course, this is not to deny that the separation has always worked best during peaceful times, since in times of war debt monetization tends to become the norm rather than the exception.[9] Thus, during World War II, Congress amended the Federal Reserve Act to authorize the Fed to purchase securities directly from the Treasury—which it did, always under at low-interest rates.[10] After the War, inflationary pressures pushed for the reinstatement of a prohibition against monetary financing—first, in a 1951 one-paragraph "Accord" between the Fed and the Treasury, and later with an amendment to the Federal Reserve

[9] Although in the United States little money was created to fund the war efforts of World War I. See Richard Sutch, Liberty Bonds, RESERVE HISTORY, FED. RESERVE BANK ST. LOUIS, https://www.federalreservehistory.org/essays/liberty-bonds ("the [United States] federal government relied on a mix of one-third new taxes and two-thirds borrowing from the general population [...] The borrowing effort was called the "Liberty Loan" and was made operational through the sale of Liberty Bonds. These securities were issued by the Treasury, but the Federal Reserve and its member banks conducted the bond sales.").

[10] G. Richardson, The Federal Reserve's Role During WWII FED. RESERVE HISTORY, FED. RESERVE BANK ST. LOUIS, https://www.federalreservehistory.org/essays/feds-role-during-wwii.

Act that allowed the Fed to buy and sell Treasury securities only in the secondary market.[11]

The point to be noted is now there is a strong movement to undo this framework of separation of fiscal and monetary policy in times of peace. To be sure, any realistic assessment must acknowledge that the line between fiscal and monetary policy is already very much blurred. To respond to the 2008 financial debacle, the Fed set to purchase unprecedented quantities of government debt under its "quantitative easing" programs—a trait that was sometimes perceived as the Fed backstopping public debt.[12]

Besides that, the Cares Act enacted in response to the Covid-19 pandemic further expanded the Fed's lending capabilities to non-bank entities by authorizing it to provide "liquidity to the financial system that supports lending to eligible business, States, or municipalities".[13] In particular, the Cares Act authorized the Secretary of the Treasury to use almost half a trillion dollars in programs with funds appropriated to a fund that belongs to the Treasury.[14] Thus, upon obtaining prior approval of the Secretary of the Treasury—a requirement also established by the Dodd-Frank Act of 2010—the Fed put in place several lending facilities to finance chosen companies, businesses, and demographic cohorts. Given the Fed's limited discretion in allocation, some scholars sustained the Fed was simply acting as a "conduit" for fiscal-policy implementation through the financial system.[15] But this, in any case, is far from a rigid separation between monetary and fiscal authority.

As such, the adoption of CBDCs along the lines that we have described herein (representing a devolution of monetary powers to the state) can be framed simply as the normalization of a situation that heretofore is

[11] Federal Reserve Act § 14(2)(b), 12 U.S.C. § 355 (2018). For a summary of the evolution of the statutory limitations to monetary financing in the United States, *see* Marcelo Prates, Money in the Twenty-First Century: From Rusty Coins to Digital Currencies, 15 Ohio State Business Law Journal 164, 197–199 (2021).

[12] J. B. Bolzani, Independent Central Banks and Independent Agencies: Is the Fed Super Independent? 2022, 22 Bus. L. Journal 195, 228.

[13] Cares Act, Section 4003(b).

[14] *Id.*

[15] See J. B. Bolzani, Has the Cares Act Expanded the Fed's Legal Mandate? The FinReg Blog, October 26, 2020, at https://sites.law.duke.edu/thefinregblog/2020/10/26/has-the-cares-act-expanded-the-feds-legal-mandate/#_ftnref5.

being treated as exceptional. Theoretically, in normal times the Fed holds operational autonomy vis-à-vis the Treasury and the executive power. Base money is created for the purpose of facilitating monetary policy to keep inflation at bay and to permit the Fed to ease economic fluctuation within the business cycle. In practice, the expansion of the Fed mandate to backstop and ever-increasing number of non-bank agents creating money-claims within the shadow banking system has rendered the Fed's independence less relevant, and debt monetization has blurred the frontier between the Fed and the Treasury.

The coming about of retail CBDCs would accordingly be the coronation of this process, one where commercial banks progressively (or perhaps rapidly) are forced to renounce their ability to produce money in response to profitable opportunities and the accommodation of the economy's needs for liquidity is shifted to the government.

6 The Choice at Hand

Foes of private money may aspire for direct retail accounts with the Fed, or a "postal bank" associated with the Fed, and lending done directly by the Federal government and some of its agencies. In this scenario, the entire financial sector is nationalized, in one way or another. Leveraging and deleveraging of the private sector become increasingly a political matter and the incentives for efficient capital allocation are severely hurt. The system of market-driven allocation of capital is undone and with that the efficiency of wealth creation in society is reduced.[16] All of that can be marshaled to justify caution in CBDCs.

A steadfast opposition to CBDCs is however a different story. It is a dangerous path, because it can accommodate a number of errors, especially self-deception in assuming that the current system, despite all its advantages, presents the endpoint of monetary history. Besides that, opposing CBDCs as a matter of principle can amount, perhaps, even to a form of neo-luddism, this time represented by oblivion to CBDCs' technological advantages and possibilities. More concretely, one should

[16] Of course, not all proposals for the creation of CBDCs are that extreme. Some of the proposals for the creation of digital "token dollars", for instance, will only marginally (although no one can know for sure by how much) reduce private banking intermediation by inducing a greater portion of the liquid holdings to be kept in cash—now, in its digital form.

recognize that current commercial bank systems are expensive and that CBDCs can offer means to streamline payments, making them cheaper and faster, particularly in international payments.

An additional point is that, with or without CBDCs, the role of commercial banks is changing. Traditional commercial banks are now in competition not only among themselves, but also with non-banking institutions that thanks to new technologies found niches in financial markets and became fintechs. In fact, when we consider the vibrancy and quick development of electronic money issuers, the financial system looks not like the retreat of financial intermediation (or "desintermediation", as discussed above) but rather like its expansion. Given the quick expansion of cryptocurrency markets, it becomes possible to envision a new payment system where CBDCs become the basis for a revamped systematic for financial intermediation.[17]

Among the different types of digital money currently being created, stablecoins seem to hold the most potential for wider adoption. Stablecoins are, in the words of the Financial Stability Board, "crypto-assets that aim to maintain a stable value".[18] They were designed as such to address the problem of extreme volatility which plagues most cryptocurrencies and harms their ability to serve as money. Stablecoins can be pegged to commodities, gold, or to other cryptocurrencies. More daringly, stablecoins can simply be backed by an algorithm that tries to keep the peg with a national currency through a complex system of arbitrage and governance tokens (this was famously the case of Terra USD, which collapsed in May of 2022). Stablecoins can also be tied to a currency basket (as intended, for example, by the Libra project advanced and then abandoned by Facebook and other companies).

Our interest here, however, lies on the stablecoins whose value is moderated with a depository receipt model, such that the stablecoin becomes a claim on a single currency. Under this model, stablecoins contain private liabilities that can be redeemable in base money, just like

[17] See M. K. Brunnermeier, H. James, and J.-P. Landau, The Digitalization of Money, Working Paper, available online at https://scholar.princeton.edu/markus/publications/digitalization-money.

[18] Fin. Stability Bd., Addressing the Regulatory, Supervisory and Oversight Challenges Raised by "Global Stablecoin" Arrangements 4, 2020, https://www.fsb.org/wp-content/uploads/P140420-1.pdf

bank deposits.[19] That is as much as a traditional form of financial intermediation done through fintechs as it is possible to conceive, except that they have been offered by entities that are considered so far as non-financial institutions.

Importantly, stablecoins are a form of credit money, that is, currency that is redeemable in something else. Here, the contrast with Bitcoin is striking, because stablecoins are an "I owe you something" form of money, whereas Bitcoin is an "I owe you nothing" form of money. Because stablecoins are a form of credit money, they can be leveraged by the issuance of more debt than what they will hold in liquid reserves. As such, they can become a source of risk of financial instability, as the recent run on Terra USD has shown.[20]

Here is not the place to discuss whether prudent management of individual issuers of money substitutes would suffice to keep the financial system stable. What should be clear is that in the presence of governmental regulation, if it is for stablecoins to be incorporated in the financial system, most likely, the issuers of stablecoins will eventually be put under the umbrella of liquidity facilities provided by the central bank, becoming "Payment Interface Processors" (PIPs) in the terminology adopted by the Bank of England, or "Currency Connectors" (CCs) as some have suggested.[21] Stablecoins would therefore create money in response to profitable business opportunities, in much the same way that is typically done by commercial banks and trustees of mutual funds.

If we endorse the entry of stablecoins into the financial system, wouldn't we simply trade six of one for half a dozen of the other?

[19] For a good description of stablecoins, see Larry White's "Should we fear stablecoins?" (White, 2021).

[20] See "Digital Currency and the Next Financial Crisis," posted by P. H. Kupiec on the Law & Liberty website on August 30, 2021, available online at https://lawliberty.org/digital-currency-and-the-next-financial-crisis. On the collapse of TerraUSD, see Stablecoins: The Collapse of TerraUSD and the Road Ahead for the "Less-Risky" Form of Cryptocurrency, from May 19, 2022, available online at https://www.mayerbrown.com/en/perspectives-events/publications/2022/05/stablecoins-the-collapse-of-terrausd-and-the-road-ahead-for-the-less-risky-form-of-cryptocurrency?utm_source=Mondaq&utm_medium=syndication&utm_campaign=LinkedIn-integration.

[21] See D. G. W. Birch "When The CBDC Revolution Comes, It Won't Be on the Blockchain," posted on August 3, 2022, at Forbes.com and available at https://www.forbes.com/sites/davidbirch/2022/08/03/when-the-cbdc-revolution-comes-it-wont-be-on-the-blockchain/?sh=7649877483af.

Wouldn't we simply replicate the same sort of fragility held by commercial banks, but now with new players and unchartered technological waters? This is a legitimate concern. As stablecoins grow and competition intensifies, stablecoin issuers will probably move to adopt more aggressive practices in their money-creating strategies. With that, runs from private to sovereign money become at some point simply expectable. To allow for more stringent regulation, one possibility would be to require these stablecoin issuers to obtain a bank charter.[22]

But to even consider extending bank charters to stablecoin issuers, we have to first understand what the issuers of stablecoins bring to the table. A good way to do that is to start by considering the role of new technologies in bringing institutional change in the payments systems. Think about the introduction of banknotes at a time when most transactions were cleared by coins or the compensation of primitive forms of debt. Coins are risky to carry around, uncertain in their value due to clipping, falsification, and debasement. Despite that, they were used for clearance because primitive forms of debt like bills of exchange from private merchants were not easily accepted outside of narrow circles of business associates. That was the situation up until the coming of the technology of security printing. With that, the institutional environment rapidly adapted to permit the creation of money substitutes in the form of banknotes. Clearance with coins progressively declined, and basically came to an end in the early 1970s with the demise of the Bretton Woods system.

Today, the clearance of commercial and financial transactions is done through by the clearing mechanisms put in place or closely monitored and regulated by central banks and other financial authorities. In the United States, dollar wholesale payments are cleared and settled through systems such as the Fedwire, Real-Time Payments systems (or RTP), and the Clearing House Interbank Payment System (or CHIPS, which is used for cross-border payments). Consumer and commercial payments occur through the Automated Clearing House System, or ACH.

The clearing of payments has over time been encumbered by an increasing number of regulations that attach political goals to that of settling monetary obligations. Chiefly among them are Anti-Money Laundering/Combating the Financing of Terrorism (AML/

[22] For a detailed articulation of this proposal, see M. Ricks, The Money Problem: Rethinking Financial Regulation, 2016.

CFT) and the economic sanctions by the Financial Crimes Enforcement Network (FinCEN). Taken together, these measures have led to a sharp decrease of correspondent banking networks and thwarted efforts to streamline cross-border payment systems. European privacy laws have been blamed for complicating the transmission of data cross-border. These policies are put in place within the systems for clearance of transactions in sovereign money and regulated money substitutes.

But just like the printing press and the evolution of communication technologies eventually led to the demise of settlement in coins, the coming about of distributed ledger may also lead to changes in the architectures for settlement of transactions. Here, stablecoins, such as USDC powered by the Ethereum blockchain, represent a new form of money substitute that may force the regulators and existing financial intermediaries to rethink their political priorities.[23] The process is not fundamentally different from ride-sharing apps such as Uber and Lyft forcing entrenched interests in the taxi business and urban transportation authorities at the local level to rethink their procedures and goals.

It is at this point that CBDCs may play a role by offering the money base to settle payments between stablecoin. To be clear, the CBDCs, here, would be wholesale, not retail, since they would not be available to the public at large. With a wholesale CBDC, the Fed would just provide an Application Programming Interface (API) for all the issuers of stablecoins and their correspondent digital wallets to be cleared in this digital form of sovereign money. Naturally, their implementation would require overcoming technological hurdles. Nevertheless, the use of wholesale CBDCs would bypass the need for correspondent banking. This would be particularly efficient in cross-border payments, where settlement currently requires a web of correspondent banking networks.

Wholesale CBDCs could also be employed at the domestic level. The roadmap we envisage here would be one where the Fed would eventually allow the issuers of stablecoins to access to its ordinary clearing mechanisms. A first step in that direction was recently taken by the Office of the Comptroller of the Currency with the enactment of several Interpretive Letters allowing national banks to use Dollar-based stablecoins as a settlement infrastructure in the US payment system. The Interpretive Letter

[23] See "Visa Becomes First Major Payments Network to Settle Transactions in USD Coin (USDC)," available online at https://usa.visa.com/about-visa/newsroom/press-releases.releaseld.17821.html.

issued in October of 2020 authorized national banks to hold stablecoin reserves as a type of service to their clients.[24] That would allow the stablecoin issuers to provide assurance to the public that they hold sufficient assets to back their stablecoins. Another Interpretive Letter, issued in January of 2021, authorized national banks to serve as independent nodes to validate transactions performed on stablecoin DLT ledgers.[25]

After the change of administration, the OCC enacted a new Interpretive Letter confirming that national banks can engage with Dollar-based stablecoins but will be subject to heightened scrutiny and will need a supervisor's letter of non-objection before they can start offering the services.[26] The topic is still surrounded by uncertainties, but a fruitful path has been established. The provision of services by national banks to issuers of stablecoins will create a communication channel between fintechs' private currency creation and the Fed. Expectedly, when facing liquidity or solvency problems, these national banks may end up discounting (i.e. selling) the stablecoin issuers' reserve assets to the Fed. It is, as we see it, a likely sequencing.

7 Politics in the Origin

It is difficult to imagine that the design of new digital monies, public or private, could achieve simultaneously both goals of becoming instruments for more efficient payments (like stablecoins premised by wholesale CBDCs, as outlined above) and instruments for financial repression (as most proposals for retail CBDCs suggest). CBDCs could probably assist in the implementation of either of these agendas, but hardly in the implementation of both at the same time. The choice is therefore essentially political.

Which way will politics point to? National indebtedness and the specter of climate change, alongside other pressures for public expenditure have been forcing US monetary authorities to accommodate the increased demand for borrowed funds by national governments—including, of course, the US government. As the process continues and fiscal deficits grow, we can expect that the Fed may be tempted to increase the

[24] Interpretative letter # 1172, October 2020.

[25] Interpretative letter # 1174, January 2021.

[26] Interpretative letter # 1179, November 2021.

crowding out of private productive investment by increasing financial repression not only in favor of the political allocation of credit to favored sectors, but above all to attend the direct fiscal needs of the Treasury.

The alternative path is nevertheless worth contemplating: CBDCs could be used to (in part, at least) disintermediate commercial banks, and to re-intermediate credit with stablecoins. For that to work, stablecoins would be privately issued but settled with wholesale CBDCs that serve as base money. The issuer of the stablecoins would extend credit in stablecoins and these credits would not be fully backed, allowing for their leverage, in the same way that commercial banks have always operated with fractional reserves.

8 Conclusion

In the old days, at the time of the gold standard, there were gold reserves in the form of bars in bank vaults, gold and silver coins issued by governments, bank notes issued by banks redeemable in coins (or bars, by other banks) and account credits to be honored with the notes issued by the banks themselves. What we contemplate here is a similar architecture with digital technology where wholesale CBDCs or tokens play a role partly similar to that of gold and silver bars and coins.

CHAPTER 12

Open Banking in the UK: A Co-opetition Scenario for Innovation and Evolution in the UK Retail Banking Sector

Nikita Divissenko

1 Introduction

"Can we win more by competing less?" asks one of the City of London banks in its poster ad in the London subway. This might appear as an odd question to raise for an incumbent in the industry traditionally characterised by a high level of concentration. Yet precisely this kind of strategies underpin the ongoing evolution in UK retail banking prompted by the implementation of the Open Banking framework.

Open Banking—the provision of retail banking services based on the sharing of customer data by account service providers (banks) with other authorised service providers—brought drastic changes to the retail

N. Divissenko (✉)
Utrecht University School of Law, Utrecht, The Netherlands
e-mail: n.divissenko@uu.nl

M. Bodellini et al. (eds.), *Commercial Banking in Transition*, Palgrave Macmillan Studies in Banking and Financial Institutions,
https://doi.org/10.1007/978-3-031-45289-5_12

banking sector. Application programming interface (API)[1] based business models, including account aggregation service providers,[2] have been emerging throughout the last decade, overhauling 'traditional' retail banking. The resulting user interface innovation and overlay services significantly altered customer demand.

The Open Banking framework adopted under the revised payment services directive (PSD2)[3] in the EU and implemented under the CMA 2017 Order[4] in the UK has been deemed as setting a new benchmark for global efforts directed at 'policy-led innovation'.[5] With Open Finance high on policy-makers' agenda and promises of further economic growth by leveraging on data-driven innovation, the effects of the UK Open Banking framework are of particular interest.[6] Based on authorised customer data sharing, it is only logical that the 'opening up' of transactional data sharing for the purposes of innovation should be designed with a demand-side interests in mind. However, the current framework for Open Banking originated from the supply-centred concern over the lack of competition. This resulted in a paradox: to tackle the lack of competition in the sector, the Open Banking framework incentivised cooperation

[1] What Is an Application Programming Interface (API)?, November 10, 2022, https://www.ibm.com/cloud/learn/api; see also, M. Zachariadis and P. Ozcan, The API Economy and Digital Transformation in Financial Services: The Case of Open Banking, SSRN Scholarly Paper, Rochester, NY, 2017, https://doi.org/10.2139/ssrn.2975199.

[2] See, I. Oliinyk and W. Echikson, Europe's Payments Revolution: Stimulating Payments Innovation While Protecting Consumer Privacy, CEPS, 2018.

[3] Directive (EU) 2015/2366 of the European Parliament and of the Council of 25 November 2015 on payment services in the internal market, amending Directives 2002/65/EC, 2009/110/EC and 2013/36/EU and Regulation (EU) No. 1093/2010, and repealing Directive 2007/64/EC.

[4] "Retail Banking Market Investigation Order 2017," GOV.UK, accessed November 25, 2022, https://www.gov.uk/government/publications/retail-banking-market-investigation-order-2017.

[5] "The Kalifa Review of UK FinTech," GOV.UK, accessed November 18, 2022, https://www.gov.uk/government/publications/the-kalifa-review-of-uk-fintech.

[6] In its essence, Open Finance will facilitate B2B data sharing beyond sector-specific the bank transaction account data sharing under Open Banking. Instead, Open Finance will aim to facilitate third-party providers offering services such as advice, optimisation solutions, or assistance with savings, lending, investments, pensions or insurance. See, Communication from the Commission to the European Parliament, the Council, the European Economic and Social Committee and the Committee of the Regions on a Digital Finance Strategy for the EU,COM(2020) 591 final, 2020, 13. Also, The Kalifa Review of UK FinTech, 17.

among competitors to jointly develop new standards which, in turn, were meant to increase competition and pose threat to incumbents.

Concerns underpinning the regulatory intervention in the UK retail banking sector involved low levels of switching (and shopping around) by banking customers, lack of transparency undermining comparison between account service providers, accompanied by barriers to entry, and obstacles to scaling up of innovative service providers within the highly concentrated sector. These issues prompted the Consumer Market Authority (CMA) to undertake a market investigation in 2014.[7]

Adopting the Open Banking framework, the CMA rolled out a package of reforms that (i) mandated common and open standards for Open Banking and (ii) obliged the largest banks in Great Britain and Northern Ireland to share their customer data with third-party service providers so as to facilitate the development of novel retail banking services that would enhance customers' ability to choose services best suiting their needs.[8]

Today, five years since the implementation of Open Banking, competition landscape in the UK retail banking sector has changed dramatically. The technological development continues at a high pace as new data-driven business models emerge, challenging the existing market structures and market actors' strategies. From the pro-competitive objective of 'opening-up' the retail banking industry, the focus has gradually shifted to 'ecosystem growth' as a paradigm for regulation that supports innovation and competition. Meanwhile, co-opetition strategies, prompted by the implementation of the Open Banking framework, continue to play an important role. Based on the analysis of these trends and changes, this chapter offers a detailed inquiry into the inception and evolution of the Open Banking framework and the change it brought to the UK retail banking sector.

The chapter begins by discussing the background and objectives of the Open Banking framework in the UK, and focuses on the 2016 market investigation and the core mandate of Retail Banking Market Investigation Order 2017. The second and main part of the chapter discusses the

[7] K. Baker, Open Banking Lessons Learned Review, Competition and Markets Authority, accessed November 23, 2022, 5, https://www.gov.uk/government/publications/open-banking-lessons-learned-review-report-by-kirstin-baker.

[8] Ibid., 9.

role of the CMA9 and the co-opetition-driven evolution and innovation in the UK retail banking sector, and puts the main trends, developments, and debates over the future of the sector in the context of the requirements of the Open Banking framework. The final section of the chapter concludes.

2 Background

The Problem: CMA Market Investigation

Retail banking market investigation launched by the CMA in 2014, had been preceded by a number of inquiries into the UK retail banking sector, and in particular, into the UK retail payments sector throughout the last decades.[9] Competition concerns and the need to promote effective competition had been raised in earlier reports, from Sir Donald Cruickshank's review in 2000,[10] to Sir John Vickers chaired Independent Commission on Banking (ICB) in 2011,[11] as well as the Parliamentary Commission on Banking Standards (PCBS) in 2013.[12]

The earlier reports outlined the need for additional efforts to address not only the concentration issues on the supply-side of the UK retail banking market, but also those on the demand-side. Thus, the ICB 2011 report underlined, that:

> *Market concentration of the supply side is coupled with weaknesses on the demand side. In particular, current account switching costs are perceived as*

[9] Competition and Markets Authority, Retail banking market investigation, Final report, 2016, ii.

[10] D. Cruickshank, Competition in UK Banking: A Report to the Chancellor of the Exchequer, London, Stationery Off, 2000.

[11] "Independent Commission on Banking," accessed November 18, 2022, https://webarchive.nationalarchives.gov.uk/ukgwa/20120827143059oe_/http://bankingcommission.independent.gov.uk/.

[12] House of Lords House of Commons, Parliamentary Commission on Banking Standards. Changing banking for good, Report of the Parliamentary Commission on Banking Standards Volume I: Summary, and Conclusions and recommendations, HL Paper 27-I HC 175-I, London, Stationery Off, 2013.

being high and product comparisons are opaque. Switching rates are remarkably low, and this is not explained by high levels of customer satisfaction with existing suppliers.[13]

The CMA market investigation, launched in 2014, focused on several competition-related issues, taking both the supply- and demand-side considerations into account. The question of 'whether there is a weak customer response due to lack of engagement and/or barriers to searching and switching reducing the incentives on banks to compete on price and/or quality and/or to innovate'[14] constituted the core of its analysis. Bridging the demand-side consideration of customer engagement (incl. consumer demand) with the supply-side concerns over competition and innovation, the 2016 final report of investigation delineated a number of important links between the three.

First, the report emphasised the importance of innovative technology that impacts several aspects of retail banking. These impacts included the cost of entry, including 'digital-only' entrants, innovation in payment methods such as contactless payments and mobile payments, and, finally, the impact on the way customers interact with their banks.[15] Furthermore, the report focused on the potential benefits from innovation for retail bank customers. Importantly, the report emphasised the link between the demand-side obstacles—low customer engagement due to search and switching costs—and the obstacle to innovation development on the supply-side. In other words, despite a number of competitors in the personal current account markets offering lower prices and higher service quality, the level of switching between service providers and market share growth by those offering lower prices and better quality—remained extremely low.[16] The report further stipulated that the behaviour of customers had led to competitive constraints on service providers, as low customer engagement reduced incentives to compete.[17]

[13] "Independent Commission on Banking," accessed November 18, 2022, 154, https://webarchive.nationalarchives.gov.uk/ukgwa/20120827143059oe_/http://bankingcommission.independent.gov.uk/.

[14] Competition and Markets Authority, Retail banking market investigation, Final report, 2016, ii.

[15] Ibid., iii.

[16] Ibid., xiii.

[17] Ibid., xiv.

The report thus underlined the mutually dependent relationship between customer engagement on one side, and innovation and effective market competition, on the other side (Fig. 1). Where customer engagement remains low, innovation uptake is slow or deemed unlikely. This, in turn, affects competition, leading to higher levels of market concentration.

The three-way dependency had been illustrated in the 2016 report by highlighting the example of aggregation services.[18] The findings of the report suggested, that if the use of aggregation services became widespread, this could raise financial awareness and subsequently increase customer engagement. However, due to several potential barriers to further development and adoption of aggregation services by users, including lack of effective competition and market concentration, at the time of the report most of the aggregation services were provided by the small number of third-party providers, limiting the awareness and wider adoption of the service. Slow adoption and use of the service by consumers, in turn, appeared to slow down innovation efforts in these services as well as the effects of this innovation on customer engagement.[19]

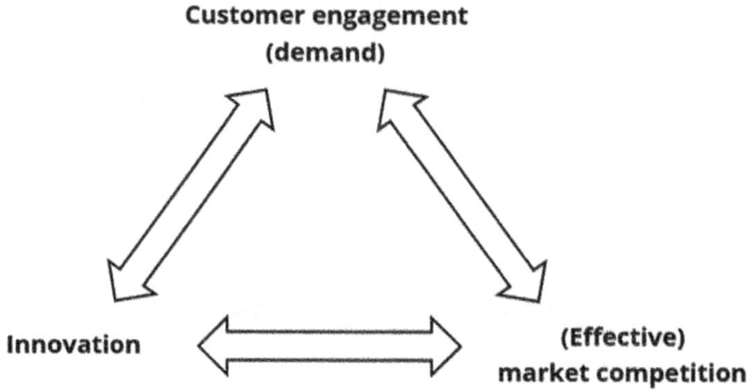

Fig. 1 Innovation, market competition, and customer engagement

[18] Today widely known as 'account information services' (AIS) in accordance with the term adopted by the revised Payment Services Directive (PSD2).

[19] Competition and Markets Authority, Retail banking market investigation, Final report, 2016, 145.

Focus of the report on innovation, such as that of the new aggregation services, further underscored the link between customer engagement and competition concerns. Aggregation services emphasised the role of customers (esp. consumers) on the demand-side, and of entrants (third-party providers) on the supply-side in the provision of those new services, and illustrated the concerns regarding the effects of low levels of customer engagement on both innovation and competition. Since in its essence, account aggregation innovation required incumbents to offer new services themselves or to provide third parties with access to customer transaction data, the lack of competitive pressure significantly reduced the incumbents' incentives for adopting and facilitating this innovation. As the findings of the report suggested, low customer engagement with services such as personal current accounts (PCAs) was often due to the existing 'barriers for customers to access and assess information and barriers to switching,'[20] that could be reduced or removed with further digitalisation and wider adoption of aggregation services. In the absence of incumbent incentives due to a lack of competitive pressure (and, to a large extent, conflicting incentives to maintain control over customers' data), such innovation efforts remained low, ultimately affecting customer engagement in the market.

Lack of effective competition was the third element in the triangle of mutually dependent forces behind the (mal)functioning of the retail banking sector in the UK, and constituted the centrepiece of the analysis. As can be seen throughout the analysis in the report, the emphasis on the need for a competitive UK retail banking sector largely stemmed from the objective to facilitate innovation to the benefit of end users. The benefits of innovation—such as third-party account aggregation services—are the diversity of choice, cost efficiency, and better quality service offered to customers.[21] Lack of competitive pressure was found to lead to reduced (incumbent) incentives to innovate, instead erecting barriers to (new entrant) innovation in the retail banking sector.[22] Example of aggregation services provided a striking manifestation of such lack of incentives with respect to innovative solutions that required significant cooperative

[20] Ibid., 193.

[21] Competition and Markets Authority, Retail banking market investigation, Final report, 2016, 251.

[22] Ibid.

efforts and, in addition, would have undermined the status quo in the concentrated market. As a result, also customer engagement, measured by the frequency and levels of switching between products and service providers, remained low. For this reason, and as the main outcome of the inquiry into competition in the markets for personal and business current accounts in the UK, the investigation concluded that the effectiveness of competition in these markets needed to be improved with the aim of facilitating innovation that enhances customer engagement.

The Solution: Retail Banking Market Investigation Order 2017

Following the publication of the report in 2016, the CMA implemented a package of reforms aimed at introducing measures for customers to benefit from technological advances and allow new entrants to compete more fairly with market incumbents.[23]

The framework, that became known as Open Banking, undertook to:

- accelerate technological change in the UK retail banking sector;
- enable individual customers and small businesses to share their data securely with other banks and with third parties;
- enable customers to manage their accounts with multiple providers through a single digital 'app' to take more control of their funds (for example to avoid overdraft charges and manage cashflow) and to compare products on the basis of their own requirements.[24]

In light of the importance of the interrelation between consumer engagement, fair and effective competition, and innovation, the cornerstone of the proposed framework - the Retail Banking Market Investigation Order 2017 (CMA 2017 Order)—was built upon stimulating competition to facilitate innovation and enhance customer engagement (Fig. 2).

The Fig. 2 illustrates how, in line with the findings of the 2016 market investigation report, the objectives of the Retail Banking Market Investigation Order 2017, albeit a competition-enhancing tool, have

[23] "CMA Paves the Way for Open Banking Revolution," GOV.UK, accessed November 18, 2022, https://www.gov.uk/government/news/cma-paves-the-way-for-open-banking-revolution.

[24] Ibid.

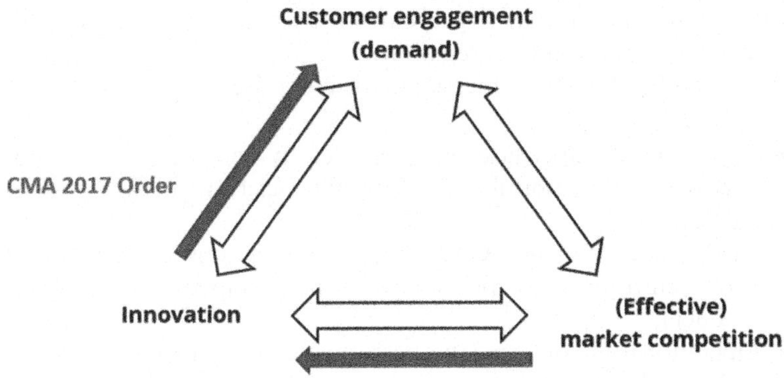

Fig. 2 Innovation, market competition, and customer engagement under CMA 2017 Order

been tangled together with the objectives of promoting innovation and customer engagement. To ensure the objectives of the framework were fulfilled, CMA 2017 Order required from the market participants in charge of implementing the order a level of cooperation. Mandated cooperation, in the (near) absence of individual incentives, had been deemed necessary to achieve the level of technological change necessary to have the desired effect on innovation and customer engagement. Thus, somewhat paradoxically, the tool adopted to enhance market competition mandated cooperation between competing market actors.

3 Open Banking: Co-opetition and Innovation in the UK Retail Banking

Open Banking

The Open Banking implementation body—Open Banking Implementation Entity (OBIE)—places standardisation at the centre of Open Banking definition. Open Banking standards allow banks and authorised third parties (third-party provides)[25] to connect in a common and secure way,

[25] This encompasses the ecosystem-centred view that focuses on the interactions between the players within the framework of open banking. See, P. Laplante and N. Kshetri, Open Banking: Definition and Description, 2021, *Computer* 54, no. 10, 122–128, https://doi.org/10.1109/MC.2021.3055909.

and enable simple and easy-to-use customer journey[26] in the use of novel services (such as account aggregation).

Accordingly, Open Banking standards comprise:

- Technical API Specifications (the security and messaging standards necessary for the transfer of sensitive financial data between regulated participants);
- Customer Experience Guidelines (the user journey standards that allow customers to provide informed consent in an intuitive manner);
- Operational Guidelines (the performance standards required of the technical infrastructure);

Together, Open Banking standards allow banks and authorised third parties to connect in a common and secure way, to exchange (share) customer data necessary for the provision of their services (e.g. account aggregation). The standards, moreover, enable simple and intuitive user journeys, which in turn foster greater adoption of open banking.[27] The mandated standardisation under Open Banking is thus deemed necessary to ensure, on the one hand, that access to data is not restrained to any regulated service providers, ensuring fair competition for the benefit of customers; on the other hand, the standards also consider that innovative services, based on customer consent to data sharing, have to meet customer (notably, consumer) demand for ease of use and convenience.[28]

Having its roots in the EU's revised payment services directive (PSD2),[29] the UK Open Banking framework chose its own path by

[26] "The OBIE's Annual Report," Open Banking, accessed November 18, 2022, https://www.openbanking.org.uk/insights/the-obies-annual-report/.

[27] The OBIE's Annual Report, 8.

[28] Finextra, Open Banking: The Next Frontier for Enhancing Financial Experiences, Finextra Research, October 24, 2022, https://www.finextra.com/the-long-read/517/open-banking-the-next-frontier-for-enhancing-financial-experiences.

[29] Comparative analysis of the framework as implemented in the EU and the UK is beyond the scope of this paper. For key institutional and governance differences, consider the framework under the oversight of the European Banking Authority (EBA industry working group on APIs under PSD2). Unlike the OBIE under the oversight of the CMA in the UK, the EBA working group brought together some stakeholders whereas the development of standards mandated under the PSD2 took place elsewhere. See, "EBA Industry Working Group on APIs under PSD2," European Banking

mandating the development of Open Banking standards to a selected group of incumbent account service providers.

CMA9

Art. 3.1.1 of the CMA 2017 Order defines the entities charged with cooperating for the purposes of implementing the Open Banking framework mandated by the Order. The addressees of the Order thus include the key incumbent players in the retail banking sectors in Great Britain and Northern Ireland (the CMA9): RBSG, LBG, Barclays, HSBCG, Nationwide, Santander in Great Britain and Northern Ireland and Danske, BoI, and AIBG in Northern Ireland.

Part 2 of the CMA 2017 Order sets out the key steps and requirements for implementing Open Banking through the developing of open application programming interface (API) standards, data format standards, and security standards for data sharing between incumbent and new market actors.[30] The order mandated the establishment of a single body—OBIE—to ensure the participating banks 'agree, consult upon, implement, maintain and make widely available, without charge open and common banking standards'.[31] In accordance with the Order, the composition, governance arrangements, budget, and funding for the OBIE were to be agreed by and implemented by the CMA9 under the mandate and oversight by the CMA.

Albeit having its roots in the implementation of the revised Directive (EU) 2015/2366 on payment services (PSD2), transposed in the UK despite the outcome of the Brexit vote,[32] the Open Banking framework as defined by the CMA 2017 Order stands out for its specific mandate,

Authority, May 22, 2019, https://www.eba.europa.eu/regulation-and-policy/payment-services-and-electronic-money/eba-working-group-on-apis-under-psd2; "Financial Services Unchained: The Ongoing Rise of Open Banking | McKinsey," accessed November 22, 2022, https://www.mckinsey.com/industries/financial-services/our-insights/financial-services-unchained-the-ongoing-rise-of-open-financial-data.

[30] Art. 10.1 and 10.2 of the CMA 2017 Order.

[31] Art. 10.1 of the CMA 2017 Order.

[32] Competition and Markets Authority, Retail Banking Market Investigation Final Report, 2016, 33.

narrow in personal scope with largely predefined organisational and governance structures.[33] The CMA9 thus subject to mandated cooperation had to embrace the challenge of accelerating technological change in the UK retail banking sector, while enabling customers to share their data securely with other banks and with third parties and enabling them to take more control of their funds.

Despite, or precisely because of, the competition concerns raised with respect to market concentration and lack of incentives to compete in the markets dominated by the CMA9, the innovation and consumer engagement enhancing agenda led the CMA to adopt an Open Banking framework based on mandated cooperation.

Co-opetition and CMA 2017 Order

The notion of co-opetition, first coined by Ray Noorda, is used to describe the situation where companies have to simultaneously pursue both objectives of creating and capturing value thus combining competition and cooperation.[34] Nalebuff and Brandenburger, who described the process and effects of co-opetition in several works, emphasise the importance of this business strategy for the digital economy, technology-intensive and innovative sectors.[35]

With its roots in game theory, co-opetition strategy implies competitors' understanding of the added-value that each player in the game brings. Nalebuff and Brandenburger distinguish between five main types of players in the market. Interestingly, in addition to the categories of competitors, their suppliers and customers, and governments laying down the rules of the game (e.g. by regulatory interventions), the

[33] For comparison with the EU framework, see EBA Industry Working Group on APIs under PSD2; Financial Services Unchained: The Ongoing Rise of Open Banking | McKinsey.

[34] B. J. Nalebuff and A. M. Brandenburger, Co-opetition: Competitive and Cooperative Business Strategies for the Digital Economy, 1997, *Strategy & Leadership* 25, no. 6, 28–33, https://doi.org/10.1108/eb054655, p. 28. Also, see A. M. Brandenburger and B. J. Nalebuff, Co-Opetition, Currency, Doubleday, 1996.

[35] Nalebuff and Brandenburger, Co-opetition; The Rules of Co-Opetition, accessed November 18, 2022, https://hbr.org/2021/01/the-rules-of-co-opetition.

authors underline the importance of another type of supply-side players—the complementors.[36] Complementors, or market actors that lead to consumers giving higher value to a service than if that service was provided by a competitor alone, are different from other competitors whose (new) offer makes the value of the service provided by other competitors lower.

Consider the example of Microsoft's cooperation with Intel, discussed by Nalebuff and Brandenburger. In the context of co-opetition, the relationship between two tech giants—one offering software (operation system—Windows 95) and another offering chips (Pentium chip) is not that of two competitors, nor of customers or suppliers. 'The Pentium chip makes Windows 95 work better, and Windows 95 gives people a reason for upgrading to the Pentium chip.'[37] Instead of resource-intensive innovation aimed at catching up with the other player to compete in its market (e.g. Microsoft engaging in chip production), the strategy chosen is that of co-opetition aimed at enhancing the added-value of the product.[38]

Examples of co-opetition can be found in different industries,[39] where these often appear as an alternative strategy to vertical integration due to the higher perceived added-value, time, or infrastructural constraints. One other example from the computer industry was IBM entry into PC market, relying on Intel chips and Microsoft operating system, with an 'open-architecture' policy that allowed its competitors (incl. Compaq and Dell) to replicate IBM products significantly increasing the size of the market and the added-value (profitability) of its products.[40]

Co-opetition is also not uncommon in retail banking, and in particular, the payments industry. Most recent examples include co-opetition between Kenyan banks and telecommunication service provider aimed at enhancing the use of mobile payments (MPESA).[41] Other example is the

[36] Nalebuff and Brandenburger, Co-opetition, 30.

[37] Ibid.

[38] Ibid., 31.

[39] See, for instance, L. Arnaudo, In Vino Auctoritas. The Wine Industry between Consortia and Co-Opetition, 2016, Mercato Concorrenza Regole, no. 2, 313–328.

[40] Nalebuff and Brandenburger, Co-opetition, 32.

[41] The study of co-opetition between telecom service provider (Safaricom) and banks shows how the strategy adopted by the latter from competing to benefiting from the success of the telecom provider's services meant for the reach and volumes of banks' own products. '[T]he banks quickly moved in and worked with the company to make the

integration of new payment methods by cooperation between payment service providers (banks) and merchants.[42] These cross-sectorial examples (telecoms and banking; retail commerce and banking), however, are distinct from co-opetition between competing companies within the same sector. A relevant example comes from a recent study of competitive and cooperative relationships between banks and mobile wallets in the Chinese market.[43] What underpinned cooperation between the upstream and downstream firms was the need for banks to ensure larger user traffic enabled by the third-party provider despite the competitive threat that those posed to the banks' business.[44] This, on the one hand, allowed banks to attract consumers to using their account services; on the other hand, the cooperation allowed users to reach both new third-party services while using their bank accounts, thus also benefiting the expansion of the third-party services. The study found, however, that banks eventually had an incentive to terminate their cooperation with downstream firms where the continued cooperation would have led to losses due to increased competition (e.g. due to increased used base of the downstream players or expansion upstream) under the market conditions in which a non-cooperative strategy was available to the upstream company (e.g. integration).[45]

As discussed and aptly shown by Nalebuff and Brandenburger, the complements are often missing or are too expensive, prompting other strategies such as vertical integration ('do it yourself'), creation of alliance with competitors, or setting up a proprietary model.[46] All these

customer withdraw the money in mpesa (mobile money transfer) through the Automatic Teller Machines […], they later on worked with Safaricom to allow their members to access their accounts and directly send their money into their accounts.' See, D.K. Kirui, P.K. Chepkuto, and J.G. Tanui, From Competition to Cooperation—Co Opetition: (A Case of Safaricom's Mobile Money Transfer (MPESA) and Commercial Banks in Kenya), 2015, European Journal of Business and Management 7, no. 30.

[42] S. Gonggrijp, M. Geerling, and P. Mallekoote, Successful Introduction of New Payment Methods through 'Co-Opetition', 2013, Journal of Payments Strategy and Systems 7, no. 2, 136–149.

[43] X. Zhang and D. Yang, When Friends Become Enemies: Co-Opetition Relationships between Banks and Third-Party Payment Providers, 2020, International Journal of Bank Marketing 38, no. 5, 1133–1157, https://doi.org/10.1108/IJBM-11-2019-0414.

[44] Zhang and Yang, 1134 and 1146.

[45] Ibid.

[46] Nalebuff and Brandenburger, Co-opetition, 32.

options are, however, unlikely to enhance competition and create value for consumers in the context of highly concentrated markets with low consumer engagement.

In seems rather unsurprising then, that creating conditions for co-opetition between competing market actors under CMA 2017 Order was deemed effective and justified in the context of the shortcomings identified in the 2016 Market investigation and the innovation-intensive environment of Open Banking.

Evolution of the UK Retail Banking Sector

Conceived as a response to the lack of incentives to compete and the slow adoption of innovation by disengaged consumers, the Open Banking framework under CMA 2017 Order has been seen as a success. Despite a number of shortcomings that came to light in the governance of the framework by OBIE since its inception,[47] the latter had recently celebrated surpassing of a 5 million user threshold of Open Banking users in the UK.[48] Indeed, the technical standards mandated under the framework have been delivered by CMA9 and continue to be upgraded to meet the needs of the growing sector. Moreover, the rates of adoption and awareness of Open Banking services have been increasing at an accelerated pace since the beginning of the global COVID-19 pandemic in 2020.

Competition and Changing Market Structure

The framework has indisputably increased market competition. Looking at the recent data from OBIE, as of December 2021 total of 337 regulated service providers were registered, with 245 third-party providers and

[47] The 'lessons learnt' report quotes, amongst others, serious governance failures and underestimating the complexity and scale necessary for the implementation of Open Banking remedy by the CMA. See, Baker, Open Banking Lessons Learned Review; A. White, Open Banking Limited Independent Investigation Report, Competition and Markets Authority, 2021.

[48] M. Paul, "5 Million Users—Open Banking Growth Unpacked," Open Banking, February 24, 2022, https://www.openbanking.org.uk/news/5-million-users-open-banking-growth-unpacked/. The number reportedly exceeded 6 million by the summer 2022. See, "The State of Open Banking in Europe—in 4 Charts," Sifted, April 5, 2022, https://sifted.eu/articles/state-europe-open-banking-uk-fintech/.

92 account providers, and 124 regulated entities with at least one proposition launched and offered live to customers.[49] This is indeed a significant increase compared to 294 in the end of 2020. Notably, the standards adopted under the Open Banking framework have thus not only increased the number of new entrants offering consumers innovative data-enabled services, but also encumber account providers that have entered the race.

Following the regulatory intervention, saturated and competitive markets increasingly manifest a number of co-opetition/cooperation features. Here, emerging newcomer companies (mostly third-party companies in open banking terms) appear to be increasingly playing the role of complementor companies to larger incumbent players. This is exemplified by the wave of recent acquisitions, investments, and partnerships in the segment. Some examples include the acquisition of RoosterMoney—a service for money management assistance—by NatWest[50]; the investment of Barclays in SME accounting software operator FreshBooks[51]; or a joint-venture by AIB, Bank of Ireland, Permanent TSB and KBC Bank Ireland aimed at allowing their customers instant person-to-person payments through a mobile app called Yippay,[52] aimed at targeting customers both in Ireland and in the UK.

The complementor role of innovative service providers has been evident also beyond the retail payment sector. Significant amount of partnerships has been witnessed in the lending sector, with lenders increasingly partnering with account information service providers (account aggregators) to produce efficiencies, reduce friction, and meet customer expectations vis-à-vis the speed of processing of loan requests, and

[49] Ibid.

[50] "NatWest Acquires Youth-Geared RoosterMoney," October 8, 2021, https://www.pymnts.com/news/partnerships-acquisitions/2021/natwest-acquires-youth-geared-fintech-roostermoney/.

[51] "Barclays Leads a $6.6M Seed Round in RESPONSIBLE | Barclays," accessed November 18, 2022, https://home.barclays/news/press-releases/2022/01/barclays-leads-a-66m-seed-round-in-responsible/.

[52] M. Staines, "The Irish Revolut? Here's All You Need to Know about Yippay," Newstalk, accessed November 18, 2022, https://www.newstalk.com/news/the-irish-revolut-heres-all-you-need-to-know-about-yippay-1356658.

at the same time ensure compliance with creditworthiness assessment requirements and accuracy of credit reports.[53]

Open Banking Technology and Innovation
Competition-enhancing Open Banking framework, leading to increased adoption of API and other data-sharing-enabling technologies, has also led to more innovation in the sector. According to the data published by the FCA Innovation Hub, Open Banking is amongst the most used technologies (alongside machine learning (ML), distributed ledger (DLT), and blockchain technology) in its regulatory sandbox,[54] is implemented to develop environmental, social, and corporate governance (ESG) propositions as well as infrastructure innovations.[55] Moreover, use cases of Open Banking technology spread across embedded finance, process innovation, and RegTech, as an important part of increasing digitalisation in the industry.[56]

Open Banking in the UK thus increasingly provides new value and potential for services offering their customers convenient, cheap and easy to use means to pay online for purchases (an e-commerce merchants to accept the payments), including conducting account-to-account payments via a third-party and not an incumbent bank or card network. Account aggregation services and related products continue to evolve, leading to further adjustment of the scope of the Open Banking framework to include the so-called sweeping services.[57] Notably, CMA mandated CMA9 to implement variable recurring payments (VRP) indispensable

[53] Finextra, "Open Banking: Has the Penny Dropped for UK Lenders?," Finextra Research, February 28, 2022, https://www.finextra.com/blogposting/21910/open-banking-has-the-penny-dropped-for-uk-lenders.

[54] Regulatory sandbox is a regulator-controlled environment allowing innovating firms to test their innovative propositions in the market with real consumers. "Regulatory Sandbox," FCA, March 1, 2022, https://www.fca.org.uk/firms/innovation/regulatory-sandbox.

[55] "Innovation Hub: Market Insights," FCA, March 23, 2022, https://www.fca.org.uk/data/innovation-market-insights.

[56] "Innovation Hub."

[57] I. Gulamhuseinwala, "Finally, a New Era in Payments Sweeps In," Open Banking, accessed November 24, 2022, https://www.openbanking.org.uk/insights/finally-a-new-era-in-payments-sweeps-in/.

for sweeping services provided by third parties, extending the existing mandate.[58]

Relatedly, the recent market analyses show that card payments continuously and increasingly dominate UK payment landscape with debit card payments amounting for 44% and 48% of the retail payments volume in the UK in 2021 and 2022 respectively, with debit cards being one of the most preferred payment methods to pay for online shopping.[59] This appears to reinforce the central importance of account service providers holding customers' funds, albeit a more complex and diverse Open Banking 'ecosystem'.[60]

Customer Engagement: From Switching to Navigating Ecosystems

Against the background of increased competition and wider adoption of Open Banking innovation in the UK retail banking sector, one could be confident to assume higher level of customer engagement to accompany the evolution in the market. However, the metric of account switching, used throughout the 2016 Market investigation report and underpinning the CMA 2017 Order, does not lead to that conclusion. In fact, according to the data reporting the levels of account switching the numbers have not increased significantly in the recent years. Against 4,5mln Open Banking users only 647,000 switched their account service provider in 2021, with the latter figure being comparable to 2014 data.[61]

[58] Manideepa Paul, "VRPs for Sweeping Timetable Agreed," Open Banking, November 16, 2021, https://www.openbanking.org.uk/news/vrps-for-sweeping-timetable-agreed/.

[59] UK Finance, "UK Payments Market Summary 2021," 2021; UK Finance, "UK Payment Markets Summary 2022," 2022.

[60] Described by OBIE as a 'a collaborative community comprising banks and financial institutions, fintechs, and technical service providers', thus both incumbents and newcomers, but also non-regulated technical service providers. See, "ECOSYSTEM," Open Banking, accessed November 24, 2022, https://www.openbanking.org.uk/ecosystem/; For the use of the term with respect to API-based business models, see M. Zachariadis and P. Ozcan, The API Economy and Digital Transformation in Financial Services: The Case of Open Banking, SSRN Scholarly Paper, Rochester, NY, 2017, https://doi.org/10.2139/ssrn.2975199; L. Brodsky and L. Oakes, Data Sharing and Open Banking, *Mckinsey*, accessed November 24, 2022, https://www.mckinsey.com/industries/financial-services/our-insights/data-sharing-and-open-banking.

[61] This is despite the introduction of Current Account Switching Service (CASS)—a switching-assistant service covering nearly the entirety of current accounts in the UK (https://currentaccountswitch.co.uk/how-to-switch/). See, D. G. W. Birch, "How Do You Measure Open Banking?," Forbes, accessed November 22, 2022, https://www.forbes.com/sites/davidbirch/2022/01/10/how-do-you-measure-open-banking/. On Open

Some suggest to replace the switching-metric with measuring the size of the Open Banking ecosystem as the ultimate evidence of the success of the Open Banking framework.[62] Considering that most of the accounts are the same (and CMA 2017 Order contributed to this by enforcing cost transparency),[63] it is the infrastructure created by Open Banking framework that allows millions of users to benefit from new products and services.[64] This narrative, also common when comparing the effects of the UK and EU respective Open Banking frameworks,[65] places the size of the ecosystem and the availability of new payment or account aggregation options based on API-fuelled data sharing framework alongside the growing number of users at the centre of the impact assessment of the frameworks on customer engagement. Although the shift may indeed be justified from the innovation perspective as a measure for the levels of innovation activities in the sector or the lack of significant entry barriers, the relevance of such a shift in focus is less evident from the customer engagement perspective. Notably, mere availability of wider choice options does not necessarily lead to a higher degree of customer (in particular, consumer) engagement. This has been addressed by numerous behavioural studies and studies of regulatory impact assessment that have described market conditions that impede informed consumer choice, and hence engagement, especially in the markets characterised by a wide variety (often similar) choice options.[66] Prevalence of debit card payments, outlined above, is pointing at this ambivalence and the challenge to accurately identify the level and causes for consumer engagement. While the growth in debit card popularity can

Banking adoption data for 2021, see M. Paul, "UK Open Banking Marks Fourth Year Milestone with Over 4 Million Users," Open Banking, January 13, 2022, https://www.openbanking.org.uk/news/uk-open-banking-marks-fourth-year-milestone-with-over-4-million-users/.

62 Ibid.

63 See, for instance, Financial Conduct Authority (FCA), Information about current account services, Consultation paper CP17/24, 2017.

64 Birch, "How Do You Measure Open Banking?".

65 "Financial Services Unchained: The Ongoing Rise of Open Banking | McKinsey."

66 See, for instance, "Payment Methods Report 2019—Innovations in the Way We Pay," accessed November 25, 2022, https://thepaypers.com/reports/payment-methods-report-2019-innovations-in-the-way-we-pay-2/r779461.

be traced to the Covid-19 pandemic that impacted consumer habits,[67] the change does not have clear effect on competition in the sector. This lack of visible effects on competition should not side-line the emphasis on customer engagement, since the innovation-competition-engagement three-way dependency maintains its relevance, even if the focus shifts to the objective of ecosystem-building.

Thus, despite a significant increase in the number of competitors in the market and higher levels of innovation, if measured by the size of the Open Banking ecosystem and the use of Open Banking technology in new products and services, the characteristics of the use of Open Banking and customer engagement in the retail banking sector underline the importance of continuous attention to the fast-paced evolution of the UK retail banking sector. This underscores the importance of the three-way dependency between competition, innovation, and customer engagement in the retail banking sector, as well as the idiosyncratic features of co-opetition-driven development of Open Banking under the CMA 2017 Order.

4 Conclusions: Co-opetition Scenario for Policy-Led Innovation and Evolution in Retail Banking

Technological innovation in retail banking is traditionally characterised by the interplay between key market forces, 'in which developers of technologies, service suppliers and customers contribute to the process of structural change of the industry' via 'a distributed process of innovation'.[68] In the case of the Open Banking framework, the regulatory intervention in the process stimulating competition and innovation incentives by mandating cooperation appears to reinforce innovation process that leads to sector development and, eventually, benefits end users.

[67] In particular, with respect to e-commerce and contactless payments. See N. Jonker et al., Pandemic Payment Patterns, 2022, *Journal of Banking & Finance* 143, 106593, https://doi.org/10.1016/j.jbankfin.2022.106593; Bank for International Settlements, "Covid-19 Accelerated the Digitalisation of Payments," December 9, 2021, https://www.bis.org/statistics/payment_stats/commentary2112.htm.

[68] D. Consoli, The Dynamics of Technological Change in UK Retail Banking Services: An Evolutionary Perspective, 2005 Research Policy 34, no. 4, 461–80, https://doi.org/10.1016/j.respol.2005.02.001.

However, the evolution of retail banking does not and will not stop at Open Banking. Already today, the sectorial borders blurred by digitalisation are further dismantled by increasing openness (and abundance) of available data and technology allowing service providers to use this data for new value propositions to their customers. Financial sector incumbents, like Visa,[69] entering the Open Banking landscape is one manifestation of ongoing change, as well as the increasing presence of Big Tech players in the markets, such as is the case of Apple.[70] The reverse trend is less and less uncommon, as exemplified by the Open Banking 'native' Klarna entering retail commerce and price comparison segments.[71] It is highly likely that this process vertical and cross-sectorial expansion by major technology and financial sector players is to further intensify with the realisation of Open Finance.

Mandated cooperation and resulting increase in co-opetition strategies adopted by market actors in the UK retail banking sector deserves cautions recognition as a global benchmark for policy-led innovation as the framework is hailed to be the driving force behind the transition to Open Finance.[72] At the same time as Open Finance aims at removing the barriers and limitations raised by the sector-specific data-sharing framework, the co-opetition strategy implemented by incumbent firms in other sectors is likely to prevail. The illustrations of cooperation between actors from banking sector with telecoms, or software with hardware sector actors' discussed above show, however, that the strategies tend to evolve (and, for instance, be replaced by vertical integration) when market conditions change. Co-opetition scenario may therefore be less prevalent as the new product and service markets in the retail banking industry mature.[73]

[69] "Visa Completes Acquisition of Tink," accessed November 18, 2022, https://tink.com/press/visa-completes-acquisition-tink/.

[70] R. Shevlin, "Why Apple Acquired an 'Open Banking' Fintech," Forbes, accessed November 18, 2022, https://www.forbes.com/sites/ronshevlin/2022/03/27/why-apple-acquired-a-uk-based-open-banking-fintech/.

[71] P. Sawers, "A 'Credible Alternative to Google and Amazon': Klarna Brings Its Price Comparison Tool to Europe," *TechCrunch* (blog), November 14, 2022, https://techcrunch.com/2022/11/14/a-credible-alternative-to-google-and-amazon-klarna-brings-its-price-comparison-tool-to-europe/.

[72] Khalifa report.

[73] Signs of this process can be seen in one of the CMA9—Danske bank—recently launching its account aggregation tool, with similar services now offered by Barclays (together with 11 other banks, including NatWest, RBS and Santander amongst others).

Reinforcing cooperation and consumer engagement seems to be crucial now that the competition in the retail banking has taken off full speed. Against this background, in line with the adjustments to the governance of the Open Banking framework[74] as well as the scope of its implementation,[75] it appears crucial to advance the framework in line with its initial objectives.

See, Finextra, "Danske Bank Brings Account Aggregation to UK Businesses," Finextra Research, May 31, 2022, https://www.finextra.com/pressarticle/92799/danske-bank-brings-account-aggregation-to-uk-businesses; "11 Banks in One App | Barclays," accessed November 23, 2022, https://www.barclays.co.uk/ways-to-bank/account-aggregation/.

[74] "Joint Statement by HM Treasury, the CMA, the FCA and the PSR on the Future of Open Banking," GOV.UK, accessed November 18, 2022, https://www.gov.uk/government/publications/joint-statement-by-hm-treasury-the-cma-the-fca-and-the-psr-on-the-future-of-open-banking/joint-statement-by-hm-treasury-the-cma-the-fca-and-the-psr-on-the-future-of-open-banking.

[75] The discussion and progress around the so-called sweeping payments is one of the recent developments in (re)defining the scope of the framework being adjusted with increasing consumer choice and engagement in mind. Sweeping—an automatic transfer of money between customer's own accounts (me-to-me payment), e.g. in case of moving excess funds into a separate savings account or to a different account to be used for a loan repayment or overdraft account. See, Paul, "VRPs for Sweeping Timetable Agreed."

CHAPTER 13

Rethinking Crypto-Regulation for Crypto-Investors in the UK

Joy Malala and Folashade Adeyemo

1 Introduction

Satoshi Nakamoto's influential Bitcoin Whitepaper of 2009,[1] started the discourse on blockchain-based digital assets. Since then, digital or crypto-assets have gravitated towards integration with the mainstream financial system and more deeply into the legal and regulatory realm. It has become difficult to dismiss crypto-assets as insignificant, and without

[1] See S. Nakamoto, Bitcoin: A Peer to Peer Electronic Cash System, White Paper. https://www.ussc.gov/sites/default/files/pdf/training/annual-national-training-seminar/2018/Emerging_Tech_Bitcoin_Crypto.pdf (Accessed September 23, 2021).

J. Malala (✉)
University of Warwick, Coventry, UK
e-mail: joy.malala@warwick.ac.uk

F. Adeyemo
University of Liverpool, Liverpool, UK
e-mail: F.Adeyemo@liverpool.ac.uk

M. Bodellini et al. (eds.), *Commercial Banking in Transition*, Palgrave Macmillan Studies in Banking and Financial Institutions,
https://doi.org/10.1007/978-3-031-45289-5_13

applicable use cases particularly in recent years.[2] Since its introduction, there has been a plethora of companies that have collapsed since, such as Terra and Luna stablecoins.[3] In light of this, some states have considered creating robust frameworks to ensure protection against investors being defrauded and to ensure the protection of their investments.[4] A once, peripheral community, has attracted the attention of financial institutions, large technology firms, institutional investors, and academic scholars who have become more involved regulatory issues. As a result, the courts have had to confront the relationship between established legal principles and these novel innovations.

Engaging with the legal and regulation of crypto-assets can therefore be seen as a crucial if blockchain is to fulfil its intended and even imagined transformative role in the financial system. The purpose of this chapter is to consider, in detail, the effectiveness of the current regulatory framework or cryptocurrencies and crypto-assets. At its core, the chapter addresses the question of whether the current infrastructure in the UK remains effective and whether the regulation adequately protects retail investors. Many have argued that the current regulatory framework is adequate in ensuring that there is no contagion from a would-be crypto-assets crisis. Crypto-assets limit contractual flexibility and transparency, which could lead to a wider market-wide financial crisis. Financial crises are frequently preceded by an asset price bubble in which one or more asset classes are traded at prices far above their intrinsic values.[5] A crypto crisis is at present highly unlikely, however, reflections on the Global Financial Crisis (GFC) 2007–2009, the COVID-19 pandemic, the Russian invasion of Ukraine, combined with the current food and

[2] Summer of De-Fi and the ICO of 2017–18. https://www.forbes.com/sites/jeffkauflin/2018/10/29/where-did-the-money-go-inside-the-big-crypto-icos-of-2017/?sh=580c8a7e261b (Accessed December 2, 2021).

[3] See S. Chipolina and G. Steer, The Terra/Luna hall of shame. FT.com, R. de Blasis, L. Galati, A. Webb and R. I. WEBB, Intelligent design: Stablecoins (in)stability and collateral during market turbulence, St. Louis: Federal Reserve Bank of St. Louis, 2022.

[4] See D. Dupuis, D. Smith, and K. Gleason, Old Frauds with a New Sauce: Digital Assets and Space Transition. 2021, Journal of Financial Crime, 12/2021; D. J. Cumming, J. Sofia and A. Pant, Regulation of the Crypto-Economy: Managing Risks, Challenges, and Regulatory Uncertainty, 2019, Journal of Risk and Financial Management, 12(3), 126.

[5] See C. P. Kindelberger and R. Z. Aliber, Manias, Panics and Crashes: A History of Financial Crisis, Palgrave Macmillan, 2005.

energy crises experienced in the UK, suggest that it remains pertinent that adequate measures be put in place to safeguard against any unexpected shocks. This would certainly position the UK in a more favourably. To support this, one of the recommendations of this chapter would be the creation of an independent regulatory agency, or alternately, independent oversight of retail investors in the crypto-asset market. The chapter will unpack these ideas by first reviewing the literature on the regulatory environment of crypto-assets, characterising the retail investor in the market and the third section will evaluate the risks abound in the cryptoverse then it will conclude by offering a regulatory framework for investor protection.

The literature on crypto-asset regulation continues to emerge and evolve. Some contributions have challenged the regulatory approaches adopted towards cryptocurrencies; chiefly, questions have been raised on whether the UK can learn from the international approaches. Particularly those taken by the US (e.g.the Stable Act[6]) or closer to the UK the EU's Regulation of Markets in Crypto-assets 2022.[7] To begin our analysis, we should consider, Motsi-Omojiade's[8] arguement for a reflective regulatory approach towards cryptocurrencies. This argument is hinged on the proposition that enforcement and compliance, are currently inadequate. Motsi-Omojiade moved forward the discussion in this regard by proposing new strategies for reflexive regulation through internal self-regulatory mechanisms. Also advanced this discussion by exploring the development of FinTech since the global financial crisis of 2008. Arner et al.[9] have considered the fintech environment within its broader evolutionary context, providing a holistic view of its status and future developments as well as the political enthusiasm it brings. This is since, fintech is an assemblage of products that transcend the traditional ways as providing core business of accepting and holding deposits, making loans or facilitating payments. In recognising fintech's evolution and the regulatory implications off growth, but particularly, the challenge that

[6] US the Stable Act 2022.

[7] Markets in Crypto-Assets Regulation 2022.

[8] See I. Motsi-Omojiade, Cryptocurrency Regulation: A Reflexive Law Approach Routledge, 2022.

[9] See D. Arner, J. Barberis, and R. Buckely, The Evolution of Fintech: A New Post-Crisis Paradigm? University of Hong Kong Faculty of Law Research Paper No. 2015/047, 2015.

this development presents for regulators and market participants. Chiu[10] focuses predominately on the construction of a 'crypto economy' and the measures that may be put in place to govern this space arguing that, for such an economy to succeed, it remains imperative for regulatory policies to cultivate and develop to enable this. Chiu also argues that it is necessary to create a new regulatory framework, supporting earlier and current assertions that one size fits all cannot work or be effective. Others have examined the potential money laundering risks posed by cryptocurrencies, such as Hillman, who in 2020, argued that the UK cannot simply transpose the pre-existing regulation and regulatory infrastructure in regulating cryptocurrencies.[11] At the same time, the current tools for Anti Money Laundering (AML) are not compatible to deal with the issues raised in this chapter. Given the very structure and evolving nature of cryptocurrencies and crypto-assets, it seems impossible to simply transpose existing legislation to regulate this. Gazi, has also proposed a *de novo* crypto regulator or a separate agency that would combine existing regulators' mandates, jurisdictions, responsibilities, and enforcement authorities over cryptocurrencies and overcome the current regulatory overlap and ambiguity. The *de novo* regime's mandate should be 'investor protection through promoting market transparency and preventing and policing fraud, market manipulation, and insider trading'.[12] This chapter not only adds to that growing literature but specifically addresses a framework through which retail investors might be protected.

[10] See I. Chiu, Regulating the Crypto Economy: Business Transformations and Financialisaton, Hart Publishing, 2021.

[11] See H. Hillman, Money laundering through cryptocurrencies: Analysing the responses of the United States and Australia and providing recommendations for the UK to address the money laundering risks posed by cryptocurrencies, PhD Thesis, University of the West of England, 2020.

[12] See S. Gazi, Reimagining a Centralised Cryptocurrency Regulation in the US: Looking through the Lens of Crypto-Derivatives, 2021, 6 Cambridge L Rev, 97.

2 Defining Crypto-Assets

It has been stated that cryptocurrencies are 'digital currencies that rely on a cryptographic protocol to regulate the way (and the extent to which) currency can be created and/or exchanged'.[13] Cryptocurrency is now used as an umbrella term depicting emerging technology. Since the launch of Bitcoin in 2009, cryptocurrencies and their underlying blockchain technology have risen to global attention. It is now clear Bitcoin, and several other cryptocurrencies were the focus of one of the largest speculative bubbles in history. In addition, the technology that they run on is a 'cryptographically secured digital representation of value or contractual rights that uses some type of distributed ledger technology and can be transferred stored or traded electronically'.[14] In other words, crypto-assets are digital ledger technologies upon which assets are transacted and useful for different purposes. Inquiries had been launched to distinguish between the different types of crypto-assets and DLT.[15] This distinction has become particularly important to separate out the different parts of the financial system in which the underlying DLT can become operationally applicable.[16] The UK Taskforce has therefore observed that, being a type of technology that enables the sharing and updating of records in a distributed and decentralised way, DLT can be used like any conventional database to store a range of data, such as ownership of existing financial assets like shares or digital assets like Bitcoin.[17] Throughout this chapter, reference is made to 'crypto-assets'

[13] See P. De Filippi, Bitcoin: A Regulatory Nightmare to a Libertarian Dream, 2014, 3(2) Internet Policy Review 1, 1.

[14] *Government consultation on broadening the regulation ...—Taylor Wessing*, https://www.taylorwessing.com/en/insights-and-events/insights/2020/07/government-consultation-on-broadening-the-regulation-of-crypto-assets. The Distributed Ledger: Blockchain, Digital Assets and Smart Contracts .... https://www.jdsupra.com/legalnews/the-distributed-ledger-blockchain-72260/ (Accessed July 10, 2022). Raskin M, 'The Law of Smart Contracts' [2017 1 Georgetown Law Technology Review 304.

[15] Crypto-assets Taskforce Final Report (2018), available at https://assets.publishing.service.gov.uk/government/uploads/system/uploads/attachment_data/file/75207/crypto-assets_taskforce_final_report_final_web.pdf (Accessed July 18, 2022).

[16] Blockchain—Emissions-EUETS.com. https://www.emissions-euets.com/internal-electricity-market-glossary/2094-blockchain.

[17] Grappling with this problem, the UK government taskforce on crypto-assets was launched up the Chancellor of the Exchequer in March 2018 bringing together HM Treasury, the Financial Conducts Authority (FCA) and the Bank of England to, among

when discussed broadly in terms of the overall technology. However, when specific reference is made to its exchange functionality, the term 'cryptocurrency' is used. Crypto-assets can be divided into three operative categories. First, crypto-assets that are intended to be used as a means of payment or value transfer (payment coins).[18] Second, crypto-assets that are designed to offer access to goods, services, or content (utility coins).[19] Third crypto-assets that purport to operate as digital representations of either tangible or intangible assets which exist outside of DLT networks, such as securities and money claims, but also real estate and art (asset coins).[20]

The difference between both terms is that although 'cryptocurrencies' are a type of crypto-asset, not all crypto-assets function as a medium of exchange, i.e., as currency. Admittedly, this taxonomy is not necessarily neat, as some crypto-asset tokens can be used at cross-purposes. For instance, Bitcoin can be used as a payment instrument to facilitate the exchange of value for goods or services it can also be used as a security tradable on a typical stock exchange. While Blockchain, the technical backbone of cryptocurrencies, is a secure ledger of transactions shared by all parties in a distributed network. Therefore, every transaction on a blockchain is recorded and stored to create an immutable (unchangeable) and auditable log of transactions.[21] This common log of transactions is in part what allows cryptocurrencies to function without the need for a trusted third party or intermediary, such as banks to verify transactions.[22] This is disputably perhaps why banks must leverage their competitiveness against the growing use of cryptocurrencies. The DLT, has multiuse possibilities as a new database technology and its scope has not fully been explored. Although, data bases have traditionally been centralised,

other things. Following this observation, the Taskforce identified three broad types of crypto-assets i.e., Exchange tokens, Security tokens and Utility tokens.

[18] See T. Adrian and T. Mancini—Griffoli, Fintech Notes: The Rise of Digital Money, International Monetary Fund, 2019.

[19] Ibid.

[20] Ibid.

[21] See A. Ahmad, M. Saad, and A. Mohaisen, Secure and Transparent Audit logs with BlockAudit, Journal of Network and Computer Applications, 145(1), 2019.

[22] Who Is Satoshi Nakamoto—Definition by CryptoDefinitions. https://cryptodefinitions.com/dictionary/satoshi-nakamoto/ (Accessed July 20, 2022).

with a sole purpose to create and maintain the original data set.[23] As a consequence, fractional copies of this master may be made available to the public, but there can be no guarantees of their accuracy and only the information in the master is determinative. Regulatory frameworks have therefore had to adapt to this technology and its complex structure and design. The DLT enables the creation of networks that support distributed databases. What is important, is that any actors in the system can obtain a copy of the database which perfectly matches that held by all other actors. Standardisation is ensured by an algorithm (commonly referred to as the consensus protocol) that incentivizes actors to update their copy of the database synchronously whenever new valid data entries are added. Albert Wenger describes DLT databases as 'logically centralized (there is only one database) but organizationally decentralized (a potentially infinite number of participants can hold identical copies of the database).'[24]

Therefore, these crypto-assets have captured the interest of the public. They have generated great interest not particularly because they, (consumers) use them as a system of payments, cryptocurrencies for instance, account for only 0.5% of the total value of all money in the UK and the Bank of England's Financial Policy Committee concluded that existing crypto-assets do not currently pose a material risk to the UK financial stability because they represent a small asset class.[25] Despite this, they are increasingly causing concern and it is becoming impossible to dismiss them as insignificant. This is largely because more and more entrants are being exposed to the crypto-market including various financial intermediaries. However, an argument can be made to show that as they continue to grow as an asset class and mainstream financial entities increase their exposure to them, they may begin to pose risks to financial stability. It can be worth asking whether regulatory tools in relation to systemic stability in conventional finance which is already heavily regulated are as applicable in crypto finance. Therein lies the distinction, that

[23] See A. Narayanan, Bitcoin and Cryptocurrency Technologies: A Comprehensive Introduction, Princeton University Press, 2016.

[24] See A. Wenger, The World After Capital 2019.

[25] Banking of England, Financial Stability in Focus: Crypto-Assets Sand Decentralised Finance,' https://www.bankofengland.co.uk/financial-stability-in-focus/2022/march-2022 (Accessed September 27, 2022).

with crypto-assets, the framework is highly reliant on decentralised participation,[26] while contagion in conventional banks may lead to runs and in some cases a collapse of a bank, the 'unravelling of social trust and run on any particular platform could be destabilising and exacerbate losses that may be suffered by every participant.'[27] However, it is worthwhile to note that, the design of cryptography is that there exist automated protocols that enable such destabilisation[28] as experienced by Maker DAO in March 2020.[29] Therefore a case can be made for their independent regulation as they are less resilient than conventional finance where key institutions can play centralised roles offering stabilisation, such as on the part of central banks, significant market makers, and central counterparties for derivatives trading. This risk is heightened by the cross-border nature of the crypto-asset markets. The interconnectivity within the spot market is now minimal, trading volumes though low, there is potential for systemic risk. Systemic risk, nevertheless, has to do with the degree of interconnectivity of the subject of concern, crypto-assets have heterogenous technical characteristics and transactional structures that are not yet fully understood. At the core of this chapter's arguments is the fact that, there exist informed traders in the retail marketplace who play a significant role in how accurate price signals are. The lack of sufficiently informed investors means that clamour is created. This clamour arguably skews price signals particularly when there is optimism which creates an environment ripe for a bubble.

For instance, the flagship crypto-asset Bitcoin has fallen sharply in value.[30] Its market capitalisation was down to roughly $390 billion as of December 2020.[31] Although many crypto investors are institutions, a lot of them are individuals who have made bets on crypto-assets in hopes to win as in a bear market. Mainly because they believe in the future of the blockchain and cryptocurrency, and others simply because they have seen

[26] See I. Chiu, Regulating the Crypto Economy, Hart, 2021.

[27] Ibid.

[28] See M. Raskin, The Law of Smart Contracts, 2017, 1 Georgetown Law Technology Review, 304.

[29] The Market Collapse of March 12–13, 2020—How it impacted Maker DAO, https://blog.makerdao.com/the-market-collapse-of-march-12-2020-how-it-impacted-makerdao/ (Accessed November 8, 2022).

[30] See C. Hafner, Alternative Assets and Cryptocurrencies, MDPI AG, 2019.

[31] Ibid., at 26.

the gains many crypto firms have made, and they want to be a part of the speculation.[32] This chapter classifies these crypto investors as either institutions such as investment funds and venture capitalists, but it will focus on retail investors, who are individuals or consumers. It also argues that the financial system may be subject to *some* level of risk to the extent that both are interconnected and the spill over effects may be transmitted to the real economy. The European Central Bank (ECB) has stated that, these risks are at present contained and manageable within the existing regulatory and oversight frameworks, however, we posit that the links with the regulated financial sector may develop and increase over time and have future implications.[33] Although investor rights are ambiguous and poorly defined, crypto-assets are a novel architecture with the potential for value storage, exchange, venture capital, and contracts. Promoters of crypto-assets (crypto influencers) lack the responsibility and governance necessary to give investors the necessary information because regulators are more reactive than proactive.[34]

3 The Current UK Regulatory Framework for Crypto-Assets

There are banking institutions established with the responsibility of regulating money and investments and this regulatory infrastructure has undergone some reform.[35] With the creation of a 'twin peak' model. These 'peaks' are the Prudential Regulation Authority (PRA), designated as a subsidiary of the Bank of England with the task of supervising banks, systematically important investment firms; and the Financial Conduct Authority (FCA). This second 'peak' which has three-pronged goals: (i) to ensure the protection of consumers; (ii) to improve, enhance and develop the integrity of the financial system in the UK; and (iii)

[32] A Pew Research Centre survey found that 16% of U.S. adults said they had invested in, traded or used a cryptocurrency.

[33] Understanding the crypto-asset phenomenon, its risks and measurement issues. https://www.ecb.europa.eu/pub/economic-bulletin/articles/2019/html/ecb.ebart201905_03~c83aeaa44c.en.html (Accessed August 12, 2022).

[34] Gary Gensler (Kim Kardashian fined by SEC).

[35] See also F. Adeyemo, Banking Regulation in Africa: The Case of Nigeria and Emerging Economies, Routledge, 2021, 43, which provides a good overview of the change of responsibilities.

to maintain competitive markets and promote effective competition in the interest of the consumer. In terms of regulating the cryptocurrency market, the FCA uses the term 'crypto-assets' and this includes 'cryptocurrencies' such as Bitcoin. Prior to the introduction of new regulatory powers to regulate in 2020, cryptocurrencies remained largely unregulated. In 2020, this marked a shift in regulatory approaches and the FCA now has the power to supervise the way a crypto-asset business manages the challenges posed of money laundering and counter-terrorist financing. This is found under the Money Laundering Terrorist Financing and Transfer of Funds (Information on the Payer) Regulations 2017.[36] Crypto-assets businesses, with the intention to trade in the UK must comply with the rules which includes becoming registered on the Temporary Registration Regime (TRR). The deadline for registration closed while the FCA conducted assessments. The FCA places a caveat that the assessment of such firms does not confirm its endorsement as fit and proper. In the UK there are primarily two main branches, 'regulated tokens' and 'unregulated tokens'. In terms of regulated tokens, we have two branches. 'Security tokens' are a type of specified type of investment, excluding e-money. In this type of investment, it could give rise to ownership rights. 'Unregulated tokens' are tokens which are *not* regarded as security tokens or e-money tokens. These are sometimes referred to as payment tokens and do not provide any type of rights as previously discussed. In the case of the UK, cryptocurrencies are only regulated to the extent that it involved money laundering. In this case, the Financial Conduct Authority is responsible for the anti-money laundering and counter-terrorist financing activities. The current regulatory infrastructure, arguably, is not designed to accommodate the regulation of cryptocurrencies and crypto-assets.

The current structure caters to banks and financial instruments—cryptocurrencies are not recognised by the FCA as items that can be regulated. There have been calls to introduce regulation for cryptocurrencies and particularly, for financial consumers. The most obvious reason is that these are, for the most part, regarded as some type of currency, given the level at which retail investors are looking to improve wealth portfolios and increase profits, it remains that such currency should be regulated in a way

[36] The Money Laundering, Terrorist Financing and Transfer of Funds (Information on the Payer) Regulations 2017. This is accessible here: https://www.legislation.gov.uk/uksi/2017/692/contents/made (Accessed August 21, 2022).

to offer protection to those engaging in such investments. It is no surprise that social media has played a large role in shaping society, and as such, it could be argued that a significant majority of investments come into play by such consumers relying on influential recommendations.[37] Although the regular financial market and the crypto-asset market are still viewed as two essentially different systems, there is a possibility that ties between the two markets may continue to develop.[38] This can be evident in entities that simultaneously possess obligations in one system and assets in the other and (directly or indirectly) use the assets as collateral for the liabilities to create a direct link between systems is one well-known example. Since companies might not be able to sustain a mismatch between their assets and liabilities over time, as soon as those interdependencies arise, major value changes in one market may have an impact on the other.

Retail investors in Europe, according to the European Central Bank's 2021 Consumer Expectation Survey indicate that as many as 10% of households in Europe may own crypto-assets although small amounts are invested (below EUR 5000).[39] The EU is the first major jurisdiction worldwide to provide a comprehensive, dedicated regulatory framework for crypto-assets, the EU Markets in Crypto-Asset Regulation (MiCA) Is intended to regulate crypto-assets, as well as stable coins which do not fall under existing EU regulations. It (MiCA) will prioritise requirements for the public offer and marketing of crypto-assets and the provision of their derivative services. In an ambitious move, aims to prevent market abuse within the crypto markets. More specifically it requires that issuers of stable coins will need to be authorised and have in place a robust and segregated reserve of assets to support it. The United Kingdom's Financial Conduct Authority's 2021 consumer research on crypto-assets reached similar conclusions and estimated the number of British adults investing into crypto-assets at around 4%, with a median investment of

[37] Such recommendations come from high net individuals such as Elon Musk see. H. Lee, Y. Kim, H. Cho, S. Jung, and J. Kim, The Credibility Cryptocurrency Valuation: Statistical Learning Analysis for Influencer Tweets, 2022 International Conference on Information Networking (ICOIN), 2022, 58–61.

[38] See L. Brainard, Crypto-Assets and Decentralized Finance through a Financial Stability Lens, a speech at Bank of England Conference, London, United Kingdom, July 8, 2022, St. Louis: Federal Reserve Bank of St. Louis.

[39] See L. Hermans et al., Decrypting financial stability risks in crypto-asset markets, 2019, Financial Stability Review, No. 1, European Central Bank.

around GBP 300.[40] While these numbers may appear minimal, they indicate a burgeoning and interest in investing in crypto-assets. Now that the UK has left the EU, this may be the right time for a reconsideration to put in place a better set of regulations, and to reframe the protection in place for retail investors.

4 Risks to Retail Investors and a Proposal for Protection

Building trust in the capital markets requires that robust, securities laws are implemented. Without regulatory intervention, it is unlikely that markets will produce efficient levels of trust, both because investors incentives to gather information are not optimal rationally and because investors' behaviour is subject to biases and distortions. There is therefore a need to protect the vulnerability of retail investors, although, it is also thought that reliable standardised obligatory disclosures increase trust and market participation. Therefore, focus should be directed towards retail investors 'ones who lack investing experience and sophistication so as to need the protection of the securities laws'.[41] This is aimed at levelling the playing field between the informed investor and the uninformed investor. The digital economy has on the one hand included very many new 'types' of consumers and conversely has created a new vulnerability. Consumer vulnerability, in the digital economy is no longer 'a vantage point from which to assess some consumers' lack of ability to activate their awareness of persuasion'.[42] In its place, consumer vulnerability occasioned by the digital technology, is 'a universal state of defencelessness and susceptibility to (the exploitation of) power imbalances that are the result of the increasing automation of commerce, data filed consumer–seller relations, and the very architecture of digital marketplaces.'[43] Similarly for

[40] See M. Karim and G. Tomova, Research note: Crypto-asset consumer research 2021, Financial Conduct Authority, 17 June 2021.

[41] See Langevoort, C. Donald, The SEC, Retail Investors, and the Institutionalization of the Securities Markets (September 2, 2008). Georgetown Law and Economics Research Paper Series.

[42] See N. Helberger, et al., Choice Architectures in the Digital Economy: Towards a New Understanding of Digital Vulnerability, 2022, Journal of Consumer Policy, 45(2), 175–200.

[43] Ibid.

retail investors, we posit that it is through these digital marketplaces that, unfair digital commercial practices exists as well as the lack of legal protections available from loss of funds. In this section, we characterise the risks that emanate from crypto-assets and identify the linkages to the financial system with a view to suggest an independent regulator. We begin by discussing the particular use cases for crypto-assets and the profile of individuals who use these assets. We then discuss the various points through which risk emanates in the crypto-market for these retail investors.

Traditionally, money has three main functions, as a unit of account, a medium of exchange and a store of value. For Bitcoin and other cryptocurrencies to achieve these they need broad-based support from consumers and businesses. Despite being in existence for almost a decade, it is still an open question whether cryptocurrency usage has reached a critical mass, or is still held back by insufficient users, lack of sellers accepting it and insufficient reason to hold it due to price volatility. Research has therefore shown that Bitcoin is mostly held for speculative rather than transactions purposes.[44] Among the most fundamental points is the fact that crypto-assets have no underlying claim this means that there is no right to a future cash flow or to discharge any payment obligation and they lack fundamental value. This makes their valuation difficult and subject to speculation. As a result, crypto-assets may experience extreme price movements (volatility risk), thereby exposing their holders to potentially large losses.

These crypto-assets such as Bitcoin are not necessarily used as digital currency.[45] Individuals acquire crypto-assets primarily as an investment which they hope will appreciate over time with increased participation in DLT networks, these individuals we are calling 'retail investors' and this behaviour is referred to as holding.[46] Additionally, the price of these, assets are extremely volatile, for instance, bitcoin was priced at about

[44] See A. Haynes, P. Yeoh, Cryptocurrencies and Crypto-assets, Taylor and Francis, 27.

[45] See A. Urquahart and B. Lucey, Crypto and Digital Currencies—Nine Research Priorities, Nature, 604, 2022.

[46] See J. Kauflin, Forbes' First List of Cryptocurrency's Richest: Meet The Secretive Freaks, Geeks and Visionaries Minting Billons From Bitcoin Mania, Forbes, 07/02/2018, https://www.forbes.com/sites/jeffkauflin/2018/02/07/cryptocurrency-richest-people-crypto-Bitcoin-ether-xrp/#7d8e14a372d3 (Accessed February 18, 2022). Yathukulan Yogarajah (2022) 'Hodling' on: Memetic storytelling and digital folklore within a cryptocurrency world, Economy and Society, 51(3), 467–488.

$29,000 at the end of 2020, surged to almost $67,000 by November 2021, and reverted to $20,000 by June 2022; moreover, during 2021, bitcoin had a daily average volatility of 4.56%.[47] These fluctuations are due to the fact that the price of these crypto-assets is primarily driven by supply and demand and profoundly influenced by market sentiment. For businesses, the volatility of bitcoin and other similar coins renders them extremely uneconomical, if not outright unworkable, as a currency to price their goods, services, assets, and liabilities.

Market volatility undermines trust, in crypto-assets. Market volatility coupled with a lack of protections or adequate risk disclosures means that the impact of losses would affect investors disparately.[48] This erosion in trust has the potential to drive the asset's price negatively. These dynamics have been repeated in the banking system, when depositors have been exposed to excessive risk taking by banks at their cost. In the early months of 2022, the crypto industry had shown continued volatility. Bitcoin prices for instance also continue to be at their lowest and some platforms have barred users from withdrawing their funds including some of the biggest crypto companies such as Coinbase and BlockFi have announced staff cuts. This volatility is serving as a stark warning to crypto investors, as the disruption is in some way causing economic turmoil through the broader market. For example, the Consumer Finance Protection Bureau (CFPB) reported Bitcoin prices falling as much as 61% in a single day in 2013, and as much as 80% in 2014 with a similar collapse in 2018. Bitcoin's fate as a currency rest on more individuals and merchants using it for transaction purposes rather than mainly for speculation. Bitcoin price volatility surged further in 2017 and then fell back in 2018 before rising steadily in mid-2019.[49] These fluctuations are because the price

[47] Crypto Prices Slip After Record Week for Bitcoin Volatility, (https://www.bloomberg.com/news/articles/2022-05-14/crypto-prices-slip-after-bitcoin-s-most-volatile-week-in-years) See Doumenis, Yianni, J. Izadi, P. Dhamdhere, E. Katsikas, and D. Koufopoulos, A Critical Analysis of Volatility Surprise in Bitcoin Cryptocurrency and Other Financial Assets, 2021, Risks 9, 207.

[48] See J. Weisenthal, Mark Cuban Calls for Stablecoin Regulation After Trading Token That Crashed to Zero, Bloomberg (June 17, 2021), https://www.bloomberg.com/news/articles/2021-06-17/mark-cuban-defi-iron-finance-crashed-100?sref=M8H6LjUF#xj4y7vzkg; E. Lopatto, The Tether Controversy, Explained, the Verge (August 18, 2022), https://www.theverge.com/22620464/tether-backing-cryptocurrency-stablecoin.

[49] M. Dematteo, Bitcoin Price History: 2009 to 2022, https://time.com/nextadvisor/investing/cryptocurrency/bitcoin-price-history/ (Accessed November 8, 2022).

of these crypto-assets is primarily driven by supply and demand and intensely influenced by market sentiment.[50] Bitcoin still leads the pack even if it no longer completely controls the cryptocurrency market as it once did because it seems to gain from an early mover advantage, brand recognition, and venture capital support. However, new technological developments in the form of an improved digital coin might always pose a danger. Because of its tremendous volatility, bitcoin and other coins of a similar nature are exceedingly uneconomical for businesses to use as a unit of account to value their products, services, assets, and obligations.[51] Still, technological breakthroughs in the shape of a better digital coin could always present a threat. For businesses, the volatility of bitcoin and other similar coins renders them extremely uneconomical, if not outright unworkable, as a currency to price their goods, services, assets, and liabilities. Stablecoins, which have recently become mainstream, were designed to overcome these two obstacles. They constitute a crypto-asset class that possesses all the technological advantages of DLT networks disintermediation, cryptographic security, transactional transparency but also the low volatility of traditional, government-backed currencies. Those who use them, are in a precarious position. For instance, Stable coins holders have limited rights against the issuers of these coins and even more limited claims should their issuers become bankrupt. Further, there is either no identifiable issuer or there can be no assets backing their stable coin. The risk is that these assets would typically collapse overnight, leaving their holders with worthless entries on a digital ledger.

In the absence of a regulatory framework for investor protection within the crypto markets, it is assumed that the default regulatory framework would be that of contract and consumer protection. The main doctrinal vehicle is the unconscionability doctrine. This posits that contracts between consumers and businesses are inherently based on defective bargaining procedures and are abound with unilateral mistakes. However, contract law is not suited to govern crypto transactions due to the fact that while, contractual enforcement and specific performance are not applicable the contracts created are automatically enforced.

[50] Ibid., Supra note 36.

[51] See A. Haynes and P. Yeoh, Cryptocurrencies and Crypto-Assets: Regulatory and Legal Issues, Routledge, 2020, 23.

This initial objective of this paper was to set out to present the current challenges attached to the lack of regulation of cryptocurrency. The introduction of cryptocurrency is received well since it has created investment opportunities for consumers. These challenges are not however without their peculiarities. This chapter takes the position that the current infrastructure is unable to accommodate appropriate and adequate regulation; it is impossible to simply transpose the use of cryptocurrency into existing regulation. This paper argues for additional layers for investor protection. The fast-paced development of this currency has unintentionally created an opportunity for criminal activity and there is a need to ensure adequate and satisfactory protection for consumers. The best approach for this is to create further regulatory oversight to support the existing infrastructure.

We proposes a separate agency, in addition to the FCA and PRA tasked with the regulation of crypto-assets with agents with the requisite expertise of the crypto ecosystem. This would ensure that investor confidence is maintained and at its core the agency should have the sole objective of protecting investors against the volatility risks, fraud, and market manipulation. This would mean that all crypto-asset companies should be registered. Gazi has argued that, in the US, for instance, a federal cryptocurrency agency would have 'exclusive jurisdiction over cryptocurrencies which can prevent price manipulation, fraud and abusive market practices by establishing a direct oversight over the cryptocurrency intermediaries including exchanges and spot markets and thereby enhance investors' protection'.[52] However, she asserts, which this chapter also agrees that while in the US it is not uncommon to 'constitute a new federal agency to protect consumers and fill in the regulatory vacuum. After the financial crisis of 2008, the Dodd-Frank Wall Street Reform and Consumer Protection Act established the Consumer Financial Protection Bureau—a single, independent consumer-focused regulatory regime consolidating the scattered financial authorities throughout the federal government and bringing them under one roof'.[53]

However, the evolving nature of cryptocurrencies however demands for an additional layer of supervision and regulation without the need to create a separate institution. A separate regulatory agency however to

[52] See S. Gazi, Reimagining a Centralised Cryptocurrency Regulation in the US: Looking Through the Lens of Crypto-Derivatives, 2021, 6 Cambridge L Rev, 97.

[53] Ibid.

practically work, it is necessary for it have short and concise objectives. In the UK retail investors have spent close to £30 Billion on crypto-assets this demonstrates a burgeoning appetite for crypto investment this can be attributed in part to a growing need to build wealth from alternative markets and because of crypto influencers. The emergence of crypto promotors or influencers however has been a major concern for regulators across the EU and the US.[54] This can be attributed to how vulnerable communities have been targeted in the past with deceptive sales tactics and marketing which some crypto-asset companies have employed.[55] These may include target advertising on social media platforms as well as brand partnerships with prominent celebrities to attract new customers. The main concern for regulators is that these products are marketed in ways that obscure their level of risk which ultimately heightens the impact in a highly volatile market. Many are marketed as safe when their volatility and lack of protections may result in even greater losses. The FCA has since announced a proposal on how firms that approve and communicate financial marketing have relevant expertise and understanding of the investments being offered. There were calls to improve risk warnings on advertisements and to ban incentives to invest such as new joiner or refer a friend bonuses. Their detailed proposals hinge on the classification of high-risk investments, application of the FCA'S financial promotion rules to qualifying crypto-assets.[56]

5 Conclusion

Crypto-assets markets materially differ from traditional capital markets and impose unique controlling, monitoring, and technological risk factors. Many questions remain unanswered about the ever-evolving crypto-market. There remains a lot of volatility speculation and 'hype'.

[54] See D. Dombey, J. Oliver, and S. Fleming, 'Spain Leads European Crackdown on Crypto Promotions' *Financial Times* (January 17, 2022), https://www.ft.com/content/a119dc9e-189d-4a87-ae02-a81a37260196#comments-anchor (Accessed October 20, 2022).

[55] Ibid., at 58.

[56] Sarah Pritchard, Executive Director of Markets at the FCA, said: 'Too many people are being led to invest in products they don't understand, and which are too risky for them. People need clear, fair information and proper risk warnings if they are to invest with confidence, which is the central aim of our consumer investments strategy.'

There have been however inconsistent and unconnected regulatory reactions to crypto-derivatives particularly in the US. The gap in regulation has left retail investors even more vulnerable to the unscrupulous practices in the spot market which erodes trust within it. This chapter addresses the need and challenges in protecting retail investors through the lens of consumer protection. This new market is complex, often heterogeneous, and almost difficult to navigate when and how to protect investors. Industry norms and standards necessitate a deeper comprehension of the distinctive and nearly bizarre dynamics of the cryptocurrency marketplaces. In addition, courts typically lack the necessary technical knowledge for deciphering and evaluating the code-based language used in blockchain transactions. As a result, courts that apply common law on a case-by-case basis are institutionally incapable of handling blockchain transactions and have a disadvantage over legislators or regulators. Therefore, many crypto enthusiasts have opposed industry regulation. Therefore, the FCA ought to create comprehensive cryptocurrency legislation that would account for both the novelty and underlying technology of crypto-assets. Many crypto-assets as we have demonstrated have no tangible value unlike traditional securities which give holders rights to future cash flows and claims in case of liquidation. Crypto-assets remain highly speculative, implying their value depends on market dynamics of supply and demand and may be subject to abuse. The public interest in crypto-assets is not waning, and a comprehensive regulation which will offer a systemic regulatory approach that reduces the risk associated with the spot markets would prevent its collapse. We additionally posit that clarity and effective monitoring of the system through embedded investor protection layers and a separate regulatory agency for crypto-assets is important as they protect both the integrity of the market as well as retail investors.

CHAPTER 14

Cross-Border Recognition of Foreign Resolution Actions: The Statutory Regime in the United Kingdom

Shalina Daved, Clare Merrifield, and Michael Salib

1 Introduction

Consider the following scenario. A major foreign bank fails and the relevant foreign authorities have to step in, taking all necessary steps to stabilise the situation by placing the firm into "resolution". This could

Any views expressed are solely those of the authors and so cannot be taken to represent those of the Bank of England or to state Bank of England policy. This paper should therefore not be reported as representing the views of the Bank of England or members of the Monetary Policy Committee, Financial Policy Committee or Prudential Regulation Committee. The authors would like to thank Neel Acharya, Chris Jackson, Jenny Khosla and Alan Newton for the helpful feedback in preparing this chapter.

S. Daved · C. Merrifield (✉) · M. Salib
Bank of England, London, UK
e-mail: Clare.Merrifield@bankofengland.co.uk

M. Bodellini et al. (eds.), *Commercial Banking in Transition*, Palgrave Macmillan Studies in Banking and Financial Institutions,
https://doi.org/10.1007/978-3-031-45289-5_14

involve "bailing-in" the liabilities or debt of the bank in order to recapitalise it or transferring the business to a private sector purchaser so that there is continuity of banking services. Now assume that the foreign bank has a significant amount of liabilities governed by English law or its operations and assets are based in the United Kingdom, then how does the foreign authority ensure that its resolution powers have effect in the UK? The answer to this question depends on international cooperation between the foreign and UK authorities and a fundamental part of this is the UK's statutory "recognition" regime for foreign resolution actions.

At the time of the 2007–2008 financial crisis, authorities in different jurisdictions had no pre-agreed means of cooperating with each other on how to respond to the failure of a major cross-border bank. Nor had they the confidence that the actions taken by foreign authorities would align with their own national interest. There was a pressing need to put formal cooperation mechanisms in place in order to respond to the oft-cited aphorism that large complex financial institutions are global in life, if not in death.[1]

Following that crisis, there is now a widespread appreciation that cross-border planning is critical to ensuring the continuity of critical services whilst delivering the orderly resolution of an international banking group. "Home and host authorities[2] need to agree, in advance, on the resolution strategy for a major cross-border banking group. Hosts need to be confident that the chosen strategy is viable and that it will respect their

S. Daved
e-mail: Shalina.Daved@bankofengland.co.uk

M. Salib
e-mail: Michael.Salib@bankofengland.co.uk

[1] Mervyn King, Governor of the Bank of England, 'Banking—From Bagehot to Basel, and Back Again' (Second Bagehot Lecture, Buttonwood Gathering, New York, 25 October 2010), https://www.bankofengland.co.uk/-/media/boe/files/speech/2010/banking-from-bagehot-to-basel-and-back-again-speech-by-mervyn-king.

[2] The home authority being the resolution authority that co-ordinates the resolution of a cross-border group, usually in the jurisdiction in which the bank is headquartered; and the host authority being a resolution authority in a jurisdiction in which the bank provides services through one or more subsidiaries or branches.

own financial stability needs".[3] Simply put, mechanisms are needed to establish trust.

The most well-known of these mechanisms are so-called international crisis management groups—or, within the EU, resolution colleges. The UK is a "strong supporter of enhancing these mechanisms for engagement with other authorities",[4] to agree in advance on the strategy for managing the failure of major international banks and for monitoring the progress in making that strategy possible by the advance removal of barriers to resolution.

But when cooperation moves from planning to execution, the focus shifts to the question of ensuring that home authority resolution actions are "recognised" by host authorities, so that they will have legal effect in all relevant jurisdictions. This chapter examines the UK's legislative regime on the recognition of foreign resolution actions, including the role of Bank of England (the **Bank**) within it. The UK's recognition regime does not simply exist on paper; it has been tested in practice (as discussed in the text box below) in what is understood to be the first time a resolution authority of one country has formally recognised a resolution action of another country.

The remainder of this chapter is structured as follows:

- **Section 2** establishes the rationale as to why statutory recognition is desirable, including the relevant international standards and the interaction with "contractual" recognition;
- **Section 3** then examines the circumstances when recognition can be granted under the UK regime and the presumption of recognition that exists within the framework;

[3] Sir Jon Cunliffe, Deputy Governor Financial Stability, 'Ten years on: Lessons from Northern Rock' (Single Resolution Board Conference, Brussels, 29 September 2017), https://www.bankofengland.co.uk/-/media/boe/files/speech/2017/ten-years-on-lessons-from-northern-rock.pdf.

[4] Sir Dave Ramsden, Deputy Governor for Markets and Banking, 'The UK's progress on resolvability' (Institute of Chartered Accountants in England and Wales (ICAEW), 26 February 2021), https://www.bankofengland.co.uk/speech/2021/february/dave-ramsden-institute-of-chartered-accountants-in-england-wales.

- **Section 4** turns to the circumstances when recognition may be refused, including where recognition would pose risks to UK financial stability or where there has been discrimination against UK creditors;
- Finally, **Section 5** summarises the legal process and effect of recognition, including the nature of the instrument and the scope of legal challenge.

2 The Rationale for a Statutory Recognition Regime

The UK Position Before the 2007–2008 Financial Crisis

In the aftermath of the failure of Northern Rock in 2007, then-Governor Mervyn King described the UK's bank insolvency regime as "markedly inferior to other countries" and argued that a special resolution regime was "the most important reform" at the time.[5] The absence of resolution powers meant that Northern Rock had to be taken into public ownership by the UK's finance ministry, HM Treasury (the **Treasury**) using emergency powers in 2008; a permanent resolution regime was later introduced into the UK via the Banking Act 2009 (the **Act**).

In addition to the resolution toolkit being inadequate, there was also no comprehensive framework for the cross-border recognition of foreign actions taken in respect of failing banks.

Depending on the nature of the foreign entity and the resolution action, it might have been possible that the provisions of the Cross-Border Insolvency Regulations 2006 would have provided some assistance,[6] but only if the action could be considered to be collective judicial or administrative proceedings pursuant to a law relating to insolvency,[7] in which the

[5] 'The Run on the Rock', House of Commons Treasury Committee, Fifth Report of Session 2007–2008, Volume II, 24 January 2008, https://publications.parliament.uk/pa/cm200708/cmselect/cmtreasy/56/5602.htm.

[6] The Cross-Border Insolvency Regulations 2006 do not apply to non-UK headquartered entities that have permission to accept deposits or issue electronic money under the Financial Services and Markets Act 2000 (***FSMA***).

[7] Cross-Border Insolvency Regulations 2006, Article 2(1) of Schedule 1.

assets and affairs of the debtor are subject to control or supervision by a foreign court, for the purpose of reorganisation or liquidation.[8]

Cases such as *Metliss*[9] however, demonstrate that the choice of English law as the governing law of a contract will shield that contract from the effect of certain law changes in a debtor's jurisdiction and the *Gibbs*[10] principle—that a foreign insolvency does not discharge liabilities under contracts governed by English law—may have potential application, even in cases where assistance might be sought under the Cross-Border Insolvency Regulations 2006 or otherwise.

In the absence of a statutory recognition framework, the legal pathways to international cooperation and recognition in the context of a foreign resolution action were somewhat unclear, or at the very least, incomplete.

The FSB Key Attributes of Effective Resolution Regimes

In the wake of the crisis, the Financial Stability Board (the **FSB**), the international body that monitors and makes recommendations about the global financial system, attempted to set out the policy objectives that needed to underpin effective resolution procedures. This culminated in the 2011 "Key Attributes of Effective Resolution Regimes for Financial Institutions" (the ***FSB Key Attributes***).[11] The FSB Key Attributes are the international standard for effective resolution regimes globally, and the arrangements for the resolution of failing banks in the UK are designed to comply with those principles, including on issues of cross-border resolution.

As noted by the FSB in its 2013 report to the G20, "Whichever resolution strategy is pursued for cross-border institutions, its effectiveness will be maximized if there is cross-border cooperation as called for by the Key Attributes...The effective implementation of resolution strategies can be

[8] Section 426 of the Insolvency Act 1986 might perform a similar function for insolvencies in certain jurisdictions, as might common-law principles of comity.

[9] *National Bank of Greece and Athens SA v Metliss [1958] AC 509.*

[10] *Antony Gibbs and sons v La Société Industrielle et Commerciale des Métaux (1890) 25 QBD 399.*

[11] Revised in 2014, https://www.fsb.org/wp-content/uploads/r_141015.pdf.

stymied if the cross-border effectiveness of bail-in and other resolution powers is uncertain".[12]

For this reason, the FSB Key Attributes place great emphasis on cooperation between resolution authorities. Key Attribute 7, in particular, provides that: "The statutory mandate of a resolution authority should empower and strongly encourage the authority wherever possible to act to achieve a cooperative solution with foreign resolution authorities" and that "jurisdictions should provide for a transparent and expedited process to give effect to foreign resolution measures". There is therefore a strong presumption in favour of resolution authorities recognising foreign procedures, wherever possible.

The FSB also accepts that contractual recognition clauses, which require a creditor to accept contractually that they will be bound by resolution action under a law other than the governing law of the contract, may provide some support for the effectiveness of a resolution in respect of liabilities governed by a foreign law. Contractual recognition clauses are commonly used to enhance the effectiveness of a write-down or conversion of liabilities in a resolution and to recognise temporary stays on early termination rights in the context of a resolution. Such clauses will generally be enforced by the courts unless contrary to public policy. They may certainly be regarded as an interim solution until statutory recognition frameworks are in place and they may also complement and support statutory recognition regimes thereafter.[13]

However, as the FSB notes in its "Principles for Cross-border Effectiveness of Resolution Actions", there are three key limitations to such clauses. First, a private law contractual approach may not achieve the same level of legal certainty as the adoption of a recognition framework set out in primary legislation. Secondly, by its very nature, a contractual approach binds only the parties that agree to it and so would need to be widely adopted by the firm and all its counterparties across all relevant contracts.

[12] FSB, 'Progress and Next Steps Towards Ending "Too-Big-To-Fail" (TBTF)' (2 September 2013), pages 12 and 13, https://www.fsb.org/wp-content/uploads/r_130902.pdf.

[13] See, for example, the 'Contractual Recognition' section in the FSB's 'Principles for Cross-border Effectiveness of Resolution Actions' (3 November 2015), https://www.fsb.org/wp-content/uploads/Principles-for-Cross-border-Effectiveness-of-Resolution-Actions.pdf.

Thirdly, if contractual recognition provisions are not included in all relevant contracts, there is an increased risk that creditors who otherwise would have similar legal rights may be treated differently in resolution.

Jurisdictional Implementation of FSB Key Attribute 7

With the FSB setting the policy direction and international standard, it fell to local jurisdictions to translate these non-binding aspirations into hard law. In the EU, this came in 2014, in the form of the EU's Bank Recovery and Resolution Directive (**BRRD**),[14] which was transposed into UK law, principally through revisions to the Act.

The BRRD's approach to recognition differed depending on whether or not a country was an EU Member State. Within the EU, with its harmonised resolution framework apparatus and apparatus for regulatory cooperation, the approach is to legally mandate *automatic* mutual recognition of resolution actions, through the amendment of Directive 2001/24/EC of the European Parliament and of the Council of 4 April 2001 on the reorganisation and winding up of credit institutions.

A more nuanced approach is taken in relation to so-called "third countries"—i.e. countries that are not EU Member States. This is to account for the fact that there may be greater differences between respective legal frameworks and a lesser, or less formal, degree of regulatory cooperation. Instead of automatic recognition, Articles 94–95 of the BRRD establish a presumption of recognition of third-country resolution actions subject to limited, prescribed exceptions.

This regime was retained by the UK following its withdrawal from the EU and is set out in section 89H of the Act, albeit with suitable adaptions.[15] For example, the EU language of "third-country" was retained

[14] Directive 2014/59/EU of the European Parliament and of the Council of 15 May 2014 establishing a framework for the recovery and resolution of credit institutions and investment firms and amending Council Directive 82/891/EEC and Directive 2001/24/EC, 2002/47/EC, 2004/25/EC, 2005/56/EC, 2011/35/EU, 2012/36/EU and Regulations (EU) No 1093/2010 and (EU) No 648/2012 of the European Parliament and of the Council.

[15] Following the UK's withdrawal from the EU, the UK and EU no longer automatically recognise each other's resolution actions; rather they would consider any recognition request from one another under their respective third-country recognition regimes (in the same way as the would consider a request from, say, the authorities in the United States).

in section 89H but has been adapted to refer to the law of a country or territory outside the UK.[16]

In terms of scope, section 89H currently covers a certain set of financial institutions, i.e. foreign firms that, if they were established in the UK, would be regarded as a bank, building society, credit union or investment firm and certain types of parents of such firms. Other kinds of financial institutions are therefore not within the scope of the statutory recognition regime. Any change to the scope of the recognition regime requires the approval of Parliament. Work is currently underway to expand the resolution regime for central counterparties (**CCPs**) and this includes provision for the recognition of third-country resolution action in respect of foreign CCPs.[17]

The provisions of section 89H are considered in the following sections. As a general point section 89H should be read in light of the context described above[18]: namely that it is a reflection, in law, of the UK's commitment to effective cross-border cooperation in general and to FSB Key Attribute 7 in particular.

3 Circumstances Where Recognition Will Be Granted

The recognition regime under section 89H is triggered when the UK authorities are notified of a putative "third-country resolution action".

The Bank and Treasury each have a role to play. The Bank is the primary decision-maker under the regime (assuming the role that previously sat with the English courts) and is obliged to make a "third-country

[16] In this chapter the term "third-country" is used interchangeably with "foreign".

[17] See Financial Services and Markets Act 2023, Part 7 (third-country resolution actions) of Schedule 11, https://www.legislation.gov.uk/ukpga/2023/29/contentshttps://bills.parliament.uk/bills/3326.

[18] For example, see Economic Secretary to the Treasury's written statement to the House of Commons on 19 May 2021: "Decisions over whether to recognise a third-country resolution action are regarded by the Financial Stability Board as a key aspect of an effective cross-border resolution regime", https://www.theyworkforyou.com/wms/?id=2021-05-19.hcws39.h. Further, the Treasury Code of Practice, which the Bank must have regard to under s.5 of the Act, includes paragraph 10.2 on effective cross-border resolution, see 'Banking Act 2009: special resolution regime code of practice (December 2020), https://assets.publishing.service.gov.uk/government/uploads/system/uploads/attachment_data/file/945165/SRR_CoP_December_2020.pdf.

instrument" which either recognises the action, refuses to recognise it or recognises some parts of the action but not others. The Treasury is required to approve the Bank's decision. Action to manage the failure of a firm, including matters of recognition, may involve consideration of the UK's compliance with its international obligations. The Government is legally responsible for ensuring that compliance is achieved and Treasury is responsible for this within the statutory framework for recognition of foreign resolution action. The Treasury is also responsible for protecting public funds in a resolution scenario, and this role is as relevant in relation to foreign resolutions as in relation to domestic resolutions, particularly given that (as explained below) material fiscal implications for the UK may be a ground for refusing recognition of such foreign resolution action.

Broadly speaking, the decision as to whether to recognise involves considering two questions. First, does the action meet the definition of "third-country resolution action"? Second, are there grounds to refuse recognition? This section discusses the first of these questions; the following section discusses the second.

The Definition of "Third-Country Resolution Action"

"Third-country resolution action' is defined in section 89H(7) as:

> "action **under the law** of a country or territory outside the United Kingdom to manage the failure or likely failure of a **third-country institution or a third-country parent undertaking**[19]**...**—
>
> (a) **the anticipated results of which** are, in relation to a third-country institution or third-country parent undertaking, **broadly comparable** to results which could have been anticipated from the exercise of a stabilisation option in relation to an entity in the United Kingdom corresponding to the institution or undertaking and
> (b) **the objectives of which** are **broadly comparable**, in relation to the country or territory concerned, to the [UK special resolution] objectives".

The statutory test involves an exercise of the Bank's expert evaluative judgement. The assessment focuses on "broad comparability" of the

[19] Under s 89H(7) of the Act, a "third-country institution" means an institution established in a country or territory other than the UK that would, if it were established within the UK, be regarded as a bank, building society, credit union or investment firm.

measure with what might have happened in a similar situation under the UK regime, looking at the anticipated results and objectives. There is also a prior question of whether the action can be said to be "under the law" of the third-country, meaning that the action was taken lawfully under the regime of the home resolution authority.

"Broadly Comparable": Objectives and Anticipated Results

The "broadly comparable" assessment would appear to involve an overall, holistic one, as opposed to a prescriptive analysis that is occasionally adopted for the purposes of "equivalence" assessments in other areas of financial regulation.[20] This gives the Bank a degree of expert evaluative judgement when determining whether the objectives and anticipated results of the relevant resolution action are "broadly comparable" to a corresponding UK resolution action.

For the purpose of assessing the comparability of objectives, the seven objectives of the UK special resolution regime are[21]:

- ensuring the continuity of banking services in the UK and of critical functions;
- protecting and enhancing UK financial stability;
- protecting public confidence in UK financial stability;
- protecting public funds;
- protecting investors and depositors to the extent covered by the Financial Services Compensation Scheme;
- protecting client assets; and
- avoiding interference with property rights in breach of the European Convention on Human Rights (**ECHR**).

[20] Equivalence is an autonomous mechanism by which one jurisdiction can recognise relevant standards in another jurisdiction as equivalent to their own (e.g. to allow for market access or preferential treatment for firms). Although the difference between "broad comparability" and "equivalence" may be less given the UK's stated preference is for "outcomes-based" equivalence (in contrast to the "line-by-line" comparisons of laws which have characterised the EU approach), see HM Treasury 'Guidance Document for the UK's Equivalence Framework for Financial Services' (November 2020), https://www.gov.uk/government/publications/guidance-document-for-the-uks-equivalence-framework-for-financial-services.

[21] The Act, s 4.

The objectives are not hierarchical and are to be balanced as appropriate in each case.[22]

In terms of the anticipated results, the Bank must look at the extent to which the UK regime would produce a different outcome. For example, under the UK regime, the Bank has the power to "bail-in" liabilities to recapitalise a failed firm but certain deposits are "protected" from being bailed in (on the basis that doing so could trigger contagion); therefore if a foreign resolution authority has bailed in protected deposits this would produce a different result from the UK regime. The better view is that this question should be analysed in the context of the specific third-country resolution action for which recognition is being sought, rather than the third-country's resolution regime more generally.

The regime envisages that the action may be notified to the Bank prior to or contemporaneously with the action taking place, for example by the reference to "anticipated" results in the "broadly comparable" test. This reflects the FSB standards that the mandate of a resolution authority should empower and strongly encourage the authority to achieve a cooperative solution with foreign resolution authorities and that cross-border recognition should occur in an expedited fashion.

In cases where notification of the foreign resolution action occurs only after the action has taken place, *ex-post* assessments of the outcome of the foreign resolution action may still be relevant and serve as evidence that a particular outcome could have been clearly "anticipated" in advance of the resolution action taking place.

4 Refusal of Recognition (in Whole or in Part)

If the action is a "third-country resolution action", section 89H(4) of the Act provides that recognition of the action (or part of it) may be refused only if the Bank and the Treasury are satisfied that one or more of the following five conditions are satisfied[23]:

(a) recognition would have an adverse effect on UK financial stability;

[22] The Act, s 4(10).

[23] See 'Recognition of third-country resolution action' on the Bank of England's 'Resolution' page, https://www.bankofengland.co.uk/financial-stability/resolution.

(b) the taking of action in relation to a UK branch of a third-country institution is necessary to achieve one or more of the special resolution objectives;
(c) under the third-country resolution action, UK creditors would not receive the same treatment as third-country creditors with similar legal rights;
(d) recognition of the third-country resolution action would have material fiscal implications for the UK; or
(e) recognition of, and taking action in support of, the third-country resolution action would be unlawful under section 6 of the Human Rights Act 1998 (public authority not to act contrary to ECHR).

Adverse Impact on UK Financial Stability

Ground (a) reflects the fact that the Bank has a statutory objective (duty) to protect and enhance UK financial stability[24] and so should not be expected to recognise a foreign resolution action where this could be jeopardised.

Independent Action Is Necessary to Resolve a UK Branch

As regards ground (b), the general assumption is that the failure of a UK branch will be managed by the relevant authorities in the jurisdiction where the bank is headquartered. This is reflected in the fact that, when a firm seeks to operate in the UK through a branch, authorisation by the Prudential Regulation Authority (**PRA**) applies to the whole firm, and will take into account the extent to which the PRA, in consultation with the Bank (acting in its capacity as resolution authority), has appropriate assurance over the resolution arrangements for the firm and its UK operations.[25] Significant efforts are being made in the international sphere to ensure that resolution authorities cooperate in the resolution of cross-border banks, through ex ante resolution planning in firm-specific crisis

[24] The Bank of England Act 1998, s 2A.

[25] See in particular Supervisory Statement | SS5/21 'International banks: The PRA's approach to branch and subsidiary supervision' (July 2021), https://www.bankofengland.co.uk/-/media/boe/files/prudential-regulation/supervisory-statement/2021/ss521-july-2021.pdf?la=en&hash=D45354116A8BB3F7DC567815C61878203300A2B1.

management groups and through cooperation agreements setting out the roles and responsibilities of each authority.

However, the Bank has back-stop powers to independently resolve the UK branch of a foreign institution, when it has refused to recognise a foreign resolution action or where the foreign resolution authority has failed to commence resolution proceedings.[26] These powers would only be used in the event that cooperation between resolution authorities proves ineffective, and where action is required to protect the public interest. In such a case, the Bank has power to transfer some or all of the business of the UK branch to a private sector purchaser, to a bridge bank or to an asset management vehicle. Following the transfer, the Bank may bail-in transferred liabilities to improve the position of the entity as necessary.

Discrimination Against UK Creditors

Refusal on ground (c) is essentially focused on a scenario where the foreign resolution authority has discriminated against UK creditors, i.e. where, under the foreign resolution action, UK creditors would not receive the same treatment as home country creditors by reason of being located or payable in the UK. Differential treatment may not be discriminatory if it is explicable on the basis of policy-based exemption considerations. It is also important to note that analysis under this ground must compare creditors who have similar legal rights prior to the foreign resolution action.

Material Fiscal Implications

Ground (d) gives the Bank and the Treasury the ability to refuse a foreign resolution if it were to have material fiscal implications for the UK. This is particularly important for the Treasury given its responsibility to protect public funds (which, as noted above, is an explicit objective under the UK

[26] The Act, s 89JA. See also HM Treasury's 'special resolution regime code of practice' (December 2020), paragraphs 10.12–10.17, https://assets.publishing.service.gov.uk/government/uploads/system/uploads/attachment_data/file/945165/SRR_CoP_December_2020.pdf.

resolution regime). The role of the Treasury here could be considered akin to the part that it plays in the resolution of a UK bank, whereby the Bank requires Treasury's express consent to exercise a stabilisation power if that would be likely to have implications for public funds.[27]

Recognition Would Be Contrary to the ECHR

To elaborate on ground (e) above, section 6(1) of the Human Rights Act 1998 states that "It is unlawful for a public authority to act in a way which is incompatible with a Convention right". In practice, there are three Convention rights that are likely to be potentially engaged: (i) the right to peaceful enjoyment of property (under Article 1 of the First Protocol, also referred to as ***A1P1***); (ii) the prohibition of discrimination (under Article 14) and (iii) the right to a fair trial (under Article 6), with A1P1 perhaps being the most relevant.

For example, if a creditor has their claim against the firm in resolution reduced or cancelled without adequate compensation, this could infringe A1P1. Whether there has been compliance with A1P1 will involve consideration of the following principles: (i) the need for a fair balance to be struck between public interest and private rights; (ii) the principle of proportionality and (iii) the doctrine of the margin of appreciation. The courts will allow a reasonably wide "margin of appreciation" and generally defer to a public body's judgement as to how to strike that balance, particularly on public policy issues.[28]

It is a nuanced point but the question under ground (e) is whether *the Bank's recognition itself* would have the effect of interfering with a Convention right in an unjustifiable way. It is arguably not determinative whether the foreign authority conducting the resolution has acted in breach of a Convention right (although this may be relevant to the question as to whether the resolution action was "under the law" of the third-country).

[27] The Act, s 78.

[28] See, for example, *SRM Global Master Fund LP & Ors v HM Treasury [2009] EWHC 227 (Admin)*.

Exercising Stabilisation Powers to Support a Foreign Resolution

In addition to recognising a foreign resolution action, the Bank may exercise one or more of the stabilisation powers in respect of a foreign institution, parent undertaking or foreign group company in order to support, or give full effect to, the foreign resolution action.[29] The Bank may, for example, use property transfer powers to transfer property of the foreign bank located in the UK to a new owner, in support of the foreign resolution.

In such cases, an additional special resolution objective is engaged, to which the Bank must have regard when using or considering such use of stabilisation powers. This is to support foreign resolution action with a view to promoting objectives which, in that other country, correspond to the UK's special resolution objectives. The resolution conditions assessment process set out in sections 7 to 8ZA of the Act does not apply to the Bank's use of stabilisation powers in support of a recognised foreign action,[30] however, there are specific conditions that apply to supporting action taken by the Bank in respect of a foreign group company.[31] In addition, a modified form of the "no creditor worse off" safeguard[32] applies.[33] This provides that pre-resolution shareholders and creditors should not receive less favourable treatment than they would have received had the foreign entity in respect of whom the Bank uses its stabilisation tools entered insolvency instead.

[29] The Act, s 89I(3).

[30] The Act, s 89I(7).

[31] The Act, s 89I(9).

[32] This safeguard is intended to ensure that shareholders and creditors of a banking institution are left in no worse position as a result of the exercise of the stabilisation powers than they would have been in had the powers not been exercised and the bank gone into insolvency.

[33] The Act, s 89I(8).

5 The Process and Legal Effect of Recognition

The Time Frame for Taking a Decision

The Act does not specify a time limit for the UK authorities to make a decision on recognition. As reflected in the FSB Key Attributes, this is expected to be an expedited process to ensure the success of the foreign resolution.

That said, the authorities may be justified in not taking a decision in short order; for example, where further information is necessary to inform the assessments the Bank is required to make in reaching a decision on recognition. To facilitate this process, and as discussed further below, the Bank has published ex ante guidance on its recognition regime.[34]

Alternatively, in a situation where a period of time has elapsed between the foreign resolution action and its notification, it may well be that the legality of the resolution action has come under challenge in the courts of the relevant home country. If it became aware of particular legal action, there would be a question for the Bank as to what sufficient confirmation of legality would look like. This is because, it will be recalled, that under the definition of a "third-country resolution action", the action must be "an action *under the law*" of the home country, meaning a lawful action under that jurisdiction's law. The Bank would look in particular at judgements which ruled that resolution action had contravened local law or resulted in a free-standing breach of the ECHR (if the state in question has ratified the Convention), in which case the Bank may only be in a position to take a recognition decision once such litigation has fully run its course.

The Recognition Instrument and Its Effect

The Act prescribes certain procedural steps to facilitate the transparency of the Bank's decision-making process. When it has reached its decision, the Bank must make a formal legal instrument that either: (i) recognises the entire action, (ii) refuses to recognise the entire action, or (iii) recognises part and refuses to recognise the remainder.[35]

[34] See 'Recognition of third-country resolution actions' section of the Bank of England's 'Resolution' page https://www.bankofengland.co.uk/financial-stability/resolution.

[35] The Act, s 89H(2).

Where an instrument recognises any foreign resolution action (or a part of it), that action (or the recognised part of it) produces the same legal effects in any part of the UK as it would have produced had it been made with due authority under the law of that part of the UK.[36]

Recognised foreign resolution actions will not trigger contractual termination rights: they are to be treated in the same way as a UK crisis prevention measure or crisis management measure and are to be disregarded in determining whether a default event provision in a relevant contract applies.[37]

The Bank's recognition instrument must be made publicly available, in a manner that is likely to bring it to the attention of those affected by the recognition decision. In particular, it must be disclosed:

- on the website of the Bank and the resolved firm in question;
- in two newspapers, chosen by the Bank to maximise the likelihood of the instrument coming to the attention of persons likely to be affected;
- via a regulatory news service (RNS) announcement, if the firm's shares trade on a regulated market[38]; and
- to Parliament, by the Treasury.

Duty to Give Reasons?

There is no statutory requirement for the Bank to give reasons for its decision and no general duty to give reasons for an administrative decision.[39] Courts can, however, imply such a duty on the basis of procedural unfairness in cases where it would otherwise be difficult or impossible for an adversely affected party to challenge a decision by a public authority. In practice, the level of detail in any reasoning, if it were to be provided, would likely be informed by a range of factors such as the sophistication of the affected parties, the urgency of the decision and the need to protect confidential information. In relation to the latter, for example, in the

[36] The Act, s 89I(2).

[37] The Act, s 48Z.

[38] Within the meaning of FSMA, s 103(1).

[39] E.g. *R v Secretary of State for the Home Department, ex p. Doody* [1994] 1 A.C. 531, 564E–F.

course of the recognition process, the Bank is likely to have received confidential firm-specific information from the foreign resolution authority. Such information is statutorily protected from disclosure[40] (subject to specific legal gateways or the consent of the person to whom it relates); this is not only to protect the commercial interests of the firm but also to encourage full and frank information exchange between resolution authorities, particularly in a crisis.

Challenging a Recognition Decision

Affected parties (such as the home resolution authority, the failed firm or impacted creditors) may wish to challenge the Bank's recognition decision. The Act does not provide for a specific procedure for doing so. However, as a public authority, the Bank is subject to public and administrative law obligations and its decisions are reviewable. Any challenge would need to be brought by way of judicial review.

Judicial review is a court procedure in which a judge reviews the lawfulness of a decision or action made by a public body. Judicial review is a way of ensuring that public bodies act within the limits of their legal powers and in accordance with the relevant procedures and legal principles governing the exercise of their decision-making functions.[41] This is a bulwark for the rule of law which lies at the heart of the English legal system.

The principal remedy under such an action would be a quashing order setting aside the decision and directing the Bank to reconsider its decision.[42]

[40] The Act, s 89L applying FSMA, s 348.

[41] *R (Rights: Community: Action) v Secretary of State for Housing Communities and Local Government [2021] PTSR 553* at [6].

[42] The Bank has statutory immunity from liability in damages in respect of its action or inaction in its capacity, inter alia, as a resolution authority; the immunity does not extend to action or inaction (a) in bad faith; or (b) in contravention of section 6(1) of the Human Rights Act 1998 (public authority not to act contrary to the ECHR), see s 244 of the Act.

There is no statutory requirement for the Bank to give reasons for its decision and no general duty to give reasons for an administrative decision.[43] Courts can, however, imply such a duty on the basis of procedural unfairness in cases where it would otherwise be difficult or impossible for an adversely affected party to challenge a decision by a public authority. In practice, the level of detail in any reasoning, if it were to be provided, would likely be informed by a range of factors such as the sophistication of the affected parties, the urgency of the decision and the need to protect confidential information. In relation to the latter, for example, in the course of the recognition process, the Bank is likely to have received confidential firm-specific information from the foreign resolution authority. Such information is statutorily protected from disclosure[44] (subject to specific legal gateways or the consent of the person to whom it relates); this is not only to protect the commercial interests of the firm but also to encourage full and frank information exchange between resolution authorities, particularly in a crisis.

Case Study: Recognition of the PrivatBank Bail-In

The Bank and Treasury applied the UK recognition framework for the first time in May 2021 in recognising the PrivatBank bail-in.[a] This is understood to be the first recognition of a foreign resolution action by a resolution authority, globally.

In 2016 PrivatBank, a systemically important Ukrainian bank, was nationalised by the Ukrainian authorities. The resolution action came in the aftermath of the economic and military unrest, including Russian annexation of Crimea, which caused stress within the Ukrainian banking sector. The IMF approved funding to assist Ukraine to tackle its economic crisis of 2013/14. This funding was subject to the country reforming its economy and banking system. As part of this, the National Bank of Ukraine (***NBU***) introduced new banking regulations and committed to monitoring banks' compliance, and to resolve banks if necessary.

Part of the reform programme involved stress testing the largest banks in 2015, following which the NBU concluded that PrivatBank had a major regulatory capital deficit. The deficit worsened in 2016 and the NBU

[43] E.g. *R v Secretary of State for the Home Department, ex p. Doody* [1994] 1 A.C. 531, 564E–F.

[44] The Act, s 89L applying FSMA, s 348.

considered there was no realistic prospect of restructuring. PrivatBank was declared insolvent and resolved by the Ukrainian authorities in December 2016. Certain liabilities were converted to equity pursuant to a bail-in and PrivatBank was subsequently nationalised.

The IMF and the European Bank for Reconstruction and Development, alongside the US Embassy in Ukraine, issued a statement confirming their support for the NBU's decision to nationalise PrivatBank as the only effective method of protecting depositors and the stability of the Ukrainian financial system.[b]

The PrivatBank resolution included the bail-in of four English law governed loans, totalling $595m, made by a UK special purpose vehicle to PrivatBank. These loans in turn were funded by notes issued by the SPV to noteholders in the international capital markets. The NBU submitted a request for recognition to the Bank in relation to the bail-in. PrivatBank did not perform banking activities or have banking customers in the UK. The request for recognition arose solely because of the existence of the four English law loans.

Pursuant to the UK resolution regime, in order to decide whether to recognise the bail-in, the Bank was required to undertake an analysis to determine whether the bail-in was broadly comparable in its objectives and anticipated results to those of the UK resolution regime. The Bank then had to consider whether any of the statutory grounds applied for refusing to recognise the bail-in.

The Bank kept relevant stakeholders, including the NBU and representatives of creditors, informed throughout the recognition process. The decision was complicated by the fact that the Bank was only notified of the PrivatBank resolution sometime after it had taken place and the resolution was subject to legal challenges in the Ukrainian courts. The Bank ultimately decided to recognise the bail-in of PrivatBank which gave effect to the bail-in of the four loans in question as a matter of English law.

[a]See Bank News Release, 'PrivatBank Bail-in: Bank of England Recognises Bail-in by National Bank of Ukraine' (14 May 2021), https://www.bankofengland.co.uk/news/2021/may/privatbank-bail-in-boe-recognises-bail-in-by-national-bank-of-ukraine.

[b]IMF, 'Statement on the Stability of the Banking System in Ukraine' (19 December 2016), https://www.imf.org/en/News/Articles/2016/12/19/pr16568-IMF-Statement-on-the-Stability-of-the-Banking-System-in-Ukraine.

6 Concluding Remarks

This chapter has sought to provide an in-depth overview of the UK's statutory recognition regime of foreign resolution actions: why it is important; when recognition will be granted or refused and the formalities and practicalities of the recognition process.

By having its recognition regime laid out in law, with a presumption of recognition, the UK has signalled its strong commitment to FSB Key Attribute 7. The regime ensures that the UK has a transparent and expedited process to give effect to foreign resolution actions; it also ensures that the statutory mandate of the Bank, as the UK's resolution authority, strongly encourages a cooperative solution with foreign resolution authorities, wherever possible.

The regime does not just exist on paper; it has been tested in practice.[45] As the IMF highlighted in its 2022 Financial Sector Assessment Programme:

> **In May 2021, the U.K. authorities applied the recognition regime for the first time—perhaps a global first**. In 2016, PrivatBank was subject to bail-in by the National Bank of Ukraine; the National Bank of Ukraine subsequently submitted a request for recognition of this resolution to the [Bank] relating to notes (loans) issued by a U.K. special purpose vehicle that were governed by English law. In May 2021, the [Bank], with Treasury approval, recognized the bail-in decisions for these loans. Whilst considering its decision, the [Bank] kept relevant stakeholders, including the National Bank of Ukraine and creditors' representatives, informed about the recognition process throughout.[46]

Following a recommendation by the IMF in its assessment and taking into account its experience on the PrivatBank case, the Bank published additional guidance to explain its approach to recognition of foreign

[45] See text box, **'Case Study: Recognition of the The PrivatBank Bail-in'**.

[46] IMF, UK FSAP, 'Recommendations on Financial Safety Net and Financial Crisis Preparedness' (March 2022), paragraph 39, https://www.imf.org/en/Publications/CR/Issues/2022/04/07/United-Kingdom-Financial-Sector-Assessment-Program-Select-Issues-in-Financial-Safety-Net-516276.

resolution actions.[47] This guidance underlines the importance of effective prior engagement between the foreign resolution authority and the Bank, in order to support the transparent and expedited process envisaged in the FSD Key Attributes. For this reason, the Bank's guidance encourages foreign resolution authorities to engage the Bank ahead of taking any resolution action that may require action from the Bank, including recognition. This gives the Bank time and flexibility to work with the foreign resolution authority when assessing the recognition request and supporting materials and aids in swift decision-making.

Resolution authorities should be actively considering recognition as part of business-as-usual resolution planning and engagement. This allows home resolution authorities, host and any other relevant authorities to consider the information and decision-making that may be required in advance. Of course, there may be cases where a foreign resolution authority is unable to engage ahead of taking a resolution action; in that situation, the Bank's guidance notes that they should engage as soon as possible after taking the measures.

To conclude, in the words of a Deputy Governor of the Bank, "resolution will not be some painless magic bullet. No matter how well prepared in advance, the resolution of a major bank, if it happens, would be a painful, protracted, and probably litigious, affair".[48] This statement is as true for the narrow issue of recognition of foreign resolution actions as it is for the broader resolution process. But the recognition framework and practical steps outlined in this chapter should all serve to make the recognition process a little less painful, protracted and litigious.

[47] See the 'Recognition of third-country resolution actions' section on the Bank of England's 'Resolution' page, https://www.bankofengland.co.uk/financial-stability/resolution.

[48] Sir Jon Cunliffe, Deputy Governor Financial Stability, 'Central Clearing and Resolution—Learning some of the lessons' (FIA International Derivatives Expo 2018, London, 5 June 2018), https://www.bankofengland.co.uk/-/media/boe/files/speech/2018/central-clearing-and-resolution-learning-some-of-the-lessons-of-lehmans-speech-by-jon-cunliffe.pdf.

CHAPTER 15

The Impact of Climate Change on the Economy and Financial System: Legal Aspects of the Bank of England's Response

Jack Parker and Anne Corrigan

1 Introduction

Climate change and the transition to net zero can create risks that threaten the stability of the financial system. These risks have unique characteristics that set them apart from the "traditional" risk types that the PRA and the firms it regulates are accustomed to. They are far-reaching

Any views expressed are solely those of the authors and so cannot be taken to represent those of the Bank of England or to state Bank of England policy. This chapter should not therefore be reported as representing the views of the Bank of England or members of the Monetary Policy Committee, Financial Policy Committee or Prudential Regulation Committee. We are grateful to Chris Faint, Alan Wright and Matthew Hartley for their input in writing this chapter.

J. Parker · A. Corrigan (✉)
Bank of England, London, UK
e-mail: Anne.Corrigan@bankofengland.co.uk

M. Bodellini et al. (eds.), *Commercial Banking in Transition*, Palgrave Macmillan Studies in Banking and Financial Institutions,
https://doi.org/10.1007/978-3-031-45289-5_15

in breadth and magnitude, foreseeable inasmuch as one can be certain they will happen and yet are largely unpredictable in their specific manifestations. It is for this reason that Andrew Bailey, Governor of the Bank of England (**"the Bank"**), has described climate change as the ultimate systemic risk.[1]

Climate change refers to long-term shifts in temperatures and weather patterns.[2] These occur naturally but are also both directly and indirectly human-induced. Climate change creates financial risks (**"climate-related financial risks"**) and has observable macroeconomic consequences. These arise through two principal channels.[3]

The first is the physical risks to the planet. These have crystallised through specific weather events such as heatwaves, floods, wildfires and storms.[4] These physical effects have also been felt through the longer-term-shifts in climate, including changes in precipitation and an increase in sea levels and mean temperatures. These can potentially result in large financial losses, impairing asset values and the creditworthiness of borrowers.[5]

J. Parker
e-mail: Jack.Parker@bankofengland.co.uk

[1] See A. Bailey, Tackling climate for real: The role of central banks, Reuters Events Responsible Business, 2021, https://www.bankofengland.co.uk/speech/2021/june/andrew-bailey-reuters-events-global-responsible-business-2021 (hereafter **"Bailey"**).

[2] Climate change is legally defined in the United Nations Framework Convention on Climate Change (1992) to mean: "*a change of climate which is attributed directly or indirectly to human activity that alters the composition of the global atmosphere and which is in addition to natural climate variability observed over comparable time periods*".

[3] 'Basel Committee on Banking Supervision: Climate-related risk drivers and their transmission channels', Bank for International Settlements (April, 2021), https://www.bis.org/bcbs/publ/d517.pdf.

[4] The IPCC Sixth Assessment Report on Climate Change 2022: Impacts, Adaptation and Vulnerability includes an assessment of the impacts of climate change on nature and humanity.

[5] To illustrate, a reduction in the valuation of a property due to greater flood risk increases the loan to value ratio of the mortgage and the credit risk on loan books through greater loss given default. Further, if damages from physical risks are not adequately insured, the financial burden could fall onto other market participants, increasing credit exposures for banks. Extreme weather events can cause significant losses for homeowners, reducing their ability to repay their loan.

The second is the transition risks which can be thought about in terms of the responsive process of adjustment made by governments, industries and consumers in pursuit of a low-carbon economy. This can be influenced by developments in policy and regulation, the emergence of disruptive technology and business models, shifting societal preferences and evolving evidence, frameworks and legal interpretations. These could prompt a reassessment of the value of a large range of carbon-intensive assets, and manifest as increased credit exposures and market[6] and operational[7] risks for banks, as the costs and opportunities become apparent.[8]

Transition risks also include litigation risks that can arise from individuals or businesses seeking compensation for losses they may have suffered from the physical or transition risks from climate change, or legal challenges taken to require a particular course of action.[9]

Climate-related financial risks have a number of distinctive elements and are relevant to multiple lines of business, sectors and geographies. Their full impact on the financial system may, therefore, be larger than for other types of traditional risks, and is potentially non-linear, correlated and irreversible.[10] The time horizons over which climate-related financial

[6] The impact of decarbonisation on carbon-intensive sectors could affect energy and commodity prices, corporate bonds, equities and certain derivative contracts. The financial risk associated with an abrupt transition could increase if portfolios are not aligned with anticipated climate pathways.

[7] Severe weather events can impact business continuity and the pricing of inputs such as energy, water and insurance could also increase.

[8] To illustrate, in the context of the Minimum Energy Efficiency Standard in the UK, properties with an energy performance certificate rating in the lowest two categories may not be rented as new leases or renewals. Landlords who do not improve the energy efficiency of these properties may be more likely to default on their buy-to-let mortgages, or the value of the property may be impaired, decreasing the value of a bank's collateral.

[9] To illustrate, refer to Milieudefensie et al. v Royal Dutch Shell (2021).

[10] See E. Stheeman, Why macroprudential policy needs to tackle financial stability risks from climate change, Queen's University Belfast, 2022, https://www.bankofengland.co.uk/speech/2022/april/elisabeth-stheeman-speech-at-queen-university (hereafter "**Stheeman**"). Climate-related financial risk management and the role of capital requirements, The PRA, Climate Change Adaptation Report, 2021, https://www.bankofengland.co.uk/-/media/boe/files/prudential-regulation/publication/2021/october/climate-change-adaptation-report-2021.pdf (hereafter "**CCAR**").

risks may be realised are also uncertain, and their full impact may crystallise outside of many current business planning trajectories.[11] The use of past data, therefore, may not be a useful predictor of future risks.

Ultimately, climate-related financial risks can only be mitigated by reducing greenhouse gas (“**GHG**”) emissions across the economy. Collaboration is crucial across sectors and between central Government, regulators and industry, both domestically and internationally. Legal and policy frameworks can facilitate a smooth transition and assist to focus on the beneficial power of green finance.

As the world goes through the transition to a net-zero economy, climate-related financial risks will continue to require action across international organisations, Government and regulatory authorities. Climate-related financial risks fall squarely within the Bank's mission to promote the good of the people of the UK. As the UK's independent central bank, the Bank is charged with maintaining monetary and financial stability. As regulator of banks, insurers, central counterparties, central securities depositories and the largest investment firms, the Bank is charged with ensuring prudential stability for the entities it regulates. Climate change is therefore central to its prudential, financial stability and monetary policy objectives and the way it runs its own operations.

This chapter will explore the development of the legal framework and central banking policy in the UK between 2015 and 2022 to show how the work of the Bank of England fits into the overall effort, including ensuring the financial system is resilient to climate-related financial risks.[12]

[11] In discussing the effectiveness and appropriateness of the capital regime for capturing climate risks, Sam Woods refers to the “regime gaps” which occur when the design, methodology or scope of the capital framework do not adequately cover these risks. To illustrate, “*some aspects of the Pillar 1 capital framework for banks use a one-year time horizon for calculating potential unexpected losses…The one-year horizon is, in effect, a modelling assumption. It may be reasonable for many risks, but seems particularly ill-suited for climate change, a risk which is structurally building over time and will not fully crystallise in a one-year horizon*”. See S. Woods, Climate Capital, Webcast hosted by the Global Association of Risk Professionals, 2022, https://www.bankofengland.co.uk/speech/2022/may/sam-woods-speech-on-the-results-of-the-climate-bes-exercise-on-financial-risks-from-climate-change (hereafter “**Woods**”).

[12] “*…to fulfil our mission going forwards we need to look ahead to the structural shifts we face over the coming years and decades. That will mean hearing central bankers like me speak about things that we have not in the past – terms like central bank digital currencies, cyber risk, and climate change are now firmly part of our lexicon. This is not about us*

2 The Legal Framework for Combating Climate Change

Climate change is a global phenomenon that, commensurately, requires international cooperation and coordinated solutions. The legal regime in relation to climate change, therefore, can be found in both domestic legislation and international law.

The United Nations Framework Convention on Climate Change (the "Convention")

The Convention was adopted in 1992 and creates the basic legal framework and principles supporting international cooperation in relation to climate change with the ultimate objective: "*to achieve ... stabilization of greenhouse gas concentrations in the atmosphere at a level that would prevent dangerous anthropogenic interference with the climate system. Such a level should be achieved within a time-frame sufficient to allow ecosystems to adapt naturally to climate change, to ensure that food production is not threatened and to enable economic development to proceed in a sustainable manner*".

The Kyoto Protocol, adopted in 1997, committed industrialised countries and countries in transition to a market economy to set and achieve quantified emissions targets reductions across six GHG emissions.

The Paris Agreement (the "Agreement")

The Agreement[13] was adopted by 196 parties at COP 21[14] in Paris in December 2015 and enshrines an aspiration to achieve a net-zero GHG emissions level during the latter half of the century. Specifically, the aim is to curb the rise in global average temperatures to well below 2, preferably

adding new things to our mission, nor is it about doing that which is rightly for others. It is about taking these new things into account alongside the old as we go about fulfilling our mission, delivering monetary and financial stability through time". Bailey (n 1).

[13] The Paris Agreement (United Nations, 2015), https://unfccc.int/files/essential_background/convention/application/pdf/english_paris_agreement.pdf (hereafter "**Paris Agreement**").

[14] The twenty-first session of the Conference of the Parties and the eleventh session of the Conference of the Parties serving as the meeting of the Parties to the Kyoto Protocol which took place from 30 November to 11 December 2015, in Paris, France.

to 1.5, degrees Celsius, relative to pre-industrial levels. It entered into force on 4 November 2016.

The Agreement includes commitments from all signatories to reduce their GHG emissions and collaborate to adapt to the impacts of climate change. It also calls on countries to strengthen their commitments over time. Signatories also committed to making finance flows consistent with a pathway of low GHG emissions and climate-resilient development.[15]

The Agreement works on a cycle whereby each country is expected to submit a nationally determined contribution ("**NDC**") every five years. The NDC is the means by which countries communicate the action they plan to take to reduce their GHG emissions to attain the objectives of the Agreement. They also communicate the actions they will take to build resilience and adapt to the impacts of rising temperatures. Unlike the NDCs, which are mandatory, the Agreement also invites countries to formulate and submit long-term low GHG emission development strategies which provide visibility on the signatory's direction of future development.

In order for signatories to support one another, particularly those most in need, the Agreement provides a framework for financial, technical and capacity building. In terms of accountability, the signatories established an "enhanced transparency framework" and, from 2024, will commence reporting on actions taken in furtherance of climate change mitigation. The collective progress under the Agreement will, in turn, be assessed via a "global stocktake" leading to recommendations for further plans in the next cycle.

R (Application of Friends of the Earth Limited and Others) v Heathrow Airport Limited (the "Heathrow Case")[16]

The legal status of the Agreement was tested in the Heathrow case and it illustrates its limited legal effect in the UK. The Heathrow case concerned whether the Secretary of State's failure to take account of the UK's commitments under the Agreement rendered a decision in favour of a third runway at Heathrow Airport unlawful. The issue before the court

[15] Article 2.1(c) (Paris Agreement n 13).

[16] *R (on the application of Friends of the Earth Ltd and others) (Respondents) v Heathrow Airport Ltd (Appellant)* [2020] UKSC 52. On appeal from: *R (on the application of Plan B Earth) v Secretary of State for Transport* [2020] EWCA Civ 214.

was whether the Government's commitments under the Agreement were tantamount to "government policy".

The Court reasoned that the ratification of international treaties gives rise to binding legal obligations on the UK in international law, and treaty commitments continue regardless of whether a particular Government remains in office. It does not constitute "*a commitment operating on the plane of domestic law to perform obligations under the treaty*" since "*law-making steps*" would be required to give effect to treaty obligations in domestic law.[17]

In addressing the arguments made by the respondents in relation to the legal framework applicable to significant infrastructure projects in the UK, the Supreme Court held that what constitutes "government policy" for the purposes of the Planning Act 2008 should be construed narrowly in order for the legislation to "*operate sensibly*".[18] The formal ratification of the Agreement did not render the Government's commitment to its "government policy" for the purpose of this legislation. Rather, the Court reasoned that government policy in the context of the Planning Act 2008 refers to readily identifiable, "*carefully formulated written statements of policy*" which have been "*cleared by the relevant departments on a Government-wide basis*".[19]

Climate Change Act 2008 (the "CCA")

Under the Kyoto Protocol, the UK was required to reduce its GHG emissions by 12.5% below 1990 levels, between 2008 and 2012, and 18% by 2020. The UK government implemented a domestic framework in the form of the CCA in order to make these commitments legally binding and deliver these reductions.[20]

The CCA requires the UK to achieve a 100% reduction in GHG emissions levels (below 1990 levels) by 2050, further to an upward revision

[17] Paragraph 108.

[18] Paragraph 105.

[19] Ibid.

[20] This legislation was also preceded by the '*Stern Review: The Economics of Climate Change (2006)*' which, in short, concluded that the benefits of strong, early action on climate change far outweigh the costs of inaction.

in 2019 from 80%.[21] This made the UK one of the first countries to embed in legislation a commitment to achieve net-zero GHG emissions by 2050. There are only limited circumstances where amendments may be made to the baseline and target amounts.[22] As such, the target can be characterised as a legislative duty rather than merely an ambition.

To that end, the Secretary of State (at the time of writing, Minister of State for Climate) must set "carbon budgets" that impose limits on the net UK carbon account 11.5 years in advance of each budgetary period.[23] In doing so, this affords the industry the needed certainty and predictability to make long-term investment decisions. There are various matters the Secretary of State must take into account when setting the carbon budget.[24] These include scientific knowledge regarding, and technology relevant to, climate as well as economic circumstances and in particular the likely impact of the decision on the economy and the competitiveness of certain sectors.

The legislation is quite inflexible as to the circumstances when a budget may be amended.[25] The Secretary of State is under a duty to ensure that the account remains within budget. The procedure to amend either the baseline, the 2050 target figures or the carbon budget is by secondary legislation laid, debated and voted upon in each House of the UK Parliament.[26]

The Committee on Climate Change (**"CCC"**), a new independent body established under the CCA, plays a central role in advising the Secretary of State in the context of setting and realising its carbon budgets. In terms of accountability, the CCC is required to deliver annual progress reports to Parliament, setting out its views on progress made.

The CCA also provides for the Secretary of State to direct certain organisations to produce reports on the current and future predicted

[21] Climate Change Act 2008 (2050 Target Amendment) Order 2019 (SI 2019/1056).

[22] The CCA, s 2(2).

[23] The CCA, s 27(1).

[24] The CCA, s 10.

[25] The CCA, s 6(2).

[26] The CCA, s 91(1).

impact of climate change. This is in relation to the organisation's functions, their proposals and policies for adapting to climate change, and an assessment of progress towards implementing policies and proposals set out in previous reports.[27]

3 The Relevance of Climate Change to the Bank of England's Remit and the Objectives of Its Statutory Committees

The mission of the Bank is to promote the good of the people of the UK by maintaining monetary and financial stability. As set out in the Bank's climate-related financial disclosure in 2022, a "*key aspect of delivering this mission is to manage the financial risks and economic consequences arising from the physical effects of climate change and the transition to net-zero emissions on our policy functions and internal operations*".[28]

Climate-related financial risks have direct implications for the global and UK economy and financial system. The Bank's international and domestic approach is driven by its objectives which relate to monetary policy and macro- and micro-prudential financial stability. It adopts policies and undertakes operations to ensure that the UK financial system, macro-economy and the Bank itself are resilient to the risks arising from climate change and a transition to a net-zero economy.[29] Hence Andrew Bailey has referred to the Bank's work in this space as "*sitting firmly within the bounds of*"[30] its mission to maintain monetary and financial stability rather than constituting an entirely new objective. The Bank also designated climate change as one of its seven strategic priorities covering the four-year period to February 2024.

[27] The CCA, s 62.

[28] The Bank of England's climate-related financial disclosure (2022), https://www.bankofengland.co.uk/prudential-regulation/publication/2022/june/the-bank-of-englands-climate-related-financial-disclosure-2022.

[29] Ibid.

[30] See A. Bailey, Tackling climate for real: Progress and next steps, BIS-BDF-IMF-NGFS Green Swan 2021 Global Conference, https://www.bankofengland.co.uk/speech/2021/june/andrew-bailey-bis-bank-of-france-imf-ngfs-green-swan-conference (hereafter "**Bailey**").

The Monetary Policy Committee ("MPC")

Since the Bank of England Act 1998 (the "**1998 Act**"), the Bank has held operational responsibility for monetary policy in the UK, which it exercises independently of government via its MPC.[31] The Bank's statutory objectives in setting monetary policy are: (a) to maintain price stability; and (b) subject to that, to support the economic policy of the government, including its objectives for growth and employment.[32] The two principal tools open to the MPC are setting interest rates and operations in the markets to purchase or sell bonds thereby effecting changes in interest rates to influence the trajectory of inflation and promote price stability.[33]

The remit of the MPC is set by the objectives in the 1998 Act and supplemented by remit letters issued by the Chancellor of the Exchequer which provide details of the economic policy of the government.[34] In a letter to the Governor of the Bank of England dated March 2021, the Chancellor updated the MPC's remit to reflect the government's revised economic strategy for achieving strong, sustainable and balance growth that is also "*environmentally sustainable and consistent with the transition to a net zero economy*".[35] This marked the first time that the UK Government policy, as expressed in the MPC remit letter, explicitly referred to

[31] The 1998 Act, s 10 and 13.

[32] The 1998 Act, s 11.

[33] The government sets the Bank an inflation target of 2%. In the event inflation moves away from the target by more than 1% in either direction, the Governor is required to send an open letter to the Chancellor explaining why and what action the Bank is taking to bring inflation back to target. In May 2020, the Office for National Statistics published data showing the Consumer Prices Index was 0.8% in April. As required by the remit for the MPC, the Governor wrote to the Chancellor accordingly on 18 June 2020 to address the reasons why, the outlook for inflation and the policy action being taken by the MPC in response.

[34] Letter from Rishi Sunak to Andrew Bailey (3 March 2021), https://www.bankofengland.co.uk/-/media/boe/files/letter/2021/march/2021-mpc-remit-letter.pdf.

[35] The government's economic policy objective was expanded to include:

> *structural reform to level up opportunity in all parts of the UK and to transition to an environmentally sustainable and resilient net zero economy, including through regulation, and an ambitious programme of investment in skills, infrastructure and innovation, in order to sustain high employment, raise productivity and improve living standards; and maintaining a resilient, effectively regulated*

climate change. This was also included in the letter to the Governor to the Bank of England dated October 2021 which, at the time of writing, is the most recent remit letter issued by the Chancellor of the Exchequer to the MPC.[36]

The Financial Policy Committee ("FPC")

The FPC exercises its functions with a view to contribute to the achievement of the Bank's financial stability objective. The FPC's objectives and responsibilities relate primarily to the identification, monitoring and taking of action to remove or reduce systemic risks,[37] with a view to protect and enhance the resilience of the UK financial system.[38] Subject to achieving this primary financial stability objective, in exercising its functions the FPC also supports the economic policy of the government, including its objectives for growth and employment.[39]

The FPC has the power to direct the PRA and FCA to take action across a number of specific policy tools[40] and to make recommendations to the government, the regulators and even to entities in order to reduce risks to UK financial stability.[41] Where risks arising from climate change have the potential to create a macro-prudential systemic impact, the FPC monitors those risks and if necessary can take action to reduce or remove those risks.

The remit of the FPC is set by the objectives in the 1998 Act and supplemented by a remit and recommendation letter issued by the Chancellor. This provides details of the economic policy of the Government and contains recommendations to which the FPC must have regard.

and competitive financial system that supports the real economy through the provision of productive finance and critical financial services, while protecting consumers, safeguarding taxpayer interests and supporting the transition to a net zero economy.

[36] Letter from Rishi Sunak to Andrew Bailey (27 October 2021), https://www.bankofengland.co.uk/-/media/boe/files/letter/2021/october/mpc-remit-october-2021.pdf.

[37] See Stheeman (n 10).

[38] The 1998 Act, s 9C(2).

[39] The 1998 Act, s 9C(1).

[40] The 1998 Act, s 9H.

[41] The 1998 Act, s 9O to 9R.

These letters have recognised that climate-related financial risks are relevant to the work of the FPC. For instance, in the March 2021 remit letter, the Chancellor confirmed:

> *... the FPC has a critical role to play in maintaining the resilience and stability of the UK financial system and supporting the government's economic objective of achieving strong, sustainable and balanced growth.*[42]

This was preceded by the letter in March 2020 where the Chancellor first set out that the FPC should "*continue to regard the risks from climate change as relevant to its primary objective*", and that in the context of its secondary objective, the FPC "*has a role to play in seeking to support the Government's Green Finance Strategy...*".[43]

These were updated in the letter of March 2021 to include the Government's revised economic strategy. The Chancellor outlined that the FPC should:

> *...continue to act with a view to building the resilience of the UK financial system to the risks from climate change and support the government's ambition of a greener industry, using innovation and finance to protect our environment and tackle climate change.*[44]

It also recommended that the FPC "*consider the potential relevance of other environmental risks to its primary objective*".[45]

In April 2022, HMT wrote to the FPC to supplement the recommendations made in its 2021 letter. In this letter, HMT recommended that the FPC should have regard to the important role that the financial

[42] Letter from Rishi Sunak to Andrew Bailey (3 March 2021), https://assets.publishing.service.gov.uk/government/uploads/system/uploads/attachment_data/file/965778/FPC_Remit_and_Recommendations_Letter_2021.pdf (hereafter "**Sunak**"). For completeness, letter of response from Andrew Bailey to Rishi Sunak setting out the action taken and further action intended to be taken in response to the recommendations (13 July 2021), https://www.bankofengland.co.uk/-/media/boe/files/letter/2021/july/2021-remit-response.pdf.

[43] Letter from Rishi Sunak to former Governor of the Bank, Mark Carney (11 March 2020), https://assets.publishing.service.gov.uk/government/uploads/system/uploads/attachment_data/file/871960/FPC_REMIT_2020_.pdf.

[44] See Sunak (n 42).

[45] Ibid.

system will play in supporting the UK's energy security, including through investment in transitional hydrocarbons such as gas, as part of the UK's pathway to net zero.[46]

The Prudential Regulation Committee ("PRC")

The PRA was originally constituted as a newly formed subsidiary of the Bank, its micro-prudential functions being transferred to it from the former Financial Services Authority by the Financial Services Act 2012. Under The Bank of England and Financial Services Act 2016, the functions of the PRA were transferred to the Bank in a process known as "de-subsidiarisation". The Bank now formally exercises the functions of the PRA through the PRC, a statutory committee of the Bank.[47] This includes rulemaking[48] and supervision in relation to PRA-regulated firms. Therefore, whereas the FPC might be described as a macro-prudential regulator of the financial system as a whole, the PRA (along with the FCA) is a micro-prudential regulator of the individual firms within that system.

The Financial Services and Markets Act 2000 ("**FSMA**") contains the statutory framework by which the PRA makes rules and regulates PRA-authorised firms. The PRA's mandate is defined in terms of its statutory objectives. The first, "*general objective*" is to promote the safety and soundness of the firms it regulates. In advancing it, the PRA focuses primarily on addressing risks to UK financial stability.[49] The second, specifically for insurers, is to contribute to the securing of an appropriate degree of protection for policyholders.[50] When the PRA discharges its general functions in a way that advances its objectives, FSMA requires that it must "*so far as is reasonably possible*" act in a way that, as a secondary

[46] Letter from Rishi Sunak to Andrew Bailey (7 April 2022), https://assets.publishing.service.gov.uk/government/uploads/system/uploads/attachment_data/file/1067016/Recommendations_for_the_Financial_Policy_Committee_April_2022_final.pdf.

[47] The 1998 Act, s 30A(1).

[48] The 1998 Act, schedule 6A, paragraph 19(9)(b).

[49] FSMA, s 2B(3).

[50] FSMA, s 2C(2).

objective, facilitates effective competition in the markets for services provided by banks and insurers in carrying on regulated activities.[51]

Any measures taken by the PRA in the course of its rule and policy-making will always be primarily informed by its statutory objectives.[52] In addition to observing public law principles[53] and practising good administration,[54] the PRA is under a duty to "have regard" to certain matters. These include "regulatory principles" set out in FSMA[55] and any matters covered in HMT's recommendations letter to the PRC.[56] The recommendations letter sets out the aspects of the economic policy of the government to which the PRC should have regard when considering how to advance the PRA's objectives[57] and it must be issued at least once in each Parliament.

In his 2021 recommendations letter, the Chancellor noted:

> *"The PRC's main contribution to this economic policy is by promoting the safety and soundness of firms, thereby maintaining and enhancing financial stability in the UK."*

The Chancellor's recommendations letter of March 2021 included a revision to the Government's economic strategy and noted that the PRC should "*have regard to the Government's commitment to achieve a net-zero*

[51] FSMA, s 2H(1).

[52] 'The PRA's Approach to banking supervision' (October 2018).
'The PRA's Approach to insurance supervision' (October 2018).

[53] Public law governs the use of power by public authorities in the exercise of their public functions. It comprises both constitutional law, which sets out what power exists and to whom it belongs, and administrative law, which governs how decisions should be made. Whilst these principles are mainly derived from common law, in the context of the PRA's functions, several are codified in FSMA.

[54] Broadly speaking, performing public duties, including decision-making, speedily, efficiently and fairly.

[55] FSMA, s 3B.

[56] Letter from Sajid Javid to Mark Carney (4 November 2019), https://assets.publishing.service.gov.uk/government/uploads/system/uploads/attachment_data/file/844467/PRC_Remit_2019.pdf.

[57] S 30B of 1998 Act permits HMT to make recommendations to the PRC about aspects of the economic policy of Her Majesty's government to which the Committee should have regard when considering how to advance the objectives of the PRA and the application of the regulatory principles in s 3B of FSMA.

economy by 2050 under the Climate Change Act 2008 (Order 2019) when considering how to advance its objectives and discharge its functions".

In April 2022, HMT wrote again to the PRC to supplement the recommendations made in its 2021 letter. In this letter, HMT recommended that the PRC should have regard to the important role that the financial system will play in supporting the UK's energy security, including through investment in transitional hydrocarbons such as gas, as part of the UK's pathway to net zero.[58]

The Financial Services Act 2021 made certain amendments to FSMA. Of particular relevance, the PRC, when exercising rulemaking powers to make "CRR rules",[59] must, among other things, have regard to the target for net-zero emissions in section 1 of the CCA.[60] In addition, this also applies when the PRC is making "CRR rules" applying to financial holding companies and mixed financial holding companies.[61]

On 20 July 2022, the Financial Services and Markets Bill was laid before Parliament. It proposes the deletion of the target for net-zero emissions as a matter to which the PRC must have regard when making "CRR rules" and, instead, proposes the inclusion of the following "regulatory principle" to which the PRA and the FCA would need to have regard when exercising all general functions, not just rulemaking powers: "*the need to contribute toward achieving compliance with section 1 of the CCA (UK net zero emissions target)*".[62]

4 Actions Taken by the Bank in Response to Climate Change

The Bank has deployed various tools from its toolkit in response to the risks posed by climate change and in pursuance of its objectives. Its actions to this end can be considered in terms of its strategic goals.

[58] Letter from Rishi Sunak to Andrew Bailey, 'Recommendations for the PRC' (23 March 2021), https://assets.publishing.service.gov.uk/government/uploads/system/uploads/attachment_data/file/972443/CX_Letter_-_PRC_Remit_230321.pdf.

[59] FSMA, s 144A.

[60] FSMA, s 144C(1)(d).

[61] FSMA, s 192XA and s 192XB.

[62] The Financial Services and Markets Bill, paragraph 25.

Ensuring the Financial System Is Resilient to Climate-Related Financial Risks

Climate-related financial risks can affect the safety and soundness of the firms regulated by the PRA as well as the stability of the wider financial system and economic outlook. An orderly transition to a net-zero economy will minimise not only the risks to climate but also the future financial risks faced by firms and the financial system.[63]

The PRA's role in supporting the transition is to ensure that firms are effectively managing the climate-related financial risks they face. The PRA explored the potential impact of climate change on the UK banking sector through two key reports in 2015 and 2018 respectively.

The 2018 report[64] found a range of responses concerning the treatment of climate-related financial risks. These ranged from inclusion as "corporate social responsibility" to their integration alongside any other financial risk, but even the best in class were found to have a long way to go to identify and measure these risks comprehensively: firms had insufficient capabilities to effectively identify, measure and manage climate-related financial risks and the approach to risk management varied widely between firms.

The report also found that although oversight of climate-related financial risks and responsibility for setting the strategy, targets and risk appetite relating to these risks were beginning to be considered at the board level, more strategic oversight and dynamic scenario analysis were required.

In response, in April 2019 the PRA became the first prudential regulator to publish a comprehensive set of climate-related supervisory

63 "*Transitioning to net zero will be a major challenge for our institutions and societies even in a benign economic environment – doing so without confidence in the basic functioning of the financial system would be near impossible. It is therefore vital that firms can withstand risks to their safety and soundness, including those that arise as a consequence of climate change...Firms therefore need to understand, at a granular level, how their balance sheets and business models are exposed to both present and future climate risks, so that they can take the right risk management actions today. This includes investing in their data and modelling capabilities, and carefully scrutinising the data they get from third parties. It means ensuring Boards and senior executives see climate risk as a strategic priority*". Woods (n 11).

64 'Transition in thinking: The impact of climate change on the UK banking sector' (September 2018), https://www.bankofengland.co.uk/-/media/boe/files/prudential-regulation/report/transition-in-thinking-the-impact-of-climate-change-on-the-uk-banking-sector.pdf.

expectations ("**Supervisory Statement 3/19**") for regulated firms to enhance their approaches to identifying and managing climate-related financial risks.[65] These expectations were designed to ensure firms adopt a strategic, holistic and ambitious approach to managing climate-related financial risks. In short, Supervisory Statement 3/19 sets out expectations for firms to embed climate risk into their governance framework, incorporate climate risk into existing risk management frameworks, undertake longer-term scenario analysis to inform strategy and risk assessment and develop an appropriate approach to climate disclosure in line with the Financial Stability Board's ("**FSB**") Taskforce of Climate-Related Financial Disclosure ("**TCFD**") framework.[66]

In July 2020, the PRA published a "Dear CEO letter" to provide additional guidance for firms in meeting the expectations in Supervisory Statement 3/19, giving industry feedback on progress to date and setting a deadline for firms to fully embed the PRA's expectations so far as possible by the end of 2021.[67] It also included an expectation that firms explain how they attained comfort that they were holding adequate regulatory capital for climate-related financial risks.

In its 2021 Climate Change Adaptation Report ("the **CCAR**"), the PRA assessed progress made by firms against the expectations in Supervisory Statement 3/19 and made preliminary comments about the role of capital in the context of climate-related financial risks.

First, the PRA noted that the expectations had helped catalyse a change in how climate-related financial risks are considered by firms. However, whilst the PRA observed a step change among senior executives and boards since the publication of Supervisory Statement 3/19, it found that further progress was needed, particularly with regard to firms' risk

[65] 'Supervisory Statement 3/19: Enhancing banks' and insurers' approaches to managing the financial risks from climate change' (April 2019), https://www.bankofengland.co.uk/-/media/boe/files/prudential-regulation/supervisory-statement/2019/ss319.

[66] The TCFD framework refers to a set of principles and adoptable recommendations, the purpose being to assist public companies and other organisations more effectively disclose climate-related risks and opportunities via their existing reporting processes.

[67] Letter from Sam Woods 'Managing climate-related financial risk—Thematic feedback from the PRA's review of firm's SS3/19 plans and clarifications of expectations' (1 July 2020), https://www.bankofengland.co.uk/-/media/boe/files/prudential-regulation/letter/2020/managing-the-financial-risks-from-climate-change.pdf.

management and scenario analysis capabilities.[68] Second, the PRA found that since 2015 firms had improved their understanding of climate-related financial risks to their business. This resulted in more investment in developing climate-related financial risk management capabilities, such as more sophisticated climate data analytics, and more resources being deployed to support the transition. Accordingly, the CCAR signposted that the PRA would be "shifting gears" from assessing implementation of its supervisory expectations to actively supervising against them.[69] In the CCAR, the PRA confirmed that firms were already required to ensure they have sufficient capital to be resilient against all material risks, including those stemming from climate change. The PRA re-iterated its expectations in Supervisory Statement 3/19 by stating that firms should incorporate judgements of their exposure to climate-related financial risks in the way they assess their own capital requirements, as they do for other drivers of financial risks. Where they fail to demonstrate this, the PRA noted that where appropriate it could use capital scalars against significant weaknesses in climate-related financial risk management and governance.

Finally, the CCAR made preliminary comments about the role of regulatory capital in the context of climate change. The PRA recognised that some aspects of the existing capital regime are not ideally positioned to capture climate-related financial risks. In consequence, the Bank has established a work programme to examine the relationship between climate-related financial risks and the capital framework, including a Climate and Capital Conference to bring together expert thinking, held at the Bank in October 2022.[70]

The FPC was also active in considering the macro-prudential effects of climate-related risks during 2021–2022. Jointly with the PRA it also launched the Climate Biennial Exploratory Scenario (**"CBES"**) exercise. The CBES was conducted in two rounds and assessed the resilience of

[68] CCAR (n 10). The PRA produced the report in response to an invitation by DEFRA to participate under the third round of the climate change adaptation reporting power. In inviting the PRA to produce this report, DEFRA did not exercise its powers under Section 62 of the CCA.

[69] This could include the appointment of a "skilled persons review" under Section 166 of FSMA.

[70] Note to support the Bank of England's Climate and Capital conference, https://www.bankofengland.co.uk/events/2022/october/climate-and-capital-conference/note-to-support-the-boes-climate-and-capital-conference.

major UK banks, insurers, and the wider financial system to three different climate scenarios by sizing financial exposures, identifying challenges to firms' business models and assessing firms' risk management. The scenarios were based on those published by the Network for Greening the Financial System (**"NGFS"**). The Bank published the results of its CBES in May 2022. The results made clear that climate risk is a "*first-order strategic issue*"[71] for PRA-regulated firms and found that an "early action" scenario, where policies are introduced in a timely manner to deliver an orderly transition to net zero by 2050 resulted in the lowest costs and greatest opportunities for the financial sector.[72]

The CBES, along with findings from PRA thematic reviews and firm supervision, have enabled the Bank to build up a body of experience and learning on firms' progress against the expectations in Supervisory Statement 3/19. In October 2022 the PRA published a second Dear CEO letter.[73] It summarised the capabilities that the PRA expected firms to be able to demonstrate by that point, provided thematic observations of firms' levels of embeddedness and set out examples of effective practices it had identified. In general, the PRA found that banks across the sector had taken concrete and positive steps to implement the expectations. These steps assisted to advance firms' capabilities and progress their ability to address the opportunities as well as the risks from climate change. Notwithstanding, the PRA also found that whilst some firms have made considerable progress, the levels of embedding varied and the assessment of supervisors was that further progress was needed by all firms.

[71] Woods (n 11).

[72] 'Results of the 2021 CBES' (24 May 2022), https://www.bankofengland.co.uk/stress-testing/2022/results-of-the-2021-climate-biennial-exploratory-scenario. The projections by UK banks also suggested the costs of transition which fall on them would be absorbable without a worrying direct impact on their solvency, in part because a significant portion of those costs may ultimately be passed on to their customers.

[73] Letter from Sam Woods, 'Thematic feedback on the PRA's supervision of climate-related financial risk and the Bank of England's Climate Biennial Exploratory Scenario exercise' (21 October 2022), https://www.bankofengland.co.uk/-/media/boe/files/prudential-regulation/letter/2022/october/managing-climate-related-financial-risks.pdf.

Supporting Firm-Led Collaboration to Enable an Orderly Transition to Net Zero

Recognising the shared challenges which building capacity to consider climate-related financial risks entails, the PRA and the FCA set up the Climate Financial Risk Forum (“**CFRF**”): a collaborative group of industry representatives that gives guidance to and shares best practice with the industry on climate risks. In June 2020, the CFRF published a guide for the financial sector containing practical tools, information and case studies on climate risk management, scenario analysis, disclosure and innovation, all with the purpose of supporting efforts by firms to develop their capabilities in this area.

The Bank has also taken steps to create conditions that facilitate investment in assets that support the transition. To illustrate, the Bank, together with HMT and the FCA, convened an industry working group to facilitate investment in productive finance.[74] This was with the aim of developing practical solutions to the barriers to investing in long-term, less liquid assets, recognising the importance of long-term growth and productivity. Within this initiative, the Bank recognised: “*investment in less liquid assets can … have broader benefits, including facilitating the financing of long-term projects, such as the transition to a net zero carbon economy*”.[75]

Supporting an Orderly Transition to Net-Zero Emissions: Contributing to a Coordinated International Approach to Climate Change

Climate-related financial risks have direct implications for the global, as well as the UK, economy and financial system. As such, the Bank works with other central banks in international fora to deliver progress towards a timely and coordinated international approach to climate change.

[74] ‘HMT, Bank of England and FCA convene working group to facilitate investment in productive finance’ (News release, 20 November 2020), https://www.bankofengland.co.uk/news/2020/november/hmt-boe-and-fca-convene-working-group-to-facilitate-investment-in-productive-finance.

[75] See A. Bailey, The Productive Finance Working Group, foreword to ‘A Roadmap for Increasing Productive Finance Investment’, September 2021, https://www.bankofengland.co.uk/-/media/boe/files/report/2021/roadmap-for-increasing-productive-finance-investment.pdf.

Internationally, central banks are working collaboratively via the international central banks and supervisors' NGFS to develop their responses. In addition, standard setters with membership drawn from central banks including the Bank, such as the Basel Committee on Banking Supervision (**"BCBS"**), are developing the internationally applicable principles and standards.

The Bank has worked internationally to help develop climate scenarios that shine a light on different transition paths, notably through acting as chair of the NGFS's macro-financial work stream which works with a consortium of climate scientists and modellers. These scenarios, actively used by over 22 global central banks, assess the financial and economic impacts of different possible temperature pathways and client policy actions consistent with those outcomes. They aim to set out what transition means in practice, providing a key tool to enable firms and policymakers to take practical steps today based on the risks they face from climate change under different climate scenarios. As such, the development of frameworks to undertake scenario analysis, and the development of the climate scenarios themselves, are central to the Bank's strategy to support the transition. The Bank has also used these scenarios in its CBES exercise.

The Bank has participated in the BCBS Task Force on Climate-related Financial Risks (**"TCFR"**). The TCFR has undertaken work on identifying gaps within the Basel framework and potential measures to better capture climate-related financial risks, including regulatory, supervisory and disclosure elements culminating in the publication by the BCBS of "*Principles for the effective management and supervision of climate-related financial risks*" in June 2022.[76] As the work of the BCBS continues, the Bank's domestic work on climate and capital will enhance and enrich the international debate.

Bridging climate data gaps, improving access to climate data sets and establishing common climate data standards are crucial to enabling effective reporting and disclosure and supporting the development of more advanced and useful climate metrics. The Bank is engaged in the NGFS and FSB work streams on climate data gaps.

[76] Progress in implementing and embedding the principles will be monitored by the BCBS. https://www.bis.org/bcbs/publ/d532.pdf.

The global nature of climate risks necessitates coherence and consistency of disclosure requirements and sustainability standards across jurisdictions in order to promote effective risk management and support climate action. The Bank has been supportive of the multilateral work, including the G20 and FSB exploring ways to promote globally comparable, high-quality and auditable standards of disclosure based on the TCFD recommendations.

The Bank supported the IFRS Foundation Trustees' proposal to establish the International Sustainability Standards Board (**"ISSB"**) for the development of global sustainability reporting standards.[77] The ISSB published its initial exposure draft of a comprehensive global baseline of sustainability-related disclosure standards in March 2022.[78]

The Bank has undertaken key chair roles and invested in furthering shared work and learnings as a thought leader. In 2021, the Bank supported the UK Government in delivering its G7 and COP26 agendas with the greatest focus on climate change to date. Under the UK presidency, the G7 has started meaningful discussions on the role of finance ministries and central banks in the transition to net zero, including how climate policies can help mobilise private finance to support the transition.

The Bank has increased the climate training it undertakes for central banks and regulators through its Centre for Central Banking Studies. In partnership with the UK's Foreign, Commonwealth and Development Office, the Bank hosted a series of workshops on climate change in 2021 and 2022. These were aimed at central bankers and financial regulators who handle climate-related issues in their institutions. In September 2021, the Bank held a global workshop on climate-scenario analysis and stress testing, with over 330 central bankers and supervisors spanning 65 countries in attendance.

The FSB's Standing Committee on Supervisory and Regulatory Cooperation, chaired by the Governor of the Bank, published a report

[77] 'The Bank's joint statement in support of the IFRS Foundation's consultation on sustainability reporting' (25 January 2021), https://www.bankofengland.co.uk/news/2020/november/boes-joint-statement-in-support-of-ifrs-consultation?

[78] 'Exposure Draft: General Requirements for Disclosure of Sustainability-related Financial Information' (IFRS Sustainability, March 2020), https://www.ifrs.org/content/dam/ifrs/project/general-sustainability-related-disclosures/exposure-draft-ifrs-s1-general-requirements-for-disclosure-of-sustainability-related-financial-information.pdf.

providing recommendations to help regulatory authorities identify relevant and useful climate-related data through supervisory and regulatory data collection.[79] Through the G20 Sustainable Finance Working Group, the Bank has helped to develop a transition finance framework that will set out high-level principles for authorities to enable financial flows to support the transition and help firms formulate consistent and credible transition plans. Moreover, through the Organisation for Economic Cooperation and Development the Bank has contributed to high-level principles for climate transition-relevant finance.

Demonstrating Best Practice Through Its Own Operations

The Bank holds itself to the same high standards that it holds the firms it regulates and the financial system it oversees and recognises that as a central bank, it must manage and mitigate the risks from climate change. As such, the Bank endeavours to ensure its own operations conform to best practices in the measurement, management and mitigation of climate risks. This includes emissions from both its physical activities (such as its buildings, production of banknotes and travel) and financial market operations. To that end, in 2021 the Bank committed to reducing emissions from its own operations to net zero by 2050 at the latest.

As a public institution, the Bank also considers it important that it provides transparency across its own policy functions, financial operations and physical operations, which it has done in its own annually published climate-related financial disclosures. Bank seniors have also delivered a number of speeches setting out the work the Bank is doing on climate change.[80]

In addition, the Bank's pension trustees have committed to have regard to climate risks when making future investments and the fund published its own TCFD-aligned disclosure in 2022.

Regarding its approach to greening the Corporate Bond Purchase Scheme ("**CBPS**"), the Bank published a detailed description of its

[79] 'Supervisory and Regulatory Approaches to Climate-related Risks' (Interim Report, 29 April 2022), https://www.fsb.org/wp-content/uploads/P290422.pdf.

[80] For example, Andrew Bailey's remarks at COP26: 'Laying the Foundations for a Net Zero Financial System' (3 November 2021), https://www.bankofengland.co.uk/speech/2021/november/andrew-bailey-speech-at-cop26-laying-the-foundations-for-a-net-zero-financial-system.

greening tools[81] and a list of issuers held in the portfolio to allow any future loss of eligibility and divestment to be publicly observable.

The inclusion of climate change within the economic policy of the government as expressed within the MPC's remit in March 2021 enabled the MPC to undertake operations that could catalyse the actions of private sector firms. Drawing on feedback following a discussion paper,[82] in November 2021 the Bank published a comprehensive and innovative framework to green the CBPS portfolio, a financial asset portfolio held for monetary policy purposes.[83] In addition to monetary policy, the objective was to incentivise economy-wide transition and take into account the climate impact of issuers in adjusting the composition of its CBPS portfolio. Under the framework, the Bank introduced new climate-related eligibility criteria that issuers had to satisfy to be included in the CBPS, with purchases then being "tilted" towards those firms that were performing relatively strongly in support of net zero and away from those that are not. A programme of reinvestment operations based on this new framework was executed between November 2021 and January 2022.[84]

The MPC announced in February 2022 that the Bank would be reducing the stock of sterling corporate bonds through a programme of bond sales to be completed no earlier than towards the end of 2023

[81] 'Greening our CBPS', https://www.bankofengland.co.uk/markets/greening-the-corporate-bond-purchase-scheme?.

[82] 'Options for greening the Bank of England's CBPS' (Discussion Paper, May 2021), https://www.bankofengland.co.uk/-/media/boe/files/paper/2021/options-for-greening-the-bank-of-englands-corporate-bond-purchase-scheme-discussion-paper.pdf.

[83] 'The Bank of England publishes its approach to greening our CBPS' (5 November 2021), https://www.bankofengland.co.uk/news/2021/november/boe-publishes-its-approach-to-greening-the-corporate-bond-purchase-scheme. Andrew Hauser, 'It's not easy being green—But that shouldn't stop us: How central banks can use their monetary policy portfolio to support orderly transition to net zero' (Bloomberg, 21 May 2021), https://www.bankofengland.co.uk/-/media/boe/files/speech/2021/may/its-not-easy-being-green-but-that-shouldnt-stop-us-speech-by-andrew-hauser.pdf.

[84] At the time of unveiling the new greening eligibility criteria, the target stock for the CBPS was already reached. While the corporate holdings are to be unwound, the Bank of England's framework, on which the subsequent reinvestments were based, supports climate transition by providing an example for other investors in the public and private sectors of how to green a corporate bond portfolio.

or in early 2024, subject to market conditions. In the market notice[85] which followed in May 2022, it was highlighted that, in designing a sales programme consistent with the MPC's instructions, the Bank took certain considerations into account, including: "*managing risks to public money by continuing to monitor the credit quality of the portfolio, and by designing sales with regard to portfolio characteristics including concentration, liquidity and – to the extent consistent with wider aims – climate considerations (or 'greening')*".[86]

In October 2022, applications opened for the joint Bank and HMT "Energy Markets Financing Scheme" ("**EMFS**").[87] This backstop scheme was designed to address the extraordinary liquidity requirements faced by viable energy firms with major operations in the UK given the unprecedented volatility triggered by Russia's invasion of Ukraine. The EMFS operates to allow commercial banks to provide larger credit lines to approved energy firms that are unable to meet extraordinary margin calls due to large moves in energy prices. These commercial lenders receive a full coverage guarantee from the Bank to ensure they have the capacity to support the UK energy sector.

In order to be eligible to access the EMFS and benefit from the guarantee, HMT requires the energy firms to agree to certain conditions. One of the conditions that applies is that the energy firms listed in the UK must disclose whether they have a net-zero transition plan and, if so, deliver it to HMT within 6 months of drawdown on the facility or before termination of the guarantee, whichever is sooner. All energy firms are required to deliver proportionate, climate-related financial information in line with the TCFD guidance to HMT, within 6 months of drawdown of the guaranteed tranche of the credit facility or before termination of the guarantee, whichever is sooner.[88]

[85] 'Asset Purchase Facility (APF): CBPS Reinvestment programme—Market Notice 5 November 2021', https://www.bankofengland.co.uk/markets/market-notices/2021/november/asset-purchase-facility-market-notice-5-november-2021.

[86] Ibid.

[87] Energy Markets Financing Scheme news release (17 October 2022), https://www.bankofengland.co.uk/news/2022/october/energy-markets-financing-scheme-opens-today.

[88] Joint HM Treasury and Bank of England Energy Markets Financing Scheme (EMFS)—Market Notice 17 October 2022, https://www.bankofengland.co.uk/markets/market-notices/2022/october/joint-hmt-boe-emfs-market-notice-17-october-2022.

5 Concluding Remarks

Climate-related financial risks constitute a significant and distinct challenge for the financial services sector and the macro-economy. Whilst it is inevitable that the legal and policy framework will continue to develop given that many of the effects of climate change remain to be seen and felt, progress to mitigate those risks, render the financial system resilient to the challenges presented and ensure an orderly transition to net-zero emissions has been marked and tangible.

As acknowledged in the preamble to the Paris Agreement, climate change is a "*common concern of human kind*"[89] and as such the road ahead will require the engagement of a number of stakeholders, each with a part to play. These include governments, inter-governmental organisations, central banks, regulators, industries, investors and consumers.

As also acknowledged in the preamble to the Paris Agreement, stakeholders will be affected not only by climate change but also by the effects of the measures taken in response to it.[90] Central to this endeavour is a stable financial system that can support households and businesses to navigate through this transition with confidence. To close with the words of Andrew Bailey, Governor of the Bank of England: "*... we have come far, but have further to go. When it comes to climate change, we cannot stand still. We need to continue to be bold and learn from our work so far to deepen our understanding and inform future actions. Greater ambition and cooperation is still needed, including wider adoption of best practices. For this reason, as well as evolving our domestic work, we also need to evolve our collective approaches*".[91]

[89] Paris Agreement (n 13).

[90] Ibid.

[91] Bailey (n 30).

PART III

China and South Korea

CHAPTER 16

Chinese Commercial Banks and Fintech-Competition and Collaboration

Ding Chen

1 Introduction

'Fintech' or 'financial technology' is used to describe technologies and innovations that transform the provision of financial services and compete with the traditional financial establishment.[1] Fintech is an umbrella term that encompasses a set of innovative technology-empowered financial services, such as mobile payment, cryptocurrency, cross-border payment,

[1] See World Bank and CCAF, The Global Covid-19 Fintech Regulatory Rapid Assessment Report, World Bank Group and the University of Cambridge, October 2020, https://www.jbs.cam.ac.uk/wp-content/uploads/2020/10/2020-ccaf-report-fintech-regulatory-rapid-assessment.pdf; The Financial Stability Board defines Fintech as 'technologically enabled financial innovation that could result in new business models, applications, processes or products with an associated material effect on financial markets and institutions

D. Chen (✉)
School of Law, University of Sheffield, Sheffield, UK
e-mail: Ding.Chen@sheffield.ac.uk

M. Bodellini et al. (eds.), *Commercial Banking in Transition*, Palgrave Macmillan Studies in Banking and Financial Institutions,
https://doi.org/10.1007/978-3-031-45289-5_16

digital banking, insurance, and wealth management. The Fintech industry is dynamic and fast-growing. In 2019, the global Fintech market was valued at about US$111 billion and it is expected to grow to US$191 billion by 2025, $325 billion in 2030.[2]

Relying on the development and use of large datasets, artificial intelligence (AI), cloud computing, and blockchain, the global boom of Fintech has fundamentally changed banking sector competition while significantly improving the services and operational efficiency. For instance, due to a boom in digital payment, conventional banks now account for only 72% of the market value of the global banking and payment industry, down from 96% in 2010[3]; online peer-to-peer lending (P2P lending) platforms enable lenders and borrowers to conduct lending activities directly without the involvement of banks; statistical models based on big-data enable Fintech companies to provide loans to firms and households without posting collateral[4] and approve loans immediately.

The rise of Fintech in China has been unmatched elsewhere. Fintech has become an integral part of public life in China. According to the 'Ernst & Young Fintech Adoption Index' published in 2019,[5] the adoption rate of consumer Fintech in China reached 87%, meaning that 87% of China's digitally active population uses at least one Fintech service in their daily life. And China has become a magnet for Fintech investments, with the total growing from US$900 million in the second half of 2020 to more than US$1.3 billion in the first half of 2021, according to an

and the provision of financial services', http://www.fsb.org/what-we-do/policy-development/additional-policy-areas/monitoring-of-fintech/; The People's Bank of China (PBOC) in its 'Fintech Development Plan (2019–2021)' describes Fintech as 'technologically enabled innovation in financial services, intended to use modern scientific and technological achievements to transform or innovate financial products, operating models, and business processes, among others, and promote the improvement of the quality and efficiency of financial development,' See http://lawinfochina.com/display.aspx?id=31101&lib=law.

[2] See The Business Research Company, Fintech Global Market Opportunities and Strategies, July 2020, https://www.thebusinessresearchcompany.com/report/fintech-market.

[3] See The Economist, Ant Group and Fintech Come of Age, 8 October 2020.

[4] See OECD, Digital Disruption in Banking and Its Impact on Competition, 2020, https://www.oecd.org/competition/digital-disruption-in-banking-and-its-impact-on-competition-2020.pdf.

[5] See https://www.ey.com/en_uk/ey-global-fintech-adoption-index.

analysis by KPMG.[6] China's Fintech sector had a market value of RMB 375.3 billion ($59.2 billion) in 2019; its Fintech market size is projected to reach RMB 543.4 billion ($85.7 billion) by 2022.[7]

China is home to the world's biggest banks. Its financial sector is heavily regulated, making life difficult for disruptive innovators. In 2008, the founder of Alibaba, Jack Ma criticized China's banking system for failing to serve small-medium-sized enterprises (SMEs) and made a famous claim that 'if the banks don't change, we will change the banks.'[8] He certainly did. Since then, China's Fintech industry, led by Jack Ma's Ant Financial (Alibaba's Fintech arm), has driven disruption into retail banking in payment, online investment, and online lending, posed a threat to the Chinese banking system. In this chapter, we will consider how the Chinese commercial banks respond to this challenge. It is structured as follows: Sect. 1 briefly outlines the structure of China's banking system; Sect. 2 reviews the development of China's Fintech sector; Sect. 3 discusses the coping strategy of big banks; Sect. 4 considers the position of small-medium-sized banks (SMBs) and then concludes the chapter.

2 Structural Overview of China's Banking Sector

The modern Chinese banking system started its evolution in 1979 with the spin-off of three banks from the People's Bank of China (PBOC).[9] It has been growing rapidly since then. Measured in total assets, its size surpassed that of the US banking system in 2010, and even all euro area

[6] See KPMG, China Attracts $1.3 billion in Fintech Investment in Best Result Since H2′19, Finds KPMG Analysis, August 2021, https://home.kpmg/cn/en/home/media/press-releases/2021/08/china-attracts-1-3-billion-in-fintech-investment-in-best-result-since-h2-19.html.

[7] See The PBOC, Fintech Development Plan for 2022–2025, http://www.gov.cn/xinwen/2022-01/05/content_5666525.htm.

[8] See J. Ma, If the Bank Does Not Change, We Will Change the Bank, Sina Finance, 7 December 2008, https://finance.sina.com.cn/hy/20081207/18215601585.shtml.

[9] Before 1979, The PBOC had sole responsibility for issuing currency and controlling the money supply. It also served as the government treasury, the main source of credit for economic units, the clearing center for financial transactions, the holder of enterprise deposits, the national savings bank, and a ubiquitous monitor of economic activities.

banking systems put together in the last quarter of 2016.[10] It is now the largest banking system in the world, with $42.7 trillion in total assets by the end of 2021.[11]

The Chinese banking system consists of various types of banks and non-bank financial institutions. Among these, the most important players are the six large state-owned banks (SOBs)[12]—Industrial and Commercial Bank of China (ICBC), China Construction Bank (CCB), Bank of China (BOC), Agricultural Bank of China (ABC),[13] Postal Savings Bank of China (PSBOC), and the Bank of Communications (BOCOM)—together, they accounted for 47% or $15.9 trillion of all commercial bank assets by the end of 2019.[14] The six large SOBs provide nationwide wholesale and retail banking services and they are all listed on both the Shanghai and Hong Kong exchanges.

Joint-stock banks (JSBs) constitute the second-largest subgroup of banks in China. Unlike SOBs, they are not majority owned by the central government, their owners include private and foreign entities, state-owned enterprises (SOEs), and various government agencies. Unlike small banks that usually serve a certain region, JSBs operate nationwide. There are currently twelve JSBs, which hold an additional 21% of total commercial bank assets.[15]

[10] See IMF, People's Republic of China: Financial System Stability Assessment, 2017, Country Report No. 17/358.

[11] See Deloitte, Forging Ahead Together for a Better Future, Chinese Banking Sector 2021 Review and 2022 Outlook, 2022, https://www2.deloitte.com/cn/en/pages/financial-services/articles/chinese-banking-sector-2021-review-and-2022-outlook.html.

[12] By April 2020, ICBC, CCB, ABC and BOC ranked from 1 to 4th place in global banks by asset value. See S&P Global Market Intelligence, 2020, https://www.spglobal.com/marketintelligence/en/news-insights/research/the-worlds-100-largest-banks-2020.

[13] They used to be referred to as 'Big Four.'

[14] See Chinese Banking and Insurance Regulatory Commission (CBIRC), List of Banking Financial Institutions (银行业金融机构法人名单), December 2018, http://www.cbrc.gov.cn/chinese/files/2019/88C2C82DFD34470D9B2D441D553B80C4.pdf; China Banking and Insurance Regulatory Commission via CEIC database.

[15] See CBIRC via CEIC database. The twelve national joint-stock banks are China Merchants Bank, Shanghai Pu Dong Development Bank, China Citic Bank, Hua Xia Bank, China Everbright Bank, China Min Sheng Bank, Industrial Bank, China Guangdong Development Bank, Ping An Bank, China Zheshang Bank, China Bo Hai Bank, and Heng Feng Bank.

There are also a multitude of regional banking institutions with various ownership structures, including 134 city commercial banks (CCBs), 3915 rural financial institutions, and other banking financial institutions by the end of 2019.[16] Regional banks are generally smaller than JSBs. Before 2006, they were only allowed to operate in their headquarter cities. The geographical restrictions were once relaxed by the China Banking Regulatory Commission (CBRC)[17] between 2006 and 2010,[18] but have been tightened up again from 2011 onwards. As a result, except for a limited number of eligible banks,[19] majority of regional banks are continuously confined to their local markets. The geographical segmentation of the banking market imposed a severe funding constraint on regional banks and effectively restricted them from competing with the larger public commercial banks. SMBs in this chapter mainly refer to regional banks.

CCBs were formerly known as the city credit cooperative, born to solve the local debt in the 1990s. They were created following the rule of one-city–one bank. Before 2006, they were located in the central cities of every province (province-level or prefecture-level cities) and operated

[16] See CBIRC via CEIC database.

[17] The regulator of China's banking sector between 2003 and 2018, it was replaced by the CBIRC from April 2018.

[18] The CBRC partially removed the market entry barrier first in February 2006 by 'Regulation of City Commercial Banks' Supra-Regional Branches' (城市商业银行异地分支机构管理办法) https://wenku.baidu.com/view/c144c63283c4bb4cf7ecd1ee.html; then further in April 2009 by 'Interim Measures in Relation to Market Entry of Small and Medium-sized Commercial Banks' Branches' (关于中小商业银行分支机构市场准入政策的调整意见 (试行)) http://www.gov.cn/gzdt/2009-04/30/content_1301338.htm. In light of these two regulations, subject to approval by the CBRC, eligible city commercial banks were allowed to establish branches in other cities in their home province, and even in other places in other provinces.

[19] The requirements included the bank's age, total capital, registered capital, capital adequacy, non-performing loans, return on assets and return on equity. Furthermore, the bank's regulatory rating had to be above Grade 2 (including Grade 2). So far, only five regional banks have established more than five trans-provincial branches (i.e. Beijing Bank, Shanghai Bank, Ningbo Bank, Hangzhou Bank and Tianjin Bank). Regional banks' supra-regional expansion was not completely banned after 2011, but it is subject to more strict approval procedures and higher standards.

within each province. For instance, the Bank of Beijing is a CCB established in Beijing, and the Bank of Nanjing is established in Nanjing (the Capital city of Jiangsu Province). After years of development, the share of CCBs in the total banking sector assets rose to 16% by 2019.[20]

Rural financial institutions (RFIs) have traditionally included rural commercial banks (1478), rural cooperative banks (28), and rural credit cooperatives (722). New types of RFIs have also emerged recently. These include village or township banks (VTBs), lending companies (13), and rural mutual cooperatives (44). With the largest number of institutions and the smallest average customer size, VTBs was designed to support SMEs and farmers. Since the pilot program of VTBs was initiated in 2006, the number of VTBs has increased rapidly and reached 1633 as of 2019, with 65.7% located in the central and western regions, covering appropriately 1300 counties of 31 provinces. RFIs account for nearly 16% of banking sector assets.[21]

In addition to commercial banks, China also has three national state-owned policy banks: China Development Bank, Export–Import Bank of China, and Agricultural Development Bank of China. The Chinese government does not publish disaggregated figures for the policy banks' assets, but the three banks' most recent annual reports reveal that their combined assets equaled about $4 trillion at the end of 2018.

3 Fintech Industry in China

China's Fintech sector started in 2004 when Alipay first came online, but the real boom did not begin until June 2013, when Ant Financial successfully launched its online money-market fund Yu'E bao. Unlike in the West, Fintech sector is overwhelmed by a large number of small companies, China's Fintech landscape is dominated by a small number of unicorn players such as Ant Financial, Tencent, Baidu, and Jingdong. In addition, in the West, much attention in the Fintech space is placed on

[20] See CBIRC via CEIC database.

[21] See CBIRC via CEIC database.

cryptocurrencies[22] and cross-border payment, in China, by contrast, the focus is on mobile payment, online lending, and online investment funds (Table 1).[23]

Mobile Payments

Mobile payment is the most prominent FinTech business in China which started as a means to support e-commerce. Alipay was initially just an escrow account to transfer money to sellers after buyers had received their goods, but it was soon launched as an app for mobile use. In 2011 it introduced QR codes for payments, which are trivially easy to generate and could be used anytime, anywhere. This means of payment proliferated, supercharging Alipay's growth. It has more than 1 billion active users and handled $16trn in payments in 2019, nearly 25 times more

Table 1 Largest big tech companies in China ranked by valuation (2020)

Company name	*Market value (USD billion)*
Alibaba	666
Tencent	638
Ant Financial	313
Meituan	211
Jingdong	130
Xiaomi	100
Baidu	65.5
Didi Chuxing	56
Toutiao	30

Quoted from Tomasz Dziawgo[24]

[22] Due to concerns about money laundering and financial instability, the Chinese authorities banned trading in cryptocurrencies and initial currency offerings (ICOs). Currently, however, the PBOC is actively exploring the issuance of its own version of sovereign digital currency—digital currency/electronic payment (DC/EP).

[23] See X. Hua and Y. Huang, Understanding China's Fintech Sector: Development, Impacts and Risk, 2020, https://core.ac.uk/download/pdf/334410228.pdf.

[24] See T. Dziawgo, Big Tech Influence on China's Financial Sector, European Research Studies Journal 2021, XXIV(Special Issue 1), 1110–1120.

than PayPal.[25] A competitor arrived in 2013 with Tencent, which added a payment function to WeChat (social media app), China's main messaging app. Together the two process some 90% of mobile transactions in China.[26]

Perhaps the most impressive development concerning mobile payment is the ecosystems built around it. Users can organize their daily lives around the payment app. These ecosystems not only make people's lives easier but also bring about significant changes to the broader financial sector and the economy. Facilitated by mobile payment, e-commerce now accounts for more than 20% of total retail sales, with major consequences for offline supermarkets and department stores. Commercial banks also started to reduce the number of branches and lay off employees.[27]

Money Market Funds

Until recently, thanks to the Chinese government's repressive financial policy,[28] Chinese savers faced two extreme options for managing their money: stash it in bank accounts, safe but interest rates were artificially low; or punt on the stock market, about as safe as playing baccarat in a casino in Macau. Something in the middle finally arrived in 2013 when Ant Financial launched its money-market funds (MMF) product, Yu'E Bao. Yu'E Bao is working like an add-on of the Alipay app as users can deposit or withdraw anytime with the ease of a few clicks on the Alipay app. MMFs have high liquidity similar to that of cash, while subscribers

[25] See The Economist, What Ant Group's IPO Says about the Future of Finance? 10 October 2020.

[26] See The Economist, What Ant Group's IPO Says about the Future of Finance? 10 October 2020.

[27] See Y. Huang, Fintech Development in People's Republic of China and Its Macroeconomic Implications, 2020, ADBI working paper series, No. 1169, https://www.adb.org/sites/default/files/publication/629396/adbi-wp1169.pdf.

[28] The Chinese government maintained widespread and heavy intervention in the financial system, such as regulated interest rates, state-influenced credit allocation and tightly controlled capital accounts, throughout the entire reform period. In 2015, China's Financial Repression Index (FRI) still ranked 14th out of 130 economies and was even higher than the average level of low-income countries. See Y. Huang and T. Ge, Assessing China's Financial Reform: Changing Roles of the Repressive Financial Policies, 2019, Cato Journal 30(1), 65–85.

can earn handsome returns paid on a daily basis.[29] As a result, Yu'E Bao became an instant success after its launch. In less than one year, the investment scheme had attracted 400 billion yuan ($59.96 billion) from Chinese savers, making it a principal rival to dominant state-owned banks.[30] Tens of millions of customers have chosen to use Alipay e-wallet and Yu'E Bao as their default banking accounts. Other Fintech firms followed Ant's footsteps and offered similar products. In 2014, Tencent launched Licaitong, an online fund platform linked to WeChat which had 100 billion yuan under management within a year; Jing Dong launched its wealth management product-Jingdong Xiao Jinku. At the end of 2015, the fast expansion of Yu'E Bao and other mobile wealth management platforms contributed to the record-breaking value of MMFs in China—4.4 trillion yuan ($659 billion).[31]

Online Lending

Another prominent FinTech business in China is online lending, mainly online consumer microloans and online bank lending.[32] In most countries, banks overlook small borrowers due to their lack of credit history

[29] The return of Yu'E bao is based on the interbank lending rate, which fluctuates freely overtime. As of March 5, 2020, Yu'e Bao had a seven-day annualized yield of 2.3%, compared to 0.3% for standard bank deposits and between 1.5 and 2.25% on one-year fixed deposits. See Global Economics, Which Bank's Time Deposit Has the Highest Interest 2020? List of Bank Deposit Interest Rates in 2020 (2020 年 哪个银行定期存款利息高? 2020 银行存款利率一览表), 8 January 2020, https://www.shiji5.com/licai/yinhang/2020-01-08/175288.html; Sina Fund, Tianhong Yu'e Bao Money (天弘余额宝货币) http://finance.sina.com.cn/fund/quotes/000198/bc.shtml.

[30] See The Economist, Foe or Frenemy? 1 March 2014.

[31] See C. Flood, China Tightens Money Market Regulation, Financial Times, 1 February 2016.

[32] In 2014, both Ant and Tencent created their own internet bank—MyBank and WeBank—respectively. Yet unlike their other financial businesses which recorded exponential growth initially, BigTechs' internet banks remain relatively small. By end-2018, the total assets of MyBank and WeBank were around RMB 96 billion and RMB 220 billion respectively, much smaller than the average of RMB 7 trillion for a medium-sized bank. Two regulatory requirements seem to have hindered the initial growth of these internet banks. First, the authorities set a 30% ownership limit on a private bank for any non-financial entity. This essentially bans any non-financial firms from having a controlling stake, which might have discouraged BigTech firms from devoting the necessary resources to the newly established bank. Second, more importantly, internet banks in China are not allowed to open deposit accounts for customers on a remote basis. Given that these new

and/or collateral. This problem is especially acute in China. China's financial system is dominated by large SOBs which have a strong preference for lending to SOEs. The absence of a mature system for assessing consumer credit risk adds to banks' reluctance to lend to SMEs and low-income households. For instance, in 2008, only about 20% of Chinese SMEs had ever received bank loans and the credit card penetration rate was only around 19%.[33] Over 70% of China's population aged 18 years and above did not own a credit card in 2019.[34]

Fintech has risen to fill this gap. Credit scoring has an important role in the financial system in advanced economies. For example, in the United States, around 80% of the population has FICO scores which are based on an individual's financial information, including payment history, amounts owed to banks or credit card companies, and how long he or she has held certain bank accounts. Developing a FICO-style system in China would be difficult as most Chinese residents have no such credit history. Yet China's Fintech companies, through their e-commerce and payment platforms, have collected a large volume of non-financial information that could be used to supplement financial data in developing credit scores for individuals. Alibaba introduced Sesame (Zhima) Credit Scoring system in 2015 after analyzing the payment history of 400 million clients. The system considers five criteria: credit history, behavior preferences, agreement honoring, personal information as well as social network. After that it gives a score between 350 and 950 and assigns one of five categories (excellent, good, fair, poor, and bad).[35] Tencent introduced its' Tencent Credit Score with similar categories and score ranges using WeChat data and WeChat Pay information.[36] Compared to the traditional

internet banks do not have a wide-reaching branch network, this is a major obstacle for them to growing their deposit base.

[33] See X. Hua and Y. Huang, Understanding China's Fintech Sector: Development, Impacts and Risk, 2020, https://core.ac.uk/download/pdf/334410228.pdf.

[34] See Fitch Ratings, The Rise of Consumer Finance in China to Bolster Consumption, 28 January 2021, https://www.fitchratings.com/research/corporate-finance/the-rise-of-consumer-finance-in-china-to-bolster-consumption-28-01-2021.

[35] See M. Chui, Money, Technology and Banking: What Lessons Can China Teach the Rest of the World? 2021, BIS Working Paper No. 947, https://www.bis.org/publ/work947.pdf.

[36] See J. Horowitz, China's Tencent Is Quietly Testing a Social Credit Score Based on People's Online Behavior, 9 August 2017, Quartz, https://qz.com/1049669/chinas-tencent-hkg-0700-is-quietly-testing-a-social-credit-score-based-on-peoples-online-behavior.

bank approach, Fintech credit scoring might work better for two reasons: First, the bank approach mainly relies on financial data, which are reliable and accurate but also easily outdated. The Fintech approach relies more on real-time data, and behavior data which is often more stable during shocks. Second, compared to the scorecard model, the Fintech machine learning model can better capture not only non-linear relations but also interactions among different explanatory variables.[37]

The credit scoring system and Big Tech's capacity of handling big-data enable speedy loan approval. For instance, Ant created the so-called '310 model': loans take 3 minutes to apply and less than 1 second for approval with zero human intervention.[38] In late 2012, Ant managed to approve a total of 100 million RMB microloans in just 36 minutes during a special promotion campaign.[39] Tencent offers Weili Dai, an online consumer microloan product accessible through WeChat and QQ's wallets. The product is currently 'by invitation' only—applicants do not have to provide any guarantee and documents. The application result can be obtained in under 5 seconds, and funds are unlocked under a minute. Ant's banking Arm, MyBank, focuses on serving small and micro enterprises and farmers. It is an online bank that operates completely on the cloud and uses Big Data to determine loan amounts and terms for borrowers. As of June 2020, MyBank has served a total of 29 million small and micro enterprises, among which 80% have never received a

[37] See X. Hua and Y. Huang, Understanding China's Fintech Sector: Development, Impacts and Risk, 2020, https://core.ac.uk/download/pdf/334410228.pdf.

[38] Ant Group's consumer lending is made up of two products, each of them operated by a subsidiary of Ant, both located in Chongqing's Liangjiang New Area, a Pilot Free Trade Zone. Ant Huabei (or Ant Credit Pay) is a consumer credit scheme that functions as a virtual credit card, offering an interest-free period of up to 41 days. Ant Jiebei (Ant Cash Now) is a consumer loan service with a loan duration of up to 12 months. The loan applications are made on Alipay, and once approved, the funds are transferred to the borrower's Alipay account. The interest rates offer to depend on the Sesame credit score of the applicant.

[39] See M. Chui, Money, Technology and Banking: What Lessons Can China Teach the Rest of the World? 2021, BIS Working Paper No. 947, https://www.bis.org/publ/work947.pdf.

bank business loan before.[40] The non-performing loan (NPL) ratio for Mybank's SMEs business loans has consistently been at around 1%, which is significantly lower than the industry average of 3.22% in 2019, according to CBIRC.[41] Thanks to Fintech companies, online lending was virtually non-existent before 2014, now accounting for about 30% of the country's consumer loans.[42]

4 Fintech Challenges and China's Big Banks

By providing customers with lower costs and higher efficiency, China's Fintech sector has posed a real threat to the monopoly of traditional commercial banks in main retail businesses. Alipay and Wechat pay charge only 0.1% of each transaction in mobile payment, less than banks do from debit cards.[43] As a result, since the launch of Alipay and WeChat Pay, bank card penetration has plateaued[44] which caused an annual loss of about $60 billion for banks.[45] With a much higher yield, Yu'E Bao and other MMFs kept attracting savings deposits away from banks-banking deposits fell by one trillion yuan in January 2014.[46]

[40] See The New Five-Year Goals Start to Be Implemented at Hu Xiaoming: MyBank Is More of a Tech Company (新五年目标首次亮相, 胡晓明: 网商银行更应是科技公司) 1 July 2020, https://t.cj.sina.com.cn/articles/view/1686546714/6486a91a0200148ng.

[41] See Business Wire, Mybank Served Over 20 Million SMEs as of 2019, Further Spurring the Growth of China's Small and Micro Businesses, 27 April 2020, https://www.businesswire.com/news/home/20200427005353/en/MYbank-Served-Over-20-Million-SMEs-as-of-2019-Further-Spurring-the-Growth-of-China%E2%80%99s-Small-and-Micro-Businesses.

[42] See Reuters, Chinese Retail Banks Gain Consumer Lending Clout as Fintech Fall Out of Favor, 28 January 2021, https://www.reuters.com/world/china/chinese-retail-banks-gain-consumer-lending-clout-fintechs-fall-out-favour-2021-01-28/.

[43] See The Economist, Foe or Frenemy? 1 March 2014.

[44] It increased only from 44.4% in the fourth quarter of 2012 to 49.04% in the third quarter of 2019. See S&P Global, Tech Disruption in Retail Banking: China Banks Are Playing Catch-Up to Big Tech, 14 May 2019, https://www.spglobal.com/en/research-insights/articles/tech-disruption-in-retail-banking-china-s-banks-are-playing-catch-up-to-big-tech.

[45] See S&P Global, Tech Disruption in Retail Banking: China Banks Are Playing Catch-Up to Big Tech, 14 May 2019, https://www.spglobal.com/en/research-insights/articles/tech-disruption-in-retail-banking-china-s-banks-are-playing-catch-up-to-big-tech.

[46] See The Economist, Foe or Frenemy? 1 March 2014.

Banks did not stand still, they struck back against the threat by lobbying regulators to introduce restrictions on Fintechs. For instance, in 2016, the Chinese Securities Regulatory Commission (CSRC) tightened rules for MMFs by imposing new requirements for minimum holdings of liquid assets and reducing allowable leverage.[47] In addition, in 2017, the CSRC introduced investor concentration limits and a cap of 10,000 yuan on T+0 settling redemptions from a single account.[48] As concerns about the sheer size of Yu'E Bao grew, Ant Financial also had to adopt voluntary measures that likely curtailed its expansion. In 2017, Tianhong Asset Management capped Yu'E Bao's individual users' daily and total subscriptions at 20,000 yuan and 100,000 yuan respectively.[49] The tightened regulations certainly relieved some of the pressure on banks.[50] Yu'e Bao's asset size declined by 33% to RMB1.13 trillion ($165.0 billion) at the end of 2018, from a peak of RMB1.68 trillion ($245.3 billion) at the end of March 2018.[51]

But banks are not as conservative as they are often thought to be. They are always the pioneers in adopting innovative technology such as computers, the internet, and big-data analysis since banks need to process billions of transactions every day. Moreover, the pace of technological progress and the burgeoning functionality of mobile devices mean that financial service providers in China have no choice but to evolve and adapt.[52] Since 2016, Fintech is an important technological driver of financial innovation and has been the consensus. In 2016, the 13th Five-Year National Science and Technology Innovation Plan issued by the State

[47] See Fitch Ratings, New Chinese Money Fund Rules Move Closer to International Standards, 2016, https://www.fitchratings.com/site/fitch-home/pressrelease?id=997998.

[48] See Fitch Ratings, China's Tighter MMF Regulations Won't Halt Sector Growth, 2018, https://www.fitchratings.com/research/fund-asset-managers/china-tighter-mmf-regulations-won-t-halt-sector-growth-12-06-2018.

[49] See Reuters, Ant Financial's Yu'e Bao Caps Daily Investment at $3000, 7 December 2017, https://www.reuters.com/article/us-ant-financial-fund-regulation-idUSKBN1E11FQ.

[50] It is also because of the increased competition from other higher-yielding wealth management products.

[51] See S&P Global, Tech Disruption in Retail Banking: China Banks Are Playing Catch-Up to Big Tech, 14 May 2019, https://www.spglobal.com/en/research-insights/articles/tech-disruption-in-retail-banking-china-s-banks-are-playing-catch-up-to-big-tech.

[52] See D. Allen, The Future of China's Fintech Boom, 1 September 2016, East West Bank, https://www.eastwestbank.com/ReachFurther/News/Article/China-Fintech.

Council of China listed the promotion of Fintech products and service innovation and the construction of a national Fintech innovation center as the guiding direction of national policies.[53] In May 2017, the PBOC further established the Financial Technology Committee, which aims to provide strategic planning and policy guidance for China's financial technology development. In October 2019, the PBOC issued the Fintech Development Plan (2019–2021), which became China's first top-level document regulating the development of financial technology.[54]

Since 2019, China's banks have started actively pursuing partnerships with tech firms to drive Fintech adoptions as part of their digital strategies. At the same time, facing an increasingly harsh regulatory environment, Chinese internet giants have begun shifting their focus from being financial services providers to being tech providers.[55] Alibaba has partnered with over 200 Chinese banks to support their digital transformation, including ICBC.[56] According to the strategic agreement, ICBC will use Ant technology and Alibaba platforms to drive its existing payments and e-commerce business. Moreover, this deal will see ICBC work with Ant to hone its capabilities in global corporate finance, scenario-based finance, and financial innovation.[57] Among the six SOBs, CCB is regarded as the most aggressive when it comes to digital transformation. It was the first to set up a Fintech department (supported by Tencent), and has pioneered a

[53] See State Council Notice on the Publication of the National 13th Five-Year Plan for Science and Technology Innovation (国务院印发十三五国家科技创新计划的通知), https://cset.georgetown.edu/publication/state-council-notice-on-the-publication-of-the-national-13th-five-year-plan-for-st-innovation/.

[54] See Moody's Analytics, PBOC Sets Out Fintech Development Plan for 2022 to 2025, 4 January 2022, https://www.moodysanalytics.com/regulatory-news/jan-04-22-pbc-sets-out-fintech-development-plan-for-2022-to-2025.

[55] For instance, Jing Dong Technology was rebranded twice, from the initial Jing Dong Finance to Jing Dong Digits in 2018, then Jing Dong technology in January 2021. Ant Financial also changed its name to Ant Technology Group Co in 2020. Bloomberg reports that before 2018, most of the investment transactions were related to retail financial products. From 2018 onwards, more than 50% of the transactions are related to technologies themselves. See Bloomberg, 14 August 2019, https://www.bloomberg.com/professional/blog/alibaba-tencent-set-pace-emerging-powers-fintech-shift/.

[56] See Pay Space Magazine, Alibaba Extends Its Partnership with Large Chinese Banks, 17 December 2019, https://payspacemagazine.com/retail/alibaba-extends-its-partnership-with-large-chinese-bank/.

[57] See DigFin, The Urgent Digitalization of China's Banks, 22 January 2020, https://www.digfingroup.com/china-banks-digital/.

real-estate marketplace app to let customers rent or buy apartments. CCB even opened an all-robot branch in Shanghai back in 2018.[58]

China's big banks have made massive investment in Fintech. In 2019, the total investments on Fintech by SOBs and JSBs amounted to 100.8 billion yuan, accounting for 2% of their total annual revenue. Among these, the Big Four (ICBC, ABC, CCB, BOC) all spent more than 10 billion yuan on Fintech. In 2021, Fintech investment by six SOBs rose to 107.49 billion yuan, and 8 JSBs made a total investment of 47.9 billion yuan.[59] Apart from a partnership with Fintech companies, China's big banks also established their Fintech subsidiaries to meet the group's internal demands. As of December 31, 2021, 12 large (five SOBs and 7 JSBs[60]) banks have founded their Fintech subsidiaries. Fintech subsidiaries leveraged their parent bank' features and advantages to develop products and solutions and provide Fintech services, commencing a wave of new technology-oriented innovation among commercial banks.[61] China's large banks have upgraded their data and technology capabilities and achieved initial results in digital products and services, digital risk control, and digital operation (Table 2).

5 Fintech Challenges and Small and Medium-sized Banks (SMBs)

Big banks are under pressure, but SMBs are certainly feeling more heat. As noted earlier, except for a limited number of eligible banks, the majority of China's SMBs are restricted to operate in their local markets and serve local clients, mainly local governments, local SMEs, and households. Fintech companies also target the same customer groups and thus launch direct competition with SMBs. In the past, SMBs had a comparative edge over large counterparts in their better connection and

[58] See DigFin, The Urgent Digitalization of China's Banks, 22 January 2020, https://www.digfingroup.com/china-banks-digital/.

[59] They are China Merchants Bank, China CITIC, Ping An, Xing Ye, Everbright, Min Sheng, Heng Feng, and Bo Hai Bank.

[60] Five SOBs (except for PSBOC), and 7 JSBs (Industrial Bank, Ping An, Everbright, China Min Sheng, Hua Xia, China Merchants Bank, and China Zhe Shang Bank).

[61] See Deloitte, Forging Ahead Together for a Better Future, Chinese Banking Sector 2021 Review and 2022 Outlook, 2022, https://www2.deloitte.com/cn/en/pages/financial-services/articles/chinese-banking-sector-2021-review-and-2022-outlook.html.

Table 2 Fintech Investment by SOBs and major JSBs in 2019

Name of bank	*Fintech Investment (RMB, Billion)*	*Percentage of Fintech investment to total revenue (%)*
CCB	17.63	2.5
ICBC	16.37	1.91
ABC	12.79	2.03
BOC	11.65	2.12
China Merchants Bank	9.36	3.72
PSBOC	8.18	2.96
BOCOM	5.045	2.57
China CITIC Bank	4.89	2.61
Pu Dong Development Bank	4.12	2.16
Xing Ye Bank	3.65	1.97
Ping An Bank	3.497	2.53
China Everbright Bank	3.4	2.56

Quoted from Zhu and Zhang (2021)[62]

understanding of local customers. However, this informational advantage could hardly sustain in facing the competition from Fintech companies whose very strength is in data collection and analysis. Zhou Xiaochuan, the former governor of PBOC, recently expressed his concern over SMBs 'If the core process of banking is replaced by the information system, small banks will have few advantages- probably just in having a banking license and taking part in deposit insurance.'[63]

To survive the increasingly fierce competition, there is an urgent need for China's SMBs to embrace financial technology to modernize their infrastructure and respond to changing customer demands and expectations. However, this requires a heavy investment in IT infrastructure

[62] See T. Zhu and Y. Zhang, A Study on Digitalization of Rural Small-medium-sized Banks (农村中小银行数字化转型), Financial Regulation Studies, 2021 (4), 36–58 (in Chinese).

[63] See X. Zhou, The Development of Information Technology and the Prospects of Small Banks (信息科技的发展与基层银行的前景) 22 February 2022, China Finance, http://www.meritsandtree.com/index/journal/detail?id=2180.

and talent. Unlike big banks, SMBs usually lack capital replenishment channels. They have low profitability, which makes them unable to generate replenishment capital internally; they are also unable to raise funds through external channels such as initial public offerings due to their small scale and poor credit ratings.[64] Hence, most SMBs cannot afford to make the investment necessary to build and maintain Fintech hardware. Moreover, SMBs, especially those located in less developed regions or rural areas, often encounter difficulty of recruiting IT, and Fintech talent due to uncompetitive salaries and unattractive locations. For instance, a survey reports that by 2020, in 68.92% of SMBs, Fintech staff account for less than 5%, in 20.27% of SMBs, Fintech staff account for less than 1%; in 56.04% of CCBs, the average monthly payment for Fintech staff is less than 5000 RMB.[65] KMPG conducted a study with 46 regional banks in 2021, it finds that the overall progress of digital transformation is slow with 52% of surveyed banks are still in the initial stage.[66]

The survival pressure[67] has led to a wave of consolidation and restructuring among SMBs in recent years. In 2020 alone, it witnessed 7 merges/consolidations involving about 30 SMBs, such as three rural commercial banks in Xu Zhou, Tong Shan, Huai Hai, and Peng Cheng merged to create a new Xu Zhou Rural Commercial Bank; a provisional commercial bank was to set up to take over six CCBs in Shanxi province: Jin Cheng, Jin Zhong, Chang Zhi, Yang Quan, Shanxi District, Da Tong

[64] There are a total of 43 SMBs listed in the stock markets, including 30 CCBs and 13 rural commercial banks. See Deloitte, Forging Ahead Together for a Better Future, Chinese Banking Sector 2021 Review and 2022 Outlook, 2022, https://www2.deloitte.com/cn/en/pages/financial-services/articles/chinese-banking-sector-2021-review-and-2022-outlook.html.

[65] See A Survey on Cultivation and Development of China's Fintech Talent (中国金融科技人才培养与发展问卷调查), 2021, https://www.nbd.com.cn/articles/2021-12-28/2063622.html.

[66] See X. Li, A Report on Digital Transformation of 46 Regional Banks: 80 Percent Are Still in the Initial Stage, Short of Core Digital Talent (46 家区域性银行数字化转型报告: 近八成处于起步阶段 数字化核心人才短缺) 10 June 2021, Economy Observer, http://m.eeo.com.cn/2021/0610/491231.shtml.

[67] The pressure is not only from Fintech competition, also from interest rate liberation, slow down of economic growth, etc.

commercial bank.[68] In 2021, Luo Yang, Ping Ding Shan, and Jiao Zuo commercial banks were merged to Zhong Yuan Bank, after the restricting, Zhong Yuan Bank's assets would amount to 1250 billion RMB, placed it to 8th place among all CCBs.[69] KMPG study finds that there is a strong correlation between the scale of banks and the speed of digitalization, with 200 billion RMB as a critical threshold. The wave of consolidation and restructuring has probably just begun. Its effect on the SMBs landscape and on the banking sector remains to be seen.

The limited resources mean that most SMBs have little option but almost entirely depend on Fintech companies for technological innovation. For instance, Ping An group provides 640 banks with cloud-computing tech[70]; Du Xiaoman offers technological solutions for fraud detection and prevention.[71] Until January 2021, the most eye-catching collaboration between SMBs and Fintech companies is selling deposit products via third-party internet platforms. Products sold online included personal time deposits, with a focus on three and five-year maturities. Interest rates on these products were close to the upper limit of banks' self-regulatory pricing mechanism, which is tied to the benchmark interest rate. Most products required an initial deposit of only 50 RMB and could be withdrawn at any time. SMBs naturally found this appealing, as it could help them effectively break through geographical restrictions and turn them into de facto national banks. By the end of 2020, 89 commercial banks, 84 were SMBs, had attracted 550 billion yuan ($81 billion) worth of online deposits through such platforms. In some cases, online deposits sold to nationwide depositors even replaced interbank financing as the primary source of funds. The PBOC found that some high-risk small banks amassed 70% of deposits from nonlocal online deposit products

[68] See W. Zhang and Q. Diao, Arrival of a Wave of Consolidation and Merges in Small-medium-sized Banks in China (我国中小银行合并重组浪潮开启), 2020, Xinhua Finance, https://www.cnfin.com/upload-xh08/2020/0930/40a79f69019348b4aeb862b4647aa60f.pdf.

[69] See X. Mao, Unpacking Zhong Yuan Bank, The Birth of a 1000 Billion Yuan City Commercial Bank (拆解中原银行, 万亿级城商行即将诞生), 29 October 2021, https://www.weiyangx.com/395746.html.

[70] See The Economist, How Ping An, an Insurer, Became a Fintech Super-app, 3 December 2020.

[71] See The official website of Du Xiaoman, https://ir.baidu.com/investor-overview?c=188488&p=irol-irhome.

sold by third-party platforms, whereas interbank financing as a percentage of total liabilities dropped from 30% to 3.2%.[72]

This collaboration was banned by the CBIRC and PBOC in January 2021 for hidden risks regarding information disclosure and product management.[73] SMBs' use of national funds could create the potential for risk contagion. SMBs often do not have the capacity to control risks for such nationally-based, large-scale deposits, especially while offering higher interest rates. Risks can spill over from one region into another as funds dry up or become volatile. SMBs create additional risks by matching high-yield assets with high-risk projects. Customer service is poor since the third-party mechanism restricts customers from inquiring about their accounts, and the transactions take place only on the platform. What is more, the platforms selling the banks' deposits do not have a financial license and remain outside of regulators' supervision.[74]

Before January 2022, SMBs were also partnered with Fintech companies in digital lending. Fintech companies use their consumer credit data to identify and assess potential borrowers, then they either extended the loans jointly with banks or passed them on to banks and charged a 'technology service fee'. Ant was the biggest beneficiary of this business model. According to its prospectus in July 2020, it had facilitated some 1.73 trillion yuan in loans, but 98% of the loans were off its balance sheet-[75] SMBs funded the bulk of online lending. SMBs welcomed this cooperation because it helped them overcome the barriers of technology and customer acquisition and quickly expand their lending business nationwide. But this also made many SMBs become a pure funding channel without fully understanding the potential credit risk and overly relying on

[72] See Z. Liu, China's Village Bank Collapses Could Cause Dangerous Contagion, 27 July 2022, Foreign Policy, https://foreignpolicy.com/2022/07/27/china-village-banks-economic-growth-dangerous-contagion/.

[73] See CBIRC and PBOC, Notice on Matters Concerning the Regulation of Internet-based Personal Deposits of Commercial Banks' (关于规范商业银行通过互联网开展个人存款业务有关事项的通知) 2021, http://www.cbirc.gov.cn/en/view/pages/ItemDetail.html?docId=961998.

[74] See S. Hsu, China's Small Banks Suffer from Platform Deposit Crackdown, 2020, China-US Focus, https://www.chinausfocus.com/finance-economy/chinas-small-banks-suffer-from-platform-deposit-crackdown.

[75] See Ant Financial Prospectus, https://www1.hkexnews.hk/listedco/listconews/sehk/2020/1026/2020102600165.pdf.

selective Fintech partners for credit assessment, therefore introducing risk to their already shaky financial ground.

Following Ant's IPO suspension in November 2020, the regulators introduced new rules on micro-lending.[76] Under the new regulations, banks' joint lending with online platforms or other partners cannot exceed 50% of their outstanding loans; lending with one partner must stay within 25% of the bank's tier-1 net capital. Regional banks are banned from tapping nationwide customers with the help of online lending platforms. Internet platforms, such as those of Ant Group or Jing Dong Digits, need to provide at least 30% of the funding themselves. The new rules will make Ant and other platform lenders look more like banks and therefore considerably transform their business model. For SMBs, the rules may strengthen their risk control, but also accelerate the sector's differentiation. Online lending requires large amounts of investment so big banks will be able to quickly improve their prowess in the field whereas small peers cannot afford to keep up.

6 Concluding Remarks

Fintech has significantly transformed the financial service industry and that is particularly so in China. China has the world's largest banking system, but it is heavily regulated, in favor of SOEs and leaves a large number of SMEs and low-income households under-served or un-served at all. Fintech companies, led by Alibaba, rose to meet this unmet demand. In less than two decades, China has become a global leader in Fintech. China's Fintech industry has driven disruption into retail banking in payment, online investment, and online lending, posing a real threat to the Chinese banking system. Chinese commercial banks respond to this threat with both competition and collaboration. They successfully lobbied the regulators imposing more stringent rules on Fintech companies to restrict competition. In the meanwhile, they have been taking active measures to evolve and adapt to financial innovation. Through heavy investment and strategic collaboration with Fintech companies,

[76] See CBIRC, Further Regulation Notice on Commercial Bank Internet Loan Business (关于进一步规范商业银行互联网贷款业务的通知) (Came into effect in January 2022, banks must comply by July 2022), 2021, http://www.gov.cn/zhengce/zhengceku/2021-02/20/content_5587989.htm.

China's large banks have upgraded their data and technology capabilities and achieved initial results in digital products and services, digital risk control, and digital operation. But China's large number of SMBs are struggling to keep up due to small scale and limited resources. Recent crackdown on online lending and online deposit reinforced the geographic restrictions over SMBs and eliminated their hope of quick expansion through digital platforms. The latest wave of consolidation and restructuring might suggest the future direction: only large banks can survive and small ones will have to go.

CHAPTER 17

Fintech and Banking Reform: A Perspective from China

Feimin Wang, Duoqi Xu, and Xuejun Cheng

1 Introduction

Since the twenty-first century, China's banking industry has faced challenges in WTO accession, technological innovation, and domestic economic restructuring. Fintech companies and platforms have disrupted traditional banks' market share and profits through their technological advantages. In response, banks have accelerated their business reform, investing in fintech departments and collaborating with platforms to enhance their financial services. This has led to a shift from offline-based

F. Wang (✉)
School of Humanities and Law, North China University of Technology, Beijing, P.R. China
e-mail: wangfeimin@126.com

Bank Recovery and Resolution Research Institute, North China University of Technology, Beijing, P.R. China

Center for Fintech and Information Security Law, North China University of Technology, Beijing, P.R. China

M. Bodellini et al. (eds.), *Commercial Banking in Transition*, Palgrave Macmillan Studies in Banking and Financial Institutions,
https://doi.org/10.1007/978-3-031-45289-5_17

banking to online service models, resulting in notable achievements such as online finance, trade finance blockchain platforms, and improved data governance.

The history of currency in ancient China highlights the evolution from commodity currency to metal coins and eventually the emergence of enterprise-based banknotes. Today, digital finance and asset transactions are driven by blockchain technology, facilitating the digitization of currency. Central bank digital currency (CBDC) has gained global attention, with various countries researching and developing their own versions. China, in particular, has made significant progress with its central bank digital currency, named Digital Currency and Electronic Payment (DC/EP or e-CNY). However, the impact of DC/EP on commercial banks and the necessary changes for banks in this context have received limited academic attention. This study aims to analyse the positive and negative influences of DC/EP on commercial banks within the operational framework of China's central bank digital currency.

The chapter explores the online finance, trade finance blockchain platforms, bank data governance, and reform path for commercial banks amidst the wave of central bank digital currency.

2 Fintech-Driven Banking Reform

Online Finance

Online finance is a major achievement of fintech to promote the digital transformation of financial institutions. Banks are empowered by the Internet, biometrics, big data credit reporting, cloud computing, artificial intelligence, blockchain, and the like, to improve transaction efficiency,

D. Xu
Fudan University Law School, Shanghai, China
e-mail: xuduoqi@fudan.edu.cn

Fudan Artificial Intelligence Regulation Lab (FAIR), Shanghai, China

Center for Law and Digital Economy, Fudan University, Shanghai, China

X. Cheng
Tongji University, Shanghai, China
e-mail: chengxuejun222@126.com

reduce costs, and enhance their risk control capabilities. In the world of online finance, banking services, such as payment and settlement, account opening and deposit, wealth management, and loans are processed online and intelligently through working from home and electronic formalities. Online finance is an innovation and transformation of financial services driven by fintech and client demand, and its full implementation has speeded up because of the increasing demand for contactless financial services during the COVID-19 pandemic.

Electronic Payment

In October 2005, the People's Bank of China promulgated the Electronic Payment Guidelines (No. 1) to regulate electronic payment. The so-called electronic payment refers to an activity of an entity, a person, or those authorized to send payment instructions through electronic terminals to pay in currency and transfer currency. Electronic payment includes online payment, telephone payment, mobile payment, POS terminal transactions, ATM transactions, and the like. As surveyed by the People's Bank of China, 274.969 billion electronic payments were made in China in 2021, involving an amount of CNY 2976.22 trillion. In these payments, mobile and online payments account for the major part; among them, there are 151.23 billion mobile payments, accounting for 55.0% of all electronic payments, and there are 102.28 billion online payments, accounting for 37.2%. However, mobile payment features "small amount and frequent payments", and the amount involved in online payments is much larger than that in mobile payments. In 2021, the amount involved in online payment in China reached CNY 2354.0 trillion, accounting for 79.1% of the total amount involved in electronic payment; and mobile payment involved CNY 527.0 trillion, accounting for 17.7%. China's third-party payment service providers in electronic payment, represented by Alipay and Tenpay, have developed rapidly since 2005, which is impressive but imposes a significant impact on the banking business. The People's Bank of China promulgated the Administrative Measures for the Payment Services Provided by Non-financial Institutions in June 2010 to regulate the third-party payment business. Third-party payment is a particularly useful supplement to the payment service provided by banks. However, the third-party payment institution has gathered a huge fund of pending payments of clients in transactions, which functions as deposits, but the third-party payment institution needs to hold none of the legal deposit reserve, and the deposit business of banks is adversely affected. Therefore, in January 2017, the People's Bank of China promulgated the Notice of the General Office of the People's Bank of China on Matters concerning Implementing the Centralized Deposit of the Funds of Pending Payments of Clients of Payment Institutions, requiring the third-party payment institution to deliver the funds of pending payments of clients generated in transactions to an account designated by the People's Bank of China, and third-party payment institutions shall not misappropriate or tie up the funds of pending payments of clients. In August 2017, the People's Bank of China approved the establishment of NetsUnion Clearing Corporation, which is responsible for operating a platform of online payment clearing for non-banking payment institutions and supervising the accounts of the funds of pending payments of clients of third-party payment institutions. As of June 30, 2018, all third-party payment institutions have been included in the NetsUnion payment clearing platform, which takes charge of online payment services initiated by third-party payment institutions involving bank accounts. Since then, third-party payment institutions have been completely disconnected from cooperative banks in terms of the direct settlement business, and banks no longer directly provide settlement channels for third-party payment institutions separately.

Offline Banking Business Moved to Online Processing
With technological support, commercial banks have moved offline business to online channels through online banking, mobile banking, and virtual business receptions, providing clients with all-weather, uninterrupted, and non-contact financial services. So far, various services, for example, most of the procedures concerning account opening, such as file review and interview for contracting, transfer of money, deposit, wealth management, sale as agency of fund and wealth management products, and bill payment agency, have all been moved to online processing. And in some further services, technologies such as artificial intelligence and remote video services are employed. Taking the advantage of their platforms, third-party payment institutions sell or sell as agency wealth management products online, which reduces the scale of bank deposits, increases the cost for banks to take in deposits, and impairs banks' profitability. In response, banks sell wealth management products through both offline and online channels to fight back against the challenges brought by third-party payment institutions and their associated licensed financial institutions. It is stipulated in Article 8 of the Interim Measures for the Administration of Sales of Wealth Management Products of Wealth

Management Companies promulgated by the China Banking and Insurance Regulatory Commission on May 27, 2021, and enacted on June 27, that "a non-financial institution or individual may not sell wealth management products as agency without the permission of the financial regulatory authorities". This article stipulates that the sale through the Internet and the sale as an agency of wealth management products are subjected to regulation, which is conducive to the steady development of wealth management business.

Online Loans

Online loans refer to a digital loan model where an application is filed online without human contact. Online loans are a product of banks responding to technological development and social needs, and the COVID-19 pandemic has promoted the full implementation thereof. After the COVID-19 outbreak, China Development Bank, together with the two non-commercial banks, six top commercial banks, joint-stock banks, local city commercial banks and rural commercial banks, and village and town banks, launched online loans to provide guarantees for the resumption of work and production. With the technological support, online loans for small, medium, and micro enterprises can be available after an application procedure that takes 3 minutes and is disbursed in 1 second, and credit review is completely completed by big data, cloud computing, artificial intelligence, hence the loans can be delivered to the mobile banking accounts of small, medium and micro enterprises at low cost, quickly and easily. Though popularized in response to the hardship of the COVID-19 pandemic, online loans are backed up by the development of fintech.

Online loans are not only the product of the development of fintech in banking, but also the product of cooperation between loan-facilitating institutions and licensed credit institutions such as banks. Loan facilitation refers to a service where loan-facilitating institutions, with certain professional and technical capabilities, provide licensed financial institutions and other funders with pre-loan services, such as target client soliciting and selection, and then the bank completes the core business such as credit review and risk control. Loan facilitation is a helpful supplement to the traditional credit system. Loan-facilitating institutions are mostly digital platforms that provide e-commerce, payment, search, and other services. The client data resources they have, such as user identities, accounts, transactions, consumption records, and social networking information, can overcome the shortcomings of traditional banks in reaching new clients, and improve the risk assessment and risk control capabilities of banks when facing small and medium-sized enterprises and individual borrowers. Nonetheless, as a form of cooperation in loan services between banks and loan-facilitating institutions, loan facilitation also has problems such as the illegal source of data and information, partial risk control model, and misconduct in debt collection. To regulate these problems, the China Banking and Insurance Regulatory Commission promulgated the Interim Measures for the Administration of Internet Loans of Commercial Banks in July 2020, which regulates the cooperation between loan-facilitating institutions and banks, clarifies the accountability, and strengthens the protection of consumers' personal information. Moreover, quota management and concentration management are prescribed for the loans provided by banks jointly with loan-facilitating institutions. It is expressly stipulated in Article 5 of the Measures for the Administration of the Credit Reporting Business, which came into effect on January 1, 2022, that "financial institutions shall not carry out commercial cooperation with market institutions that have not obtained legal credit reporting business qualifications to obtain credit reporting services". Therefore, Internet platforms or big data companies, and fintech companies must provide data to banks through credit reporting agencies and can no longer directly provide big data credit reporting services to banks in the form of "loan facilitation". Such a measure is commonly known in the industry as" disconnection of facilitation". "Disconnection of facilitation" is not conducive to exerting the positive role of microfinance in supporting the development of the real economy and goes against the trend of mutual benefit under comparative advantage. However, it plays a positive role in strengthening the protection of personal information and promoting the collection of alternative data by banks, which reduces the risk of overreliance on loan-facilitating institutions in serving "long tail" clients. Herein the alternative data includes public information such as taxation, commercial registration, judicial proceedings, and administrative penalties, as well as information on public utility expenses such as water, electricity, natural gas, communication, and network fees.[1] Although "disconnection of facilitation" does

[1] See G. Lei, Loan Facilitation: Realistic Dilemma, Social Value, and Advice for Regulation. https://baijiahao.baidu.com/s?id=1743786523885779626&wfr=spider&for=pc, accessed Sep 15, 2022.

not cut off data supply, and even helps to form a larger big data set, it truly gets rid of the scenario and traffic-attracting advantages of loan-facilitating institutions. Consequently, additional links with Baihang Credit increase the cost, which hinders the implementation of online loans to serve the real economy for inclusive finance.

Trade Finance Blockchain Platform

In China, blockchain has been applied to trade finance platforms to meet the financing needs of supply chain platforms. Banks and other financial institutions, as funders in trade finance, understand the financing needs of companies participating in trade, but they "dare not to lend even though they intend to" in the face of the risk control cost and information asymmetry with clients, which ties the hands of them up. Currently, 70% of trade enterprises have no access to trade finance services.[2] The huge corporate financing deficit and credit market demand have prompted banks to seek technical help to break through business bottlenecks.

Trade Finance Blockchain Platform Led by Banking Consortium
The China Trade Finance Union Platform (CTFU platform) is planned by the China Banking Association and co-sponsored by 14 large commercial banks including CDB, ICBC, ABC, and Bank of China. Also, the CTFU platform takes blockchain as the underlying technology and meets the digital transformation and development needs of banking services for trade finance with its characteristics of openness and transparency, tamper-proofness, collective maintenance, and privacy protection. Mr. TIAN Guoli, President of the China Banking Association and Chairman of CBC, pointed out that the CTFU platform would play a role in the following four aspects. Firstly, the CTFU platform enables the standardization, electronization, and intelligentization of transaction information of inter-bank trade finance products to promote the development of supply chain finance. Secondly, the CTFU platform improves the efficiency of trade financing, reduces financing costs, and enhances the quality and efficiency of financial services for the real economy. Thirdly, with the characteristics of blockchain like "distributed storage, transaction traceability, and tamper-proofness", the CTFU platform effectively prevents and controls

[2] See IBM.we.Trade. https://www.ibm.com/case-studies/wetrade-blockchain-fintech-trade-finance, accessed Dec 3, 2021.

risks in trade finance. Fourthly, the CTFU platform is conducive to resource sharing and utilization and improves the performance of the association in serving its members.[3]

The trade finance blockchain platform led by the banking consortium, as a comprehensive blockchain platform based on financial institutions, is jointly established by multiple initiators, and it can make the best use of existing corporate client resources of banks and give full play to the effect of the Internet to help the construction of inclusive finance. However, as a platform co-established by multiple parties, the coordination and mutual trust mechanism in the stage of setting up the underlying technology is particularly important. The lack of a joint action plan with enough incentives will render the application of the platform inefficient; business competition among multiple bank entities will hinder the establishment of a mechanism for sharing core data and information; given the fact that trade finance is mostly dominated by core enterprises and they are few, the financial institutions that can shake the entire industry must be large banks. As a result, from the perspective of keeping a fair competition order in the market, large banks gain further dominance with the help of a consortium empowered by advanced technology, and the existing power inequality among large, medium, and small-sized banks is further exacerbated in the face of fierce market competition. Small and medium-sized banks bear a greater burden of survival, and so do small and medium-sized enterprises. The competition landscape will be farther from a fair one.

Trade Finance Blockchain Platform Led by Public Sector

Public services provided by government departments and private institutions such as customs, taxation, arbitration and rating authorities, and professional associations are necessary for a successful trade finance scenario. The public sector, as a party in trade finance, is primarily engaged in providing public services and maintaining trade order. Therefore, the trade finance blockchain platform led by the public sector is distinctive for its social public attributes.

[3] See Z. Ding, Banking Consortium and Five Top Banks to Jointly Build CTFU Platform. http://bank.xinhua08.com/a/20200831/1953409.shtml, accessed Aug 31, 2021.

A typical representative is the "eTradeConnect" platform initiated and established by the Monetary Authority of the Hong Kong Special Administrative Region of China (Hong Kong Monetary Authority, HKMA), formerly known as the "Hong Kong Trade Finance Platform". With blockchain as its underlying technology, the "eTradeConnect" platform is a trade finance platform jointly developed by a consortium of twelve major banks in Hong Kong. The main functions of "eTradeConnect" are reflected in three aspects. Firstly, "eTradeConnect" helps trade participants effectively verify and transmit trade documents on the platform through digitalization; secondly, "eTradeConnect" adopts encryption technology to ensure that only trade participants can share trade information and then can take trade materials to apply for financing from financial institutions such as banks; thirdly, "eTradeConnect" automates the transaction process of issuing delivery receipts and purchase orders, receipt reconciliation, etc. As stated by HKMA, these functions can boost the confidence of both parties, improve transaction efficiency and accuracy, and reduce financing risks, including human operational risks. Moreover, the transparency of capital sources and use is better to avoid repeated financing and financing fraud.[4]

The development of the People's Bank of China Trade Finance Blockchain Platform (the "PBC Trade Finance" platform) is led by the Digital Currency Research Institute of the People's Bank of China and the Shenzhen Central Branch of the People's Bank of China based on blockchain technology. The "PBC Trade Finance" platform is oriented to solve the problem of limited access and high costs for small and medium-sized enterprises to finance and serve the real economy. With the concept of "inclusiveness, openness, sharing, and minimal interest rate", the platform has three goals, that is, "information penetration, trust transfer, and credit sharing", and serves as a financial infrastructure that provides public services for trade finance based on the model of co-construction, co-management, and co-governance.[5] As a financial infrastructure launched by the People's Bank of China, the "PBC Trade Finance" platform not

[4] See L. Dazhi, HKMA Officially Launched "eTradeConnect", A Blockchain Trade Finance Platform. http://www.diankeji.com/blockchain/43686.html, accessed Nov 25, 2021.

[5] See C. Rongguo and L. Jie, Promotion and Application of Blockchain Technology and "PBC Trade Finance" Platform in Trade Finance in Gansu, GANSU FINANCE, 2020(05), 13–19.

only has the functions of enhancing trust, promoting trade flows, and easing corporate financing tensions that are common to other similar platforms, but also shares the social and public responsibility of the People's Bank of China, as a government agency, to regulate financial activities. In this practical case of applying regulatory technology, regulatory authorities can conduct penetrative regulation of the entire process and life cycle of trade finance through the "PBC Trade Finance" platform, whereby their regulatory capabilities are improved to prevent the accumulation and outbreak of financial risks. Financial innovations are promoted while the function of maintaining financial stability is duly done, which is also the embodiment of the social and public attributes of the trade finance blockchain platform.

It is to be noted that since trade finance blockchain platforms led by the public sector have the same duty to "perform social and public functions" and are driven by the same, exchanges and cooperation between platforms are readily possible. For example, "on November 3, 2020, Shenzhen Fintech Research Institute, a subsidiary of the Digital Currency Research Institute of the People's Bank of China, and Hong Kong Trade Finance Platform Co., Ltd., a subsidiary of Hong Kong Interbank Clearing Limited, jointly announced that the 1st stage of the project for communicating the trade finance blockchain platform with the 'eTradeConnect' platform has completed, and then the project officially entered the trial operation stage."[6] Because of the efforts paid by the government and the public sector, the platform resolves disputes over the responsible party for the construction and the governance mechanism. In one platform, barriers among users, scenarios, and public services are removed, and interconnection is enabled. Resources are integrated, and regulatory efficiency is improved; moreover, progress is made in the interaction between platforms and scenario integration. However, in the course of building a global trade finance blockchain platform, a platform consisting of state authority elements can hardly be effectively recognized and practiced globally due to sovereignty disputes, international tax interests, international trade barriers, and other factors. In addition, from the perspective of the relationship between the government and the market, it is inherent

[6] Digital Currency Research Institute of the People's Bank of China. First Stage of the Project for Communicating the Trade Finance Blockchain Platform with the "eTradeConnect" Platform Completed. http://www.lianmenhu.com/blockchain-22842-1 (accessed Jan 25, 2022).

to such a business model, as a matter of rule of law, to consider how to "give full play to the decisive role of the market in resource allocation, and better play the role of the government", and regulate the administrative power of the public sector rationally and legally to keep its measures neutral.

Data Governance in Banks

Commercial banks attach great importance to the role of data in banking, as well as the role of data in bank governance. The data of commercial banks come from two sources, one is credit data, mainly from the Credit Reference Center of the People's Bank of China, and the other is alternative data, mainly from the public sector and public enterprise sector, as well as client data obtained in bank services. Through big data credit reporting, commercial banks not only fulfill their business needs, but also improve the performance of client risk control, and the effectiveness and efficiency of their governance mechanisms. In the new model of banking with data, network, and financial information as the core, new security challenges have also been shown. Hackers attack a bank's network and database online, steal and tamper with data information, and transfer account funds or other assets, which brings severe challenges to the transaction security, data security, and network security of the bank. A compliance system of the bank for personal client information protection accountability has become a new issue. The Cybersecurity Law, the Data Security Law, and the Personal Information Protection Law are the fundamental rules that banks must follow in the era of big data credit reporting for personal information protection.

3 The Influence and Reform of Central Bank Digital Currencies in China (e-CNY) to Commercial Banks

The Theoretical Basis of Central Bank Digital Currency

Looking back at history, the development of money has evolved from personal credit (such as commodity currency) to enterprise credit (such as bank currency) and then to national credit (legal paper currency). It is inevitable for the development of the times to evolve into digital currency based on social consensus in the future.

The Theoretical Connotation of Digital Currency

Digital currency is a product driven by blockchain technology. Unlike the third-party payment application platforms (WeChat, Alipay, etc.) based on the centralized database ledger technology, the blockchain technology is based on the decentralized database and adopts the collaborative bookkeeping and account checking of all nodes in the network, and each bookkeeping forms a new block. Each block can only have one node for packaging. After the hash algorithm determines that the information is legal, it is broadcast to the whole network, added to the tail of the previous block and recorded by other nodes, according to the chronological order of the ledger chain formed by this, which is known as the blockchain. In order to motivate bookkeepers on the blockchain system, the system will give bookkeepers certain digital currency rewards, which is mining.[7] However, the total supply of some digital currencies is limited, for example, the maximum number of Litecoin is 84 million. Therefore, with the deepening of digital currency mining by "miners", the competition for digital currencies will be more intense, and the rewards will be increasingly reduced. In the context of limited supply, the demand for digital currency is enormous, forming the consensus that digital currencies have value.

There are still significant differences in the definition of digital currency in academic and industrial circles. However, it is generally accepted that digital currency refers to a kind of currency presented in digital form rather than in the materialization of traditional currency (paper currency, coin, and so on). To a certain extent, it bears the function of physical currency and can support the transfer of currency ownership without geographical and time restrictions. It has a significant degree of the value attribute. For this reason, the International Monetary Fund (IMF) defines digital currency as "the digital expression of value".[8]

[7] See Y. Q. Zhao, Development Trend, Contingent Risks and Regulatory Considerations of Digital Currencies in the Public and Private Sectors, Economist, 2020(8), 110–119.

[8] See A. M. Qi and Z. Zhang, On the Concept and Legal Nature of Digital Currency, Science of Law, Journal of Northwest University of Political Science and Law, 2021, 39(2), 80–92.

Classification and Characteristics of Central Bank Digital Currency

Since the rise of blockchain technology in 2008, it has been deeply applied to various social scenarios, of which digital currency is the most important application scenario at present.[9] From the perspective of the category of digital currency (see Fig. 1), it can be divided into non-legal digital currency and legal digital currency according to whether it is determined by law. Among them, non-legal digital currency can be divided into private digital currency and stable digital currency. The former includes bitcoin (BTC), ETH, and EOS, and the latter includes USDT and Libra. The legal digital currency mainly includes central bank digital currency (CBDC) and central bank digital account (CBDA), among which central bank digital currency is the digital manifestation of legal tender. Specifically, central bank digital currency is a digital currency directly issued by the central bank of the country based on the national credit. From the technical perspective, central bank digital currency adheres to the principle of technology neutrality. It can be issued based on the traditional central bank database ledger technology or the decentralized blockchain technology, and it is not necessarily issued using blockchain technology. Moreover, central bank digital currencies in different countries and regions can be divided into the wholesale type and retail type according to different application scenarios. The former includes Canada (Jasper project), Singapore (Ubin project), Japan (Stella project), European Union (digital Europe project), etc., and the latter includes Uruguay (E-Peso) and China (DC/EP).[10] Among them, the central bank digital currency in China (DC/EP) is very representative. It refers to the digital legal currency issued by the People's Bank of China according to the central database ledger technology. It takes the encrypted digital string representing the specific amount as the specific form and adopts the retail application scenario mode. It can be used for the storage, transfer, payment, and investment of digital currency.

Firstly, central bank digital currency is legal tender, not contractual currency. The agreed currency is the currency gradually formed by the trading subjects within a specific range. All the issues can be recognized within the field through commodity trading habits. The law does

[9] See X. J. Cheng, International Experience and China's Strategy of Blockchain Technology Regulation, China Business and Market, 2021, 35(3), 31–43.

[10] See D. D. Zhao, The Impact of the Central Bank's Digital Currency on Commercial Banks and Countermeasures, Enterprise Economy, 2021, 40(2), 143–149.

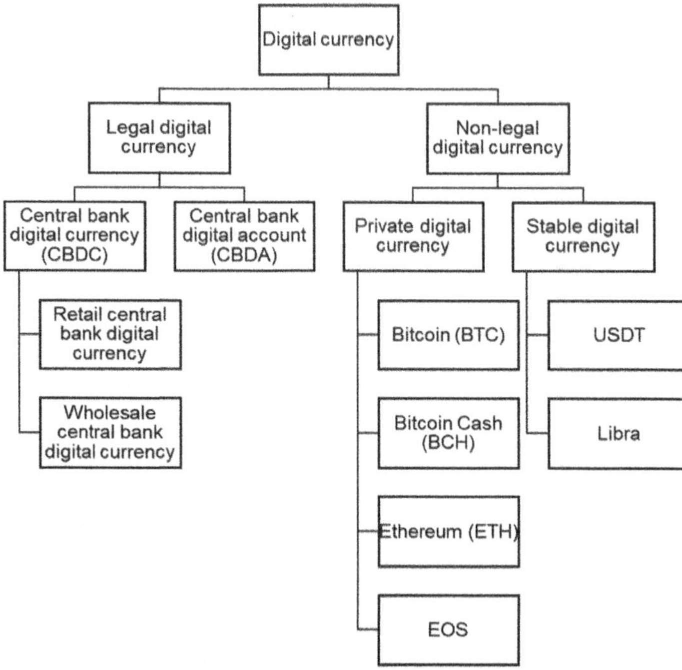

Fig. 1 The classification of digital currency

not acknowledge its current status and it has no legal force. Therefore, it is also called non-legal currency. For example, Bitcoin (BTC) is not recognized by the law as a currency and belongs to the agreed currency. Correspondingly, legal currency refers to the currency specially stipulated by national or regional laws, which has a binding effect on regulation. For example, within the jurisdiction of China, both the RMB in physical form and the DC/EP in digital form shall be legal currency and have the force of law.

Secondly, central bank digital currency is digital currency, not cash currency. Cash currency refers to money existing in paper or similar form (coin, etc.), which is the counterpart of digital currency in the way of existence. Digital currency is the currency existing in electronic equipment in the form of electromagnetic symbols. The main difference between central bank digital currency and cash currency lies in their different forms of existence. One represents the national credit behind the central bank in physical form, while the other represents the national credit behind the central bank in electronic form. From the perspective of the historical evolution of currency, it has gone through the forms of "commodity currency—bronze currency—gold and silver currency—paper currency—digital currency". The issuance of central bank digital currency is the inevitable development of the times, and mankind will inevitably enter the "cashless society". Of course, with the current level of digital technology, the current form is in a middle zone, and central bank digital currency is unlikely to completely replace cash.[11] The social economy will show the relationship of "coexistence" between central bank digital currency and cash currency for a long time.

Thirdly, central bank digital currency is legal electronic currency, not deposit electronic currency. Legal electronic money refers to electronic money in the form of electronic money in the customer account of the central bank; Deposit e-money refers to deposit money in the form of electronic money, such as deposit money deposited in third-party payment platforms such as Alipay and WeChat. According to the Law of the People's Bank of China, "the legal currency of China is RMB". The vast majority of the legal tender will be converted into deposits. Although electronic deposit money (such as Alipay) is the conversion form of legal tender, there are essential differences between them in legal nature. The external forms of the two are similar, both need to complete payment through mobile phones and other devices, central bank digital currency represents the national credit behind the central bank, and the electronic deposit currency represents the credit of commercial banks. However, there are also many differences between these two currencies: the first difference is that the central bank digital currency is loosely coupled to the account, while the electronic deposit currency is tightly coupled to the account, and its capital transfer must be completed through the account; the second difference is that the electronic deposit currency in the account is the deposit currency of the commercial bank, which is the transformation form of legal currency and represents the credit of the commercial bank. If the commercial bank goes bankrupt, these monetary funds will become the bankruptcy property, and the depositor will have the right to obtain interest; the central bank digital currency in the account represents

[11] Digital Currency Research Group of the People's Bank of China. China's Road to Legal Digital Currency, China Finance, 2016(17), 45–46.

the national credit behind the central bank. If the commercial bank goes bankrupt, these monetary funds will not become the bankruptcy property. Only after the central bank goes bankrupt will it become the bankruptcy property. At the same time, the holder has no right to obtain interest income,[12] and the legal currency has no value-added attribute. As for the last difference, under the background of electronic deposit currency, commercial banks have the right to use the depositor's account funds to invest abroad, obtain investment income, pay interest to the depositor, and commercial banks will charge custody fees and pay settlement fees; under the digital currency of the central bank, commercial banks have no right to use the digital currency of the central bank to make the foreign investment, and their custody, payment, and settlement are also free.[13]

Finally, central bank digital currency is an unlimited legal tender, not non-legal tender. The digital currency issued by the central bank is a new type of legal currency that replaces cash in circulation (M0). It has the exact legal nature of the RMB. It has the perfect nature of legal tender that no one can refuse to accept the payment; otherwise, it will be regarded as an illegal act. The corresponding is non-legal-tender, the currency without legal payment effect. This type of currency has no absolute payment effect. If the creditor's rights and debts are settled with the non-legal-tender, the other party has the right to refuse to undertake the payment obligation based on the non-legal-tender.

The Influence Mechanism of Central Bank Digital Currency on Commercial Banks in China

The *Experimental Research on Central Bank Digital Currency Prototype System*, published by the Digital Currency Research Institute of the People's Bank of China, has made a profound analysis of the operational framework of the central bank digital currency in China (DC/EP) (see Fig. 2): On the one hand, the core elements of the central bank digital currency are "one currency, two vaults and three centers": One currency refers to central bank digital currency (CBDC), that is, the encrypted digital string representing the specific amount guaranteed and signed by

[12] See F. R. Zeng, Research on the Motives and Impact of Issuing Legal Central Bank Digital Currency, Financial Development Review, 2018(5), 26–39.

[13] See S. J. Liu, Study on the Legal Principles and the Distribution of Rights and Duties of Legal Digital Currency, Journal of CUPL, 2018(3), 165–179, 209.

the People's Bank of China; two vaults refers to the issuance vault of the People's Bank of China and the bank vault of commercial banks; three centers refer to certification center, registration center and big data analysis center.[14] On the other hand, the digital currency of the People's Bank of China adopts a "two-tier operation system": the first layer is the central bank to the operating institutions (mainly commercial banks), and the second layer is the operational institutions to connect users. Commercial banks, as an important part of the DC/EP two-tier operation system, play an essential role in the "delivery" of the central bank digital currency. Under the collaborative development of blockchain technology and the digital economy, the issuance and circulation of China's DC/EP will significantly influence commercial banks, including both constructive and negative effects.

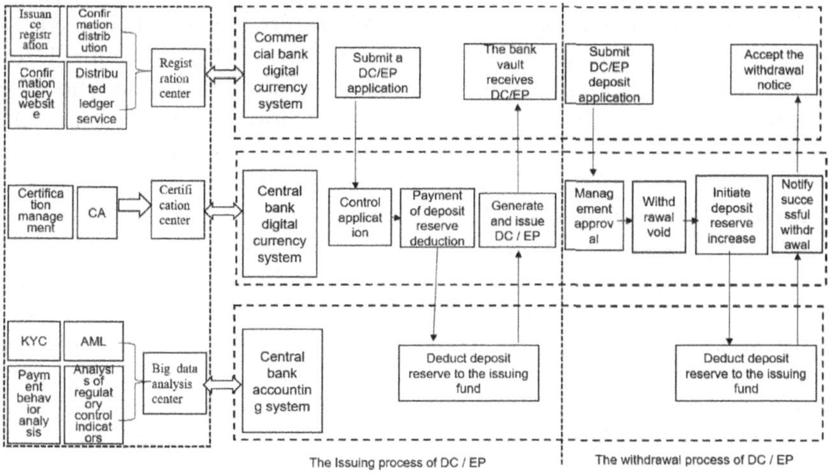

Fig. 2 The operational framework of the central bank digital currency in China (DC/EP)

[14] See Q. Yao, Experimental Study on Prototype System of Central Bank Digital Currency, Journal of Software, 2018(9), 2716–2732.

The Positive Influence of China's Central Bank Digital Currency on Commercial Banks

Driven by blockchain technology, digital finance has become a production factor in promoting social and economic development, among which digital currency is an essential component of digital finance. In this regard, the central bank of China actively embraces digital currency and actively responds to the influence of blockchain technology by issuing DC/EP, which will positively influence commercial banks. That is, DC/EP is conducive to preventing financial disintermediation of commercial banks, helping commercial banks reduce operating costs, and helping commercial banks improve the level of financial risk prevention.

DC/EP Helps Commercial Banks Reduce Operating Costs

The position of central bank digital currency is the digitization of cash (M0) in circulation. It is a digital currency of the central bank based on the encryption algorithm, which effectively meets the objective needs of users' portability and anonymity. In China, DC/EP will eventually be applied to small and high-frequency retail scenarios rather than wholesale scenarios. Therefore, it will be the best financial instrument to replace M0 without directly affecting the monetary multiplier and derivative deposits of M1 and M2. DC/EP will also comply with all legal norms related to anti-money laundering and other legal norms.

DC/EP is equivalent to cash in circulation (M0), which refers to the total amount of cash held by all units and individuals outside the banking system. Currently, the main business of commercial banks is deposits and loans, so the cash business of banks is very complicated. To ensure the safety of funds, many resources will be spent on counting and inspecting cash, exchanging large and small denominations, and the links between income and expenditure. As for the bank cash handover link, it is also necessary for staff to use professional machines to bind and package, and the cash cost of vehicle maintenance and personnel training needs to be paid between commercial banks and the issuance vaults of the People's Bank of China, central vaults and various business branches. Due to the physical properties of traditional currency, banks must devote a great deal of energy to protecting their security to guarantee depositors' assets' safety.

However, once the central bank digital currency in China is successfully implemented, China can reduce the operating costs of banks in this area.

At that time, DC/EP will only appear in the digital wallets of commercial banks. It is a kind of currency utilizing powerful data encryption, but in a sense, it is also a technical symbol. Once DC/EP enters the circulation stage, it will not have the traditional cash storage, transportation, and counting links, which will help reduce the daily operating burden of commercial banks. In other words, the successful issuance of DC/EP will help commercial banks' cash business become electronic and digital, and the cash management cost of commercial banks will be significantly reduced.

DC/EP Is Conducive to Preventing Financial Disintermediation of Commercial Banks

Currently, most countries and regions (such as the United Kingdom, Canada, Singapore, etc.) are willing to take the initiative to research and develop central bank digital currency. Some countries even officially issue central bank digital currency. On the one hand, it is to protect the currency sovereignty of their countries and regions and improve the utilization rate of currency payment; on the other hand, it is to prevent the aggravation of financial disintermediation, especially the financial disintermediation of commercial banks. The so-called financial disintermediation refers to a capital flow state in which the market participants bypass financial institutions (mainly commercial banks) to conduct capital transactions under financial control. The capital supplier bypasses the commercial banking system and directly delivers the funds to the capital demander to complete the external circulation of funds, which brings significant challenges to the development of commercial banks. Unlike the developed countries in the United Kingdom and the United States under the maritime law system, China's direct financing market is more developed. As a representative country under the civil law system, China's indirect financing market represented by commercial banks is more developed,[15] and it pays more attention to the financial intermediary role of commercial banks. Therefore, if digital currency is allowed to cause a direct influence on commercial banks, it is likely to bring adverse effects to China's commercial banking system and even the financial system.

With the acceleration of the technological and marketization process of the social economy, the importance of commercial banks as financial

[15] See X. J. Chen, The Development Risk, International Comparison and Governance Path of Residents' Leverage Ratio, Economist, 2021(11), 43–51.

intermediaries is relatively decreasing. In the environment of continuous innovation of financial instruments and products, the financial deepening will continue to strengthen, which will also lead to financial disintermediation. At present, China's non-cash payment (some scholars call it cashless society[16]) has gone through four stages: firstly, the traditional bank card payment stage (before 2005), which was marked by the establishment of China UnionPay. At that time, digital payment and transactions were mainly dominated by commercial banks, and the phenomenon of financial disintermediation was not obvious. Secondly, the traditional Internet payment stage (2005–2012), which started with the independent operation of Alipay, opened the door to the development of China's traditional Internet, especially e-commerce, and shook the position of commercial banks as a systematic financial intermediary. Thirdly, the mobile Internet payment stage (2012–2020),[17] which is marked by bar-code payment, has formed mobile Internet payment platforms such as Alipay and WeChat payment. These large platforms have further aggravated the financial disintermediation of commercial banks. Fourthly, the central bank digital currency stage (after 2020), China has accelerated the implementation and development of DC/EP, and the digital payment industry is ushering in a new development direction, returning to a new era dominated by commercial banks instead of the Internet in the past 15 years. In the new stage of the central bank digital currency, China's DC/EP adopts the two-tier operation system of "central bank—commercial bank" (see Fig. 3). As an important operation institution in the circulation link of DC/EP, commercial banks connect the issuing institution of DC/EP (the People's Bank of China) upward and effectively connect the user group of DC/EP downward, which makes commercial banks in the middle position under the two-tier operation system of DC/EP, compared with other financial institutions. It plays an important role in DC/EP "delivery". At this time, under the background of DC/EP issuance, commercial banks will play an important role as financial intermediaries again to effectively prevent the aggravation of financial disintermediation.

[16] See D. D. Garcia-Swartz, R. W. Hahn and A. Layne-Farrar, The Move Toward a Cashless Society: A Closer Look at Payment Instrument Economics, Review of Network Economics, 2006, 5(2), 4–20.

[17] See D. Xu, S. Tang, and G. Dan, China's Campaign-Style Internet Finance Governance: Causes, Effects, and Lessons Learned for New Information-Based Approaches to Governance, Computer Law & Security Review, 2018, 35(1), 3–14.

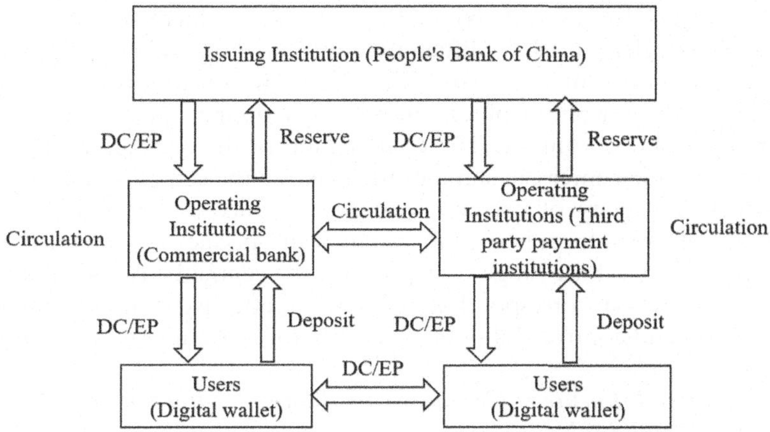

Fig. 3 Two-tier operation system of central bank digital system in China (DC/EP)

DC/EP Improves the Financial Risk Prevention Level of Commercial Banks

Commercial banks play a fundamental role in anti-money laundering (AML). However, at present, the anti-money laundering business is highly dependent on manual operation, and the system's processing capacity is weak. Based on the fact that it is difficult to identify the actual controller of the accounting system, such as the commercial bank card, the criminals will choose to purchase the bank accounts of other people's identities as a tool for money laundering and launder money through repeated inter-bank, cross-regional transfers and remittances through online banking, mobile banking, third-party payment, and other devices. Commercial banks can only examine the transaction information within their banks and cannot obtain the transaction flow information across banks. Reviewing the financial institutions and counterparties to which the funds ultimately flow is challenging, which brings obstacles to the transaction measurement and investigation of anti-money laundering.

However, once the central bank digital currency is launched, commercial banks can rely on the central bank's "one currency, two vaults, three centers" operational framework and data processing ability to strengthen anti-money laundering work and prevent financial risks. Firstly, the registration center, certification center, and big data center can form a credit exchange mechanism with commercial banks and increase data source channels, which reduces the difficulty of anti-money laundering. Secondly, the certification center can store the change information of the digital wallet of the transaction object into the system and update the ownership information promptly. The combination of the big data center and the certification center can significantly enhance the central government's management ability of currency circulation. Once it is found that the amount of central bank digital currency in specific accounts changes beyond the typical use range of depositors, the central bank and commercial banks can take corresponding measures to effectively improve the risk prevention and control ability of potential money laundering activities.

The Negative Influence of China's Central Bank Digital Currency on Commercial Banks

Undeniably, the innovative development of central bank digital currency is bound to positively influence financial institutions led by commercial banks. However, any innovation is two-sided. Under the situation that the promotion of the pilot programs of central bank digital currency is in full swing, central bank digital currency will also bring some negative effects to commercial banks.

DC/EP May Bring Governance Risks to Commercial Banks

The implementation of central bank digital currency will significantly influence the governance of commercial banks, because the "material" basis of legal currency has changed substantially. It is not the traditional category of cash currency but the digital form of currency. Admittedly, compared with the "blind zone" of financial governance of standard legal tender (paper currency and coin), the issuance of central bank digital currency does have inherent advantages, which can reduce the launch and circulation cost of traditional legal tender and improve the convenience and transparency of economic activities. Availing the digital characteristics of central bank digital currency is helpful to realize the accurate supply and counter-cyclical regulation of money and solve the dilemma of being in the "negative interest rate" liquidity trap.[18] Therefore, central bank digital currency will reverse or even end the competitive advantage of

[18] See Q. Yao, Analysis of the Economic Effects of Fiat Digital Currencies: Theoretical and Empirical Demonstration, Studies of International Finance, 2019(1), 16–27.

private digital currencies (such as Bitcoin, Litecoin, etc.) over traditional fiat currencies.

However, central bank digital currency is an innovative financial product. It adopts a two-tier operation system, which can directly connect the user's identity without binding the commercial bank account. Therefore, it also eliminates the dependence on the traditional retail bank account system, which may bring risks at the governance level.[19] On the one hand, for such new financial products, central bank digital currency carries external legal and regulatory governance risks to commercial banks. China's legislation on central bank digital currency is almost blank. Neither the basic laws such as *Law of the People's Republic of China on the People's Bank of China* and *Law of the People's Republic of China on Commercial Banks* nor other norms such as *the Measures for Payment and Settlement* and *the Measures for Handling the Business of Large Sum Payment Systems* clearly define the legal issuance right of central bank digital currency. Is there any law for the People's Bank of China to issue DC/EP? Can citizens' relevant rights, such as the right to privacy, be protected when they use central bank digital currency? Are there corresponding legal remedies for the losses faced by citizens when using central bank digital currency? All these problems need to be considered by legislators and solved in practice. On the other hand, central bank digital currency brings internal governance risks to commercial banks. Central bank digital currency will indeed improve commercial banks' financial risk prevention level to a certain extent. However, central bank digital currency is a brand-new financial product, which is relatively unfamiliar and inadaptable to commercial banks. It is not hard to predict that the issuance and circulation of DC/EP will inevitably harm the traditional internal governance of commercial banks, such as anti-money laundering, anti-terrorist financing, anti-corruption, and anti-counterfeiting currency, due to the imbalance between the innovation and development of digital currency by the central bank and the internal governance of commercial banks, which puts forward higher requirements for commercial banks to improve their inner risk management ability.

[19] See X. X. Wen and P. Zhang, The Impact of Digital Currency on Monetary Policy, China Finance, 2016(17), 24, 26.

DC/EP Reduces the Traditional Business Income of Commercial Banks

From the technical design point of view, central bank digital currency has the inherent characteristics of no transaction cost, settlement upon payment, and offline use. With the pilot implementation of DC/EP in Shenzhen, Suzhou, Xiong'an, Chengdu, and other places in China, it is expected to be implemented nationwide soon. This is bound to affect the main business of commercial banks, resulting in a sharp reduction in the income of a traditional business.

Firstly, the issuance of digital currency by the central bank may challenge commercial banks' payment and settlement products. Traditional commercial bank card consumption, payment, third-party account binding, bank card particular account, and other products may have a substitution effect with central bank digital currency. However, central bank digital currency has the force of law, which is paid through the unified wallet application. It has the advantages of convenience, security, and uniformity, which will significantly replace the payment and settlement business of traditional commercial banks to a considerable extent.

Secondly, the issuance of digital currency by the central bank may reduce the scale of demand deposits of commercial banks and increase the debt cost of commercial banks. Given the convenience of daily payment of commercial banks, although the withdrawal and redemption of time deposits and financial products of commercial banks face certain costs and formalities restrictions, residents are always willing to hold a part of high liquidity demand deposits for payment. However, once a central bank digital currency is issued, even though it does not pay interest (currently, DC/EP is designed not to pay interest), since the central bank digital currency payment has the advantages of convenience and high platform compatibility, ordinary users may be more inclined to convert some current deposits in commercial banks into central bank digital currency and deposit it in digital wallets for payment at any time. Or, with the broad application of central bank digital currency, the employees' salaries of enterprises may be paid in the form of central bank digital currency in the future. Many Internet platform enterprises (such as JD, Didi in China, etc.) have recently tried to pay their employees through the central bank digital currency. Under such a development trend, to a certain extent, this has led to the partial replacement of current deposits of commercial banks, which may reduce the scale of recent deposits of commercial banks and affect the source of funds on the liability side of commercial banks. To maintain the stability and scale of demand deposits, commercial banks may attract depositors by raising deposit interest rates, which increases the cost of liabilities of commercial banks to a certain extent. Ultimately, the increase or decrease of demand deposits of commercial banks depends on whether central bank digital currency pays interest, residents' daily payment habits, and their preference for digital currency and electronic cash.

DC/EP Weakens the Function of Physical Branches of Commercial Banks

In terms of design concept, the digital currency of the People's Bank of China (DC/EP) is positioned at the digitization of the cash in circulation (M0) and focuses on the replacement of M0. It does not calculate and pay interest in the system design and is non-profit. It mainly pursues the maximization of social efficiency and welfare. It can be seen that what the People's Bank of China wants to establish is a financial infrastructure based on the value transfer system of free central bank digital currency (DC/EP), and it does not charge relevant circulation fees from commercial banks in the issuing layer, and commercial banks do not charge users with the service fees for the withdrawal and return of central bank digital currency.

However, in the development process of traditional commercial banks, they have many offline physical branches, which is incompatible with the development orientation of central bank digital currency. It is not difficult to predict that the demand for deposits, withdrawals, and loans provided by the offline physical branches of commercial banks will inevitably decrease with the increasing popularity of central bank digital currency, which will lead to the gradual weakening of the functions of the physical branches of commercial banks: On the one hand, the issuance of central bank digital currency will lead to the gradual reduction of the cash deposit, withdrawal and loan services of the physical branches, automatic teller machines (ATMs) or counters of commercial banks, and even some offline physical units will be canceled. According to the General Situation of Payment System Operation released by the People's Bank of China, in 2015, when the demand for ATMs in China was at its peak, the number of newly added ATMs was as high as 252,000, which rapidly dropped to 58,000 and 36,000 in 2016 and 2017, showing a rapid downward trend. Even if the People's Bank of China adjusted the statistical caliber of ATMs in 2018, the number of ATMs in 2019 still decreased by nearly 40,000 compared with that in 2018. If central bank digital currency is vigorously promoted throughout the country, it is not difficult to predict that the physical branches of China's commercial banks will be further weakened. On the other hand, with the issuance of central bank digital currency, the personnel structure of retail bank branches will change. That is, those traditional financial talents (tellers, cashiers, and staff engaged in other cash business) will be increasingly reduced, while the financial technology talents will gradually increase.

DC/EP Brings Pressure to the Financial Infrastructure Construction of Commercial Banks

Under the background of the deep application of blockchain technology, especially central bank digital currency, DC/EP will significantly influence the traditional financial infrastructure, directly affecting commercial banks' business operations. Currently, the central bank digital currency of China (DC/EP) adheres to the principle of technology neutrality, insists on the centralized database ledger technology, and fully draws on the decentralized blockchain technology concept. To overcome its technical loopholes, it is necessary to strengthen the technical construction in all aspects of its issuance, transaction and use, especially in the payment terminal. It can learn from the mature experience of the existing third-party payment to ensure the security and stability of storage and payment. In terms of information connection between the central bank, commercial banks, and various financial institutions, it is also required to have a complete data transmission infrastructure to realize the system compatibility of all links of the central bank digital currency circulation.[20] However, in the face of the rapid development of central bank digital currency, commercial banks still have little to do with the financial infrastructure construction of central bank digital currency.

From the technical design concept perspective, China's central bank digital currency adopts the two-tier operation system of "central bank—commercial bank", which mainly focuses on replacing cash in circulation. However, in the future, society will still retain cash and legal currency (notes and coins, etc.), and there will be a parallel circulation of cash legal currency and central bank digital currency. Therefore, in the face of

[20] See W. Liu, Mechanism Exploration and Risk Prevention of Digital Currency Issuance Based on International Experience, Southwest Finance, 2017(11), 51–58.

such a parallel circulation situation, commercial banks need to reconstruct or update the current basic information system and currency database and constantly expand the service chain of digital currency of commercial banks to meet the needs of the circulation of cash legal currency and central bank digital currency. Moreover, each commercial bank needs to build its own digital currency business library to receive and store the central bank digital currency issued by the central bank. To a certain extent, this has prompted the commercial banks to increase their research and development investment in the secure storage, confidentiality, and efficient settlement of central bank digital currency. In the short term, strengthening the financial infrastructure construction will increase the investment, operation, and maintenance costs related to the central bank's digital money business. However, in the long run, strengthening the construction of financial infrastructure and commercial banks issuing and custody of the central bank digital currency through agents will effectively expand the service chain of commercial banks in blockchain finance, especially in digital currency, constantly enrich the business types of commercial banks and improve the added value of commercial banks.

The Reform Path of China's Commercial Banks Under the Wave of Central Bank Digital Currency

The issuance of central bank digital currency will bring all kinds of positive and negative influences to commercial banks. Commercial banks need to seize this important development opportunity, make full use of the advantages and avoid the disadvantages, and realize the development and reform under the wave of central bank digital currency.

Promoting the External Regulation and Internal Governance of Commercial Banks Orderly

Central bank digital currency is highly dependent on various digital technologies, which makes it easier to spread various risks generated when the financial system plays the role of infrastructure. Moreover, the technical density and anonymity of central bank digital currency also deepen the difficulty of risk assessment and early warning in digital currency. Under the wave of digital currency development by the central bank, commercial banks, as essential participants in the market, urgently need to reform the regulation theory of traditional single administrative management and change from government regulation to diversified governance.[21]

Firstly, strengthening the external legal and regulatory governance of commercial banks. Currently, China's legislation in the field of digital currency is almost blank, and the legislation cannot cover the digital currency level of the central bank. The controllable anonymity of the central bank digital currency leads to weakening the central bank's regulation and media efficiency, and it is impossible to take strict rules over it. On the one hand, China needs to accelerate the legal governance of the central bank digital currency, establish the legal status of the central bank digital currency from the legal system and regulatory framework, and develop special regulatory departments and market access systems. Only by separating central bank digital currencies from non-legal digital currencies (private digital currencies, institutional digital currencies, etc.) at the legal level can the monetary functions of central bank digital currencies be played, and the adverse effects of non-legal digital currencies on the financial market order be excluded.

On the other hand, China needs to build a sound and targeted regulatory system for the central bank digital currency. Because of the rapid development of the central bank digital currency, China needs to ensure that the central bank has the necessary data, to strengthen the monitoring and trading of the central bank digital currency in commercial banks, prudential regulation and anti-money laundering regulation, etc. At the same time, China should actively use the deposit reserve, interest rate, and other monetary policy tools to regulate commercial banks, so that monetary policy can better promote the development of the real economy and realize the effectiveness of monetary policy under the new financial form. In addition, China needs to learn from international experience and strengthen international cooperation. In terms of the governance practice of the central bank digital currency, the United Kingdom, Singapore, and other countries have adopted the "regulatory sandbox" method to conduct innovative regulation on the digital currency, which is of reference significance for the immature central bank digital currency regulation. Meanwhile, cooperation at the international level needs to be strengthened. The central bank digital currency is issued and circulated

[21] See D. Q. Xu, From Regulation to Governance: The Global Pattern and Practical Consensus of Digital Currency Regulation, Science of Law, Journal of Northwest University of Political Science and Law, 2021(2), 93–106.

by digital technology, closely related to currency digitization and financial globalization. Applying the central bank digital currency will gradually penetrate international finance, foreign exchange, foreign trade, and other fields. At this time, the financial regulation of a country is not enough to supervise central bank digital currency, and it is necessary to strengthen cooperation at the level of international economy and law.[22] China can actively deal with the global financial market risks faced by the central bank digital currency in circulation and effectively prevent the illegal and criminal movements of the central bank digital currency abroad.

Secondly, strengthening the internal risk management of commercial banks. Implementing the central bank digital currency has put higher risk management requirements for commercial banks to carry out anti-money laundering (AML), anti-corruption and anti-counterfeiting, and anti-currency alteration. Adhering to the centralized database ledger technology, together with fully drawing on the decentralized blockchain technology concept of DC/EP, can supervise the whole process of the central bank digital currency transaction process. Specifically, the central bank digital currency can improve the processing and execution efficiency of anti-money laundering activities and solve the timeliness problem through the technical design of the database ledger. Through the development of artificial intelligence technology, commercial banks can strengthen the self-learning ability of artificial intelligence, learn the new characteristics and trends of money laundering activities in the operation process, and update the smart contract in time. This can also improve the weak learning ability caused by the current overreliance on the manual anti-money laundering process. In the process of promoting the issuance and circulation of the central bank digital currency, commercial banks need to sum up their development experience, adopt a micro-prudential development attitude, make a set of feasible risk prevention plans, and consolidate the internal risk management of commercial banks. In addition, commercial banks can enhance cooperation and establish a set of unified digital currency technical standards; by strengthening cooperation with relevant government institutions, commercial banks help them explore a central bank digital currency regulatory system that conforms to China's national conditions and realize the two-way promotion of the development and governance of the central bank digital currency.

[22] See J. S. Yu, International Economic Law (2rd Edition), Beijing: Higher Education Press, 2019, 16–17.

Promoting the Product Application and Comprehensive Business Development of Commercial Banks

The implementation of central bank digital currency is a "double-edged sword" for the development of commercial banks. It may not only reduce the traditional business of commercial banks (payment and settlement, deposits and loans, etc.) but also bring many development opportunities to commercial banks.

On the one hand, the Central Bank of China adopts a "two-tier operation system" for digital currency: the first layer is the central bank to the operating institutions (mainly commercial banks), and the second layer is the operational institutions to users. Among them, commercial banks, which are essential components of the "two-tier operation system", play an important role in the "delivery" of digital currency by the central bank. Commercial banks compete with third-party payment platforms (such as WeChat and Alipay, etc.) to regain their advantages. The fundamental function of the central bank digital currency lies in innovative payment. It can achieve "interconnected" with various industries through the Internet of Things (IoT) technology. At that time, commercial banks could make full use of the payment function of the central bank digital currency to provide users with various comprehensive financial services around their payment scenarios.

On the other hand, for commercial banks, the central bank digital currency can be extended to the retail scene. Currently, the central bank digital currency is mainly issued to commercial banks. Commercial banks play an essential role in the central bank digital currency system and effectively connect the People's Bank of China and its customers. Therefore, commercial banks need to fully seize the development opportunities provided by the central bank digital currency, effectively obtain various types of active flows, and continuously augment the number of customers and customer stickiness of commercial banks. The issuance of central bank digital currency will help motivate commercial banks to build an open digital platform, gather different kinds of scene partners, effectively infiltrate end users, and promote them to use the services of commercial banks in daily life through various media and channels, and effectively promote the transformation of scientific and technological achievements and innovative business development of commercial banks. In addition, commercial banks can develop new off-balance sheet businesses such as agency of digital currency issuance and wallet custody to comprehensively support the development of various types of businesses.

Accelerating the Strategic Transformation of Commercial Banks from Offline Outlets to Online Platforms

The influence of central bank digital currency on the offline physical branches of commercial banks mainly includes the business of physical branches and the staff of physical branches. Under this direct influence, commercial banks need to reform internally, keep open to the outside world, and realize the strategic transformation from offline physical branches to online digital platforms.

Firstly, commercial banks should rearrange the distribution of offline physical branches based on reducing the number of offline physical branches due to the decline in demand. It seeks a balance between maintaining the most basic need of commercial banks and controlling the costs of commercial banks to fully optimize the benefits of offline physical branches of commercial banks.

Secondly, as the reduction of physical branches of commercial banks will inevitably have an influence on the existing counters, cashiers, and other cash business-related staff, commercial banks can base on adequately arranging the original staff and actively promoting job transfer, increase the reserve of talents due to the increase of related online finance, especially financial technology business in the future.

Finally, commercial banks should plan the construction of digital network-related infrastructure and coordinate the construction of digital currency issuance, circulation, and payment system. Guided by the transformation from offline physical branches to online digital platforms, the central bank will make complete preparations for the technical research and development, staffing, and network distribution of the central bank digital currency to be issued and circulated, and actively build an online digital platform, to seek a new digital competitive advantage from the perspective of central bank digital currency.

Strengthening the Construction of Information Systems for Commercial Banks and Promoting the Upgrading of Financial Infrastructure

From the analysis of the issuance and circulation mechanism of central bank digital currency, commercial banks need data coding and blockchain format trans-coding for the issuing end of the central bank; for the user end, the commercial bank needs to receive the central bank digital currency transaction request. The introduction of central bank digital currency is bound to reshape the current information system of commercial banks.

Under the background that it is difficult for the information system of commercial banks to adapt to a brand-new central bank digital currency, commercial banks need to promptly respond, transform the information system with the help of digital banking projects, upgrade and update their information system to a new system suitable for central bank digital currency, actively promote the financial infrastructure construction of commercial banks, and focus on increasing the investment in blockchain talents and funds. In addition, with the deep application of central bank digital currency, the user's trading habits and behavior patterns may change substantially. Commercial banks need to actively invest in the central bank digital currency research, deeply analyze the possible influence of central bank digital currency on the commercial banks' existing business models, increase research and development investment in information systems, make changes to the existing commercial banks' operation models, to bring better user experience and minimize the business influence.

Every technological development and evolution will more or less influence the traditional social economy. When technology is deeply applied to the currency field and combined with the credit dimension, it will lead to the development of currency from personal credit (such as commodity currency) to enterprise credit (such as bank currency), national credit (such as legal tender), and further evolution to central bank digital currency (CBDC) based on social consensus. This is the necessity of the technology development level, and it is also necessary to deepen credit rating.

At present, human society is moving forward from the era of Internet technology to the era of blockchain technology. Various cryptocurrencies, from private digital currencies (Bitcoin, Litecoin, etc.) to institutional digital currencies (Libra, USTD, etc.), have achieved rapid development driven by technology, forcing countries to accelerate the research and development process of central bank digital currencies. This is because there is fierce competition among various types of digital currencies, and there is also a dispute between sovereign currencies and international discourse power among central banks of different countries. Major countries and regions around the world have accelerated the research and development of their central bank digital currencies for objective reasons such as maintaining currency sovereignty, improving monetary efficiency, and reducing monetary costs. In response, China began to develop DC/EP in 2014 and began to conduct pilot tests on DC/EP in Shenzhen, Suzhou, Xiong'an, Chengdu, and the Winter Olympic Games in 2020, effectively coping with the fierce competition of other digital currencies and grasping the development trend of central bank digital currency.

From the technical design of China's central bank digital currency, it is based on the national credit issuance, which can make the transmission effect of China's monetary policy more efficient, improve the discourse power of RMB in the digital currency, and safeguard China's monetary sovereignty. From the perspective of the operation framework of DC/EP, it adopts a two-tier operation system of "central bank—commercial bank", which helps commercial banks to reduce operating costs, slow down financial disintermediation and improve the level of financial risk prevention. However, any innovative financial product is not perfect, and it may also bring a negative influence on the traditional social economy. Similarly, DC/EP will also harm commercial banks. It may bring about governance risks to commercial banks, reduce the conventional business income of commercial banks, weaken the function of physical branches of commercial banks, and add pressure to the financial infrastructure construction of commercial banks.

The road on the development of central bank digital currency is tortuous, but the future is bright. This is also a "tortuous" and "bright" choice for commercial banks. If commercial banks follow the development wave of central bank digital currency and actively change on the "tortuous" road: orderly promoting the external regulation and internal governance of commercial banks, enabling the application of commercial banks' products to promote the development of comprehensive business, accelerating the strategic transformation of commercial banks from offline branches to online platforms and strengthening the construction of commercial banks' information systems to promote the upgrading of financial infrastructure, then the future development of commercial banks will inevitably lead to "bright".

4 Conclusion

In conclusion, the banking industry in China has been undergoing significant transformations driven by fintech and the adoption of digital technologies. The shift toward online finance has revolutionized banking services, improving transaction efficiency, reducing costs, and enhancing risk control capabilities. The utilization of technologies like big data, cloud computing, artificial intelligence, and blockchain has played a crucial role in achieving major milestones in China's fintech-driven banking innovations, such as online finance, trade finance blockchain platforms, and data governance. To navigate these challenges and protect consumer rights, commercial banks must adhere to fundamental rules and regulations related to cybersecurity, data security, and personal information protection.

Furthermore, the introduction of China's central bank digital currency (DC/EP or e-CNY) has both positive and negative implications for commercial banks. While enhancing convenience and promoting financial innovation, the adoption of DC/EP brings governance risks, challenges traditional revenue streams, and puts pressure on existing financial infrastructure. In response to the wave of central bank digital currency, commercial banks in China must actively embrace the opportunities and mitigate the potential drawbacks. This involves accelerating strategic transformations, strengthening information systems, and transitioning from offline outlets to online platforms. By capitalizing on their strengths, collaborating with fintech companies and platforms, and aligning their strategies with the evolving landscape, commercial banks can adapt to the changing paradigm and ensure their continued growth and competitiveness.

Overall, the development of online finance, trade finance blockchain platforms, and data governance in banks, combined with the advent of central bank digital currency, presents both challenges and opportunities for commercial banks in China. With a proactive approach and strategic reforms, commercial banks can thrive in the digital era and effectively navigate the changing dynamics of the banking industry.

CHAPTER 18

Prudential Regulation of the Banking-Like Business of Fintech Companies in China

Yangguang Xu and Zhirou Li

1 Introduction

FinTech refers to the innovation of financial products and services through the use of emerging technologies such as big data, blockchain, cloud computing, and artificial intelligence (AI). The development of FinTech drives the transition of commercial banks, the banks not only compete but also cooperate with each other. On the one hand, China's banks are increasingly investing in FinTech, on the other hand, FinTech companies are engaged in banking-like business. FinTech companies' banking-like services have higher efficiency and lower operating costs than traditional banks, but they are less regulated and more risky. The

Y. Xu
Renmin University of China, Beijing, China

Z. Li (✉)
Centre for Commercial Law Studies, Queen Mary University of London, London, UK
e-mail: zhirou.li@qmul.ac.uk

M. Bodellini et al. (eds.), *Commercial Banking in Transition*, Palgrave Macmillan Studies in Banking and Financial Institutions,
https://doi.org/10.1007/978-3-031-45289-5_18

rapid expansion of third-party payment platforms and the FinTech companies behind them affected the deposit base, revenue, and profitability of China's banking industry. Some FinTech giants have become systemically important; however, their financial risks have not been effectively regulated. Problems such as regulatory vacuums and regulatory gaps remain unresolved.

This chapter aims to examine the situation of China's FinTech companies, and discuss how to prevent the systemic risks brought by FinTech companies' banking-like business from the perspective of prudential regulation. To find effective solutions, this paper will analyze the operation models of FinTech companies' banking-like business, as well as its potential risks and consequences, and the causes of risks. This chapter will propose regulatory recommendations for regulating Fintech companies.

Definition of FinTech

The Oxford Dictionary defines FinTech as "computer programs and other technology used to support or enable banking and financial services".[1] The technology areas covered by FinTech include big data, artificial intelligence (AI), cloud computing, blockchain, and quantum computing.[2] A FinTech company is defined as "the ones offering technologies for banking and corporate finance, capital markets, financial data analytics, payments and personal financial management".[3] These companies usually focus on four main areas: payment-related services, wealth management, peer-to-peer lending, and crowdfunding.[4] The advantages of FinTech companies mainly lie in: (i) lower search costs and thus more efficient matching in financial markets, (ii) economies of scale in collecting and processing large data Samples, (iii) lower cost and higher security of

[1] See T. Vasiljeva and K. Lukanova, Commercial Banks and FINTECH Companies in the Digital Transformation: Challenges for the Future, 2016, 11 Journal of Business Management, 25.

[2] See Y. Wang, S. Xiuping and Q. Zhang, Can Fintech Improve the Efficiency of Commercial Banks?—An Analysis Based on Big Data, 2021, 55 Research in International Business and Finance, 101338.

[3] Ibid., n1.

[4] Ibid.

transmitting information, and (iv) lower verification cost.[5] Not only that, FinTech innovations may change industry structures, blur industry boundaries, and lead to disintermediation.[6]

The Application and Impact of FinTech on the Banking Industry

Application of FinTech in Banking Industry

The impact of FinTech on the banking industry mainly comes from two aspects: one is the use of FinTech by banks in their own business, and the other is the competition between FinTech companies' services and traditional banking business. The application of FinTech is considered to have greatly improved the operational efficiency of commercial banks.[7] Therefore, more and more commercial banks are adopting FinTech in their business. Commercial banks can lower bank operational costs, increase efficiency of service, improve risk control abilities, and make business models more customer-oriented through FinTech, which can improve bank's competitiveness overall.[8] For example, FinTech can improve credit processes and customer evaluation models,[9] speed up lending, lower corporate financing costs, and increase the economic efficiency of financial services,[10] especially for small and micro enterprises and private companies.[11]

[5] See G. B. Navaretti and others, 'Fintech and Banking. Friends or Foes?', available at https://papers.ssrn.com/abstract=3099337 (accessed 22 July 2022).

[6] See A. Admati and M. Hellwig, The Bankers' New Clothes: What's Wrong with Banking and What to Do About It: With a New Preface by the Authors, Princeton University Press, 2014.

[7] 'Under the new pattern, how to change the focus of commercial banks' FinTech applications? (新格局下，商业银行金融科技应用着力点如何转变, translated)', available at http://bank.hexun.com/2021-05-11/203578127.html (accessed 26 August 2022).

[8] See Y. Wang, S. Xiuping and Q. Zhang, Can Fintech Improve the Efficiency of Commercial Banks?—An Analysis Based on Big Data, 2021, 55 Research in International Business and Finance, 101338.

[9] See E. Bouri, B. Lucey and D. Roubau, The Volatility Surprise of Leading Cryptocurrencies: Transitory and Permanent Linkages, 2020, 33 Finance Research Letters, 101188.

[10] Ibid.

[11] See Y. Wang, S. Xiuping and Q. Zhang, Can Fintech Improve the Efficiency of Commercial Banks?—An Analysis Based on Big Data, 2021, 55 Research in International Business and Finance, 101338.

These advantages have led to a growing demand for FinTech applications by banks. Not to mention the ongoing COVID-19 crisis further increased financial institutions' demand for digital services.[12] The development of FinTech has produced a "catfish effect"[13] and promoted the transformation of commercial banks.[14]

Many banks are expanding their digital businesses by investing in or acquiring FinTech companies, and their areas of greatest interest are payments, big data, and trading.[15] China's banking industry is increasing its investment in FinTech. China's commercial banks have incorporated FinTech development into their mid- and long-term strategies.[16]

China's large commercial banks' investment in FinTech is increasing year by year. Bank of China, China Construction Bank, Bank of Communications, Agricultural Bank of China (ABC), and Industrial and Commercial Bank of China (ICBC) all have their own FinTech subsidiaries. For instance, as of the end of 2021, the ICBC has invested the most, with a value of 25.987 billion yuan. Compared with 2020, the investment has increased by 9.10% year-on-year, accounting for 2.76% of operating income. ICBC also has the largest number of FinTech talents among China's large commercial banks. According to ICBC's 2021 annual report, as of the end of 2021, ICBC has 35,000 FinTech personnel, accounting for 8.1% of the bank's employees. ICBC has the

[12] See A. Boot and others, Fintech: What's Old, What's New? 2021, 53 Journal of Financial Stability, 100836.

[13] The "catfish effect" means that the arrival of a strong competitor (catfish) forces other weaker participants (sardines) to improve themselves. For example, new FinTech products are the catfish, and banks' traditional products are the sardines. New FinTech products force traditional bank to innovate and avoid losing customers in the competition. See Zhu, Yueteng, and Jiajun Lu, FinTech and Bank Intermediation–Evidence From the Deposit Market in China, 2021, Available at SSRN 4030108.

[14] See S. Nie and Y. Liu, Research on the Transformation of Traditional Commercial Banks in the Background of Science and Technology Finance_Based on the Influence of Third-Party Payment (科技金融背景下传统商业银行转型问题研究_基于第三方支付的影响, translated), 2021, 4 Northern Economy and Trade, 82.

[15] See T. Vasiljeva and K. Lukanova, Commercial Banks and FINTECH Companies in the Digital Transformation: Challenges for the Future, 2016, 11 Journal of Business Management, 25.

[16] 'Analysis of the current situation and trend of the construction of financial technology system in commercial banks (商业银行金融科技体系构建的现状与趋势分析, translated)', available at https://baijiahao.baidu.com/s?id=1649005653662205033&wfr=spider&for=pc (accessed 26 August 2022).

largest number of patents in the industry, ranking first among large Chinese commercial banks.[17] ICBC's FinTech Research Institute, established in November 2019, has FinTech innovation laboratories including blockchain, big data, AI, cloud computing, distributed, 5G, Internet of Things, information security, and other technical fields.[18] ICBC's technological capability far exceeds other Chinese banks.

Regarding the application of FinTech, ICBC uses FinTech to improve its information security system. For example, it established anti-fraud systems such as external fraud risk information systems, e-banking transaction anti-fraud systems, and credit card risk monitoring systems. ABC cooperated with Baidu, it used AI technology to launch the first face-recognition cash withdrawal application in the industry. Additionally, it uses blockchain technology in the credit accounting within the ABC.[19] In order to alleviate the difficulty of farmers getting loans, the ABC has designed a simple and fast peasant household small credit loan product "Jin Sui Kuai Agricultural Loan (金穗快农贷)" with the help of the Internet and big data. "Jin Sui Kuai" mainly distribute credit to farmers in relatively developed and stable operating industries with easy measurable input and output. It develops specific credit models for different types of farmers, with the combination of online and offline methods, implementing automatic system review and approval.[20] However, many banks

[17] L. Jiao, 'Fintech for the big six banks in 2022 (2022 年六大银行的金融科技, translated)', available at https://www.sohu.com/a/572746112_411876 (accessed 22 October 2022).

[18] 'ICBC Financial Technology Research Institute was formally established', available at http://www.icbc.com.cn/icbc/%E5%B7%A5%E8%A1%8C%E9%A3%8E%E8%B2%8C/%E5%B7%A5%E8%A1%8C%E5%BF%AB%E8%AE%AF/%E5%B7%A5%E5%95%86%E9%93%B6%E8%A1%8C%E9%87%91%E8%9E%8D%E7%A7%91%E6%8A%80%E7%A0%94%E7%A9%B6%E9%99%A2%E6%AD%A3%E5%BC%8F%E6%88%90%E7%AB%8B.htm (accessed 29 June 2022).

[19] 'How FinTech affects banks: Into the ABC Data Center', available at https://baijiahao.baidu.com/s?id=1627894664180340429&wfr=spider&for=pc (accessed 29 June 2022).

[20] 'Technological innovation promotes the transformation and upgrading of agricultural inclusive financial services', available at http://www.abchina.com/cn/special/jrkjz/jrcx/201705/t20170515_1069209.htm (accessed 29 June 2022).

only use FinTech for business accounting and maintenance, FinTech has not yet become a management tool.[21]

Compared to large banks, small and medium-sized banks are even more eager to use FinTech because they want to make up the competitive disadvantage with large banks in terms of customer acquisition capabilities. However, small and medium-sized banks might not have sufficient capacity to equip infrastructure to support Fintech business.

Some investigation suggests that FinTech has significantly lower the credit risk of China's commercial banks, mainly through the use of FinTech to achieve the following three purposes: (i) Improve the efficiency of risk management, (ii) Enhance the internal governance and control of the bank, and (iii) Improve the degree of bank diversification. However, at the same time, the technical and regulatory risks brought by FinTech may increase bank credit risk to some extent.[22] Application of FinTech has also had a certain negative impact on commercial banks and created some new regulatory issues.

The Impact of FinTech Companies on Banking

The impact of FinTech companies on commercial banks is mainly through competition effects and technology spill over effects.[23] FinTech and commercial banks have a relationship of cooperation and competition. In terms of cooperation, commercial banks cooperate with leading FinTech companies such as Ant Financial, Tencent, Baidu, JD Finance, etc. Their cooperation projects include consumer finance, product innovation, capital settlement, electronic payment, inclusive finance, and small and medium-sized enterprises credit services. By cooperating with FinTech companies, the business scope of commercial banks has been continuously expanded, and the customer base has become more and more diverse.[24]

21 'Under the new pattern, how to change the focus of commercial banks, FinTech applications? (新格局下，商业银行金融科技应用着力点如何转变, translated)', available at http://bank.hexun.com/2021-05-11/203578127.html (accessed 26 August 2022).

22 See M. Cheng and Y. Qu, Does Bank FinTech Reduce Credit Risk? Evidence from China, 2020, 63 Pacific-Basin Finance Journal, 101398.

23 Ibid.

24 See S. Nie and Y. Liu, Research on the Transformation of Traditional Commercial Banks in the Background of Science and Technology Finance_Based on the Influence of Third-Party Payment (科技金融背景下传统商业银行转型问题研究_基于第三方支付的影响, translated), 2021, 4 Northern Economy and Trade, 82.

In terms of competition, some FinTech giants have business similar to banks, namely taking deposits and lending. Some FinTech companies attract customers with lower loan interest or even interest-free, leading some deposits to leave commercial banks and transfer to money market funds.[25] The strong information capabilities of large FinTech companies may enable them to be more competitive than traditional banks in financial services. For example, Ant Financial, a subsidiary of Alibaba, has extended credit lines in China's rural areas which have less banks.[26]

Financial innovation may affect financial market stability. For instance, payment services provided by FinTech companies may result in funds in deposit accounts being transferred to non-bank payment service providers. This could have implications for bank financing. In addition, new FinTech companies have captured market share in the payment services market that formerly belonged to banks. This disintermediation could affect the profitability of banks and the effectiveness of the central bank to transmit monetary policy to the real economy.[27] Empirical results show that the impact of third-party payment[28] on the profitability of commercial banks is significantly negative, and the impact on the commercial banks' proportion of non-interest income is significantly positive.[29] But the development of FinTech's third-party payment also promotes the optimisation of commercial banks' profit structure.[30] This further proves that the relationship between FinTech companies and commercial banks includes competition and cooperation.

[25] Ibid.

[26] See A. Boot and others, Fintech: What's Old, What's New?, 2021, 53 Journal of Financial Stability, 100836.

[27] See B. Van Roosebeke and R. Defina, Five Emerging Issues in Deposit Insurance, 2021. Available at SSRN 3919974.

[28] Third-party payment refers to an online payment model in which an independent institution with certain strength and reputation guarantees facilitates transactions between both parties through the Internet. Y. Wang, Research on the Development of Third-Party Payment Based on the Background of Internet Finance——Taking WeChat Tenpay as an Example (基于互联网金融背景下第三方支付的发展研究——以微信财付通为例, translated), 2019, 31 Times Finance, 62.

[29] See S. Nie and Y. Liu, Research on the Transformation of Traditional Commercial Banks in the Background of Science and Technology Finance_Based on the Influence of Third-Party Payment (科技金融背景下传统商业银行转型问题研究_基于第三方支付的影响, translated), 2021, 4 Northern Economy and Trade, 82.

[30] Ibid.

However, although these FinTech giants are engaged in banking-like business, they are not subject to the same strict regulation as commercial banks. More importantly, the rapid development of FinTech has made some FinTech companies already systemically important. Some studies even worry that FinTech companies may replace banks in the future.[31] These concerns could lead to prudential risks of financial market. In addition, due to regulatory arbitrage and the platform economy, there are heightened concerns about financial instability and negative impact on fair competition caused by FinTech. This presents new challenges for supervisors and deposit insurers.[32]

The Rationality of Choosing China as a Sample Study

This article focuses on China's FinTech market, because China's FinTech is developing rapidly in a large market. First, there is a huge market demand for FinTech in China. China has a large number of small savers, and digital payments are already widely used.[33] For recent several years, young people and many middle-aged Chinese people usually do not carry cash with them in their daily life, but only use Alipay or WeChat to pay on their mobile phones.

Second, the development of FinTech has made the financial service accessible to more people. In China, due to the insufficient financial universality, it is not easy for individuals, small and medium-sized enterprises, and clients in rural areas to obtain loans from commercial banks due to many restrictions. As a result, many of them turn to financial services provided by FinTech companies on the Internet. This changed the business model of traditional banking and created a new

[31] See T. Vasiljeva and K. Lukanova, Commercial Banks and FINTECH Companies in the Digital Transformation: Challenges for the Future, 2016, 11 Journal of Business Management, 25.

[32] See B. Van Roosebeke and R. Defina, Five Emerging Issues in Deposit Insurance, 2021. Available at SSRN 3919974.

[33] Zsee hu, Yueteng, and J. Lu, FinTech and Bank Intermediation–Evidence from the Deposit Market in China, 2021. Available at SSRN 4030108.

industry, namely internet banking[34] industry where all financial services are provided online.[35]

Third, China's Internet banking has formed a unique self-ecosystem. For instance, Alibaba Group owns online shopping platforms Taobao and Tmall, which are tied to the Alipay and provide customers with financial services on Alipay. Alibaba Group established MYbank in 2015. Another internet giant, Tencent Group, owns WeChat, the instant messaging software with the most users in China. It established WeBank in 2014. The two groups have a large number of customers and a variety of business types. More importantly, the logistics services, and information flow in their business enable them to have a complete interlocking operating ecosystem. MYbank and Webank combine AI and big data for accurate analysis, provide customers with a variety of innovative and more convenient financial services to achieve inclusive finance.[36] In addition, China's FinTech developed more than one billion anonymous samples as early as 2009, and validated and improved customer identification models in practice.[37]

Despite the increasing influence of FinTech in China's banking industry, the regulatory regime on FinTech is still not sound enough, which will lead to regulatory inefficiency, and bring many risks. Therefore, improving FinTech-related legislative system is a top priority for FinTech regulators and policymakers.[38] In such a large market with high demand

[34] Internet bank has two meanings, one is the online service system provided by traditional banks, such as online banking and mobile banking of physical commercial banks; the other is pure online banking established based on the Internet and FinTech. In this article, Internet bank refers to the latter meaning.

[35] See K-C. Chen, Implications of Fintech Developments for Traditional Banks, 2020, 10 International Journal of Economics and Financial Issues, 227. China's banking system is dominated by four big state-owned banks (including Industrial and Commercial Bank of China, Bank of China, China Construction Bank, Agricultural Bank of China), some joint-stock commercial banks, and numerous regional banks. Internet banking entered the banking industry in 2014.

[36] Ibid.

[37] See F. Bickenbach and others, Adjustment After the Crisis: Will the Financial Sector Shrink and Entrepreneurship Boom?, Kiel Policy Brief, 2009.

[38] See M. Cheng and Y. Qu, Does Bank FinTech Reduce Credit Risk? Evidence from China, 2020, 63 Pacific-Basin Finance Journal, 101398.

but without perfect regulatory system, research on China's FinTech and banking industry is valuable, it can provide important experience and inspiration for other countries' financial regulation.

2 Banking-Like Business Among China's FinTech Companies

Overview of China's FinTech Companies

As a country with one of the biggest FinTech market, China accounts for more than half of the global digital payments market and three-quarters of global online lending transactions.[39] Among them, Alipay and WeChat Pay together account for 94% of the third-party mobile payment market in China. Alipay users exceeded 1 billion, while WeChat Pay users reached 1.2 billion.[40] A potentially risky phenomenon in China's financial markets is that Internet companies are engaging in banking-like activities, namely deposits and loans, through their financial services groups and payment platforms.

Ant Financial

Alibaba Group is a leading internet company in China. Ant Financial, Alibaba's affiliated company, owns Alipay, Yu'E Bao, Ant Credit Payment, Ant Wealth (mobile wealth management), Mybank (internet bank), Sesame Credit (big data credit rating), and other sub-business sectors. The development of Ant Financial has benefited from the advanced technical level of Alibaba Group, and the huge customer base and personal data reserves from Alibaba's online shopping platforms Taobao and Tmall.[41]

Ant Financial is involved in the retail deposit and loan business. Yu'E Bao provides funds management services for customers. It attracts clients to transfer money in Alipay, a third-party payment platform, to invest

[39] The Economist, "The Age of the Appacus: FinTech in China" (25 February 2017), 65.

[40] 'iResearch: Alipay and Tenpay's 2019Q3 Market Share Reached 94%', available at https://baijiahao.baidu.com/s?id=1656342003872731698&wfr=spider&for=pc (accessed 26 August 2022).

[41] See L. Lu, Decoding Alipay: Mobile Payments, a Cashless Society and Regulatory Challenges, 2018, Butterworths Journal of International Banking and Financial Law, 40.

in monetary funds. The investment threshold of Yu'E Bao is extremely low, the income is higher than deposit in banks, and the investment can be redeemed immediately, so as to rapidly expand and absorb the deposits of retail investors. Compared with commercial banks, Yu'E Bao offers depositors higher interest and borrowers lower interest. Additionally, the "currency" in Yu'E Bao can be directly used for online shopping. Compared with bank deposits, Yu'E Bao can replace bank deposits to a large extent.[42] The market size of Yu'E Bao in 2017 even exceeded the total deposits of China Merchants Bank which was the fifth largest bank in China. Obviously, Ant Financial has significantly affected the payment and deposit business of commercial banks, and this fierce competition has undermined the profitability of China's banks in recent years.[43]

In terms of loan business, Ant Credit Pay provides installment payment services for consumers. MYbank provides credit to small businesses settled on Alibaba's shopping platforms. Ant Financial uses the big data accumulated on the platforms to grant credit lines to small businesses.[44] Through Alipay, Ant Financial uses big data technology to accurately profile customers in the loan relationship. It can be aware of when the client needs money, how well the repayment ability is, and how the income is, so as to reduce the bad debt rate and encourage people to consume more. With the help of efficient and convenient internet platform technology, Ant Financial gives loans quickly. It only took 4 years for Ant Financial to recycle the loans 40 times, it used about 3 billion RMB to issue more than 360 billion RMB online loans, forming a high rate of nearly 120 times.[45]

[42] See Zhu, Yueteng, and J. Lu, FinTech and Bank Intermediation–Evidence from the Deposit Market in China, 2021. Available at SSRN 4030108.

[43] See L. Lu, How a Little Ant Challenges Giant Banks? The Rise of Ant Financial (Alipay)'s FinTech Empire and Relevant Regulatory Concerns, 2018, International Company and Commercial Law Review, Sweet & Maxwell, available at https://papers.ssrn.com/abstract=3052318 (accessed 22 July 2022); L. Lu, Decoding Alipay: Mobile Payments, a Cashless Society and Regulatory Challenges, 2018, Butterworths Journal of International Banking and Financial Law, 40.

[44] See R. M. Stulz, FinTech, BigTech, and the Future of Banks, 2019, 31 Journal of Applied Corporate Finance, 86.

[45] See F. Kong, Reflections on the Supervision of FinTech Enterprises_Taking Ant Financial as an Example (对金融科技企业监管的思考_以蚂蚁金服为例, translated), 2020, 12 Shanxi Cai Shui, 35.

Despite the fierce competition between Ant Financial and commercial banks, Ant Financial is still beneficial to the development of the banking industry in some aspects. For example, Mybank has provided loan services for a large number of small and micro enterprises. More importantly, the development of Sesame Credit is conducive to the establishment of China's personal credit system. The services provided by Sesame Credit can help banks to more accurately evaluate personal and small business credit, improve the efficiency of bank lending. In this regard, the business of Ant Financial is complementary to traditional commercial banks.[46]

Nonetheless, these operations of Ant Financial are not as regulated and supervised as the traditional activities of commercial banks, and third-party payment systems are also exposed to liquidity risks. Scholars believe that the huge scale of Yu'E Bao may pose serious liquidity and systemic risks to financial markets.[47] The current resolution mechanisms have not covered how to address these issues.

Tencent

Another internet giant in China is Tencent Group. Similar to Alibaba's Alipay, Tencent Group owns the third-party payment platform Tenpay, which provides online payment services for Internet users and various enterprises. Tenpay was launched in 2005, it relies on the strong technology background of Tencent, as well as large scale of users of Tencent's QQ and WeChat (both instant messenger). Tenpay competed with Alipay in the Internet payment market, and developed into the second-largest third-party Internet payment platform under Alipay.[48] Because WeChat has a wide range of users, it innovatively combines WeChat chat with funds income and expenditure settlement services. The launch of WeChat Red Envelopes has made the circulation of small funds faster. The maximum amount of WeChat Red Envelopes sent in a single time is 200

[46] See L. Lu, How a Little Ant Challenges Giant Banks? The Rise of Ant Financial (Alipay)'s FinTech Empire and Relevant Regulatory Concerns, 2018, International Company and Commercial Law Review, Sweet & Maxwell, available at https://papers.ssrn.com/abstract=3052318 (accessed 22 July 2022).

[47] See Zhu, Yueteng, and J. Lu, FinTech and Bank Intermediation–Evidence from the Deposit Market in China, 2021. Available at SSRN 4030108.

[48] See Y. Zhou, A Comparative Study of Major Third-Party Mobile Payment Platforms in China (中国主要第三方移动支付平台的比较研究, translated), 2017, 20 Shangchang, 49.

RMB, which shows that WeChat payment is still focusing on the market of micropayment.[49] In terms of risk prevention and control, Tenpay has a unique "millisecond recognition" system, which is a mechanism based on the AI model to quickly and automatically intercepts various risks, and continuously improves the accuracy and precision of risk identification, aiming to effectively protect the safety of users' property.[50] However, due to the customer's security concern, people tend to conduct commercial transactions with large amounts through bank transfers rather than Tenpay.[51]

In addition to payment service, Ant Financial and Tencent are more willing to attract users to other financial services. Tenpay also provides financial services such as credit and monetary funds for clients.[52] Once users enter an App on their platform, they can easily access mutual funds, insurance products, virtual credit cards, and online banks specializing in microloans on their mobile phones. While these derivative businesses bring profits to FinTech companies, they also bring credit risk.

WeBank is a world's leading digital bank owned by Tencent Group, it was opened in 2014. WeBank is the first digital bank in China with technology as the core development engine. It is committed to meeting the diversified financial service needs of individuals and small and micro enterprises to realize inclusive finance. International rating agencies Moody's and Standard & Poor's rated WeBank "A3" and "BBB+" respectively.[53]

[49] See Y. Wang, Research on the Development of Third-Party Payment Based on the Background of Internet Finance——Taking WeChat Tenpay as an Example (基于互联网金融背景下第三方支付的发展研究——以微信财付通为例, translated), 2019, 31 Times Finance, 62.

[50] Tenpay, Available at https://posts.tenpay.com/posts/16db756f630c6a7f12c4392f1532be31.html (accessed 26 August 2022).

[51] See Y. Wang, Research on the Development of Third-Party Payment Based on the Background of Internet Finance——Taking WeChat Tenpay as an Example (基于互联网金融背景下第三方支付的发展研究——以微信财付通为例, translated), 2019, 31 Times Finance, 62.

[52] See L. Jiao, Research on the Profit Model of My Country's Third-Party Payment Platform——Taking Tenpay as an Example (我国第三方支付平台盈利模式研究——以财付通为例, translated), 2019.

[53] Webank, available at https://www.webank.com/#/about (accessed 26 August 2022).

Other FinTech Companies

There are some other FinTech companies that have similar business in China. For instance, JD Group owns JD Finance (京东金融) and the products and services of JD Finance cover three major business segments: personal finance, consumption installment, and insurance. In the field of FinTech, JD Digital provides financial institutions with solutions for digital and sustainable growth, and serves the digital upgrade of financial institutions in payment settlement, wealth management, consumer finance, corporate finance, and asset management.[54] JD shopping platform is the first Internet credit payment service provider in China."Jingdong Baitiao" assesses credit through big data, consumers can enjoy installment shopping services in JD.com and some offline shops, with interest rates lower than bank credit cards.

Duxiaoman (度小满) Financial belongs to Baidu Group, providing micro-credit (maximum 200,000 RMB), wealth management, insurance brokerage, payment, personal FinTech, supply chain FinTech, and other services.[55] Credit FinTech and Wealth Management FinTech are the two major strategies of Duxiaoman Financial. Based on the accurate portrait identification of small and micro enterprises, Duxiaoman Financial has established a FinTech system with risk management as the core: its AI algorithm can reduce credit risk by 25%. It can realize automatic loan approval in seconds, and strive to achieve zero mortgage, low risk, and high efficiency.

Suning Financial Services (苏宁金融服务) was a FinTech company under Suning Group, with third-party payment, supply chain finance, wealth management, insurance sales, fund sales, crowdfunding, and other financial services. Through a complete financial service chain, it promoted Suning's industrial ecosystem and provided comprehensive financial services for consumers and micro enterprises. It has six core technologies of data risk control, financial AI, Internet of Things, financial cloud, and biometric identification. Suning Financial Services has been acquired by the Bank of Nanjing in 2022.[56]

[54] JD Financial, available at https://jrhelp.jd.com/ (accessed 26 August 2022).

[55] Duxiaoman Financial, available at https://www.duxiaoman.com/ (accessed 26 August 2022).

[56] 'Bank of Nanjing: Completed the equity acquisition of Suning Consumer Finance Co., Ltd.', available at https://baijiahao.baidu.com/s?id=1742583666444488352&wfr=spider&for=pc (accessed 26 August 2022).

3 Summary of FinTech Company's Banking-Like Business

In sum, the operating model of FinTech company's banking-like business is usually that Internet companies engage in activities like payment, wealth management, making loans through their financial services companies. These financial service companies rely on the strong technical support of Internet technology groups, the group's large and stable customer base, and complete business chain (such as shopping platform and logistics chain).

The interest rate of monetary funds provided by third-party payment platforms is higher than that of commercial banks' demand deposits, which attracts a large number of funds and customers, resulting in a lot of funds leaving the banking system and affecting the deposit business of commercial banks. In terms of loan business, third-party payment platforms take advantage of technology to accurately assess customer credit through big data, and then carry out precise loans to seize the personal consumer credit and small and micro-enterprise credit markets. Compared with bank loans, the third-party payment platform has a lower threshold and faster approval speed, which fills the shortcomings of commercial banks to a certain extent, and also brings competition to commercial banks and affects the profitability of commercial banks.[57] Additionally, the impact of FinTech on China's commercial banks has accelerated the trend of financial disintermediation.[58]

However, these banking-like businesses have not been incorporated into a strict and sound regulatory system, and there are unsolved challenges like liquidity risks. If the popularity and customer base of big tech groups are used to sell illegal financial products, it will cause more losses to more consumers.

[57] See S. Nie and Y. Liu, Research on the Transformation of Traditional Commercial Banks in the Background of Science and Technology Finance_Based on the Influence of Third-Party Payment (科技金融背景下传统商业银行转型问题研究_基于第三方支付的影响, translated), 2021, 4 Northern Economy and Trade, 82.

[58] 'Looking at the future development of China's commercial banks from the perspective of financial technology', available at https://baijiahao.baidu.com/s?id=1631475084026528136&wfr=spider&for=pc (accessed 26 August 2022).

4 Pros and Cons of FinTech Companies Engaging in Banking-Like Business

Positive Effect

First, FinTech companies have stronger information analysis capabilities which can reduce the risk of default. For instance, the accuracy of Latin American online marketplace MercadoLibre's internal ratings outperformed credit scores in predicting default risk. There is also evidence that BigTech Finance is most effective when traditional financial intermediaries provide insufficient service.[59] FinTech companies promote competition and diversity in the banking industry through the "catfish effect", which contributes to wealth management product innovation. Many FinTech companies have captured significant market shares in the financial market, which further intensifying competition in the retail financial services industry.[60] To avoid losing customers in the competition, banks have increased investment in financial product innovation, and improved the cost efficiency and technical level. Because of the low cost and high efficiency of FinTech, the application of new technology can reduce the operating cost of the bank. FinTech improves the utilization of financial resources and information symmetry.[61] Due to the "catfish effect", FinTech can facilitate competitive innovation and encourage banks to do better in financial intermediation, rather than replacing banks. FinTech promotes the cooperation between commercial banks and third-party payment platforms, and forces commercial banks to transform.[62] By influencing banks' pricing strategies, FinTech competition can also promote welfare redistribution, transferring more benefits from banks to depositors

[59] See A. Boot and others, 'Fintech: What's Old, What's New?' 2021, 53 Journal of Financial Stability, 100836.

[60] Ibid.

[61] See C. C. Lee and others, Does Fintech Innovation Improve Bank Efficiency? Evidence from China's Banking Industry, 2021, 74 International Review of Economics & Finance, 468.

[62] See S. Nie and Y. Liu, Research on the Transformation of Traditional Commercial Banks in the Background of Science and Technology Finance_Based on the Influence of Third-Party Payment (科技金融背景下传统商业银行转型问题研究_基于第三方支付的影响, translated), 2021, 4 Northern Economy and Trade, 82.

and borrowers. Although this reallocation may reduce the bank's profitability, FinTech also promotes commercial banks to expand intermediary business and optimize profit structure.

Second, the banking-like business of FinTech companies helps to achieve inclusive finance by providing more financing opportunities for small and micro enterprises and promotes the development of the private economy. With the popularization of big data finance, Internet finance, and blockchain technology, the application and development of FinTech can allow more people to obtain financial services at a lower cost. FinTech companies enhance the disintermediation of financial resources. It can meet the diverse financial needs of more consumers in a more convenient and efficient way. Additionally, e-money products increased access to financial services on digital platforms for people who did not have equal chances to be served by traditional banking in the past.[63]

Potential Risks

Liquidity Risk

Third-party payment systems also face liquidity risks. A large number of depositors transfer funds from savings accounts in banks to FinTech E-wallets such as Alipay and Yu'E Bao, which will no longer be protected by deposit insurance. Most FinTech E-wallet users are not fully aware of this risk. Based on their trust in Big Tech's brands, they regard Yu'E Bao as a safe alternative to bank savings.[64]

FinTech companies, such as Tencent, Alibaba, JD.com, Baidu, etc., do not have banking franchises, but they have a history of providing services to a large and stable corporate and retail customer base, which makes it easy for them to gain customer trust. However, compared to traditional banks, FinTech companies have weaker capabilities to deal with market risks or unfavorable public rumors during a crisis. Customers have lower trust in FinTech companies than in traditional banks, making FinTech companies more vulnerable to runs during a crisis.

[63] See B. Van Roosebeke and R. Defina, Five Emerging Issues in Deposit Insurance, 2021. Available at SSRN 3919974.

[64] See L. Lu, Decoding Alipay: Mobile Payments, a Cashless Society and Regulatory Challenges, 2018, Butterworths Journal of International Banking and Financial Law, 40.

Non-Performing Loan Risk

In the past, it was difficult for many small and medium-sized companies and individuals to obtain loans from banks. After Internet banking has entered the financial market, small and micro enterprises and individuals have greater opportunities to obtain loans. This has relieved the credit pressure faced by traditional banks to some extent. However, the analysis results show that the asset-liability ratio of Internet banks is high, and the risk of default increases.[65] Because FinTech companies, the parent companies of internet banks, usually only act as brokers, leaving the credit risk of the loans they provide to investors.[66]

Moreover, China has not yet established a personal insolvency system to resolve the risk of non-performing loans, and China's current regulatory policies are insufficient to supervise these FinTech companies to effectively manage non-performing loan risks. As a result, China's banks, especially Internet banks, have more prominent risks in this regard, and they should be worthier of the attention of the regulatory authorities.

Regulatory Arbitrage

As an emerging hybrid business, it is sometimes difficult for regulators to classify all FinTech services into the existing financial regulatory system, resulting in these FinTech activities not being fully and accurately covered by regulation.[67] This may lead to regulatory arbitrage. On one hand, FinTech companies may earn a lot of benefits in the legal gray area; on the other hand, under the competitive pressure of FinTech, commercial banks may also take advantage of regulatory arbitrage opportunities and take more risks.[68]

The banking-like business of FinTech companies avoids the strict supervision on commercial banks. Financial innovations can be mis-sold to consumers who do not have accurate understanding of the risks or do not have ability to take that risk. Additionally, the privacy issue of

[65] See K-C. Chen, Implications of Fintech Developments for Traditional Banks, 2020, 10 International Journal of Economics and Financial Issues, 227.

[66] See G. B. Navaretti and others, Fintech and Banking. Friends or Foes?, available at https://papers.ssrn.com/abstract=3099337 (accessed 22 July 2022).

[67] See L. Lu, Decoding Alipay: Mobile Payments, a Cashless Society and Regulatory Challenges, 2018, Butterworths Journal of International Banking and Financial Law, 40.

[68] See G. B. Navaretti and others, Fintech and Banking. Friends or Foes?, available at https://papers.ssrn.com/abstract=3099337 (accessed 22 July 2022).

new technologies is an ongoing concern.[69] Lack of effective safety net, resulting in the potential leak of personal data, and online fraud are major vulnerabilities in FinTech's business model.[70]

Oligopoly

While the banking-like business of FinTech companies can promote banking competition and diversity to a certain extent, it may also create large tech oligopolies. Big FinTech companies may use market positions to harm consumers and generate new financial stability risks.[71] For example, FinTech companies may develop into "too big to fail" in the financial market. Regulators should balance promoting competition and maintaining financial stability. In theory, a looser regulatory approach is conducive to promoting competition in financial markets. However, the risks to financial stability posed by the rapid expansion of FinTech cannot be ignored.[72]

In recent years, China has attached great importance to the legislation and enforcement of the anti-monopoly law, especially the anti-monopoly of the platform economy. The development of anti-monopoly law facilitates the regulation of FinTech oligopoly to some extent. But the platform economy is a new thing, the anti-monopoly regulation of the platform economy needs to be further studied, so the problem of FinTech oligopoly remain unsolved.

[69] See F. Restoy, Regulating Fintech: What Is Going on, and Where Are the Challenges?, 2019, Bank for International Settlements, 1.

[70] See Adebayo, S. Oyetoyan and Ajiboye Wale Thomas, Impact of Regulation of Financial Technology (FinTech) Services on The Performance of Deposit Money Banks in Nigeria.

[71] See F. Restoy, Regulating Fintech: What Is Going on, and Where Are the Challenges?, 2019, Bank for International Settlements, 1.

[72] See G. B. Navaretti and others, Fintech and Banking. Friends or Foes?, available at https://papers.ssrn.com/abstract=3099337 (accessed 22 July 2022).

5 Prudential Regulation on Banking-Like Business of FinTech Companies

The Necessity of Prudential Regulation on FinTech Companies

Current regulation of FinTech activities focuses more on consumer protection and data protection than on preventing prudential risks. One possible reason is that regulators may believe new technologies themselves will not pose a significant threat to financial stability.[73] However, the combination of deposit-taking and venture capital in the business of FinTech companies is exactly the object of prudential supervision. Banks are familiar with how to balance liquidity needs, but it is doubtful whether FinTech companies can effectively manage liquidity needs. In particular, if FinTech companies raise deposit-like funds to make illiquid loans, they are engaging in the business of banking, so they should be subject to the same regulation as banks.[74]

The more FinTech companies carry out banking-like activities, the higher their systemic importance. The rapid development of FinTech makes some FinTech giants such as Ant Financial become systemically important.[75] This means that the crisis of FinTech giants will be contagious in the wider financial market, causing systemic risks, which necessitates prudential supervision of FinTech giants.

Even if they are also engaging in deposits taking and loans issuing, FinTech companies may pose different forms of systemic risk than commercial banks. Existing prudential regulation such as current capital or liquidity requirements may not be able to adequately control these risks. Cybersecurity, for example, could be a new risk for the operation

[73] See F. Restoy, Regulating Fintech: What Is Going on, and Where Are the Challenges?, 2019, Bank for International Settlements, 1.

[74] See G. B. Navaretti and others, Fintech and Banking. Friends or Foes?, available at https://papers.ssrn.com/abstract=3099337 (accessed 22 July 2022).

[75] See L. Lu, How a little ant challenges giant banks? The rise of Ant Financial (Alipay)'s FinTech empire and relevant regulatory concerns, 2018, International Company and Commercial Law Review, Sweet & Maxwell, available at https://papers.ssrn.com/abstract=3052318 (accessed 22 July 2022).

of digital financial products and for financial stability in general.[76] Significant cyber incidents may become new sources of systemic risk, which will need to be addressed through new regulatory approaches.[77]

Regulatory authorities are making progress in improving understanding of FinTech and addressing potential related prudential risks, but there are still several concerns: (i) Regulation of cloud computing service providers (corruption or service interruption may cause systemic risk); (ii) the level of capital and liquidity of FinTech companies; and (iii) how to resolve FinTech companies that are failing or likely to fail.[78]

China's Current Regulatory Approach to FinTech Companies' Banking-Like Business

Since 2015, the People's Bank of China and relevant Chinese authorities have issued *Guiding Opinions on Promoting the Healthy Development of Internet Finance* and *FinTech Development Plans*. These policy documents aim to guide the compliant and sustainable development of FinTech, clarify the requirements for risk prevention, and strengthening supervision. From 2020 to 2021, China's banking regulator, the China Banking and Insurance Regulatory Commission, and the central bank, issued the *Interim Measures for the Administration of Internet Loans in Commercial Banks, Interim Measures for the Administration of Online Micro-loan Business (Draft for Comment)*, and *Notice on Regulating the Issues Concerning the Regulation of Commercial Banks to Carry out Personal Deposit Business through the Internet*.[79]

The regulatory responses to the risk brought by FinTech giants include restrictions on the amount of Ant Financial users' investment or withdrawal per day, and the limitation on the deposit of WeBank and

[76] See B. Van Roosebeke and R. Defina, Five Emerging Issues in Deposit Insurance, 2021. Available at SSRN 3919974.

[77] See F. Restoy, Regulating Fintech: What Is Going on, and Where Are the Challenges?, 2019, Bank for International Settlements, 1.

[78] See C. Taylor, 'Prudential Regulatory and Supervisory Practices for Fintech: Payments, Credit and Deposits', available at https://policycommons.net/artifacts/1265971/prudential-regulatory-and-supervisory-practices-for-fintech/1843204/ (accessed 22 July 2022).

[79] See M. Cheng and Y. Qu, Does Bank FinTech Reduce Credit Risk? Evidence from China, 2020, 63 Pacific-Basin Finance Journal, 101398.

MYbank.[80] From 2017 to 2019, the central bank gradually stipulated that 100% of the reserves of third-party payment platforms should be centrally deposited with the People's Bank of China, and payment of interest will be canceled. For customers, such a series of measures reduces the risk of capital loss, but for third-party payment institutions, the platform completely loses the income from sedimentary money which seriously decrease the profitability of the entire industry. However, for Alipay and Tenpay, the industry duopoly, they have already developed a variety of profit models, and the overall profits will not be greatly affected.[81] Regulations stipulate that "the amount of funds raised by the company in the form of standardized securities assets shall not exceed 4 times its net assets",[82] which directly limits the financing ability of Ant Financial, which is known for its high-leverage operation.

In recent years, some small and medium-sized banks have absorbed deposits through Internet platforms, and the scale of deposits has grown rapidly. This phenomenon has attracted the attention of the regulators. Chinese regulators are sending a clear signal: If technology companies are doing banking business, they must follow the same rules as banks. From December 2020, according to the requirements for the Internet deposit industry, Alipay, Tencent Wealth Management, Duxiaoman Finance, JD Finance, Didi Finance, and other platforms have removed Internet deposit products. Users who have purchased the product are not affected.

Although China has some regulations on FinTech, the current prudential supervision of FinTech in China is still not sound enough. China's previous separate regulatory system has the boundaries of different industries, these new financial activities fall into the regulatory gap, resulting

[80] China Daily, Transformation Under the Supervision of Alipay and Tenpay: Emphasis on "Technology" and Light on "Finance" (支付宝和财付通们监管下的转型: 重 "科技" 轻 "金融", translated), 2019, 28 China Daily, 5.

[81] See L. Jiao, Research on the Profit Model of My Country's Third-Party Payment Platform——Taking Tenpay as an Example (我国第三方支付平台盈利模式研究——以财付通为例, translated), 2019.

[82] 'Interim Measures for the Administration of Online Micro-Loan Business (Draft for Comment)', available at http://www.gov.cn/xinwen/2020-11/03/content_5556884.htm (accessed 5 September 2022).

in the failure of regulators to incorporate them into the regulatory framework in a timely manner. This leads to inefficient regulation and many risks. Therefore, improving the legislation is a top priority.[83]

Improving Prudential Regulation of FinTech Companies' Banking-Like Business

Macroprudential policy focuses on the stability of the entire financial system. To address potential systemic risks from FinTech companies, regulators may conduct appropriate macroprudential regulation.

Regulatory Sandbox and Authorization

First, as innovative products, FinTech services can first be tested in the regulatory sandbox. Regulatory sandbox is a temporary relaxed regulatory environment in which companies can test new products, services, or business models and delivery mechanisms,[84] without serious repercussions on financial markets and without overhauls of the current regulatory system. The regulatory sandbox was first adopted by the UK, which is seen as the most FinTech-friendly jurisdiction in the world.[85] The regulatory sandbox appears to be beneficial for FinTechs, financial regulators, and consumers, and it saves time and effort to implement.

If the new products of FinTech companies can enter the normal financial market, regulators need to have a strict authorization system. For example, the European Central Bank requires FinTech banks to apply for the license of any bank within a single regulatory mechanism, ensuring that FinTech banks are licensed to operate and control risks.[86] In the past, China's FinTech industry had low barriers to entry. Most FinTech companies engage in traditional and even illegal financial activities under

[83] See M. Cheng and Y. Qu, Does Bank FinTech Reduce Credit Risk? Evidence from China, 2020, 63 Pacific-Basin Finance Journal, 101398.

[84] See G. B. Navaretti and others, Fintech and Banking. Friends or Foes?, available at https://papers.ssrn.com/abstract=3099337 (accessed 22 July 2022).

[85] See L. Lu, How a Little Ant Challenges Giant Banks? The Rise of Ant Financial (Alipay)'s FinTech Empire and Relevant Regulatory Concerns, 2018, International Company and Commercial Law Review, Sweet & Maxwell, available at https://papers.ssrn.com/abstract=3052318 (accessed 22 July 2022).

[86] See G. B. Navaretti and others, Fintech and Banking. Friends or Foes?, available at https://papers.ssrn.com/abstract=3099337 (accessed 22 July 2022).

the banner of financial innovation, they did not have long-term risk planning. Therefore, once it experienced liquidity risk, it would be difficult to effectively solve the problem, resulting in bankruptcy of the enterprise, bringing greater risks to consumers or investors. Therefore, Chinese regulators need to raise the threshold of FinTech market. In addition, the FinTech market also needs to have a sound exit mechanism, formulate contingency plans, effectively resolve failing FinTech companies, and minimize the negative impact on the financial market.[87]

Preventing Liquidity Risk

In response to the liquidity risk of FinTech platforms, regulator could limit the upper limit of funds that depositors can hold on third-party payment platforms. For instance, China Banking and Insurance Regulatory Commission lowered the maximum amount each depositor can hold in a Yu'E bao account, from 1 million yuan ($1,439,926) to 100,000 yuan ($14,399). In addition, central banks and financial regulators can require FinTech platforms to establish reserve funds to compensate customers for losses in emergencies and to deal with liquidity risks.[88] Moreover, the FinTech platform should announce the status of the reserve fund to investors to reduce information asymmetry. Because the more confident investors are in the solvency of FinTech platforms, the less likely a run will occur.

Reducing Regulatory Arbitrage

To reduce regulatory arbitrage, regulators should first include the banking-like activities of FinTech companies within the scope of supervision. Second, Financial regulators should level the playing field and avoid regulatory arbitrage that could lead to serious financial instability.[89] Both engaged in financial services, the banking-like activities of FinTech

[87] See H. Huang, FinTech's Extraterritorial Governance Experience and Its Enlightenment to My Country (金融科技域外治理经验及对我国的启示, tranlated), 2021, 40 Enterprise Economy, 153.

[88] See L. Lu, How a Little Ant Challenges Giant Banks? The Rise of Ant Financial (Alipay)'s FinTech Empire and Relevant Regulatory Concerns, 2018, International Company and Commercial Law Review, Sweet & Maxwell, available at https://papers.ssrn.com/abstract=3052318 (accessed 22 July 2022).

[89] See G. B. Navaretti and others, Fintech and Banking. Friends or Foes?, available at https://papers.ssrn.com/abstract=3099337 (accessed 22 July 2022).

companies are subject to more relaxed supervision, but banks are subject to many restrictions. This creates both unfair competition and risks for financial markets. Effective regulation should prevent risky businesses from seeking more benefits from looser regulation.

Financial regulators should adopt activity-based regulation. Although FinTech companies are not registered as financial institutions, they should be regulated to the same standards as financial institutions based on their financial services activities. However, the execution of the same activity by different entities (banks and non-banks, small FinTech firm, and large FinTech firm) may create different risks, so activity-based regulation should be viewed as a complement to entity-based regulation rather than alternative. Because the systemic risk from large FinTech firm not only comes from the size of their business, but also from the interplay between the risks generated by each activity. Hence the a need for a more holistic approach to regulation that simultaneously focuses on entities, activities, and the wider ecosystem.[90]

Applying RegTech in FinTech Regulation

China was relatively tolerant of FinTech development before 2015, after a few years, FinTech companies have grown from "too small to care" to "too big to fail".[91] It created new concepts such as data sovereignty and algorithm supervision, so the sustainable development of FinTech requires the application of regulatory technology.[92]

Regulatory technology (RegTech) is defined as the application of FinTech in regulation, which can help banks reduce compliance costs, improve internal risk management efficiency, and achieve regulatory goals such as consumer protection or anti-money laundering.[93] RegTech has near real-time data functions, automated advanced algorithm processes, and other AI technologies, making supervision capabilities more comprehensive and fast, so RegTech is more suitable for regulating FinTech

[90] See F. Restoy, Regulating Fintech: What Is Going on, and Where Are the Challenges?, 2019, Bank for International Settlements, 1.

[91] See D. W. Arner, J. Barberis and R. P. Buckey, FinTech, RegTech, and the Reconceptualization of Financial Regulation, 2017, 37 Northwestern Journal of International Law & Business, 371.

[92] Ibid.

[93] See G. B. Navaretti and others, Fintech and Banking. Friends or Foes?, available at https://papers.ssrn.com/abstract=3099337 (accessed 22 July 2022).

innovation than traditional regulatory methods. It can also help regulators to better enforce prudential regulatory behavior[94] and Strengthen monitoring of emerging risks.[95] China should adopt more RegTech in the regulation of FinTech companies, and innovate regulatory tools to strengthen systemic financial risks prevention. For example, applying big data, cloud computing, AI, and other technologies to regulatory tools to supervise the risks of FinTech companies in real time. Key applications are in areas prone to systemic risks, such as anti-money laundering and regulatory arbitrage. At the same time, given the limited technical capabilities of financial regulators, it is possible to rapidly improve the RegTech level of financial regulators by cooperating with technology companies in the early stage. In addition, FinTech can also be used to improve regulatory efficiency. For example, using the smart contract function of the blockchain to set up a warning line for violations of FinTech companies. That is, as long as the FinTech performs certain violations, the system can automatically monitor and record them.[96] Similarly, when a risk indicator is detected to reach a certain level, a regulatory action is automatically triggered by the smart contract of RegTech. In this way, risks can be detected in a timely manner, and cover-up behavior in supervision could be significantly avoided.

Timing is particularly important in the prudential regulation of FinTech. A FinTech crisis can cause a bank run and undermine the banking market, which can happen within hours or even minutes. For example, the May 6 flash crash in the United States in 2010 exhausted market liquidity within 20 minutes, causing panic in the US financial market. Regulators should first intervene early with real-time risk alerts of supervisory technology (Suptech) similar to RegTech.[97] Handling the data flows and more difficult analytical needs from regulated firms in

[94] See I. Anagnostopoulos, Fintech and Regtech: Impact on Regulators and Banks, 2018, 100 Journal of Economics and Business, 7.

[95] Ibid.

[96] See H. Huang, FinTech's Extraterritorial Governance Experience and Its Enlightenment to My Country (金融科技域外治理经验及对我国的启示, tranlated), 2021, 40 Enterprise Economy, 153.

[97] See B. Van Roosebeke and R. Defina, Five Emerging Issues in Deposit Insurance, 2021. Available at SSRN 3919974.

normal times more efficiently.[98] In crisis management, the Prudential supervisory disclosure model can be used to effectively protect banks from runs caused by the impact of FinTech crises.[99] Both FinTech and RegTech are data-centric, which represents a shift from a Know-Your-Customers approach to Know-Your-Data objective, which is still underdeveloped. Although the application of RegTech is still in its early stages, it has great potential for RegTech in the area of macroprudential policy in the future.[100]

In addition, it is necessary to prevent local banks from absorbing deposits from the whole country through Internet financial platforms, which violates the geographical restrictions on the operation of local banks. It may lead to unclear division of regional regulatory responsibilities and lag in supervision. Regulators should also scrutinize the compliance of wealth management products that banks sell through FinTech companies' internet platforms. Banks may use the branding of FinTech companies to gain customer trust and gain more retail customers. These products often have high interest and high risk, and may even imply illegal factors. In the event of a serious product crisis, FinTech companies do not take responsibility, making it difficult for investors to defend their rights, and FinTech companies encountering a reputational crisis, which may further lead to a run on the bank or FinTech companies.

Supervision of FinTech companies should try to strike a balance between protecting the industry's innovation motivation and financial stability goals. It should equip prudential supervision tools and mechanisms to quickly respond to systemic risks.[101] For example, to prohibit speculation in the name of FinTech innovation. However, over-regulation of the FinTech industry may stifle the motivation of innovation. In this

[98] See C. Taylor, 'Prudential Regulatory and Supervisory Practices for Fintech: Payments, Credit and Deposits', available at https://policycommons.net/artifacts/1265971/prudential-regulatory-and-supervisory-practices-for-fintech/1843204/ (accessed 22 July 2022).

[99] See S. Zeranski and I. E. Sancak, Prudential Supervisory Disclosure (PSD) with Supervisory Technology (SupTech): Lessons from a FinTech Crisis, 2021, 18 International Journal of Disclosure and Governance, 315.

[100] See D. W. Arner, J. Barberis and R. P. Buckey, FinTech, RegTech, and the Reconceptualization of Financial Regulation, 2017, 37 Northwestern Journal of International Law & Business, 371.

[101] See F. Restoy, Regulating Fintech: What Is Going on, and Where Are the Challenges?, 2019, Bank for International Settlements, 1.

regard, a FinTech risk red line can be created. For instance, it should prohibit illegal fundraising in the name of financial innovation.[102]

Enhancing Regulatory Cooperation

In the context of China's expanded financial opening, Chinese regulators should collaborate and share experiences with other jurisdictions, especially in areas such as cybersecurity and monitoring macro-financial risks. This will reduce divergence between new regulatory frameworks and reduce the possibility of cross-border regulatory arbitrage. Regulatory cooperation can also help reduce the negative impact of risk cross-border contagion.

6 Conclusion

This article discusses the impact of FinTech companies engaged in banking-like business on the financial market. There is a relationship of cooperation and competition between FinTech and commercial banks, which has a positive impact on the financial market but also brings potential prudential risks. Because these FinTech giants, while engaged in banking-like businesses and already systemically important, are not as tightly regulated as commercial banks.

This paper suggests that the prudential supervision of FinTech's banking-like businesses can be improved in terms of regulatory sandboxes, authorization and exit mechanisms, liquidity risk, regulatory arbitrage, and RegTech. For example, the smart contract function of the blockchain can be used to detect risks in time and avoid concealment in supervision. In particular, regulators should prevent local banks from exploiting the brand of FinTech companies to acquire more retail clients and taking deposits across the country, which may lead to regulation difficulty and run on bank or FinTech companies. Regulators need to be equipped with prudential tools to respond quickly to systemic risks, also pay attention to the balance between protecting the industry's motivation to innovate and financial stability goals, and cooperate with foreign regulators.

[102] See H. Huang, FinTech's Extraterritorial Governance Experience and Its Enlightenment to My Country (金融科技域外治理经验及对我国的启示, tranlated), 2021, 40 Enterprise Economy, 153.

CHAPTER 19

Recent Changes and Prospects of Banking Services Regulations and Supervision in Korea

Sung-Seung Yun and GiJin Yang

1 Introduction

Recently, banking business environment has been rapidly changing in Korea. Especially, FinTech innovations as well as the Covid-19 pandemic and the UN SDGs have made a huge impact on banking business strategies and supervision in Korea.

Sung-Seung Yun: Author of Sects. 3 and 4 of this chapter.

GiJin Yang: Author of Sect. 2 of this chapter.

S.-S. Yun (✉)
Ajou University School of Law, Suwon, South Korea
e-mail: ssyun@ajou.ac.kr

M. Bodellini et al. (eds.), *Commercial Banking in Transition*, Palgrave Macmillan Studies in Banking and Financial Institutions,
https://doi.org/10.1007/978-3-031-45289-5_19

These days, digital innovation is rapidly progressing in all directions promoting FinTech business. The Financial Stability Board's working definition for FinTech is "technologically enabled financial innovation that could result in new business models, applications, processes, or products with an associated material effect on financial markets and institutions and the provision of financial services".[1] According to the BCBS survey of its members in 2017, the highest number of FinTech service providers are in the payments, clearing and settlement category (retail or wholesale), followed by credit, deposit, and capital-raising services.[2] This indicates that FinTech is replacing the substantial part of traditional commercial banking services and raises questions about the future of commercial banking. With a high level of financial accessibility and well-developed digital payment systems, Korea experiences advanced financial inclusion and efficiency of payment services.[3] The transition to digitalized finance is progressing smoothly as well in Korea, with a high smartphone penetration rate (95%) and a steady increase in the number of both internet and mobile banking users.[4]

Since the beginning of the Covid-19 pandemic, the banking industries in Korea have rapidly adapted their operations in response to the pandemic. They increased transactions through digitalized services on the online or cellphone. Banks have confronted huge non-performing loan possibility of SMEs, whose businesses are suspended or restricted by the government, and the government intervened to support them by arranging the pandemic emergency financing and debt relief measures.

G. Yang
Jeonbuk National University School of Law, Jeonju, South Korea
e-mail: gjyang@jbnu.ac.kr

[1] FSB, Financial Stability Implications from FinTech, Supervisory and Regulatory Issues that Merit Authorities' Attention (27 June 2017), at 7.

[2] BIS, Sound Practices: implications of fintech developments for banks and bank supervisors (19 Feb. 2018), at 9–10, available at https://www.bis.org/bcbs/publ/d431.htm.

[3] The account ownership in Korea currently stands at 95%, and Korea has a sophisticated fast payment system as it launched in 2001. J. Bae, The Bank of Korea's CBDC Research: Current Status and Key Considerations, BIS Papers No. 123 (14 April 2022), at 107–108, available at https://www.bis.org/publ/bppdf/bispap123.htm.

[4] Ibid.

How to deal with these potential non-performing loans are a very critical current issue because we are still in the Covid-19 pandemic and the business recovery is quite slow.

The SDGs are also impacting banking and financial industry in Korea. The ESG guidance and regulation changing plans by the Korean financial supervisory authority (Financial Supervisory Commission) make banks to consider ESG issues in their businesses as well as financial services.

2 FinTech Innovations and the Changes of Banking Business and Supervision in Korea

BigTechs in Korea Competing with Commercial Banks

Many large technology firms (BigTechs) are on the rapid rise in the business. Like the GAFA in the Western world and the BAT (Baidu, Alibaba, and Tencent) in China, there are also some BigTechs in Korea, such as Kakao, Naver, and Toss (Viva Republica). These BigTechs are arousing considerable challenges to banks in Korea, thereby causing Korean banks inevitably to respond to them.

Once these Korean BigTechs started from small IT firms, now they have grown up so quickly that they are building mutual cooperation or competing with existing banks. As the Basel Committee on Banking Supervision (BCBS) suggested five scenarios[5] with respect to future relationships between banks and BigTechs, Korean incumbent banks are on the way to change, for instance, by digitizing and modernizing themselves to retain the customer relationship, yet leaving a lot of possibilities that such relationship will change as well.

One of the characteristics of Korean BigTechs is that they are seeking growth as comprehensive financial platforms through SNS services, search services, and/or simple payment/remittance services. First of all, Naver Group, one of the Korea's BigTechs, is a conglomerate consisting of one listed company and 53 unlisted companies (as of the end of Dec. 2022).[6]

[5] For the five scenarios of future banks' roles by the BCBS, *see* BIS, *supra* note 2, at 16.

[6] Naver Q4 2022 Business Report disclosed in the Korean Dart disclosure system.

It is a mammoth group with a large market capitalization ($26.1[7] billion, as of end of 2022), which greatly exceeds that of the KB Financial Group ($17.0 billion, as of the end of Dec. 2022), the largest financial group in Korea. At the end of 2022, Naver Group spun off its payment service platform (Naver Pay) which provided the simple payment service, and established it as a subsidiary (Naver Financial) and registered it as the electronic financial business with the Korean financial supervisory authority, the FSC (Financial Services Commission). As an electronic financial transaction company under the Korean Electronic Financial Transactions Act (EFTA), Naver Financial provides such limited service as loan, insurance brokerage, and financial investment in cooperation with other financial companies without obtaining a financial business license.

Meanwhile, Kakao Group, another well-known Korean BigTech, with a market capitalization of $17.6 billion (as of the end of Dec. 2022) has affiliates of five listed companies and 170 unlisted companies (as of the end of Dec. 2022).[8] In order to enter the traditional financial industry, Kakao Group has launched a non-life insurance company (Kakao Pay Insurance) as well as a securities company (Kakao Pay Securities), through which it is expanding its businesses to the financial services of securities and insurance, too.

Toss (Viva Republica) group is a relatively newborn platform BigTech established as a FinTech start-up in August 2013. Like other BigTechs, Toss group has grown significantly as its simple remittance service (Toss) has gained its popularity in Korea making its corporate value of $6.6 billion (as of July 2022). Toss group's main source of income is commission gained from Toss Payments' electronic payment and settlement service, and commission from advertising and brokering various financial products by Toss Securities and Toss Insurance (Fig. 1).

Changes of the Legal Framework for Data Protection

Recently, financial institutions such as banks and credit card companies, and non-financial companies such as BigTechs, have been introducing more convenient such digital services as simple payment services and

[7] In Sect. 2, see the Korean Exchange (KRX) data for market capital data for Naver, Kakao and KB financial group, and the preseneted market capital was calculated on the won-dollar exchange rate of 1,274.6 which was so as of the end of 2022.

[8] Kakao Q4 2022 Business Report disclosed in the Korean Dart disclosure system.

	Payments		Banking		Securities		Insurance		MyData	
License Held	L	P	L	P	L	P	L	P	L	P
kakao	√		√1		√		√2		√	
NAVER	√			√		√	-		√	
toss	√		√1		√		√3		√	

Fig. 1 Korean BigTechs' operations in financial services (L = BigTech has entity within group that holds financial license in respective sector. P = market presence in particular or joint venture with other financial institutions. √1: License of bank (Internet-only bank).[9] √2: License of non-life insurance company. √3: License of insurance brokerage agency.—: License withdrawn in March 2023)

simple remittance services. In particular, the new open banking service launched in Korea in April 2021 is facilitating competition among banks and FinTechs/BigTechs over payment and remittance services. With the introduction of the open banking, the participating FinTech/BigTech companies can access all financial companies without a separate partnership with existing banks for transfer and remittance; and costs to provide payment service by FinTechs/BigTechs have been greatly reduced. Open banking service is active in Korea and it is causing more intensive competition between banks and FinTechs/BigTechs as well as between banks because it makes easier for users to change their main financial platform from one to another.[10]

Another recent change in the financial business environment that has been fortifying competition between banks and BigTechs is the introduction of the MyData business. Under the current revised Credit

[9] The Act on Special Cases concerning Establishment and Operation of Internet-only Banks enacted on 19 May 2020 in Korea allows BigTechs in Korea to operate banking business in the presence of their major shareholders thereby trimming existing legal barriers for launching of internet-only banks.

[10] As of November 2021, approximately 20 million transactions worth KRW 1 trillion are processed through Open Banking every day. Not only 19 banks but also 19 financial investment companies, 8 credit card companies and 68 small and large fintechs are participating in the open banking system. Financial Services Commission, Digital Financial Innovation Achieved in 2 Years of Open Banking—2 Years of Full Implementation of Open Banking, Exceeded 30 Million Net Subscribers, Press Release (21 Dec. 2021).

Information Use and Protection Act (CIP Act) which came into be effective in August 2020, one who gets permission of MyData business from the FSC is allowed to collect personal information (data) from individuals and to transmit it to another participating company, thereby facilitating exchange of personal information across the financial industry and FinTechs/BigTechs.

Recent Responses of Commercial Banks in Korea

In order to respond to the business threat incurred by BigTechs and to attract and/or maintain customers, Korean commercial banks are also taking advantage of digital technology to create their own mobile banking apps and mobile platforms. KB Kookmin Bank, the largest commercial bank (based on total assets) in Korea, launched its consolidated banking app, i.e., KB Star Banking service in October 2021 and included the services of its financial affiliates in that app which uses the in-app browser method. Shinhan Bank, another Korean large commercial bank, launched a non-financial product delivery platform which has the characteristics of a non-financial platform in January 2022 and is selling its credit loan products and savings products to individual business store owners who have logged in its delivery app.

In addition, Shinhan Bank is building its own Metaverse platform where its beta service began in March 2022. It prepares to provide services to its customers in a virtual space by expanding and connecting the Metaverse platform both to financial and non-financial areas. Shinhan Bank's Metaverse platform provides users with a variety of virtual financial contents and aims to become a comprehensive service platform which provides various services by collaborating with non-financial partners, such as convenience stores and art-pieces trading platforms.

Ongoing Debates Surrounding Introduction of Pseudo-Banking Business

The FSC is in the process of revising the EFTA. The EFTA bill backed by the FSC tries to reorganize the existing license system for electronic financial business providers[11] as well as the introduction of a comprehensive payment and settlement business (CPS business).

However, the EFTA bill is controversial, in that it introduces the CPS business as the CPS service providers are likely to operate in a pseudo-banking way. Compared to the Electronic Money Institution (EMI) in the UK or the EU, the CPS service providers will be likely to play a role overlapping to a considerable extent with the role of traditional banks; the CPS service providers can independently open their own accounts to their customers without affiliation with banks, participate directly in financial settlement networks, and provide small credit loans. Concerns are being raised about this kind of significant benefit as CPS service providers will be highly likely to enjoy regulatory arbitrage compared to traditional banks.[12]

On the other hand, the US is strict to allow FinTech companies to act like banks. For instance, the Special Purpose National Bank (SPNB) license system by the OCC in the US allows FinTech companies to conduct banking business only with acquiring national banking license for the SPNB.[13]

[11] The EFTA bill introduces consolidated business categories such as payment instruction delivery business (so-called MyPayment business), payment agency business and payment business, and money transfer business, thereby replacing the current seven categories of businesses.

[12] As for the regulatory arbitrage that will be enjoyed by CPS providers conducting banking business in reality, see G. Yang, Some Legal Issues on Introduction of Comprehensive Payment and Settlement Business under Revised Bill on Korean Electronic Financial Transactions Act, Journal of Law and Business Research vol. 11, no. 2, Seoul, Sogang University Law Institute, 2021.

[13] See OCC, Comptroller's Licensing Manual Supplement: Considering Charter Applications From Financial Technology Companies (July 2018), available at https://www.occ.gov/publications-and-resources/publications/comptrollers-licensing-manual/files/considering-charter-apps-from-fin-tech-companies.html.

Issues to Be Discussed More in the Future

As BigTechs continue to gain prominence in the financial system, additional policy responses could be necessary to comprehensively address risks incurred by them. In order to maintain BigTechs' stability and resilience, efforts are underway for paradigm shift of the regulation approach for BigTech groups.[14] As overall regulation has been long enforced for the financial holding companies (FHC) group in Korea, FHCs are supervised as a whole under the Financial Holding Companies Act. In addition, for the efficient supervision of large non-FHC financial conglomerates in Korea, the Act on the Supervision of Financial Conglomerates (SFCA) was recently introduced.[15] The SFCA aims entity-based supervision on non-FHC financial conglomerates with more than a certain size (KRW 2 trillion or about $1.53 billion in assets) that have financial companies as affiliates. According to the SFCA, those large non-FHC corporate groups are indicated as "financial conglomerate groups" and they are subject to a duty to designate a representative financial company,[16] a duty to carry out group-wide risk management and insider transaction management, and a duty to disclose transparently important matters that financial consumers need to know and to report those matters to the FSC. Currently, seven Korean large corporate groups (Samsung, Hanwha, Mirae Asset, Kyobo, Hyundai Motor, DB, and DaouKiwoom) have been designated as financial conglomerates under the SFCA in 2022, but Kakao Group and Naver Group which are large enough and already engaged in financial businesses have not been designated as financial conglomerates yet as of 2022.[17]

Secondly, lots of virtual assets including crypto-assets are being actively traded in Korea. However, they have not been appropriately regulated from the point of investor/consumer protection. The current Act on Reporting and Using Specified Financial Transaction Information (RUSFTIA) which came into effect on March 25, 2021 mainly aims to address anti-money laundering issues by forcing real-name verification to

[14] See J. C. Crisanto, et al., Bigtech Regulation: What Is Going On?, FSI Insights on Policy Implementation No. 36, Financial Stability Institute, BIS (Sept. 2021) 2–6.

[15] The SFCA was enacted on 29 Dec. 29, 2020 and effective on 30 June 2021.

[16] A representative financial company is selected in consideration of the investment relationship of the affiliated financial company, total assets and capital, etc.

[17] This can be a blind spot of the current SFCA.

virtual assets traders. The RUSFTIA is far from being enough although it imposes some entry barriers and basic business conduct regulations on the virtual asset service providers. Therefore, the Korean National Assembly worked for fully-edged legislation of virtual asset transactions and it has enacted the Virtual Asset User Protection Act (VAUPA) on June 30, 2023, which includes the protection of users in the virtual asset market and regulation of unfair trade practices and this Act will take effect in July 2024. In the process of enacting VAUPA, the EU Markets in Crypto-assets (MiCA) gave many implications on it, which addresses the issue of narrowing the regulatory gap with other financial products and protecting users (consumers).

The third issue is a traditionally controversial one that is about the challenge to the separation policy of banking and commerce.[18] Although BigTechs are now gradually penetrating the financial industry, typical financial companies like banks are unable to engage in non-financial businesses due to the long-lasting Korean policy of banking and commerce separation. Therefore, the argument that the business environment of BigTechs is relatively advantageous in terms of regulation, the so-called "unlevel playing field" between financial companies and BigTechs, has recently gained strength in Korea.

Lastly, the Korean central bank, the Bank of Korea (BOK), is in the process of developing Central Bank Digital Currency (CBDC) and this development is expected to affect future digital payment in many aspects in Korea. As recent innovation in the payment and settlement sector has been accelerating movement onto CBDC, in August 2021, the BOK has advanced its CBDC project into a stage of kicking-off a pilot testing. CBDC is expected to play a role in introducing a virtuous cycle of competition and service improvement and, as an open platform, it may be expected to be able to help lessen BigTechs' exercise of their market power such as imposition of excessive fees or creation of barriers to entry, etc.[19]

[18] Korea's policy of separation of banking and commerce has been enforced since 1995. This policy has been enforced in Korea not by a single law but by several laws such as Fair Trade Act, Banking Act, and Financial Holding Company Act.

[19] See Bae, *supra* note 3, at 111.

3 Pandemic Emergency Financing and Debt Relief in Korea and the Implication on Banking Industry[20]

Pandemic Emergency Financing and Debt Relief in Korea

The Need of Moratorium or Debt Relief in Korea

If there is no special agreement between the parties regarding force majeure in the loan agreement, especially consumer loan or mortgage-based real estate loans, Korean Civil Code relevant provisions will be applied to the non-performing loans. Since, under the Korean Civil Code,[21] force majeure or non-negligence cannot be used as a defense in the default of monetary debt without any special agreement between the parties, there is a need of moratorium or suspension of interest and repayment under the extreme financial crisis like a pandemic.[22]

Even Pandemics cannot be an excuse for the non-performance. For the reason, if the Covid-19 pandemic makes it very difficult for the debtor to pay back the principal or interest on time, alternative solutions need to use

[20] This part was modified and revised from the article, Sung-Seung Yun, *COVID-19 Impact on Financial Contracts and Pandemic Emergency Financing and Debt Relief*, Korean Journal of Financial Law vol. 18 no. 2 (2021).

[21] Loan agreement under Civil Code is as follows:
Article 397 (Special Rules as to Non-performance of Monetary Debt)

(1) The amount of damages for non-performance of a monetary debt shall be determined by the legal rate of interest: Provided, that in a case where there exists an agreed rate of interest which does not exceed the limitation provided by Acts and subordinate decrees, that agreed rate of interest shall prevail.

(2) With regard to the damages mentioned in the preceding paragraph, the obligee is not bound to prove the actual damages nor can the obligor assert the absence of negligence as a defense.

[22] During the Covid-19 pandemic, force majeure issues is reexamined because traditional force majeure clause has not included pandemic as an example of force majeure event. However, from the experience of the Covid-19, there is need to specify pandemic as a force majeure even to prepare any future huge pandemic situation like the Covid-19. Since the courts are very stringent to allow force majeure defense to excuse the obligation, definition of the force majeure to include pandemic in the international financial contract will be a better contractual solution to the parties to prepare the disputes of failure of performance in any current and future pandemics considering the uncertainty of court's decision in any jurisdiction.

to aid the financially distressed debtors as well as to protect the financial system.

To protect the financial system, during the emergency such as an economic turmoil caused by the worldwide pandemic, it may need a moratorium and/or suspension of interest or loan repayment by the government to resolve the emergency situation. Instead of a moratorium, the government can give debt relief measures. The government can supply the pandemic emergency financing or debt relief such as modification of loans.

Korean Government Debt Relief Measures During the Covid-19 Pandemic

a. Disaster Emergency Payment

The disaster emergency payment is a kind of grant that the government provides money to the emergency situation like a pandemic or natural disaster without repayment obligation. It is similar to a stimulus check in the US during the Covid-19 pandemic. The Korean government has provided disaster emergency payments 3 times up until now.

As the 1st Disaster Emergency Payment, a total of KRW 14.2 trillion (USD 13 billion) was paid to all the households nationwide, up to about USD 900 per household depending on the number of household members in May 2020.[23]

As the 2nd Disaster Emergency Payment, a total KRW 2.8 trillion was paid by the end of November, 2020 to the impacted business and vulnerable group only.[24] Any small business owners with annual sales of less than KRW 400 million, whose sales declined due to the spread of the Covid-19, were provided with KRW 1 million.[25] If such business owners in restricted businesses by the social distance order, KRW 1.5 million were provided. If such owners in prohibited businesses, KRW 2 million was provided.[26] It was a direct cash-based support and can be applied online

[23] See J. Kim, Disaster Emergency Payment and its Economic Effect and Future Tasks, Current Issue Analysis vol. 182, NAR, Dec. 30. 2020.

[24] Ibid.

[25] Korea Policy Briefing, Economic Measures to Covid-19, Jan. 6, 2021, https://www.korea.kr/special/policyCurationView.do?newsId=148872965.

[26] Korea Policy Briefing, *supra* note 25.

without submitting any supporting documents and the payment started from Sep. 25, 2020.[27]

As the 3rd Disaster Emergency Payment, KRW 9.3 trillion targeting approximately 5.8 million people, including small business owners, self-employed people, and the underprivileged was paid in January 2021.[28] For each small business owner, it was paid about USD 900 payment for loss of business revenue in general, and about an additional USD 1800 for the Suspension of the Shop Order or USD 900 for the Limit of Opening Shop Order.

b. Extension of Loan Repayment Schedule

As an extension of loan repayment program, the loan maturity to small businesses was extended at least 6 months from April, 2020. A deferment of interest payment for 6 months was supposed to be allowed from the time of application for the interest which interest payment due date was reached by Sep. 30, 2020. These extensions of loan repayment schedule were introduced as a temporary emergency measure which would last only for 6 months. However, such extension of loan repayment and interest payment has been renewed 4 times until Sep. 30, 2022 since the pandemic situation is still going on in Korea.[29] The National Assembly and the government are considering extending it for additional 6 months after Sep. 30, 2022. The total amount of principal and interest that the repayment was extended from Apr. 2020 to Jan. 2022 is about $224 billion and the balance of deferred loans as of Jan. 31, 2022 is still about $86 billion.[30]

The FSC announced that there is no discussion or review of the government's "expanding loan maturity extension and interest repayment deferral programs from current SME loans to household loans".[31]

[27] Ibid.

[28] Kim, *supra* note 23.

[29] The Hankyoreh, COVID Financing Loan 'Soft Landing' for 1 Year... Only 7% Started Repaying, March 15, 2022, https://www.hankyung.com/economy/article/2022030702541.

[30] FSC, *Extension of Maturity and Repayment Deferment by 6 Months in the Financial Sector*, Press Release, Mar. 23, 2022.

[31] Covid-19 Economic Support-Emergency Economic Meeting, *Plans to Expand the Loan Maturity Extension and Interest Repayment Deferral Program from the Current*

c. Low-Interest Emergency Financing to Small Business Owners

Low-interest emergency financing was given to the small business owners impacted by the Covid-19 pandemic. As the First Emergency Loan Program for small businesses (SB), the Small Business Emergency Loan of KRW 10 million is for low-credit small business owners with a credit rating of 4 or lower. The loan period is 5 years (2 years deferred and 3 years repayment) with the interest rate 1.5%.[32]

As the Second Emergency Loan Program, total KRW 10 trillion, was provided starting on May 18, 2020 for small business owners[33]: Its eligibility is all small business owners (excluding those who has received the 1st program). The loan interest rate depending on central credit rating is 3~4% per year. Application limit was KRW 10 million per case. Loan period is total 5 years (2 years deferred, 3-year installment repayment). Guarantee ratio is 95% (Credit Guarantee Fund consignment guarantee). Application organizations are 6 commercial banks (KB Kookmin, NH Nonghyup, Shinhan,·Woori,·and Hana Bank) and local banks (Daegu and other banks are implemented sequentially when software development is completed). Applications for the loan started from May 18, 2020.

d. Loan for the Rent Payment

Special low-interest rate loans for small business owners in prohibited and restricted businesses were provided starting from Dec. 29, 2020. The loan program provides KRW 1 trillion at a low-interest rate of 1.9% to 100,000 people in prohibited businesses, and KRW 3 trillion at an interest rate to the business in restricted businesses in the range of 2–4% through credit

SME Loans to Household Loans Are Not Being Considered, April 6, 2020, https://www.moef.go.kr/sns/2020/emgncEcnmyMtg.do?category1=nes.

[32] Korea Policy Briefing, *Small Business Owner 10 Million KRW Emergency Loan Starts*, April 1, 2020, https://www.korea.kr/special/policyFocusView.do?newsId=148871062&pkgId=49500742.

[33] Ministry of Economy and Finance, Covid-19 Economic Support-Emergency Economy Commission, https://www.moef.go.kr/sns/2020/emgncEcnmyMtg.do?category1=detail&type=02#02.

guarantees, etc. The current guarantee fee of 0.9% is exempted for the first year and reduced to 0.6% for the second to fifth year.[34]

e. Reduction of the Debt Burden Only for the Vulnerable Groups

A debt repayment suspension (interest-free) for up to six months applied to the debtors if "a reduction in income due to the Covid-19" is recognized to the debtors who are fulfilling the debt adjustment agreements with the Credit Counseling and Recovery Service and Korea Asset Management Corporation (including the National Happiness Fund). Even if there is no monthly payment or default during the repayment suspension period, there are no additional disadvantages such as credit rating changes.[35]

If a micro-financial loan user has a "reduction in income due to the Covid- 19", he or she can receive a six-month deferment in repayment of principal. Even if there is no monthly payment during the repayment suspension period, there are no additional disadvantages such as credit rating changes.[36]

f. Guaranty

A special guaranty for SMEs and small business owners was provided in total KRW 5.5 trillion with a low guarantee fee and with an increased guarantee rate.[37] The full amount guaranty on the emergency funds for April-September period in 2020 of limiting store's opening hours was provided to a small business with annual sales of KRW 100 million or less. The total guaranty was KRW 3.0 trillion for such losses directly or indirectly caused by the Covid-19.

[34] Korea Policy Briefing, Economic Measures to Covid-19, Jan. 6, 2021, https://www.korea.kr/special/policyCurationView.do?newsId=148872965.

[35] FSC, Reduction of debt burden for the vulnerable groups under the Covid-19 will be push forward, Press Release, March 11, 2020.

[36] FSC, *supra* note 35.

[37] Ministry of Economy and Finance, *supra* note 33.

Implication on Banking Industry and Supervision

Increase of Debt Level

By the special emergency loan programs, the total loan assistance amount for SMEs and individuals is about KRW 250 trillion.[38] Among them, the total amount of new loans and maturity extensions is KRW 198 trillion (New loans are KRW 88.1 trillion, and maturity extension is KRW 11.2 trillion). The remaining KRW 52.7 trillion is guaranteed support (New guarantees of KRW 19.7 trillion and extension of guarantee maturity of KRW 33 trillion were provided by designated financial institutions).[39] However, since the huge increase of debt level for the relevant borrowers was resulted from the emergency loan program, the government is also considering how to repay it with less side effects, as debts from the Covid-19 crisis have increased. Even an official from the FSC said, "Because it is a debt that must be paid someday, we are thinking about a plan to induce a soft landing so that it can be repaid without arrears."[40] The FSC announced for soft landing that the debtor will be allowed to do the loan modification, subject to the consultation of the lending bank, which defers the repayment of the principal and the interest one more year, extends maturity up to three years, and then five-year installment repayments of them as well as loan modifications.[41]

Credit Crunch Risk

The rapid increase of total loan amount during the Covid-19 financial emergency in a short period of time can be a huge burden to both the financial institutions and debtors. All the loan needs to be repaid someday in the future, and the plan to induce a soft landing to prevent non-performing loans is required. If a soft landing will be unsuccessful, the loan modification may be needed for the huge non-performing loans. In a worst-case scenario, a credit crunch of a decline in lending activity by financial institutions can occur from the sudden shortage of funds to lend.

[38] ChosunBiz, *The Amount of COVID Pandemic Financing to Be Repaid Someday Exceeds KRW 250 trillion (about USD 189 million)*, https://biz.chosun.com/site/data/html_dir/2020/11/29/2020112900194.html, Nov. 29, 2020.

[39] Ibid.

[40] Ibid.

[41] FSC, *Maturity Extension, Deferment of Repayment, and Assisting Soft Landing*, Press Release, Sep. 27, 2022.

Companies and individuals will be nearly impossible to borrow money with a reasonable interest rate because lenders are scared of debtors' bankruptcies or defaults, resulting in higher rates.[42]

The FSC announced its plan to request to the banks to increase the loan loss provision for the potential non-performing loans in case for the very slow recovery of the businesses of SMEs.[43]

Implication to the Supervision

Various pandemic emergency financing and debt relief measures by the government of each country or global organization like IMF, was very helpful to respond the Covid-19 financial crisis in the relevant area. However, the emergency financing made a huge increase of debt ratio for the individual and the business, which was heavily impacted by the business closure and the restriction of operations. The extension of loan or interest maturity is only for the temporary relief. As the Covid-19 pandemic continues and it takes some time for businesses and households to recover after the pandemic, non-performing loans are huge burden for the financial institutions. Even credit crunch may be expected in such situation. To prevent such situation in advance, it is urgent to prepare legal measures before such problem becomes a reality.

4 SDGs in Korean Banking Business

The SDGs are very important current issues and concerns for the big companies in general as well as for the banking industry in Korea. The Korean government has stressed the importance of sustainability of the environment and business. The government policy impacts on the business, especially on the big companies as well as financial industry. Since banks and financial institutions provide financial resources through lending and investment, it has a huge impact on the financial decisions and the behavior of every business sector in Korea.

The Korean government gives the guidance, regulation, and plans on Environmental, Social, and Governance (ESG) reporting, disclosure, and

[42] See C. Reinhart, The coming COVID-19 credit crunch (worldbank.org), Dec. 2, 2020; Loren Crow, *Carmen Reinhart on the Consequences of the Pandemic*, The World Ahead, The Economist, Nov. 17, 2020, https://www.economist.com/the-world-ahead/2020/11/17/carmen-reinhart-on-the-consequences-of-the-pandemic.

[43] FSC, *supra* note 41.

business operation. The ESG is the Korean version of the SDGs. Such guidance and regulations are also gradually influencing the policy and the business of banking industry.

The Impact on Baking Business Model by ESG

Before the ESG emerges as a critical issue of the banking, the banking industry has focused mainly on the financial performance. However, now financial institutions including banks have to consider environment, social, and governance as well when they make a policy on a lending and investment decision. It is very important for them to have the comparative advantage of the reputation and to avoid any indirect sanctions from the government and the public. Now most large financial institutions provide their ESG reports at their websites each year voluntarily. However, regarding the corporate governance report in contrast to the ESG report, the listed company, with the asset of KRW 1 trillion Korean or more, should disclose a corporate governance report at the Data Analysis, Retrieval and Transfer System (DARTA) for listed companies, operated by the Financial Supervisory Service (FSS), the other Korean financial supervisory authority.[44]

The corporate governance of financial institutions has been heavily regulated in Korea, even before the ESG becomes important issues, since the previous financial crises gave the government the lesson that the governance of banks and financial institutions impacts the behavior and decision-making process of the financial institutions, which is crucial to maintain the financial stability and prevent the moral hazard and the bank failure. The statute to regulate the governance of financial institutions in Korea is the Act on Corporate Governance of Financial Companies of 2016 and the most recent amendment is effective Dec. 31, 2021. However, regarding environment or social issues of banking, there is no special act or legal regulation on financial institutions until now in Korea.

On social responsibility issues, the Social Enterprise Promotion Act (SEPA) was enacted on Dec. 8, 2006 and became effective on Jul. 1, 2007 and was amended on Jun. 8, 2010.[45] Under the SEPA, the legal

[44] KRX, Securities Disclosure Regulation Art. 24–2 and its enforcement rule Art. 7–2(1).

[45] See K. Taek Lee, Social Enterprise Promotion Act: The Case of South Korea, Asian Dialogue on Oeconomy, 2010, http://www.socioeco.org/bdf_auteur-957_en.html.

form of the social enterprise is not limited to the non-profit organization and it ranges between an association in the Civil Code and a company in the Commercial Code.[46] The State or local governments can support the social enterprises with benefits such as renting the state-owned or public land, and reducing or exempting taxes.[47]

Current SDGs Supervision on the Banking Industry and the Prospect of SDGs Regulation

Currently ESG is regulated by self-regulation and the Korea Exchange (KRX) announced the ESG Disclosure Guidance for that purpose in 2021. It is not mandatory rule, but a recommendation and suggestion for the companies on how to make and prepare the ESG reports and to disclose to the public annually.

Through such voluntary mechanism, Korean banks provides ESG-linked financial products, such as donating some funds to the organization related to responding the climate changes or reducing carbon emissions from the proceeds of selling deposits, trusts, or credit cards services and providing more interest rate to open a bank account without papers (KB bank) and special green loan program for the green industry (Woori bank and Hana Financial Group). Those financial products are for the reputation of the banks that show they have concerns on ESG sensitivity.[48] Even some large Korean banks raced in 2021 to get an endorsement from the international assessment organization, such as The Science Based Targets initiative (STBi) on their green goal to show off their ESG leadership in banking industry for their reputation.[49]

However, the FSC announced its comprehensive improvement and change plan on the Korean corporate disclosure system, which includes encouragement of voluntary disclosure of the ESG report and the staged mandatory disclosure on the ESG report in the coming years.[50] It

[46] Ibid.

[47] Ibid.

[48] E-media, Financial Industry strives to ESG management, Dec. 6, 2021.

[49] See J. Min-kyung, *S.* Korean Banking Groups Race for Global ESG Approval, The Korean Herald, Nov. 9, 2021, at https://www.koreaherald.com/view.php?ud=20211109000787.

[50] FSC, the Comprehensive Improvement Plan on the Corporate Disclosure System, Jan. 21, 2021.

contains three-staged plan on the ESG disclosure.[51] The first stage is increasing the number of voluntary ESG disclosures by encouragement (from now until 2025). The second stage is making mandatory ESG disclosure only for the big listed companies such as companies with KRW 2 trillion or more assets (from 2025 until 2030). The third stage is making it mandatory to disclose the ESG report for all the KOSPI listed companies (on and after 2030).

The FSC plan regarding SDGs shows the trend that current regulation on the ESG, which is basically based on reputational mechanism and soft-laws, will be gradually changed to some mandatory regulations on ESG in the future in Korea.

5 Conclusion

Fintech innovations as well as the Covid-19 pandemic and UN SDGs have made a huge impact on banking businesses and supervision in Korea. Fintechs are replacing and challenging the substantial part of traditional commercial banking services. With a high level of financial accessibility and well-developed digital payment systems, Korea experiences advanced financial inclusion and efficiency of payment services. In Korea, BigTech companies are now competing with traditional financial companies as BigTechs are making full use of big data under the revised Korean Personal Information Act system to facilitate the processing of personal information. However, there are still ongoing debates on issues of how to deal with banking industry under the changing digital environment, such as pseudo-banking issue, regulation of BigTechs as large financial conglomerates under SFCA, virtual asset (mostly crypto-assets) regulation, issue of separation of banking and commerce, and CBDC.

During the Covid-19 pandemic, various pandemic emergency financing and debt relief measures made a huge increase in debt ratio for the individuals and SMEs in Korea. Since the economic recovery from the pandemic takes some time and the extension of loan or interest maturity is only for the temporary relief, when the extension of such loan repayment schedule is over, non-performing loans will be a significant burden for the financial institutions. Even credit crunch may be expected in such

[51] Ibid., at 16.

a situation. In order to prevent such situation in advance, it is urgent to prepare legal measures before such problem becomes reality.

In Korea, currently ESG disclosure and reporting are not mandatory and regulated by self-regulation, the ESG Disclosure Guidance in 2021. However, Korean FSC announced its comprehensive plan to change on the Korean corporate disclosure system, which includes the staged mandatory disclosure on ESG report in the coming years. The current regulation on the ESG, based on reputational mechanism and soft-laws, will gradually include some mandatory regulations in the future in Korea.

PART IV

Looking Ahead

CHAPTER 20

Final Remarks

Antonella Brozzetti

a. The contributions included in this co-edited book provide a comprehensive overview of the most critical issues relating to commercial banking and banking institutions. The considerations on both the present and future of banks allow to identify their distinguishing features relative to the functions reserved to them, thereby envisaging their prospective evolution. The international and comparative approach taken by the co-authors of this book makes this work particularly interesting to those who deal with commercial banking from a legal and regulatory perspective.

Over the last 20 years, exogenous shocks and inherent economic transitions have affected the predominant model of capitalism based on economic liberalism and led to the search for newly established relations between law and economics. Past and ongoing socio-economic changes are re-designing the commercial banking business model as well as the perimeter of banking intermediation.

b. It is well known that banks have been blamed for being co-responsible for the global financial crisis of 2007–2008 and the following

A. Brozzetti (✉)
Business and Law Department, University of Siena, Siena, Italy
e-mail: antonella.brozzetti@unisi.it

M. Bodellini et al. (eds.), *Commercial Banking in Transition*, Palgrave Macmillan Studies in Banking and Financial Institutions,
https://doi.org/10.1007/978-3-031-45289-5_20

economic downturn triggered by the failure of Lehman Brothers. National and international rule-makers and standard setters have reacted by trying to limit banks' giantism, while bringing under the regulatory radar shadow banking on the basis of the latter being deemed responsible for the excesses resulting from the securitization of subprime mortgages. Such excesses in turn caused the transformation of several banking systems from the 'originate-to-hold' business model to the 'originate-to-distribute' business model.

The economic consequences of the global financial crisis have brought the bank-centrism featuring several financial systems, including the European one, under the spotlight, while emphasizing the importance of financing sources different from the ones provided by banks. The mutation of the global financial crisis into the sovereign debt crisis in Europe in turn showed the perverse link (so-called doom loop) between bank crises and public finance. Such doom loop impacted on the ability of banks established in countries with high public debt to get funding, while hindering the correct functioning of monetary policy measures due to the key role of banks in providing financial support to economic activities.

The new rules and regulations adopted in the aftermath of the global financial crisis aimed at enhancing and increasing bank's capital while lowering their leverage. Also, structural ring-fencing measures have been (re-)introduced in the US and UK with a view to separating commercial banking from investment banking in order to more effectively support economic growth. Yet, the persistence of extremely low (and even negative) interest rates until the beginning of the war in Ukraine in February 2022 has substantially reduced bank revenues, thereby pushing the latter to engage in investment banking activities. This move has found some regulatory support in the European initiative to create the so-called Capital Markets Union.

c. From the institutional perspective, the global financial crisis has also been one of the main reasons for the creation in the EU of the so-called European System of Financial Supervision, which focuses on both the micro dimension, through the European Supervisory Authorities, and the macro dimension, through the European Systemic Risk Board. The European experience is also an interesting example of efforts of centralization of functions and shifts of sovereignty from the national dimension to the continental dimension. Centralization of bank supervision and crisis management is the by-product of the so-called Banking Union—a new institutional architecture based on three pillars: European supervision (single supervisory mechanism), European crisis management (single resolution mechanism), and European deposit insurance (European Deposit Insurance Scheme). Such a result has been achieved through the involvement of prominent institutions; the European Central Bank has accordingly become one of the most important bank supervisors across the world and the European Commission has been playing a key role in drafting banking and financial regulation.

At the international level, efforts have been made to enhance coordination and cooperation; a clear example has been the creation of the Financial Stability Board (successor of the Financial Stability Forum). Against this background, the Financial Stability Board has been given the crucial function and inherent powers to draft global standards aimed at preserving system stability. Along with the latter, the G20 and the Basel Committee on Banking Supervision now play a crucial role in shaping banking regulation through an ever-increasing plethora of recommendations and best practices, that, after being drafted as international soft-law principles, are expected to turn into national hard law provisions through legislative and regulatory action.

d. All this is to say that the new legal framework, aimed at enabling to manage traditional banking and financial risks, has caused universal banks to be subject to complex, sophisticated, and multi-level regulations, to a large extent, still in the making. Nevertheless, those issues which affected the banking industry before the global financial crisis have not been fully solved yet: accordingly international standards setters keep on warning on systemic risks and on issues potentially caused by shadow banking.

Importantly, such regulatory reforms have been taking place together with tremendous technological innovations which have been applied also in the provision of financial services thereby redefining the main features of the industry and the market. Newcomers, extensively relying on fintech applications, have entered the market exploiting regulatory loopholes and hitting the market monopoly of banks and traditional financial intermediaries.

Along with the advent of fintech, the new era of post-crisis banking and financial regulation has also been affected by the emergence of new principles and values potentially capable to change the traditional functioning of the market. Several tragedies caused by climate-related extreme events as well as the Covid-19 pandemic have brought under the spotlight the need to amend the traditional economic development model with a view to integrating sustainability by paying attention to ESG (environment, social, governance) factors.

Interestingly, the pandemic has shown the crucial role of banks which often acted as the main transmission channel between the expansionary monetary policy measures implemented by central banks and the real economy. The key role of financing economic activities has acquired new centrality and has also shown the public interest underlying the correct exercise of banking intermediation, further reinforced by huge packages of public support distributed by governments.

e. Recent times have seriously tested the role of banking and banks, thereby raising the question of which function such entities could and should play to support economic growth.

History of banking shows how banks are in fact changing creatures capable to adapt to the peculiarities of their times. I have witnessed myself the different stages of development of traditional universal banking and I taught classes discussing the bank as a physical structure when business was only conducted through branches, self-service banking prompted by the advent of ATMs, and eventually virtual banking with services provided via the internet. We now live in the age of digital banking, which has gained momentum also due to the covid-19 pandemic and fintech innovations; today, banks operate relying extensively upon apps and their websites. Digital banking is a reality which dominates several banking systems across the world, from China to Saudi Arabia, United Arab Emirates, and Brazil. Fast-growing trends are also registered in this field in the US, UK, France, and Switzerland. Every country sooner or later will face the new digital reality.

From the legal perspective, over time I have taught my students that the very essence of the banking activity, although still resulting from the link between collecting deposits and extending loans which allow for money creation, has seen such two legs losing their functional characterization. Partly because of the competition from other financial intermediaries, partly because of the advent from outside the financial market of newcomers offering banking services (e.g. payments) via sharing mechanisms (e.g. open banking) and partly because of the growing importance gained by digital platforms which intermediate finance, banks have been losing market shares.

Based on historical lessons, I have always remained of the opinion that the banking institution is a *sui generis* entity that exercises an activity of public interest (at least because of its money creation function) and that can survive difficulties transforming and adapting itself. Banks will survive and adapt even this time. Thinking about the young generations, however, I hope that banks will play a leading role in supporting the transition to sustainability, which cannot be postponed any longer.

Index

M. Bodellini et al. (eds.), *Commercial Banking in Transition*, Palgrave Macmillan Studies in Banking and Financial Institutions,
https://doi.org/10.1007/978-3-031-45289-5

L

M

N

O

P

T

U

V

W

SPRINGER NATURE

GPSR Compliance

The European Union's (EU) General Product Safety Regulation (GPSR) is a set of rules that requires consumer products to be safe and our obligations to ensure this.

If you have any concerns about our products, you can contact us on ProductSafety@springernature.com

In case Publisher is established outside the EU, the EU authorized representative is:

Springer Nature Customer Service Center GmbH
Europaplatz 3
69115 Heidelberg, Germany

The manufacturer's authorised representative in the EU is Springer
Nature Customer Service Centre GmbH, Europaplatz 3, 69115 Heidelberg,
Germany. If you have any concerns regarding our products, please
contact ProductSafety@springernature.com

Printed and bound by CPI Group (UK) Ltd, Croydon, CR0 4YY
30/09/2026
02225311-0017